Gregg Herman

101+ Practical Solutions for the Family Lawyer

Sensible Answers to Common Problems

Second Edition

Section of Family Law
American Bar Association

Cover design by Catherine Zaccarine.

Library of Congress Cataloging-in-Publication Data

101+ practical solutions for the family lawyer / by Gregg Herman, editor.—2nd ed.
    p. cm.
        ISBN 1-59031-173-6
        1. Domestic relations—United States. 2. Attorney and client—United States. I. Title: One hundred one plus practical solutions for the family lawyer. II. Title: One hundred and one plus practical solutions for the family lawyer. III. Herman, Gregg M. IV. American Bar Association. Section of Family Law.

KF505.A2A15 2003
346.7301'5—dc21

2002156495

Contents

PART IV: MALPRACTICE AVOIDANCE

PART V: OFFICE PRACTICES

PART IX: RETIREMENT PLANS

PART X: VALUATION

PART XI: SETTLEMENT

PART XII: TORTS

PART XIII: TRIAL TACTICS

Introduction to New Edition

Welcome to the Second Edition of 101+ Practical Solutions. The response to the first edition was wonderful. My favorite comment was from an attorney who told me that the length of the chapters made the book perfect bathroom reading!

This edition eliminates some hot tips from the first edition which are no longer relevant, replaces some tips with improved versions, and includes over 25 new hot tips which were presented after the publication of the first edition.

I hope you find this Second Edition interesting and helpful—wherever you choose to read it!

Gregg Herman
Editor

Introduction to the First Edition

Every year, on the Sunday morning of the American Bar Association (ABA) annual meeting, there is a program that draws standing room only. The program is fast-moving, informative, and highly entertaining. After all, what else can get lawyers out of bed early on a Sunday morning?

The program is called "Hot Tips from the Experts." Unlike most continuing legal education (CLE) programs with droning speakers or competing panelists, each speaker gets no more than five minutes. And I do not mean five and a half minutes. The *Gong Show* had nothing on the bell that rings to signal the end of each presentation. If the speaker still does not get the idea, the microphone is turned off. The ABA Family Law Section is anything but subtle.

Each year, the presenters of the hot tips are carefully chosen from among the experts in family law. Most are lawyers—not just any lawyers, but experienced lawyers, the cream of the family law bar across the country. These are not academics, they are lawyers with real-life, hands-on experience. And certified public accountants (CPAs), judges, and psychologists as well. Each has five minutes to give one succinct tip to help family lawyers with their practices.

This book is a select compendium of the top tips of the past five years. Not every tip, of course, is included here. Some are outdated, others were intended for presentation and do not translate well into a book. Many, however, contain brief outlines that, in a very few pages, can make you a better family law practitioner.

A few acknowledgments are necessary. First, to Mark Soboslai, who took the first crack at organizing five years of material. Thanks also to Eliot Nerenberg for asking me to edit the book, Don Gecewicz of ABA Publications, Barbara Stark Kahn, chair of the Publications Board, and Glenda Sharp and her splendid staff. And, of course, thank you to the many speakers and moderators who have donated their time and efforts into developing the greatest CLE program on the face of the earth. It is our pleasure to share the best of these hot tips with you.

PART

I

Client Relations

IS THERE ANY AREA OF LAW more intensely client-related than family law? After all, no emotions are more intense than those of the family, and the breaking of those ties triggers the release of great emotional energy. There is a saying that criminal courts see bad people at their best and family courts see good people at their worst.

As a result, client relations in family law cases are extremely complicated. The emotional levels are extreme, and it is not difficult for the lawyer to be swept up in the emotions. At the same time as attempting to keep a distance, the lawyer also must be sympathetic and understanding. He or she is walking a tightrope.

Clients, of course, react in different ways. Some are looking for a surgical approach to the divorce: They want to be put to sleep and awakened when it's over. The problem with this approach is that if they are unaware of the process, they cannot understand the result. More important, the client's knowledge of the facts and of the other party cannot be used.

Some clients go to the opposite extreme: They want a mouthpiece. They will dictate the action and the lawyer will mouth the words, like a ventriloquist's dummy. This approach is similarly inappropriate. Emotions should not be used to suppress intellect. Part of the lawyer's role is to provide an objective point of view, unclouded by emotion.

There is a middle course: The client and the lawyer work together as a team toward a common goal. This is easier said than done. Few, if any, legal arenas present the challenges of client handling that family law does.

The following tips examine various aspects of client management and suggest mechanisms for working together.

1   The emotional stresses experienced by a family law client frequently require a mental health professional. **Bob Moriarty** describes how his firm uses a resource counselor to be the mental health support, so that the lawyer can be the legal support.

2   Of all law practitioners, family lawyers are among those most often targeted with ethical grievance complaints. Are family lawyers less ethical? I do not think so. This is merely one other manifestation of the emotional nature of cases we deal with on a daily basis. **Sam Goodman** gives his "Ten Commandments" on how to avoid being the target of a grievance.

3   When **Jim Preston** starts a new divorce action, he provides the client with five request forms that may help with tax issues. While these forms may have to be modified for different jurisdictions, the concept is a wonderful client service.

4   **Geoffrey Hamilton** and **Thomas Merrill** suggest a Client Assessment Scale to attempt to quantify the emotional difficulty of the case. Since forewarned is forearmed, using their scale is a great way to become armed.

5   Many client misunderstandings can be answered simply: The law does not allow what the client wants. **Harold Field**'s tip is so simple that I can't believe I didn't think of it. By giving a new client a copy of selected state statutes, the lawyer can help the client focus on what remedies are allowed by law.

6   The client must be part of a team, not a separate player or, worse yet, an observer. **Terry Kapp** shares his methods for putting the client to work at the beginning of the case.

7   Many clients feel that they hold no cards—that the spouse is totally in control. Actually these clients possess great knowledge that must be utilized. **John Finnerty** calls it "empowering the client" and suggests several valuable and easy ways to establish the teamwork with the client that is so essential.

8   Another tip from **Bob Moriarty:** Send the client a letter at the beginning of the case informing him or her of the philosophy of your office and the routine proceedings in the case. Bob offers his letter as a sample that can be adapted and personalized.

9   **Gary Skoloff** stresses the importance of promptly returning a client's telephone calls. If you are not already convinced of the importance of it, well, just read Gary's comments.

10   Divorce clients seem to do a lot of Monday-morning quarterbacking. **Lewis Kapner** calls it "postparting depression" and lends several suggestions on how to avoid it.

11   No lawyer, of course, can predict the future. How do you educate the client, then, without promising what you may not be able to deliver? **Bob Moriarty** suggests several form letters and provides outlines that can be individualized at the start of a case and again at the end.

12   Of course, spending substantial time to educate a client can be quite costly. **Jan Warner** suggests some easily available and economical means of client education, pointing out that educated clients are satisfied clients and that "there is no better advertisement than a satisfied client."

13   **Bill DaSilva** calls it homework for the client. The client is the lawyer's greatest asset and the client should be involved in every step of the case. After all, the client never will appreciate the result unless he or she is involved in the process. Bill provides examples of assignments to be given clients to assist in the case.

14   Some clients are chronically upset and it seems there is nothing the lawyer can do. **Grier Raggio Jr.** examines several different types of upset clients, tells how to identify them, and suggests tips for handling them.

15   For clients, the most important relationship in their lives is breaking down. Many clients see this as a sign of failure. Failing in the critical role of spouse leads to self-doubt on other issues and, for some, a total loss of self-esteem. **Cheryl Karp** discusses this concept with concrete ideas on how the lawyer can help the client recover the sense of self-worth so necessary for the divorce and for the life to follow.

16   Every once in a while, we are lucky enough to have the excitement of a high-profile divorce case. While the experience can be thrilling, there are some different techniques which should be applied to preserve privacy and confidentiality. **Sandra Little** describes some of these techniques.

1

Using a Resource Counselor

Robert B. Moriarty

DURING THE PAST YEAR our firm has begun to utilize the services of a resource counselor to help clients handle the stresses and strains of divorce. Referrals by lawyers to mental health professionals are common, but how we use our resource person and our relationship with her is not common and I want to share it with you.

Our counselor has her own practice, called Client Resource Services. She is an independent contractor and is not on our payroll. For a fixed retainer, paid to her on a weekly basis, she provides an agreed number of hours of counseling for our clients. The service is provided at our office, where she meets with our clients in the library, a conference room, or a partner's or associate's office as may be available. Her primary function is to assess the client's needs and concerns, to provide support, and if necessary to refer him or her to such others—therapists, community agencies, or support groups—as may be appropriate. In other words, in addition to a supportive counseling role, she acts as a liaison to the services of others. She also recommends specific reading materials that focus on individual client issues.

The process is initiated by any of the four of us (my partner, our two associates, and myself) who form the matrimonial law core of our firm, or even other staff members, including secretaries and paralegals. At any time any of us feels a client needs professional help with respect to a mental or emotional problem, a secretary is asked to send a "resource" letter that advises the client of our service and that invites the client to take advantage of it. We forward a copy of the letter to our resource person. If a client does not respond, the resource person is authorized to follow up on the letter and contact the client directly.

As noted, the counselor–client contact takes place at the office. We feel meeting at our office enhances the value of this service to us because it more fully associates the counselor's services with us. Normally when an appointment is made between the counselor and the client, the lawyer is neither involved nor for that matter even aware of the appointment being scheduled. If a legal question arises, however, and the resource counselor sees the value of providing the client with an answer, she might well pop her head into the office of the lawyer handling the case and ask if he or she is available to answer a quick question, and of course if we are available we do so.

The resource counselor regularly supplies to us, every week to ten days or so, a Client Contact Report that details her contacts with the client and that keeps us posted about the client's feelings and problems, her advice to the client, and things we can do to help.

Even those of us who want to give time and attention to a client's emotional problems find it difficult and sometimes even impossible to do so on a regular basis. And even when we do find the time, we are not well equipped to do much more than hand-holding. There is no doubt that our relationship with our resource counselor and our utilization of her services has substantially improved our ability to handle many cases with sensitivity, particularly difficult cases. By providing our clients with a trained professional who can listen and be understanding under our own roof, we signal to our clients our sensitivity to this need and our willingness to stay in touch with those problems.

In terms of expense, as noted previously, we provide this as a free service to our clients. Other firms might wish to enter into an agreement with a counselor in which the counselor bills the clients.

Resource Letter

Dear _____:

Because Moriarty & Condon will be representing you in your present matrimonial matter, I want to make you aware of one of the services I provide to its clients.

The lawyers in this firm are keenly aware of the personal difficulties that often trouble clients as they go through separation or divorce proceedings.

To deal with the frequent and normal stresses that may occur during this major transition in your life, I provide counseling services at the firm's offices to help you with matters that may be affecting you and/or your children. The personal concerns that you may have during the legal process never are too trivial to be discussed, and I urge you to contact me for an appointment. It often is very helpful to "talk out" situations that may be causing you concern.

My professional background includes working with adults and children concerning family, marital, and crisis issues, and providing personal and career counseling for clients going through separation, divorce, or widowhood.

There is no fee for this confidential service and I will be calling you to see if you wish to make an appointment. If you do not wish an appointment at present, we will at least be acquainted and you may feel free to call me at a later date. I look forward to the possibility of meeting you.

Sincerely,

Resource Counselor

2

The Ten Commandments of Client Management (or All You Ever Wanted to Know about Avoiding Grievances but Were Afraid to Ask)

Samuel J. Goodman

EVEN TO THE SAINTS AMONG US, a certified letter marked "personal" from the Disciplinary Commission evokes a sinking feeling in the pit of your stomach; sweaty, shaking palms; a racing heartbeat; and an ominous feeling of impending doom. The purpose of this tip is to enable you, whether saint or not, to stop grievances before they start. The following Ten Commandments of Client Management contain very basic instructions, yet they are violated continually by family law practitioners, and these violations are the "stuff" of which grievances are made.

THE FIRST COMMANDMENT: THOU SHALT RETURN THY TELEPHONE CALLS

The most frequent complaint against family lawyers is their failure to return telephone calls. This can be a difficult complaint to overcome because of the overwhelming number of telephone calls lawyers receive on a daily basis. Pledge to return telephone calls within twenty-four hours. Explain to the clients that there will be days when you are not available to answer their calls. Set up an office system for the return of telephone calls by associates and/or paralegals when you are in trial, on vacation, or otherwise unavailable.

THE SECOND COMMANDMENT: THOU SHALT KEEP THY CLIENT INFORMED

Your client must know everything that is happening during the proceeding. The best way to keep a client informed is to send him or her copies of everything that comes into or goes out of the office, including pleadings, correspondence, and memos. Take the time during your initial interview to explain to your client the divorce process, especially focusing on those factors that may occur that may extend the time needed to conclude the matter or that may increase the costs. Do not give your client a false sense of optimism. Complaints occur when you "promise the moon, only to deliver green cheese." Tell the client the truth, be realistic in your prognosis, and do not encourage unrealistic goals.

THE THIRD COMMANDMENT: THOU SHALT DISCUSS THY LAWYER'S FEES

Your initial conference must include a thorough discussion of lawyer's fees, including how you charge, who pays, the potential litigation expenses, your minimum time charges, and the like. Once you and the client have discussed this issue, and the client understands, the fee agreement must be reduced to a written contract. Do not quote estimates or ballpark figures. These figures tend to metamorphose into the "final fee" and come back to haunt you. Do not ever tell a client that his or her spouse will be responsible for the payment of your fees.

THE FOURTH COMMANDMENT: THOU SHALT BILL THY CLIENT REGULARLY

Frequent itemized billing, generally on a monthly basis, prevents the shock of a close-of-file bill, informs your client on a regular basis of your work on the matter, and keeps him or her advised of the cost of continuing the litigation. A client will have difficulty disputing the final fee when he or she has received regular monthly billing statements during the course of the proceeding. Monthly bills should be sent even in situations where your client's spouse will be ordered to pay fees.

THE FIFTH COMMANDMENT: THOU SHALT INVITE THY CLIENT TO COMMUNICATE TO THEE WHEN HE OR SHE IS DISPLEASED

Advise your client that you want him or her to have a better relationship with you than he or she has with the spouse. A festering client will invite a grievance. Ask your client to let you know when he or she is upset with you so that you can have the opportunity to explain what you have or have not done.

THE SIXTH COMMANDMENT: THOU SHALT CALENDAR EVERYTHING

You should not blow a statute of limitations, miss a hearing date, or lose a file because of your failure to properly document times and dates. If you do not have a calendaring system, you must create one immediately. Once a calendaring system is created, a backup system must be developed for your calendaring system. Once that is in place, you must develop a backup system for your backup system. There is no response to a grievance for blowing a statute, missing a hearing, or losing a file.

THE SEVENTH COMMANDMENT: THOU SHALT INTRODUCE CLIENTS TO ASSOCIATES AND PARALEGALS WHO WILL BE WORKING ON THE CASE

Make sure that your client has met all the personnel who will be working on his or her case. If you are going to assign a client to another lawyer in your firm, obtain that client's permission. Similarly, if you are going to have someone in your firm second-chair you at trial, make sure that your client understands the benefit and agrees to the double billing.

THE EIGHTH COMMANDMENT: THOU SHALT AVOID CONFLICTS AND BEWARE OF PRO-SE LITIGANTS

If it looks like a conflict, smells like a conflict, and sounds like a conflict, chances are it is a conflict, and representation should be declined. If you cannot resist accepting representation, then you must fully disclose potential conflicts to all parties and counsel, request written waivers of potential conflicts prior to commencing representation, and actually receive them in hand before proceeding. Similarly, make sure that the pro-se litigant clearly understands that you do not represent him or her. Urge the pro-se litigant to seek independent counsel and set a very clear paper trail to the pro-se litigant that you do not, in any manner, represent him or her.

THE NINTH COMMANDMENT: THOU SHALT BEWARE OF THE "RED FLAG, BELLS RINGING, WHISTLES BLOWING, CANNONS BOOMING" POTENTIAL CLIENT

If, during the first fifteen minutes of your initial consultation with a potential client, you realize that this client will send you straight to the aspirin bottle, or worse, do not take the case. No matter how large the retainer or how meager your present income, do not take the case. It is not worth it. You are looking at a grievance waiting to be filed.

THE TENTH COMMANDMENT: THOU SHALT CLOSE THY CASE

All cases have loose ends, which can range from the simple preparation of a quitclaim deed to application for Consolidated Omnibus Budget Reconciliation Act (COBRA) benefits. Do not conclude the trial or settlement of the case and forget those miscellaneous items. Prepare a close-of-file checklist and make sure that you have tied up all loose ends. Do not assume that your client will take care of these things, because, invariably, he or she will believe that you are taking care of them.

CONCLUSION

These Ten Commandments may not have been brought down from the mountain, but they warrant adherence nonetheless. This humorous attempt conveys an extremely serious message: When lawyers treat clients with common sense and common courtesy, we may not go to heaven, but we will avoid most grievances before the Disciplinary Commission, and this can be heaven on earth.

3

Client Information Letter

James B. Preston

CERTIFIED
FAMILY LAW SPECIALIST

LAW OFFICES
JAMES B. PRESTON
A PROFESSIONAL CORPORATION
309 NORTH WEST STREET
VISALIA, CALIFORNIA 93291
TELEPHONE (209) 625-5181

ABA/NET
ABA 11113
FAX
(209) 625-3460

Dear Client:

Attached are five (5) request forms that may assist you in your pending case. Before using any of the forms, you should review them with me and/or your tax adviser.

I will briefly explain each form:

1. *Social Security Request*—This form is a request to the Social Security Administration for your earnings and benefit estimate statement. By requesting this information, you will be able to estimate your qualifications to receive Social Security and estimated benefits. There is no charge for this information. (Form SSA-7004-SM)

2. *Earned Income Credit*—You may qualify for a tax credit of up to $1,235 per year if your income was under $21,245 and you had at least one child living with you. You must fill out this form and file it with your employer. There are detailed instructions on the form. (Form W-5)

3. *IRS Change of Address Form*—This form is the official notification to the Internal Revenue Service (IRS) that you have changed your mailing address from the address you used on your last tax return. If the IRS receives this form, any deficiency notices or other IRS communications must be sent to you at your designated address. Even if you do not move, you might need to file this form anyway, for your spouse may be receiving all notices at a new address. Before filling out this notice and mailing it, you should consult with me, because circumstances may exist wherein such filing might not be appropriate. (Form 8822)

4. *Request for Federal Tax Return*—This is an easy and inexpensive method to obtain your federal tax returns directly from the IRS, if you do not have ready access to them or if you want to verify that your copies are the same as were filed with the IRS. (Form 4506)

5. *Request for California Tax Return*—This also is an easy method to obtain copies of your filed California tax returns. There is no charge for this service. (Form FTB 3516)

As stated previously, you should discuss with me the consequences of each form before sending them. These forms change from time to time and you always should make sure you have the current version.

If you have any questions regarding these forms or anything else concerning your case, please feel free to call the office at your convenience.

Sincerely yours,

James B. Preston
Attorney at Law

ps
Enclosures

Form Approved
OMB No. 0960-0466

Request for Social Security Statement

Please check this box if you want to get your statement in Spanish instead of English.

Please print or type your answers. When you have completed the form, fold it and mail it to us. (If you prefer to send your request using the Internet, contact us at *www.ssa.gov*)

1. Name shown on your Social Security card:

First Name

Middle Initial

Last Name Only

2. Your Social Security number as shown on your card:

☐☐☐ - ☐☐ - ☐☐☐☐

3. Your date of birth (Mo.-Day-Yr.)

☐☐ - ☐☐ - ☐☐☐☐

4. Other Social Security numbers you have used:

☐☐☐ - ☐☐ - ☐☐☐☐

☐☐☐ - ☐☐ - ☐☐☐☐

5. Your Sex: ☐ Male   ☐ Female

For items 6 and 8 show only earnings covered by Social Security. Do NOT include wages from State, local or Federal Government employment that are NOT covered for Social Security or that are covered ONLY by Medicare.

6. Show your actual earnings (wages and/or net self-employment income) for last year and your estimated earnings for this year.

A. Last year's actual earnings: *(Dollars Only)*

$ ☐☐☐ , ☐☐☐ . 0 0

B. This year's estimated earnings: *(Dollars Only)*

$ ☐☐☐ , ☐☐☐ . 0 0

7. Show the age at which you plan to stop working.

☐☐ *(Show only one age)*

8. Below, show the average yearly amount (not your total future lifetime earnings) that you think you will earn between now and when you plan to stop working. Include performance or scheduled pay increases or bonuses, but not cost-of-living increases.

If you expect to earn significantly more or less in the future due to promotions, job changes, part-time work, or an absence from the work force, enter the amount that most closely reflects your future average yearly earnings.

If you don't expect any significant changes, show the same amount you are earning now (the amount in 6B).

Future average yearly earnings: *(Dollars Only)*

$ ☐☐☐ , ☐☐☐ . 0 0

9. Do you want us to send the statement:
   - To you? Enter your name and mailing address.
   - To someone else (your accountant, pension plan, etc.)? Enter your name with "c/o" and the name and address of that person or organization.

"C/O" or Street Address (Include Apt. No., P.O. Box, Rural Route)

Street Address

Street Address (If Foreign Address, enter City, Province, Postal Code)

U.S. City, State, Zip code (If Foreign Address, enter Name of Country)

NOTICE:

I am asking for information about my own Social Security record or the record of a person I am authorized to represent. I understand that if I deliberately request information under false pretenses, I may be guilty of a Federal crime and could be fined and/or imprisoned. I authorize you to use a contractor to send the Social Security Statement to the person and address in item 9.

▲

Please sign your name (Do Not Print)

Date _____ (Area Code) Daytime Telephone No.

Form **SSA-7004-SM** (6-2002) EF (08-2002)
Destroy prior editions

Request for Social Security Statement

Thank you for requesting this statement.

After you complete and return this form, we will -- within 4 to 6 weeks -- send you:

- a record of your earnings history and an estimate of how much you have paid in Social Security taxes, and
- estimates of benefits you (and your family) may be eligible for now and in the future.

We're pleased to furnish you with this information and we hope you'll find it useful in planning your financial future.

Social Security is more than just a program for retired people. It helps people of all ages in many ways. Whether you're young or old, male or female, single or married -- Social Security can help you when you need it most. It can help support your family in the event of your death and pay you benefits if you become severely disabled.

If you have questions about Social Security or this form, please call our toll-free number, **1-800-772-1213**.

About The Privacy Act

Social Security is allowed to collect the facts on this form under section 205 of the Social Security Act. We need them to quickly identify your record and prepare the statement you asked us for. Giving us these facts is voluntary. However, without them we may not be able to give you a statement. Neither the Social Security Administration nor its contractor will use the information for any other purpose.

Paperwork Reduction Act Notice and Time It Takes Statement

The Paperwork Reduction Act of 1995 requires us to notify you that this information collection is in accordance with the clearance requirements of section 3507 of the Paperwork Reduction Act of 1995. We may not conduct or sponsor, and you are not required to respond to, a collection of information unless it displays a valid OMB control number. We estimate that it will take about 5 minutes to complete this form. This includes the time it will take to read the instructions, gather the necessary facts and fill out the form.

20**03** Form W-5

Department of the Treasury
Internal Revenue Service

Instructions
Purpose of Form

Use Form W-5 if you are eligible to get part of the EIC in advance with your pay and choose to do so. See **Who Is Eligible To Get Advance EIC Payments?** below. The amount you can get in advance generally depends on your wages. If you are married, the amount of your advance EIC payments also depends on whether your spouse has filed a Form W-5 with his or her employer. However, your employer cannot give you more than $1,528 throughout 2003 with your pay. You will get the rest of any EIC you are entitled to when you file your tax return and claim the EIC.

If you do not choose to get advance payments, you can still claim the EIC on your 2003 tax return.

What Is the EIC?

The EIC is a credit for certain workers. It reduces the tax you owe. It may give you a refund even if you do not owe any tax.

Who Is Eligible To Get Advance EIC Payments?

You are eligible to get advance EIC payments if **all three** of the following apply.

1. You expect to have at least one qualifying child. If you do not expect to have a qualifying child, you may still be eligible for the EIC, but you **cannot** receive advance EIC payments. See **Who Is a Qualifying Child?** on page 2.

2. You expect that your 2003 earned income and AGI will each be less than $29,666 ($30,666 if you expect to file a joint return for 2003). Include your spouse's income if you plan to file a joint return. As used on this form, **earned income** does not include amounts inmates in penal institutions are paid for their work, amounts received as a pension or annuity from a nonqualified deferred compensation plan or a nongovernmental section 457 plan, or nontaxable earned income.

3. You expect to be able to claim the EIC for 2003. To find out if you may be able to claim the EIC, answer the questions on page 2.

How To Get Advance EIC Payments

If you are eligible to get advance EIC payments, fill in the 2003 Form W-5 at the bottom of this page. Then, detach it and give it to your employer. If you get advance payments, you **must** file a 2003 Federal income tax return.

You may have only **one** Form W-5 in effect at one time. If you and your spouse are both employed, you should file separate Forms W-5.

(continued on page 2)

▼ *Give the bottom part to your employer; keep the top part for your records.* ▼
--- Detach here ---

Form **W-5**	**Earned Income Credit Advance Payment Certificate**	OMB No. 1545-1342
	▶ **Use the current year's certificate only.**	
	▶ **Give this certificate to your employer.**	20**03**
Department of the Treasury Internal Revenue Service	▶ **This certificate expires on December 31, 2003.**	

Print or type your full name	Your social security number

Note: *If you get advance payments of the earned income credit for 2003, you **must** file a 2003 Federal income tax return. To get advance payments, you **must** have a qualifying child and your filing status must be any status **except** married filing a separate return.*

1 I expect to have a qualifying child and be able to claim the earned income credit for 2003, I do not have another Form W-5 in effect with any other current employer, and I choose to get advance EIC payments . . ☐ **Yes** ☐ **No**

2 Check the box that shows your expected filing status for 2003:
☐ Single, head of household, or qualifying widow(er)   ☐ Married filing jointly

3 If you are married, does your spouse have a Form W-5 in effect for 2003 with any employer? . . . . . . ☐ **Yes** ☐ **No**

Under penalties of perjury, I declare that the information I have furnished above is, to the best of my knowledge, true, correct, and complete.

Signature ▶ _____   Date ▶ _____

Cat. No. 10227P

15

Questions To See if You May Be Able To Claim the EIC for 2003

You **cannot** claim the EIC if you plan to file either **Form 2555** or **Form 2555-EZ** (relating to foreign earned income) for 2003. You also **cannot** claim the EIC if you are a nonresident alien for any part of 2003 unless you are married to a U.S. citizen or resident and elect to be taxed as a resident alien for all of 2003.

1   Do you expect to have a qualifying child? Read **Who Is a Qualifying Child?** that starts below before you answer this question. If the child is married, be sure you also read **Married child** on page 3.

☐ **No.** (STOP) You may be able to claim the EIC but you **cannot** get advance EIC payments.
☐ **Yes.** *Continue.*

If the child meets the conditions to be a qualifying child for both you and another person, see **Qualifying child of more than one person** on page 3.

2   Do you expect your 2003 filing status to be married filing a separate return?

☐ **Yes.** (STOP) You **cannot** claim the EIC.
☐ **No.** *Continue.*

TIP   If you expect to file a joint return for 2003, include your spouse's income when answering questions 3 and 4.

3   Do you expect that your 2003 earned income and AGI will each be less than: $29,666 ($30,666 if married filing jointly) if you expect to have 1 qualifying child; $33,692 ($34,692 if married filing jointly) if you expect to have 2 or more qualifying children?

☐ **No.** (STOP) You **cannot** claim the EIC.
☐ **Yes.** *Continue.* But remember, you **cannot** get advance EIC payments if you expect your 2003 earned income or AGI will be $29,666 ($30,666 or more if married filing jointly) or more.

4   Do you expect that your 2003 investment income will be more than $2,600? For most people, investment income is the total of their taxable interest, ordinary dividends, capital gain distributions, and tax-exempt interest. However, if you plan to file a 2003 Form 1040, see the 2002 Form 1040 instructions to figure your investment income.

☐ **Yes.** (STOP) You **cannot** claim the EIC.
☐ **No.** *Continue.*

5   Do you expect that you, or your spouse if filing a joint return, will be a qualifying child of another person for 2003?
☐ **No.** You may be able to claim the EIC.
☐ **Yes.** You **cannot** claim the EIC.

This Form W-5 expires on December 31, 2003. If you are eligible to get advance EIC payments for 2004, you must file a new Form W-5 next year.

TIP   You may be able to get a larger credit when you file your 2003 return. For details, see **Additional Credit** on page 3.

Who Is a Qualifying Child?

Any child who meets **all three** of the following conditions is a **qualifying child.**

(continued on page 3)

1. The child is:

• Your son, daughter, adopted child, stepchild, or grandchild; or

• Your brother, sister, stepbrother, stepsister, or a descendant of your brother, sister, stepbrother, or stepsister (for example, your niece or nephew), whom you cared for as your own child; or

• A foster child (any child placed with you by an authorized placement agency whom you cared for as your own child).

Note: *An **adopted child** is any child placed with you by an authorized placement agency for legal adoption even if the adoption is not final. An authorized placement agency includes any person authorized by state law to place children for legal adoption. A **grandchild** is any descendant of your son, daughter, adopted child, or stepchild.*

2. At the end of 2003, the child is under age 19, or under age 24 and a full-time student, or any age and permanently and totally disabled.

3. The child lives with you in the United States for over half of 2003.

Exception to "Time Lived With You" Condition. The child does not have to live with you for over half of 2003 if either of the following applies.

1. The child was born or died during the year and your home was this child's home for the entire time he or she was alive in 2003.

2. The child is presumed by law enforcement authorities to have been kidnapped by someone who is not a family member and the child lived with you for over half of the part of the year before he or she was kidnapped.

Note: *Temporary absences, such as for school, vacation, medical care, or detention in a juvenile facility, count as time lived at home. Members of the military on extended active duty outside the United States are considered to be living in the United States.*

Married child. A child who is married at the end of 2003 is a qualifying child only if you may claim him or her as your dependent, **or** the following **Exception** applies to you.

Exception. You are the custodial parent and would be able to claim the child as your dependent, but the noncustodial parent claims the child as a dependent because-

1. You signed **Form 8332,** Release of Claim to Exemption for Child of Divorced or Separated Parents, or a similar statement, agreeing not to claim the child for 2003 **or**

2. You have a pre-1985 divorce decree or separation agreement that allows the noncustodial parent to claim the child and he or she gives at least $600 for the child's support in 2003.

Qualifying child of more than one person. If the child meets the conditions to be a qualifying child of more than one person, only one person may treat that child as a qualifying child for 2003. If you and the other person(s) cannot agree on who will treat that child as a qualifying child for 2003, special rules apply to determine who may do so. For details, see the 2002 revision of **Pub. 596,** Earned Income Credit (EIC). However, these rules do not apply if the only other person is your spouse and you plan to file a joint return for 2003.

Reminder. A qualifying child must have a social security number unless he or she was born and died in 2003.

What if My Situation Changes?

If your situation changes after you give Form W-5 to your employer, you will probably need to file a new Form W-5. For example, you must file a new Form W-5 if any of the following applies for 2003.

• You no longer expect to have a qualifying child. Check **"No"** on line 1 of your new Form W-5.

• You no longer expect to be able to claim the EIC for 2003. Check **"No"** on line 1 of your new Form W-5.

• You no longer want advance payments. Check **"No"** on line 1 of your new Form W-5.

• Your spouse files Form W-5 with his or her employer. Check **"Yes"** on line 3 of your new Form W-5.

Note: *If you get the EIC with your pay and find you are not eligible, you must pay it back when you file your 2003 Federal income tax return.*

Additional Information

How To Claim the EIC

If you are eligible, claim the EIC on your 2003 tax return. See your 2003 tax return instruction booklet.

Additional Credit

You may be able to claim a larger credit when you file your 2003 tax return because your employer cannot give you more than $1,528 throughout the year with your pay. You may also be able to claim a larger credit if you have more than one qualifying child. But you must file your 2003 tax return to claim any additional credit.

Privacy Act and Paperwork Reduction Act Notice. We ask for the information on this form to carry out the Internal Revenue laws of the United States. Internal Revenue Code sections 3507 and 6109 and their regulations require you to provide the information requested on Form W-5 and to give it to your employer if you want advance payment of the EIC. As provided by law, we may give the information to the Department of Justice and other Federal agencies. In addition, we may give it to cities, states, and the District of Columbia so they may carry out their tax laws. We may also disclose this information to other countries under a tax treaty or to Federal and state agencies to enforce Federal nontax criminal laws and to combat terrorism. Failure to provide the requested information may prevent processing of this form; providing false information may subject you to penalties.

You are not required to provide the information requested on a form that is subject to the Paperwork Reduction Act unless the form displays a valid OMB control number. Books or records relating to a form or its instructions must be retained as long as their contents may become material in the administration of any Internal Revenue law. Generally, tax returns and return information are confidential, as required by Code section 6103.

The time needed to complete this form will vary depending on individual circumstances. The estimated average time is: **Recordkeeping,** 6 min.; **Learning about the law or the form,** 12 min.; and **Preparing the form,** 25 min.

If you have comments concerning the accuracy of these time estimates or suggestions for making this form simpler, we would be happy to hear from you. You can write to the Tax Forms Committee, Western Area Distribution Center, Rancho Cordova, CA 95743-0001. **Do not** send the form to this address. Instead, give it to your employer.

Form 8822
(Rev. December 2002)
Department of the Treasury
Internal Revenue Service

Change of Address

▶ **Please type or print.**

▶ **See instructions on back.**   ▶ **Do not attach this form to your return.**

OMB No. 1545-1163

Part I   Complete This Part To Change Your Home Mailing Address

Check **all** boxes this change affects:

1 ☐ Individual income tax returns (Forms 1040, 1040A, 1040EZ, TeleFile, 1040NR, etc.)

     ▶ If your last return was a joint return and you are now establishing a residence separate from the spouse with whom you filed that return, check here . . . . ▶ ☐

2 ☐ Gift, estate, or generation-skipping transfer tax returns (Forms 706, 709, etc.)

     ▶ For Forms 706 and 706-NA, enter the decedent's name and social security number below.

     ▶ Decedent's name   ▶ Social security number

3a Your name (first name, initial, and last name)	**3b** Your social security number
4a Spouse's name (first name, initial, and last name)	**4b** Spouse's social security number

5 Prior name(s). See instructions.

	Apt. no.
6a Old address (no., street, city or town, state, and ZIP code). If a P.O. box or foreign address, see instructions.	
6b Spouse's old address, if different from line 6a (no., street, city or town, state, and ZIP code). If a P.O. box or foreign address, see instructions.	Apt. no.
7 New address (no., street, city or town, state, and ZIP code). If a P.O. box or foreign address, see instructions.	Apt. no.

Part II   Complete This Part To Change Your Business Mailing Address or Business Location

Check **all** boxes this change affects:

8 ☐ Employment, excise, income, and other business returns (Forms 720, 940, 940-EZ, 941, 990, 1041, 1065, 1120, etc.)
9 ☐ Employee plan returns (Forms 5500, 5500-EZ, etc.).
10 ☐ Business location

11a Business name	**11b** Employer identification number

	Room or suite no.
12 Old mailing address (no., street, city or town, state, and ZIP code). If a P.O. box or foreign address, see instructions.	
13 New mailing address (no., street, city or town, state, and ZIP code). If a P.O. box or foreign address, see instructions.	Room or suite no.
14 New business location (no., street, city or town, state, and ZIP code). If a foreign address, see instructions.	Room or suite no.

Part III   Signature

Daytime telephone number of person to contact (optional) ▶ ( )

Sign Here ▶

Your signature Date	If Part II completed, signature of owner, officer, or representative Date
If joint return, spouse's signature Date	Title

For Privacy Act and Paperwork Reduction Act Notice, see back of form.   Cat. No. 12081V   Form **8822** (Rev. 12-2002)

18

Purpose of Form

You may use Form 8822 to notify the Internal Revenue Service if you changed your home or business mailing address or your business location. If this change also affects the mailing address for your children who filed income tax returns, complete and file a separate Form 8822 for each child. If you are a representative signing for the taxpayer, attach to Form 8822 a copy of your power of attorney.

Changing Both Home and Business Addresses? If you are, use a separate Form 8822 to show each change.

Prior Name(s)

If you or your spouse changed your name because of marriage, divorce, etc., complete line 5. Also, be sure to notify the **Social Security Administration** of your new name so that it has the same name in its records that you have on your tax return. This prevents delays in processing your return and issuing refunds. It also safeguards your future social security benefits.

Addresses

Be sure to include any apartment, room, or suite number in the space provided.

P.O. Box

Enter your box number instead of your street address **only** if your post office does not deliver mail to your street address.

Foreign Address

Enter the information in the following order: city, province or state, and country. Follow the country's practice for entering the postal code. Please **do not** abbreviate the country name.

Signature

If you are completing Part II, the owner, an officer, or a representative must sign. An officer is the president, vice president, treasurer, chief accounting officer, etc. A representative is a person who has a valid power of attorney to handle tax matters or is otherwise authorized to sign tax returns for the business.

Where To File

Send this form to the **Internal Revenue Service Center** shown next that applies to you.

 If you checked the box on line 2, see **Filers Who Checked the Box on Line 2 or Completed Part II** for where to file this form.

Filers Who Checked the Box on Line 1 and Completed Part I

IF your old home mailing address was in. . .	THEN use this address. . .

Florida, Georgia, Mississippi, North Carolina, South Carolina, West Virginia	Atlanta, GA 39901
Colorado, Kentucky, Louisiana, Montana, New Mexico, Oklahoma, Texas, Wyoming	Austin, TX 73301
Alaska, Arizona, California, Hawaii, Idaho, Nevada, Oregon, Washington	Fresno, CA 93888
New York (*New York City and counties of Nassau, Rockland, Suffolk, and Westchester*)	Holtsville, NY 00501
New York (*all other counties*), Maine, Massachusetts, Michigan, New Hampshire, Rhode Island, Vermont	Andover, MA 05501
Illinois, Indiana, Iowa, Kansas, Minnesota, Missouri, Nebraska, North Dakota, South Dakota, Utah, Wisconsin	Kansas City, MO 64999
Alabama, Arkansas, Ohio, Tennessee, Virginia	Memphis, TN 37501
Connecticut, Delaware, District of Columbia, Maryland, New Jersey, Pennsylvania	Philadelphia, PA 19255
American Samoa	Philadelphia, PA 19255
Guam: Permanent residents	Department of Revenue and Taxation Government of Guam P.O. Box 23607 GMF, GU 96921
Guam: Nonpermanent residents Puerto Rico (or if excluding income under Internal Revenue Code section 933) Virgin Islands: Nonpermanent residents	Philadelphia, PA 19255
Virgin Islands: Permanent residents	V. I. Bureau of Internal Revenue 9601 Estate Thomas Charlotte Amalie St. Thomas, VI 00802
Foreign country: U.S. citizens and those filing Form 2555, Form 2555-EZ, or Form 4563 Dual-status aliens All APO and FPO addresses	Philadelphia, PA 19255

Filers Who Checked the Box on Line 2 or Completed Part II

IF your old business address was in. . .	THEN use this address. . .
Connecticut, Delaware, District of Columbia, Illinois, Indiana, Kentucky, Maine, Maryland, Massachusetts, Michigan, New Hampshire, New Jersey, New York, North Carolina, Ohio, Pennsylvania, Rhode Island, South Carolina, Vermont, Virginia, West Virginia, Wisconsin	Cincinnati, OH 45999

Alabama, Alaska, Arizona, Arkansas, California, Colorado, Florida, Georgia, Hawaii, Idaho, Iowa, Kansas, Louisiana, Minnesota, Mississippi, Missouri, Montana, Nebraska, Nevada, New Mexico, North Dakota, Oklahoma, Oregon, South Dakota, Tennessee, Texas, Utah, Washington, Wyoming	Ogden, UT 84201
Outside the United States	Philadelphia, PA 19255

Privacy Act and Paperwork Reduction Act Notice. We ask for the information on this form to carry out the Internal Revenue laws of the United States. We may give the information to the Department of Justice and to other Federal agencies, as provided by law. We may give it to cities, states, the District of Columbia, and U.S. commonwealths or possessions to carry out their tax laws. We may give it to foreign governments because of tax treaties they have with the United States. We may also give this information to Federal and state agencies to enforce Federal nontax criminal laws and to combat terrorism.

Our legal right to ask for information is Internal Revenue Code sections 6001 and 6011, which require you to file a statement with us for any tax for which you are liable. Section 6109 requires that you provide your social security number on what you file. This is so we know who you are, and can process your form and other papers.

You are not required to provide the information requested on a form that is subject to the Paperwork Reduction Act unless the form displays a valid OMB control number. Books or records relating to a form or its instructions must be retained as long as their contents may become material in the administration of any Internal Revenue law. Generally, tax returns and return information are confidential, as required by section 6103.

The use of this form is voluntary. However, if you fail to provide the Internal Revenue Service with your current mailing address, you may not receive a notice of deficiency or a notice and demand for tax. Despite the failure to receive such notices, penalties and interest will continue to accrue on the tax deficiencies.

The time needed to complete and file this form will vary depending on individual circumstances. The estimated average time is 16 minutes.

If you have comments concerning the accuracy of this time estimate or suggestions for making this form simpler, we would be happy to hear from you. You can write to the Tax Forms Committee, Western Area Distribution Center, Rancho Cordova, CA 95743-0001. **Do not** send the form to this address. Instead, see **Where To File** on this page.

Form **4506**
(Rev. May 1997)

Department of the Treasury
Internal Revenue Service

Request for Copy or Transcript of Tax Form

▶ **Read instructions before completing this form.**

▶ **Type or print clearly. Request may be rejected if the form is incomplete or illegible.**

OMB No. 1545-0429

Note: *Do not* use this form to get *tax account information*. *Instead, see instructions below.*

1a Name shown on tax form. If a joint return, enter the name shown first.	1b **First social security number on tax form or employer identification number** (see instructions)
2a If a joint return, spouse's name shown on tax form	2b **Second social security number on tax form**

3 Current name, address (including apt., room, or suite no.), city, state, and ZIP code

4 Address, (including apt., room, or suite no.), city, state, and ZIP code shown on the last return filed if different from line 3

5 If copy of form or a tax return transcript is to be mailed to someone else, enter the third party's name and address

6 If we cannot find a record of your tax form and you want the payment refunded to the third party, check here . . . . . . ▶ ☐

7 If name in third party's records differs from line 1a above, enter that name here (see instructions) ▶

8 Check only one box to show what you want. There is **no charge** for items 8a, b, and c:

a ☐ Tax return transcript of Form 1040 series filed during the **current calendar year** and the **3 prior calendar years** (see instructions).

b ☐ Verification of nonfiling.

c ☐ Form(s) W-2 information (see instructions).

d ☐ Copy of tax form and all attachments (including Form(s) W-2, schedules, or other forms). **The charge is $23 for each period requested.**
  Note: *If these copies must be certified for court or administrative proceedings, see instructions and check here* . . . . . ▶ ☐

9 If this request is to meet a requirement of one of the following, check all boxes that apply.
  ☐ Small Business Administration   ☐ Department of Education   ☐ Department of Veterans Affairs   ☐ Financial institution

10 **Tax form number** (Form 1040, 1040A, 941, etc.)	**12** Complete only if **line 8d** is checked. Amount due:	
	a Cost for each period	$ **23.00**
11 **Tax period(s)** (year or period ended date). If more than four, see instructions.	**b** Number of tax periods requested on line 11	
	c Total cost. Multiply line 12a by line 12b. .	$
	Full payment must accompany your request. Make check or money order payable to "Internal Revenue Service."	

Caution: *Before signing, make sure all items are complete and the form is dated.*

I declare that I am either the taxpayer whose name is shown on line 1a or 2a, or a person authorized to obtain the tax information requested. I am aware that based upon this form, the IRS will release the tax information requested to any party shown on line 5. The IRS has no control over what that party does with the information.

Please Sign Here

▶ Signature. See instructions. If other than taxpayer, attach authorization document.   Date

▶ Title (if line 1a above is a corporation, partnership, estate, or trust)

▶ Spouse's signature   Date

Telephone number of requester
( )

Best time to call

TRY A TAX RETURN TRANSCRIPT (see line 8a instructions)

Instructions

Section references are to the Internal Revenue Code.

TIP: If you had your tax form filled in by a paid preparer, check first to see if you can get a copy from the preparer. This may save you both time and money.

Purpose of Form.—Use Form 4506 to get a tax return transcript, verification that you did not file a Federal tax return, Form W-2 information, or a copy of a tax form. Allow 6 weeks after you file a tax form before you request a copy of it or a transcript. For W-2

information, wait 13 months after the end of the year in which the wages were earned. For example, wait until Feb. 1999 to request W-2 information for wages earned in 1997.

Do not use this form to request Forms 1099 or tax account information. See this page for details on how to get these items.

Note: *Form 4506 must be received by the IRS within 60 calendar days after the date you signed and dated the request.*

How Long Will It Take?—You can get a tax return transcript or verification of nonfiling within 7 to 10 workdays after the IRS receives your request. It can take up to 60 calendar

days to get a copy of a tax form or W-2 information. To avoid any delay, be sure to furnish all the information asked for on Form 4506.

Forms 1099.—If you need a copy of a Form 1099, contact the payer. If the payer cannot help you, call or visit the IRS to get Form 1099 information.

Tax Account Information.—If you need a statement of your tax account showing any later changes that you or the IRS made to the original return, request tax account information. Tax account information lists

(Continued on back)

For Privacy Act and Paperwork Reduction Act Notice, see back of form.   Cat. No. 41721E   Form **4506** (Rev. 5-97)

certain items from your return, including any later changes.

To request tax account information, write or visit an IRS office or call the IRS at the number listed in your telephone directory.

If you want your tax account information sent to a third party, complete **Form 8821, Tax Information Authorization.** You may get this form by phone (call 1-800-829-3676) or on the Internet (at http://www.irs.ustreas.gov).

Line 1b.—Enter your employer identification number (EIN) **only** if you are requesting a copy of a **business** tax form. Otherwise, enter the first social security number (SSN) shown on the tax form.

Line 2b.—If requesting a copy or transcript of a joint tax form, enter the second SSN shown on the tax form.

Note: *If you do not complete line 1b and, if applicable, line 2b, there may be a delay in processing your request.*

Line 5.—If you want someone else to receive the tax form or tax return transcript (such as a CPA, an enrolled agent, a scholarship board, or a mortgage lender), enter the name and address of the individual. If we cannot find a record of your tax form, we will notify the third party directly that we cannot fill the request.

Line 7.—Enter the name of the client, student, or applicant if it is different from the name shown on line 1a. For example, the name on line 1a may be the parent of a student applying for financial aid. In this case, you would enter the student's name on line 7 so the scholarship board can associate the tax form or tax return transcript with their file.

Line 8a.—If you want a tax return transcript, check this box. Also, on line 10 enter the tax form number and on line 11 enter the tax period for which you want the transcript.

A tax return transcript is available only for returns in the 1040 series (Form 1040, Form 1040A, 1040EZ, etc.). It shows most line items from the original return, including accompanying forms and schedules. In many cases, a transcript will meet the requirement of any lending institution such as a financial institution, the Department of Education, or the Small Business Administration. It may also be used to verify that you did not claim any itemized deductions for a residence.

Note: *A tax return transcript **does not** reflect any changes you or the IRS made to the original return. If you want a statement of your tax account with the changes, see **Tax Account Information** on page 1.*

Line 8b.—Check this box only if you want proof from the IRS that you did not file a return for the year. Also, on line 11 enter the tax period for which you want verification of nonfiling.

Line 8c.—If you want only Form(s) W-2 information, check this box. Also, on line 10 enter "Form(s) W-2 only" and on line 11 enter the tax period for which you want the information.

You may receive a copy of your actual Form W-2 or a transcript of the information, depending on how your employer filed the form. However, state withholding information is not shown on a transcript. If you have filed your tax return for the year the wages were earned, you can get a copy of the actual Form W-2 by requesting a complete copy of your return and paying the required fee.

Contact your employer if you have lost your current year's Form W-2 or have not received it by the time you are ready to prepare your tax return.

Note: *If you are requesting information about your spouse's Form W-2, your spouse must sign Form 4506.*

Line 8d.—If you want a certified copy of a tax form for court or administrative proceedings, check the box to the right of line 8d. It will take at least 60 days to process your request.

Line 11.—Enter the year(s) of the tax form or tax return transcript you want. For fiscal-year filers or requests for quarterly tax forms, enter the date the period ended; for example, 3/31/96, 6/30/96, etc. If you need more than four different tax periods, use additional Forms 4506. Tax forms filed 6 or more years ago may not be available for making copies. However, tax account information is generally still available for these periods.

Line 12c.—Write your SSN or EIN **and** "Form 4506 Request" on your check or money order. If we cannot fill your request, we will refund your payment.

Signature.—Requests for copies of tax forms or tax return transcripts to be sent to a third party must be signed by the person whose name is shown on line 1a or by a person authorized to receive the requested information.

Copies of tax forms or tax return transcripts for a jointly filed return may be furnished to either the husband or the wife. Only one signature is required. However, see the line 8c instructions. Sign Form 4506 exactly as your name appeared on the original tax form. If you changed your name, **also** sign your current name.

For a corporation, the signature of the president of the corporation, or any principal officer and the secretary, or the principal officer and another officer are generally required. For more details on who may obtain tax information on corporations, partnerships, estates, and trusts, see section 6103.

If you are **not** the taxpayer shown on line 1a, you must attach your authorization to receive a copy of the requested tax form or tax return transcript. You may **attach a copy of the authorization document** if the original has already been filed with the IRS. This will generally be a **power of attorney** (Form 2848), or **other authorization,** such as Form 8821, or evidence of entitlement (for Title 11 Bankruptcy or Receivership Proceedings). If the taxpayer is deceased, you must send Letters Testamentary or other evidence to establish that you are authorized to act for the taxpayer's estate.

Where To File.—Mail Form 4506 with the correct total payment attached, if required, to the **Internal Revenue Service Center** for the place where you lived when the requested tax form was filed.

Note: *You must use a separate form for each service center from which you are requesting a copy of your tax form or tax return transcript.*

If you lived in:	Use this address:
New Jersey, New York (New York City and counties of Nassau, Rockland, Suffolk, and Westchester)	1040 Waverly Ave. Photocopy Unit Stop 532 Holtsville, NY 11742
New York (all other counties), Connecticut, Maine, Massachusetts, New Hampshire, Rhode Island, Vermont	310 Lowell St. Photocopy Unit Stop 679 Andover, MA 01810
Florida, Georgia, South Carolina	4800 Buford Hwy. Photocopy Unit Stop 91 Doraville, GA 30362
Indiana, Kentucky, Michigan, Ohio, West Virginia	P.O. Box 145500 Photocopy Unit Stop 521 Cincinnati, OH 45250
Kansas, New Mexico, Oklahoma, Texas	3651 South Interregional Hwy. Photocopy Unit Stop 6716 Austin, TX 73301
Alaska, Arizona, California (counties of Alpine, Amador, Butte, Calaveras, Colusa, Contra Costa, Del Norte, El Dorado, Glenn, Humboldt, Lake, Lassen, Marin, Mendocino, Modoc, Napa, Nevada, Placer, Plumas, Sacramento, San Joaquin, Shasta, Sierra, Siskiyou, Solano, Sonoma, Sutter, Tehama, Trinity, Yolo, and Yuba), Colorado, Idaho, Montana, Nebraska, Nevada, North Dakota, Oregon, South Dakota, Utah, Washington, Wyoming	P.O. Box 9941 Photocopy Unit Stop 6734 Ogden, UT 84409
California (all other counties), Hawaii	5045 E. Butler Avenue Photocopy Unit Stop 52180 Fresno, CA 93888
Illinois, Iowa, Minnesota, Missouri, Wisconsin	2306 E. Bannister Road Photocopy Unit Stop 6700, Annex 1 Kansas City, MO 64999
Alabama, Arkansas, Louisiana, Mississippi, North Carolina, Tennessee	P.O. Box 30309 Photocopy Unit Stop 46 Memphis, TN 38130
Delaware, District of Columbia, Maryland, Pennsylvania, Virginia, a foreign country, or A.P.O. or F.P.O address	11601 Roosevelt Blvd. Photocopy Unit DP 536 Philadelphia, PA 19255

Privacy Act and Paperwork Reduction Act Notice.—We ask for the information on this form to establish your right to gain access to your tax form or transcript under the Internal Revenue Code, including sections 6103 and 6109. We need it to gain access to your tax form or transcript in our files and properly respond to your request. If you do not furnish the information, we will not be able to fill your request. We may give the information to the Department of Justice or other appropriate law enforcement official, as provided by law.

You are not required to provide the information requested on a form that is subject to the Paperwork Reduction Act unless the form displays a valid OMB control number. Books or records relating to a form or its instructions must be retained as long as their contents may become material in the administration of any Internal Revenue law. Generally, tax returns and return information are confidential, as required by section 6103.

The time needed to complete and file this form will vary depending on individual circumstances. The estimated average time is: **Recordkeeping,** 13 min.; **Learning about the law or the form,** 7 min.; **Preparing the form,** 26 min.; and **Copying, assembling, and sending the form to the IRS,** 17 min.

If you have comments concerning the accuracy of these time estimates or suggestions for making this form simpler, we would be happy to hear from you. You can write to the Tax Forms Committee, Western Area Distribution Center, Rancho Cordova, CA 95743-0001. **DO NOT** send the form to this address. Instead, see **Where To File** on this page.

REQUEST FOR COPY OF PERSONAL INCOME TAX OR FIDUCIARY RETURN

Please see other side of this form to request Bank & Corporation (100, 100S, 100WE or 199), Partnership (565) or Limited Liability Company (568) Returns.

NAME AND ADDRESS PHOTOCOPIES ARE TO BE MAILED TO	NAME AND ADDRESS OF TAXPAYER(S) AS SHOWN ON TAX RETURN/CLAIM

TAX RETURN REQUESTED *(Check box)*	TAX YEAR(S)	SOCIAL SECURITY NUMBER(S) (If Joint return enter spouse's SSN below)
☐ 540 ☐ 540A ☐ 540EZ ☐ 540ADS or ☐ 540NR PIT Return		
☐ 541 — Fiduciary Income Tax Return		SPOUSE'S SSN

SIGNATURE OF TAXPAYER	TYPE OR PRINT NAME	DATE
SIGNATURE OF SPOUSE		
DAYTIME TELEPHONE NUMBER ( )		

Tax returns are available ONLY for the last 3 years.

You must sign this request. Without proper authorization, we will be unable to provide you with the requested copies. If you are not the taxpayer, you must provide appropriate authorization to receive copies of tax returns or claims. Appropriate authorization includes one of the following:

- A letter signed by the taxpayer authorizing Franchise Tax Board (FTB) to release the requested material to you;

  OR
- A Power of Attorney (FTB 3520) currently in effect;

  OR
- An Internal Revenue Service (IRS) Power of Attorney stating that it applies to FTB (above limitations still apply);

  OR
- Form FTB 3516 signed by the taxpayer;

  OR
- In the case of a deceased taxpayer, a certified copy of the letters of administration or testamentary, dated within the past 12 months. If the letters are more than 12 months old, a clerk of the court must recertify them stating they are still in effect.

If a bankruptcy is involved and you are not the taxpayer, you must:

- Provide court documents appointing you as trustee;

  OR
- Provide a letter signed by the trustee authorizing you to receive this material and a copy of the court documents appointing the trustee;

  OR
- Provide appropriate authorization.

There is no charge for a copy of your personal income tax return if the tax year requested meets the following criteria:

- The copy of the return is requested during or after an audit or collection activity related to an audit.
- You have been a victim of a designated California state or federal disaster.

If you do not meet either of the above criteria, send a check payable to the Franchise Tax Board for $10.00 for each tax year requested.

Mail your request to:
Franchise Tax Board
RID Unit
PO Box 942867
Sacramento CA 94267-0001
For additional information call (916) 845-5375.

FTB 3516 (REV 11-1998) SIDE 1 – PIT

REQUEST FOR COPY OF BANK & CORPORATION, PARTNERSHIP OR LIMITED LIABILITY COMPANY RETURN

Please see other side of this form to request Personal Income Tax (540, 540A, 540EZ, 540ADS or 540NR) or Fiduciary (541) Returns.

NAME AND ADDRESS PHOTOCOPIES ARE TO BE MAILED TO	NAME AND ADDRESS OF TAXPAYER(S) AS SHOWN ON TAX RETURN/CLAIM

TAX RETURN REQUESTED *(Check box)*	TAXABLE OR INCOME YEAR(S)	CALIFORNIA SECRETARY OF STATE NUMBER	FEDERAL EMPLOYER IDENTIFICATION NUMBER
☐ 100 — Corporation Return			
☐ 100WE — Water's Edge Corporation Return			
☐ 100S — S Corporation Return			
☐ 199 — Exempt Organization Return			
☐ 565 — Partnership Return			
☐ 568 — Limited Liability Company Return			

I declare under penalty of perjury, I am a current authorized representative for the above taxpayer.

SIGNATURE AND TITLE OF OFFICER OR TRUSTEE	TYPE OR PRINT NAME	DATE
DAYTIME TELEPHONE NUMBER ( )		

A current authorized representative of the taxpayer must sign this request and provide the business title. Without proper authorization we will be unable to provide the requested copies.

If a suspended corporation is involved, any amounts owed must be paid prior to disclosure of the requested information. To determine the amounts owed call one of the following numbers: from within the United States, (800) 852-5711; from outside the United States (not toll-free), (916) 845-6500; or for the hearing impaired (800) 822-6268.

If a bankruptcy is involved and you are not the taxpayer, you must:

- Provide court documents appointing you as trustee;

OR

- Provide a letter signed by the trustee authorizing you to receive this material and a copy of the court documents appointing the trustee;

OR

- Provide appropriate authorization.

Send no money for requests for copies of Bank & Corporation, Partnership or Limited Liability Company returns. If there are any charges, you will receive a bill.

Mail your request to:
Franchise Tax Board
RID Unit Corp
PO Box 942857
Sacramento CA 94257-0560

For additional information call (916) 845-5375.

FTB 3516 (REV 11-1998) SIDE 2 – B&C

4

What Happens Emotionally in a Divorce and Why You Should Care
and
How Do You Know How Your Client Is Faring during the Divorce Litigation?

Geoffrey Hamilton
Thomas S. Merrill, Ph.D.

WHAT HAPPENS EMOTIONALLY IN A DIVORCE AND WHY YOU SHOULD CARE

In the most simple terms, clients go through three chronological emotional stages in a divorce. These stages are *deliberation, transition* ("crazy time"), and *recovery* or *reemergence of self*. The best books for clients to read in this area that we have found are *Crazy Time, Surviving Divorce* (Trafford, 1982), and *Second Chances* (Wallerstein and Blakeslee, 1988). Practicing lawyers also may be interested in *Divorce Mediation* (Hayes), especially Chapter 2, which deals with the emotional stages of divorce.

The divorce litigation we are all familiar with usually starts out at the end of the deliberation phase, at the earliest, and at the latest may come as an afterthought—well after the parties have completed their emotional recovery from the physical and emotional separation.

The emotional stages generally are not chronologically in lockstep for both parties. In a normal case, the initiator of the divorce—the one who wants the divorce and is pushing for it—generally goes through the stages first, and the noninitiator generally lags behind chronologically.

The deliberation phase starts when the initiator first contemplates divorce and ends generally at the point of marital no return. The path between those two points generally is twisted and tortuous. There may be covert destructive behavior on the part of the initiator to somehow make the divorce inevitable. Almost invariably, there is considerable ambivalence in a back-and-forth fashion with efforts made to make the relationship work on the one hand and to initiate the divorce on the other. The deliberation phase generally ends on separation, although all of us know couples who have separated repeatedly before getting divorced.

The transition phase is, of course, the time of most of the "nutty" behavior we see in our practice. It commences on separation and lasts an indefinite period of time, depending on the length of the marriage and the nastiness of the divorce, among other things. Basically, the process during this phase is simply one of completing the rites of passage between being a couple and being relatively well-adjusted as a single person. The process involves anger, guilt, fear of failure, fear of rejection, hopelessness, grief, and other painful emotional states. Anger, in particular, seems to be a key ingredient, for it contributes to breaking down the attachment to the "coupleness" the parties experienced before.

Recovery or redirection or reemergence of self occurs when the parties seem to be able to act and to support themselves emotionally, independently of each other. They no longer consider themselves as married.

The litigation process, of course, generally starts at the end of the deliberation phase and may go all the way over to the redirection phase. As such, the litigation occurs in a time of turbulent changes for the client and is permeated by the emotions that go with them.

Our tip is simply that your ability to practice will improve to the degree that your sensitivity to the emotional aspects of divorce is enhanced. If you can recognize the initiator and the noninitiator and recognize what stage they are in, your settlement efforts will be better timed and will be more effective. Generally, parties buried in the convolutions of "crazy time" and the bizarre behavior that goes with it will not be amenable to either sending or receiving reasonable settlement offers. They simply have to pass to the next emotional phase before they can focus responsibility on settlement. In general, the further the emotional stages of divorce have progressed for both parties, the easier the case will be to settle, simply because the emotional fervor has died down and the parties are intent on getting on with their lives. Finally, your life will be easier and your clients will be better adjusted if they know what to expect in the emotional stages they and their spouses may go through. Take the time to tell them about this area.

HOW DO YOU KNOW HOW YOUR CLIENT IS FARING DURING THE DIVORCE LITIGATION?

We have stressed the importance of identifying the stages of divorce as a predictive tool to assist you in your offer–negotiation–settlement process. As we have said, the transition phase is that time in the process that you are most likely to encounter the bizarre, weird, and/or nutty behavior in your client and/or his or her spouse. The degree to which you are able to accurately identify and assess the stage and the concomitant nutty behavior is the degree to which you will be successful in the process.

So you ask, how do I tell where they are psychologically, and when do I need to call for help? Our Client Assessment Scale has been designed to help you in this regard. It is the starting point for you to use as a framework, a tool to begin to get a handle on your client's behavior and/or potential behavior.

DIRECTIONS FOR USE AND INTERPRETATION

Determine the points to be assigned for each of the seven categories of the scale. Place the points for each category in the appropriate space in the right-hand column. Total the points to determine the Divorce Quotient Rating and plan accordingly.

1. Determine whether your client is the divorcer (DOR) or the divorcee (DEE). Place the appropriate points in the right-hand column, e.g., five points if he or she is the DOR and ten if the DEE.

2. Determine the duration of marriage, assign points accordingly, and place in the space in the right-hand column.

3. Self-esteem is a direct function of the feedback one gets from work, play, and primary relationships. The numbers in this section refer to how many of the three areas are nonfunctional. If only one area, e.g., relationship, is nonfunctional, then no points are assigned. If two areas are nonfunctional, then ten points are assigned, and if all three areas are out, then twenty points are assigned. Place the appropriate number in the space in the right-hand column.

4. Determine the time since separation; move to the right and determine the appropriate column for points (the first column if your client is the DOR and the second column if your client is the DEE). Place the points in the space in the far right-hand column.

5. If your client's income has been dependent on the spouse, assign the appropriate points. As in 4, select points from the appropriate DOR or DEE column and place in the space in the right-hand column.

6. If this is the first marriage for your client, assign the appropriate points from the DOR or DEE column and place in the space in the right-hand column.

7. How much emotional support does your client have? If he or she receives no support from family, friends, church, etc., then give the client ten points. If he or she receives support from only one of these areas, give the client five points, and if he or she receives support from two of the three areas, give the client one point. If the client has all three covered, he or she is given no points. Place the points in the space in the right-hand column.

Total the points:

- 20–30 points, and your client is in the borderline range. He or she will, for the most part, act appropriately with a minimal amount of nutty behavior noted.
- 30–40 points, and you will most likely experience problems with this client as a function of the emotional condition. You may want to get psychological help for him or her.
- 40–50 points, and you have a client who is/will be in need of help. Get it for him or her.
- 50+ points, and you have a client at serious risk. Mandate that he or she be in active therapy.
- This format also can be used to estimate what shape your client's spouse is in to anticipate how he or she is going to act throughout the process.

CLIENT ASSESSMENT SCALE

		DOR	DEE	
DIVORCER (DOR) 5				_____
DIVORCEE (DEE) 10				_____

DURATION OF MARRIAGE: POINTS
        1-3 YEARS   1
        3-6 YEARS   3
        7-10 YEARS   5
        11-20 YEARS   8
        20+   10   _____

SELF ESTEEM: RELATIONSHIP_____ 1=0
               WORK   _____ 2=10
               PLAY   _____ 3=20   _____

TIME SINCE SEPARATION:

	DOR	DEE	
0-3 MONTHS	1	10	
4-6 MONTHS	1	10	
7-12 MONTHS	2	8	
1-2 YEARS	3	5	
2+ YEARS	3	3	_____
INCOME DEPENDENT ON SPOUSE	5	10	_____
FIRST MARRIAGE	5	10	_____

EMOTIONAL SUPPORT SYSTEM:
        FAMILY_____   0=10
        FRIENDS_____   1=5
        SPIRITUAL_____   2=1   _____

GRAND TOTAL   _____

RATING:
        20-30   BORDERLINE
        30-40   PROBLEMATIC
        40-50   IN NEED OF HELP
        50-   AT RISK

© Copyright 1989

29

5

Narrowing Your Client's Focus

Harold G. Field

FOR MOST CLIENTS, divorce is the greatest tragedy they have suffered—for a greater number, the most imminent. If it is also their first encounter with the judicial process or a lawyer, they have additional apprehensions.

Clients anticipating divorce dread the first meeting with a lawyer. They have to discuss the failure of their marriage. It is natural for them to have mixed emotions of hate, love, shame, guilt, fear, anguish, or revenge that they may find inexplicable. While they are ostensibly listening to the answers you give to their questions, they often are so engulfed in remorse and self-pity that they cannot absorb the responses.

We all know it is best to discuss fees at the first meeting even if the client is too shy to broach the subject. This prevents future misunderstandings.

In addition, most (but not all) clients would like you to discuss the ultimate question concerning their litigation, such as, "In addition to your bill, what am I likely to get when this is all over?"

Obviously, just as you cannot predict the total legal fee after the first meeting, you cannot tell the client the likely division of property or income. But you can discuss the possibilities in the same broad way that you discuss your fees.

This helps the clients focus on the end of the case instead of on their daily emotional misgivings. Tell them the best and worst scenarios. You certainly know within 20 percent to 30 percent how judges will divide the marital property. Child support and perhaps even maintenance will fall within a smaller percentile of difference. You should explain that maintenance and unequal divisions of property intertwine and tend to offset each other. The percentages you set must be wide enough to include the client's situation but close enough to be reasonably definitive.

In addition to discussing the brackets of likelihood of recovery, my tip is to give clients a photocopy of your state's divorce statute. Underline the statutes that clients frequently question, including child support guidelines, elements considered for maintenance, and whether fault is considered in the division of property or the amount of support. After leaving the office and during the proceedings, the clients will be able to review the statute. This will help them understand the judicial process and your esoteric legalese.

This also has the added benefit of reminding people that the legislators whom they voted into office, not judges and lawyers, made these rules. They then may be able to understand that the statutes are the structure used to resolve legal problems. By narrowing your clients' concentration to ultimate goals, you will help them to cope with their interim apprehensions.

6

Put Your Client to Work

C. Terrence Kapp

EXPERIENCED DIVORCE LAWYERS ask the new client to bring to the initial interview various financial documents. At this point, however, the client's focus is on his or her pain, confusion, and worries about the future, not about the divorce process. Therefore, even if the client is able to bring some of the requested documents, talking intelligently and informatively at that initial interview is most difficult for the client. It is the rare client who comes to an interview fully aware of and conversant about the extent and value of the marital property.

Regardless of how many financial documents the client brings to the initial interview, at the close of the interview, you should present the client with two documents. Rather than just handing the forms to the client, it is better practice to sit down next to the client and go over these forms page by page. Personalizing your interest and emphasizing the value of the forms will greatly enhance the benefits that follow, especially benefit number 12. The first document requires the client to produce a comprehensive listing of all monthly expenses of the client, the client's spouse, and the client's children. In addition, the client is required to go through the marital home and inventory its contents room by room and categorize each item by source, cost, and approximate value. The purpose of this exercise is to educate the client about marital and nonmarital property and to educate the client about the exact age and condition of the household goods and furniture.

The client also is given a comprehensive form to complete that requires the client to search for and obtain documents regarding detailed financial information. This form is to be completed in the client's own handwriting. Again, this is done even if the client has brought various documents to the initial interview. The form to use is more than twenty pages long and contains two pages of detailed but easy-to-understand instructions. I obtained the basis for it from *Family Law Tax Guide*, published by Commerce Clearing House. This form covers the following:

1. Tax returns;
2. Net-worth statements;

3. Retirement plans;
4. Retirement accounts;
5. Real estate—legal descriptions;
6. Receipted real estate tax bills;
7. Real estate appraisal;
8. Life insurance;
9. Medical insurance;
10. Bank accounts;
11. Securities;
12. Business interests;
13. Estate or trust interests;
14. Safety deposit box; and
15. Client's appraisers and professional advisers.

Requiring the client to work or to attempt to work on these financial matters provides the following benefits:

1. It immediately impresses the client with the complexity of a divorce case and of your thoroughness as the lawyer.
2. The client feels as if he or she is doing something positive on his or her own behalf.
3. It increases the client's awareness of the lawyer's job of discovery; that is, if the client is unable to obtain the information, the client appreciates the discovery process the lawyer has to go through to obtain the financial data.
4. It educates the client regarding the true financial picture if the documents are obtainable.
5. If the documents are not available, the client immediately realizes the serious degree to which he or she is uninformed about his or her financial status.
6. It highlights the reasons why the lawyer needs the information and must analyze it.
7. The client becomes acutely aware that essential information is missing and must be obtained.
8. It gives the client a good impression of what you, the lawyer, are doing.
9. The client feels as if he or she is part of a team.
10. The client who cooperates in this process becomes a much more intelligent and informed client and is more likely to listen to, understand, and accept your advice.
11. The client becomes a better witness.
12. Finally, the odds are that if the client is interviewing or has interviewed other lawyers, the client will retain you at the close of the interview.

7

Empowering Clients

John E. Finnerty

MANY PEOPLE WHO COME TO US, especially women, are terrified of the process upon which they are about to embark. Usually they have heard stories from friends of how the court system is out of control and runs amuck over people's lives. This exacerbates their own terror about divorce, particularly if they have been the "out-of-control economic spouse." They feel they have no knowledge of business, investments, or money and, therefore, that they have no power.

We find we can help assuage the clients' anxiety by enlisting them in a client/lawyer "fact-gathering presentation team." We remind them that although what they are about to embark upon seems foreign and overwhelming, they are not as impotent as they feel. In fact, they have more knowledge than they realize. In effect, clients receive a pep talk and gain insights into the knowledge they have and *how* they can help the lawyer obtain information that can be put to use for their benefit. We find this approach helps abate the client's feelings of impotence and anxiety. How do we typically do this?

PENDENTE LITE APPLICATIONS AND BUDGETS

This is one of the most critical parts of a case. In complex asset cases, there is need for much documentary and other discovery and investigation by experts. During this time, the lifestyle previously enjoyed must be continued as closely as possible if clients are not to be worn down and to give up because of the frustrations of not having sufficient money to do the things that had become a normal part of their lives. Initially, when we ask how much money was spent for budget items, clients throw up their hands at the traditional budget form, claiming that they have no idea how much things cost on a weekly or monthly basis. We then pick a few line items and take them through a day or week in their lives and help them reconstruct how often they went out to dinner, what the typical cost was, how it was paid for, etc. We divide the total cost by the number of people present and multiply that result by 4.3 (the number of weeks per month) and show clients that they can re-create a marital lifestyle by simply approaching the task as a review of daily customs and habits. This process is repeated for different expenditures.

We know most law firms like to have the client budget forms filled out by the client with the assistance of a paralegal, senior experienced secretary, or junior associate. However, we feel that these forms are of crucial importance for the litigation. In New Jersey, they are called Case Information Statements (CIS) and are sworn. Careless preparation of a CIS will expose your client to impeachment and the perception that he or she is a blithering idiot. In addition, the interaction between client and lawyer on this issue helps reinforce the client's confidence in your ability by lessening anxiety. In short, you have made the client feel better because he or she feels in control. We usually find that after the lawyer has begun the process with clients, the clients can, on their own, repeat that process for other budget items with the assistance of a well-trained paralegal. The process should be begun, however, with a lawyer.

LIFESTYLE PROOF

When a substantial lifestyle was created and the tax return does not show the earned wealth, then you have a lifestyle proof problem. Something concrete must be latched onto to persuade the court to accept as credible your version of the facts. This is very difficult to do without objective documentary proof. We remind clients that their lifestyles during better times probably were demonstrated by scores of photographs. Photographs of the house in an exclusive neighborhood on rolling hills with lakes, swimming pools, or tennis courts probably will support the inference of income greater than $50,000 per year; photographs of expensive cars in the driveway and luxurious family vacation settings demonstrate the same thing. (Hopefully, this tip will not cause the removal of all marital photographs from the control of both spouses when a divorce is planned.) Also, documents that are submitted in support of applications to banks usually have very positive assertions concerning financial circumstances, and we send clients scouting out for these documents.

8

Communicating with the Client

Robert B. Moriarty

THE SAMPLE FORM LETTER that follows provides the client with an overview of your office's philosophy and routine proceedings in the case. It will take little time to adapt the letter to the specifics of your office and your jurisdiction. Its use will save you time spent answering telephone calls, save you the need to repeat advice previously given, give your client a better idea of what is happening in his or her case, and work to improve the lawyer–client relationship.

Dear Client:

The goal of our office is to provide courteous, competent, professional service to our clients. As specialists in the field of matrimonial law, we are well qualified to represent you in matrimonial matters, and we pledge to you the best result that can be obtained by hard work and ethical representation.

Just a few words about our firm. We limit our practice to divorce, custody, and family law. Our firm of ten people—three lawyers and seven support staff—is dedicated to producing maximum results for you.

Members of our firm frequently lecture to other lawyers on divorce, custody, and related matrimonial law issues. During the past year, for example, Mr. Moriarty spoke on the Continuing Legal Education Satellite Network to lawyers across the country on the laws governing international and interstate child abduction and child custody, spoke to the American Bar Association on matrimonial law, and made several other speaking appearances to lawyers' groups. Ms. Condon spoke on different aspects of matrimonial law to the State University of New York at Buffalo School of Law, the Fund for Modern Courts, the New York Women's Bar Association, and the Child and Adolescent Psychiatric Clinic.

Members of our firm write professionally. Mr. Moriarty is co-author of the *New York Practice Guide* on divorce law published for Matthew Bender & Company, the nation's largest law publisher. In addition, articles by Mr. Moriarty or Ms. Condon have been published in the *American Bar Association Section of Family Law Annual Compendium,* the *New York Family Law Review,* the *Erie County Bar Bulletin,* the *Buffalo Business Journal, Family Concerns,* and other publications. We relate these accomplishments to you not to pat ourselves on the back, but simply to assure you that we are specialists in matrimonial law and are particularly well trained and skilled to represent you in these matters.

At this point a few words on the philosophy of our firm in handling matrimonial matters are in order.

Let us begin by noting that we fully support efforts toward reconciliation. If, at any time during the course of your action, you feel the need to reconsider your decision for divorce or separation, please do not hesitate to advise us of your desire not to proceed. If you wish, we can supply you with the names of marital counselors, psychiatrists, psychologists, and others who may be able to counsel with you regarding reconciliation, divorce, custody, and visitation problems, or any of the other wide range of problems parties in the process of divorce or separation might experience.

With respect to counseling, please be aware that we are not marital counselors. Although many years of practicing divorce law enables us to provide some answers, serious marital counseling problems are something for which we are not trained. If either you or we recognize the need for professional help, please do not hesitate to obtain it.

Our goal in handling your case is to resolve it quickly. Although the expeditious handling of a case requires the cooperation of both sides and the courts, we work hard to move a case along in a speedy and efficient manner. We realize the toll litigation takes and the psychological burden it places on parties and children, and you can be assured that we will make every effort to resolve your matter at the earliest possible moment without sacrificing your interests.

Please note that our approach to matrimonial litigation always will be to act in such a way as not to make a bad situation worse. We always will conduct ourselves in a civilized, courteous manner and conduct negotiations to make every effort to defuse tensions, avoid hostility, and maximize the ability of the parties and lawyers to arrive at a fair and reasonable settlement. It is our belief, supported by numerous studies and our own experience, that a negotiated agreement between the parties serves both parties best because it allows the parties to "fine-tune" matters between themselves in a way the courts often are unable to do. The court never will know a case as well as the parties and the lawyers do, and it always is prudent to work out a settlement if at all possible.

At times, however, despite the best efforts of lawyers and clients, settlement cannot be reached. In our experience, this is less than 5 percent of the time. Settlement may be impossible to achieve for a number of reasons, including the unrealistic expectations of the parties, disputes about the facts or the law, the existence of novel and as yet undecided issues, or the desire on the part of a party to deny a divorce to the spouse. In those instances, where trial is necessary, we are well qualified to represent you. Our ability to try cases when necessary allows us to negotiate from a position of strength.

Clients often ask whether being in litigation prevents discussion of settlement. Settlement discussions can proceed at any time—before, during, or even after trial. Ordinarily, it is better to conduct settlement negotiations after an action has been commenced to obtain the advantage of disclosure and discovery devices and so that the time spent in negotiation is not lost in the event settlement is not achieved. This is a tactical position that depends on the facts and circumstances of your case, however, and we will advise you if we feel your case should proceed otherwise. Settlement discussions may take place at the courthouse or at the lawyers' offices, and may be conducted with or without clients. Some clients wish to take an active part in settlement discussions and wish to be present at all times; some clients prefer to leave all matters to the lawyers or prefer to minimize contact with a spouse. Please advise us on your feelings about participating and we will act accordingly.

In the event litigation is commenced, certain formal stages will occur. In New York State an action for divorce is commenced by the service of a Summons in an Action for Divorce by one party upon the other. The summons may be accompanied by moving papers seeking temporary relief and/or by the "Complaint," which is a formal, written document itemizing the grounds for divorce.

New York State is a "grounds" state and it *may* be necessary in your case for you to supply us with a detailed marital history, with particular emphasis on the problems occurring in the past five years of the marriage, to assist us in drafting the complaint. As a general rule, our need for a full marital history will depend on whether your spouse is contesting your right to a divorce, the length of the marriage, and the presence of children. If your spouse is not going to contest the divorce, the grounds for divorce are not meaningful in the ordinary case. If your marriage is a marriage of short duration without children, again, the grounds for divorce are not meaningful in the ordinary case. If you are asked by us to supply a detailed history of the marriage, please do so as quickly as possible.

After the service of a complaint by the plaintiff, the defendant is entitled to serve a "Counterclaim," which is the defendant's equivalent of a complaint. The same rules govern the counterclaim.

Both sides also are entitled to what is commonly called "discovery" or "disclosure." Discovery refers to the right and responsibility of both parties to obtain and provide information, primarily financial, to the other side. Several types of discovery proceedings may be utilized in your case, but the most commonly used discovery device is the deposition or examination before trial (sometimes called EBT). This proceeding involves taking sworn testimony of you, your spouse, or both of you at one of the lawyers' offices. Usually, both clients, both lawyers, and a court reporter are present.

The deposition is an important part of your case. In connection with your own testimony, you normally will be required to bring a large number of financial documents with you, some of which you may already have provided to us. In the event that we are requested to provide your testimony at a deposition, we will write to you in advance of the date scheduled and provide to you a copy of the notice of documents requested by your spouse's lawyer. (A typical list of documents required is enclosed with the packet of information we provided to you earlier and will serve as a useful guide for you to follow as a head start in compiling this information now.) Please review this notice carefully and bring two copies of every document requested with you on the date of the scheduled deposition. When we advise you of the date of the deposition, we will give you a letter telling you more about the deposition and other information you should know about it. Please read this letter carefully.

To prepare for the deposition, we normally will schedule a meeting with you shortly before the deposition begins, at which time we will review the subject matter of your testimony and discuss several simple rules to be observed. To assist us in preparing you for the deposition and to familiarize you with this procedure, we have available for your viewing a videotape of a mock deposition that you may watch at our office at any time between 9:00 A.M. and 3:00 P.M. To do so, simply contact our receptionist, who then will make arrangements for you to view the videotape. Please allow approximately one half hour for viewing the tape.

In most cases, an EBT can be completed at the first session. In many cases, however, either because of the complexity of issues or the failure to produce documents, several sessions are required.

Finally, depositions are of necessity adjourned from time to time, either because of engagement of counsel in trial, other proceedings that the courts mandate take priority, or for other good reason. We will give you as much notice of any adjournments as possible, but inevitably there will be times when we are unable to give more than short notice. It always is a good idea to check with our office on the afternoon before a morning deposition, or in the morning of a day when a deposition is scheduled for the afternoon, to make certain the examination is continuing as scheduled.

After all pretrial discovery has been completed, your case will be certified for trial and a pretrial conference will be scheduled.

The pretrial conference is a mandatory procedure that serves to bring lawyers and clients together, in the presence of the court, for the purpose of settlement. If we can reach settlement on all matters in dispute between you and your spouse on the scheduled date, your divorce on other issues in dispute might become final on that date. If settlement is not reached, the matter will be scheduled for a further pretrial, a report back to the court, or for trial.

The pretrial conference is not a trial itself, and no witnesses need be alerted.

Because of scheduling conflicts and the priority of hearings and trials that may be ordered in other cases, pretrials may be adjourned. Please confirm with us the day before a pretrial is scheduled to make certain the proceeding will proceed as scheduled.

We will, from time to time, provide other information about your case to you. Please read this letter and other information supplied to you closely. Your attention to these matters and your cooperation will help us to serve you efficiently and professionally.

We thank you for having entrusted this matter to us for handling.

Very truly yours,

MORIARTY & CONDON

By

9

The Importance of Keeping Your Clients Current

Gary N. Skoloff

IT IS A PRACTICE IN OUR LAW FIRM to return client telephone calls within twenty-four hours. Nothing can be more frustrating to litigants who are in the emotional throes of a divorce than to be unable to reach their lawyers. As a result, it is an unwritten rule in our law firm that telephone calls should be returned that day if possible, and in no event later than twenty-four hours.

This simple rule does much for us in developing our law practice. On many occasions, clients telephone us and ask that we substitute ourselves into cases where they are represented by good and competent matrimonial lawyers. The client's major complaint is that his or her lawyer does not return telephone calls and is not accessible. This is frustrating to the litigant who, as a result, loses faith in his or her counsel.

It is not unusual for couples going through divorces to meet each other and talk about their lawyers. The biggest complaint they may have is that their lawyers do not return telephone calls. Those going through divorce who speak to our firm's clients quickly find out that we have a reputation for returning telephone calls, and this is a vehicle for referrals.

One more very important point: A litigant who is contemplating a divorce usually will have the names of three divorce lawyers to interview. Many clients have told me that the reason they hired our firm was that we were the only law firm to return their telephone calls within a matter of hours to set up that initial interview. It is so basic that the initial contact be pleasant and take place quickly; yet, how many lawyers fail to return a potential client's telephone inquiry promptly? All the time, our firm is selected to represent a litigant solely on the basis that of three lawyers telephoned, we were the only firm to make contact within a few hours and we were the only firm that did not require the litigant to wait a week or two before making the initial appointment.

Therefore, we should think about how our services are perceived by the clients and not ourselves. We should practice law from the client's chair and not our own desk chair as a way of developing our reputation and a successful law practice.

10

Avoiding "Postparting Depression"

Lewis Kapner

WE HAVE ALL SEEN IT. You have just hammered out a brilliant settlement for your client. Everybody (on your side anyway) is weary but pleased. Yet, when you arrive at your office the next morning, you are greeted with a "While-You-Were-Outer" with a big "X" next to the "URGENT" block. You are about to call your client, but the matter is so pressing that your client has called you before you have had a chance. "What about the spa membership—who gets it? You [never the client, but you] forgot to bring it up."

How to avoid this?

First, you must, of course, do your best to make sure all the odds and ends are taken care of, and we all have (or should have) appropriate forms or procedures to make sure we cover everything. Usually, though, it is not so much a matter of having forgotten to cover it as it is dealing with the emotional letdown that inevitably follows the end of a marriage. Therefore, to best assure that all the jits and jots are covered, and to make sure that you have a satisfied client, I would suggest you put the major onus on your client to remember those personal items that are of great importance to him or her. Fully explain to your client what you are doing and why. Explain that it is impossible for a lawyer to be aware of every personal matter of importance, that you will be focusing on the "big picture" and you are going to have to rely on him or her to fill in the important details. Preferably, have the client write down a "wish list" that can be kept in a separate folder and given a final review before everything is agreed on.

Second, I would suggest that you explain the emotional ramifications of what is happening. I have found, particularly right before the signing of a settlement, that anticipating this postparting depression alleviates the aftershock. I explain to the client that these feelings surely will occur and the only way to avoid them is to delay the settlement and think about it overnight. (No one wants to do that.) Also, I explain to the client that if he or she does wake up at 3:00 A.M. panicking because the spa membership was not addressed, the client should go right back to sleep because a deal is a deal and it cannot be changed; however, the chances are the other party will be going through the same process, so if there is something of real importance, I encourage the client to tell me about it. So long as the client understands that the deal cannot be backed out of, and the other side has no obligation to provide anything that is not part of the agreement, I explain that I will do my best to accomplish some sort of trade-off. If not, I explain that that is simply the price to be paid for avoiding the rigors and uncertainty of a trial.

11

Setting the Stage and Closing the Curtain

Robert B. Moriarty

THE PROBLEM

From the very start every client asks one or more of the same questions: What am I going to get? What are my chances? Will I get custody, get the house, keep my pension, get enough support, be able to pay the support I am supposed to? These are just some of the questions asked. In today's information age and the age of consumerism, clients want to and need to know as much about their cases as possible.

Usually, the client's desire to know conflicts with the lawyer's hesitation to give an answer until he or she has a better command of the facts. The answer depends, of course, on what is learned from financial statements, depositions, family and home evaluations, real estate, pension, business and personal property appraisals, and much other information not immediately available.

Eventually all necessary information is obtained and the case is certified for trial. The lawyer now has the opportunity, for the first time, to put all of the pieces together. The case is ready for pretrial negotiations and, if necessary, trial. The stage is set.

SETTING THE STAGE: THE PRENEGOTIATION LETTER

This is the time to give the client your opinion on what he or she can expect. Do not pass the opportunity by. Write the client a letter that summarizes the facts and your opinion on them. The letter will serve many useful purposes. At a minimum, however, it should do the following:

1. It should advise the client of the procedures and proceedings that will follow. In states where pretrials are mandatory, it should explain the purpose of the pretrial, convey that it is an opportunity for the parties and their lawyers to come together before trial in the presence

of the court to negotiate settlement, advise that testimony will not be taken (unless settlement is reached) and witnesses need not attend, explain the role of the court, and tell the client what documents, if any, the client will be expected to bring. The client should have a clear understanding that the pretrial may be the last and final step in his or her case.

2. It should outline the goals to be achieved. By this stage, the lawyer should be familiar with the client's goals and priorities, and should recap them in the prenegotiations letter to confirm for both client and lawyer what the negotiations seek to achieve.

3. It should outline the rules and guidelines that govern: child-support guidelines, duration-of-marriage-to-length-of-maintenance rules of thumb, counsel fee award guidelines, and others that apply. For example, if your jurisdiction generally sets one year of support for each three years of marriage, that rule should be explained, with the appropriate caveat, if necessary. This is so despite the fact that you might on many occasions have explained the rule to your client orally.

4. The prenegotiation letter should outline the offers made to date by the other side. If no offers of settlement have been made, it should so state.

5. Where different options exist, particularly options that are complex or may confuse, the different options should be explained. For example, if a pension interest is divisible both by formula (percentage of payments on maturity) and by offset (present value in exchange for other assets), the letter should explain briefly these distribution approaches and the advantages of each.

6. It should explain to the client that the negotiation process is a fluid one, that goals are and must be flexible, and that there is a give-and-take in the flow of negotiations that is routine and expected.

7. The letter should explain the significance of viewing as a whole the economic package sought. For example, if major medical insurance family coverage is a goal, and the annual expense for it is $1,500, the letter should point that fact out.

8. The letter should invite the client to respond in writing with questions, suggestions, changes, and revisions prior to the first settlement conference.

9. When appropriate, the letter should be revised from pretrial to pretrial when negotiations are protracted and more than one pretrial takes place.

10. Last but not least, if the client is bent on a course of conduct the lawyer advises against—surrender of custody, waiver of right to pension or claim for maintenance, less than equitable distribution of property, for example—the lawyer should render an opinion on the inadvisability of that action.

POSTSETTLEMENT

The client's need for information does not end with settlement or decision. Typically, clients come away from the final determination, whether achieved by settlement or otherwise, with mixed feelings—happy that they have obtained some of the goals sought but disappointed that other points were lost or surrendered. They are not sure they received a fair deal. Things moved too fast. They are not certain what happened. They do not know what is going to happen next. Am I divorced? When will it become final? When does support start? When does the medical coverage cease? When do I start to pay the mortgage? It is time to close the curtain.

CLOSING THE CURTAIN

After settlement has been achieved, the lawyer should seize the opportunity to buttress both the advice given during pretrial negotiations and the settlement with a closing letter.

The prudent lawyer will take the initiative by affirming to the uncertain client that the settlement achieved was a good one and the best possible under the circumstances. He or she also will continue to satisfy the client's need to know what is going on. The best way to do that is by letter.

The closing letter should do several things:

1. It should recap the financial terms and provisions of the settlement or decision and place a total dollar value on the financial package.

2. It should outline the rules and guidelines that applied in achieving settlement, and the extent to which the settlement exceeded them, if applicable.

3. It should convey the lawyer's belief that the settlement was fair and reasonable. If the settlement can be characterized as a particularly good result, the lawyer should say so, within the appropriate bounds of modesty. A short statement to the effect the lawyer is pleased to recommend the settlement and the settlement achieved is, in the lawyer's opinion, the best that might have been obtained is sufficient. In no circumstances, of course, should the letter reflect negatively on the opposing counsel or the other client, or on their negotiation tactics or strategies.

4. The letter should explain that the matter is now at a conclusion. If housekeeping items remain, such as the execution of real property instruments, the drafting of a Qualified Domestic Relations Order (QDRO), the execution of stock transfer forms, the obligation of the client to exercise his or her option for medical insurance coverage within thirty days of the filing of judgment, or otherwise, the letter should advise the client what to do or advise what the lawyer will be doing to finalize matters.

5. The letter should recap the fee arrangements and include a final bill to the client, if appropriate. Frankly, there is no better time to present

a bill. Where matters remain to be resolved, the letter should explain that the billing includes an estimate for remaining matters, and that if the remaining matters cannot be resolved in the time estimated, a further billing will be rendered.

6. Finally, the letter should wish the client well and thank the client for the opportunity to have been of service.

It will take little time and effort to devise a form letter that will give the basic information that you want to supply. Once you have a "master," or perhaps several different masters, it will be simple enough to tailor the master to the requirements of a particular case.

The prenegotiations letter and the closing letter are, like much else we do to service our clients, marketing tools as well as a means of keeping our clients informed.

These letters are also, however, of great benefit to the lawyer—their use will save you time spent answering telephone calls, save you the need to repeat advice previously given, give your client a better idea of what is happening, and work to improve the lawyer—client relationship.

12

Client Education

Jan Warner

TODAY, CONSUMERISM IS RUNNING RAMPANT throughout the United States. The mystique of the professions is disappearing as more and more Americans demand to be informed of their options and to be included in the decision-making process.

"Informed consent," the requirement that physicians first apprise the patient of all treatment options and alternatives and then help the patient make the best decision, is fast being transported to the practice of law.

People hire lawyers for two main reasons: expertise in legal procedures and familiarity with the local courts and personnel. Although clients do not want their involvement to hinder lawyers from using their legal expertise, clients do want to be involved because it is their future everyone is talking about. And because the client ultimately bears the risk of the actions of the lawyer as reflected in the results of the case, the client is entitled to be informed—and, as lawyers, we should want them to be informed.

We, as lawyers, should provide each client with access to the "whos," "whats," "wheres," and "whys" and should encourage each client to participate in the management of the case as a partner in the process. A motivated, well-organized, interested, diligent client is a benefit to the lawyer and to the case, while an uninterested client is nothing but trouble.

Although the specific laws and time limits in each state may vary, the basics of alimony, child support, division of property, custody, health insurance, retirement, and taxation are the same. So, by making sure each of your clients is both knowledgeable about the basics and involved in the decision-making process, you can increase your productivity and reduce the risks of client discontent and allegations of malpractice. And there is no better advertisement than a satisfied client.

But who has the time to sit there and give this basic information—that we take for granted and assume each client already knows—to every client? The answer: none of us. So how can we make sure our clients are educated?

Developing an information resource for your clients can be accomplished in two ways: You can do it yourself, but this is difficult and expensive—and you probably will never have the time to get around to it; or, to use a buzz-word of the 1990s, you can outsource this important assignment to those who understand your needs and those of your clients and who advocate a strong lawyer–client relationship. By outsourcing, you can make sure your client is informed without time expenditure on your part. Here's how to do it:

1. You can purchase resource materials in bulk and give them to your clients on an individual basis.
2. You can maintain a library of client informational programs and materials that can be used by your clients on a rotating or loan basis.
3. You can inform your clients how to secure the information themselves and suggest that they make the purchase.

Because 3 is the worst choice—clients often lose sight of the ultimate goals—you should examine economical resources you can purchase for your clients that will help you save hours of time.

One of the best sources of information available to you for your clients is brought to you by your section: *Family Advocate* has published a number of issues geared to the basic informational needs of your clients about taxes, father's custody, relocation, and what the client should expect in the divorce process. The Summer 1999, Spring 2000, and Summer 2001 issues are Handbooks for Clients. Purchased in volume, these are very affordable resources. These issues can be ordered at www.abanet.org/family/advocate.

By providing your client with these economical yet vitally important information products, you will not only differentiate yourself from other practitioners in your area, but also provide a real "value-added" service to your clients.

By using these easy-to-understand resources that have been designed to talk to your clients in their language and to teach them the basics, you will be able to offer your clients what they need, when they need it. And as fully informed partners, they will be better equipped to participate in their cases and to prepare for their futures.

13

Homework for the Client

Willard H. DaSilva

CLIENT INVOLVEMENT IN A CASE is critical to a good working relationship between the client and the lawyer and office staff. A common complaint by a client is that he or she is unaware of activity in the case, that the lawyer has taken a step without the knowledge of the client, or that the lawyer is doing little or nothing, while in fact much work is being performed on the file.

To help lessen the client's feeling of frustration at not being told what is going on, and to assist the lawyer to perform necessary work on the case, it is extremely beneficial from all points of view to solicit, encourage, and even insist on client participation in the case in a way that will benefit all. The beginning of client participation can and should occur when the lawyer is first retained. At the retainer conference, after the retainer letter is read, explained, and signed, the very next step is to put the client to work right then and there.

RETAINER CONFERENCE ASSIGNMENTS

Client's Net Worth Affidavit

Perhaps the most important document in a typical equitable distribution case is the client's net worth affidavit. It normally consists of several items: background, expenses, income, assets, and liabilities. It is simple enough for the client to bring in a shopping bag or carton full of checkbook stubs, canceled checks, and statements, along with innumerable (and usually unsorted) bills. At this point, the wise lawyer sends the client back home with all of the papers with the homework assignment of collating and organizing the papers into income, expense, asset, and liability categories. Then, they are used to generate and, more important, document the items under those categories. By assigning the client this laborious task, the lawyer has saved time, and the client has saved money.

Client's Standard of Living

A form should be furnished to the client to assist in categorizing the various items of expenditures that characterize and quantify the preseparation standard of living for the entire family. This standard becomes the basis for the determination of proper support requirements for the client (and children, if they remain in the care of the client) and also identifies the level of support that the adverse party has the right to expect, whether from his or her own income or from contributions from the other spouse or a combination of both.

Prospective Budget

This form is identical to the standard-of-living form, but it is filled out differently. Instead of containing the expenses of both spouses and all of the children as the family previously lived, this form is filled out by the client, keeping in mind his or her needs commencing from the conclusion of the case into the future. In some cases, the expense categories may be the same. In others, however, there may be drastic changes, such as in the case where the client plans to live in a different house or location. Some items will not be applicable, such as the spouse's clothing, while there may be additional items because the spouse will not be a family member.

Documentation

At the retainer conference a further assignment to the client should include instructions to photograph the house, its contents, and its environs, and to keep a log of expenditures and a record of support money and benefits given by or received from the other spouse. Documentation by way of diaries and other methods should be a part of the client's job to establish a record of events that may become important at the time of trial, particularly if custody and visitation are expected to become issues to be tried. Another form of documentation is a request that the client maintain diaries of events of importance in the case, where entries are made on a contemporary basis. Still another request is that the client obtain certified copies of the parties' joint income tax returns for the past five years from the Internal Revenue Service (IRS). The request is made on IRS Form 4506 and requires several weeks for a response. The certified copies, however, may reveal amendments and changes to the returns and may even be different from the copies furnished by the spouse.

LITIGATION ASSISTANCE

During the course of the case, the client may be of considerable help. If discovery is pursued, the client can suggest questions for interrogatories and for depositions. As the trial approaches, the names of witnesses and their areas of knowledge of facts can be outlined by the client. Always invite the client to attend a deposition of the other spouse and witnesses, unless there is a compelling reason not to have the client present. Give the client a pad and pencil on which to write comments and suggestions during a deposition and, especially, during a trial.

ASSISTANCE WITH EXPERTS

Have the client interview the accountant, appraiser, and other experts. Afford the client the opportunity to provide input of ideas and facts, which could be very helpful to the expert. An accountant or business appraiser will welcome the spouse's thoughts on where to look for hidden assets or personal expenses hidden in the business expense records.

SETTLEMENT NEGOTIATIONS

No settlement offers should be made without the prior knowledge and understanding of the client. Having the client participate, not in the settlement discussions but in the preparation for those discussions, will give the lawyer the direction in which to proceed as well as provide the parameters of what a client may desire and what may be acceptable. The discussions should include a consideration of the risks, advantages, and disadvantages, on both the financial and the emotional levels, of going to trial.

THE ADVANTAGES

The benefits derived by client involvement in the case are both numerous and obvious. A closer relationship between the client and the lawyer will exist. With that feeling of working together, the client will have a better appreciation of all of the work that the lawyer has performed in the case. This certainly improves the attitude of the client on receipt of the lawyer's bill. By keeping the client busy and productive, much of the work that otherwise might have been performed by the lawyer and paralegals can be accomplished without much of that expense, thus effectuating a cost saving for the client. If the client is aware of this saving, the lawyer's image is enhanced, and the lawyer's credibility is improved immeasurably. A client who feels part of a team effort can be a happy client and an appreciative one—all too rare today. Pile on the homework and give good grades for work well done. The rewards will be shared by both client and lawyer.

14

Dealing with the
Chronically Upset Client

Grier H. Raggio Jr.

THIS OVERVIEW of some psychological characteristics that, when found in divorce clients, present major challenges to the lawyer derives from discussions between the author and Robert Schachter, Ed.D., and Risa Ryger, Ph.D. Drs. Schachter and Ryger are therapists in New York City who treat families in divorce. All comments that follow are generalized and simplified and are not intended to be clinically accurate descriptions.

THE DEPRESSED CLIENT

Identification

The client may express feelings such as excessive guilt, hopelessness, helplessness. The tone of voice, mannerisms, and facial expression may broadcast depression. The client may be easily distracted and may lack the will to take what seem to be appropriate actions.

Risks

The depressed client, as a result of temporary passivity, may allow himself or herself to be led or pushed into an unfair settlement. He or she may have difficulty truly understanding the implications of the decisions made in the divorce process. Once the divorce is over, his or her depression may turn to anger at the lawyer for not furnishing better protection.

Tip

Send the severely depressed client to a good therapist and get the client's written consent to talk with the therapist before you sign off on any settlement. Patiently explain choices that need to be made in litigation or in settlement, and explain them in small pieces.

THE PARANOID CLIENT

Identification

This client may incessantly read dark meanings into trivial behavior, often is overly suspicious of almost everyone, and often is ready to find conspiracies against his or her interests.

Risks

Anything the lawyer does for the client may be misinterpreted as evidence of disloyalty or incompetence. Realistic goals agreed to by the client should be set at the outset of representation, for this client may decide that the lawyer intentionally undermined the case if the client's internal result expectations are not met.

Tip

Avoid this client if you can. Once committed, give the client as much information as possible and make him or her participate in all important decisions. Set conservative goals and tactfully suggest a therapist.

THE DEPENDENT CLIENT

Identification

This client may project helplessness and seek direction from the lawyer on even very small decisions. He or she may want to speak with you several times a day, at home as well as at the office, though continually apologizing for his or her needs for your time and attention.

Risks

Underneath the client's seeming helplessness and need, there is probably much anger and frustration. If the lawyer allows the client to leave all the decisions to the lawyer, and the results later seem unsatisfactory to the client, the lawyer may become the object of rage that the client has previously repressed.

Tip

Insist that the dependent client act as an adult responsible for his or her life rather than as a passive child. Discourage this client from bringing advisers, such as parents, to meetings with you. Encourage client decision making by laying out options simply and discussing pros and cons in an adult-to-adult manner.

THE PASSIVE-AGGRESSIVE CLIENT

Identification

The client's words and actions frequently do not seem to match. He or she may talk of a desire to settle the divorce case amicably, then undermine movements toward resolution in subtle ways. The lawyer may notice that he or she is angry and frustrated after conversations with the client who passively expresses concealed aggressions.

Risks

The client's tendency to hide dissatisfaction and anger under a veneer of pleasant behavior will lead to sabotage of actions the lawyer takes in reliance on the client's words. It also may mean difficulty in getting legal fees paid after the case is decided.

Tip

Discuss frankly, but calmly, with the client your perception of the client's inconsistent words and delaying, sabotaging behavior. If you cannot reach a comfortable understanding, get out of the relationship.

THE BORDERLINE CLIENT

Identification

The borderline client may exhibit impulsive behavior, mood instability, and intense personal relationships that go up and down between idealization and then angry rejection of the same person.

Risks

The client initially may put the lawyer on a pedestal. Invariably the client will be disappointed later when the lawyer does not meet the client's unrealistic expectations. This client may experience intense rage when he or she feels let down and frequently has the energy to pursue litigation, sometimes against the formerly sainted lawyer.

Tip

Limit contact with this client and discourage him or her from repeated demands that you solve small problems the client sees as emergencies. Encourage this client to talk about his or her emotional issues with a therapist, not with you as the lawyer.

15

Self-Esteem and the Divorce Client

Cheryl Karp

WHAT EXACTLY IS SELF-ESTEEM? It is pride in oneself, self-respect. In other words, self-esteem is a state of being on good terms with one's superego. Self-esteem also is defined in terms of empowerment. Persons with a healthy "sense of self" feel empowered to make decisions in their life that affect their well-being as well as the well-being of their dependents.

When a client is undergoing a divorce, it is rather easy to understand why the sense of self is damaged. The client is experiencing one of the more traumatic events of his or her life. Often the lawyer forgets this and treats the client as if everything is normal in the client's life other than this temporary "inconvenience."

The divorce lawyer is put to the test when he or she represents an "emotionally battered client" going through the grueling decision to end his or her marriage. The emotionally battered client may not even realize that he or she has been abused, for there are no "bruises." Research has documented that emotional abuse often is more difficult to endure than physical abuse. The ego has been so damaged by repeated insults, put-downs, and threats that the client actually feels inferior and unable to assert himself or herself in an adversarial situation. There is a sense that the client is "helpless."

What can the divorce lawyer do to increase self-esteem in his or her client? First of all, I suggest the lawyer make the client part of "the team." This means sitting with the client at the beginning of the case and asking where the client wants to be three to four years from now and utilizing that information in the overall scheme. This teaches the client to plan for the future rather than obsessing about the past.

Second, involve the client in gathering documents, preparing the case, and understanding the issues, because this is not only less costly to the client, but it is therapeutic—the client gains a sense of empowerment that was lost during the marriage.

Strike quickly and decisively so that the client and spouse can see immediate results. This may seem simplistic, but obtaining an order restraining the other spouse from certain actions, providing exclusive possession and use of the family residence, or temporary support and maintenance will illustrate to the client that being a team player will produce positive results.

The psychological impact of such tactics on the client can be tremendously important. It is amazing how quickly the practitioner can win the confidence of the client by helping him or her obtain an order of protection at the outset of the case. The client feels that the lawyer is listening, that the lawyer believes the client when he or she says that the spouse may hurt the client, and that the lawyer is capable of acting quickly and effectively to prevent this abuse. Such confidence also can pay off for the client in the long run. By forcing a separation and providing the spouse with the exclusive use of the home, along with other remedies, the spouse may feel for the first time that he or she is on an equal footing with his or her partner. He or she often feels less intimidated by the spouse and gains significant confidence in the lawyer to negotiate for a more advantageous settlement or, in the alternative, to go to trial on the divorce action with more confidence in his or her ability to succeed in the end.

I cannot stress enough the importance of listening to your client and validating his or her concerns. Returning telephone calls is vital—nothing insults a client more than being ignored. You will find that a sense of being "heard" will go a long way to building confidence in your opinions. The last thing you want to do is "revictimize" your client.

Self-esteem involves getting on with one's life. If you feel your client is really struggling with this concept, refer him or her to a mental health professional. Remember, the best public relations is a happy client.

REFERENCE

L. Karp and C. Karp, *Domestic Torts: Family Violence, Conflict and Sexual Abuse.* Colorado Springs, Colo.: Shepard's/McGraw-Hill, 1989.

16

Managing the High-Profile Case

Sandra Morgan Little

SPECIAL CONSIDERATIONS ARE REQUIRED to manage a high-profile case. Extra precautions must be taken to maintain the safety, privacy, and confidentiality of clients who are "famous." Celebrities, professional athletes, and international entrepreneurs expect considerable attention and extra efforts to be instituted on their behalf.

Our law office has established a number of procedures when handling a high-profile case:

- *Locked cabinets:* Each case is given a coded, locked file cabinet. The attorney, legal assistant, and secretary each have a key, which is also coded, to access the locked file. The secretary is responsible for making sure at the end of the day that all documents pertaining to the case are filed and locked in the cabinet.
- *Shredder:* A paper shredder is essential to maintaining confidentiality in the high-profile case. Extra copies of documents should never be left out in the open. All extra copies are slashed with a highlighter and, after being reviewed, are shredded by the secretary.
- *Document control:* The highlighting system works very well for determining how many copies are circulated throughout the firm. All attorneys and legal assistants on a case are copied with each document, draft, or pleading that is being circulated. The front page of the document is slashed with a colored highlighter, along with the initials of the individual receiving the copy. At the end of the day, the secretary can determine whether all extra copies have been collected and shredded. The original document is immediately filed in the locked cabinet.
- *Computer passwords:* All software programs have password options that should definitely be employed in the high-profile case. A list of each operator's password should be maintained in the locked file at a readily accessible spot, such as the inside front cover of the main file.

- *Blocked phone calls:* Identification of phone callers can compromise the lawyer's private intentions when placing calls to the client, so we maintain a "blocked" status on our phone system. Although it creates inconvenience when Caller I.D. will not accept blocked calls, it ensures that a phone call cannot be traced to our firm.

- *Coded facsimiles:* When sending faxes to high-profile clients, we give them a code name on the cover sheet as an added protection. We emphasize with our staff the seriousness of double-checking the fax number that is dialed before sending it through. Clients are called beforehand to confirm that they are available and, afterwards, to confirm that the fax was successfully transmitted.

- *Mail:* All classes of mail, even hand-delivered express mail, are vulnerable to public interference. As a general rule, we do not mail documents to our high-profile clients unless specific circumstances require it and arrangements are made previously with the client.

- *Airport security:* Efforts must be devised to maintain maximum security when clients are being met or left at the airport. Make certain you are *early* at the airport, that the meeting place has been previously determined, and that there are at least two of you from the firm, one to drive and one to greet the client. Do not use the airport intercom system or tell any airport personnel who it is you are meeting.

- *Building access:* Your law office may be more unprotected ground where a famous client needs security. Avoid elevators, if possible, or, if not, request building management to allow private access to the maintenance elevator. Stay with your client until he or she is safely in a car, cab, or limousine.

- *Media inquiries:* From the very start, alert each staff person on the first day he or she is hired to decline any inquiries from the media.

Fees

MUCH AS WE LIKE TO THINK of the practice of law as a profession, there is a definite business aspect to it. Few of us practice law just for the fun of it—we have mortgages to pay and families to support.

Collecting fees in divorce cases is not easy. In criminal cases, usually the taxpayers pay the lawyer. In personal injury cases, the lawyer is paid by "found money" or by an insurance company. In business law, the fees are a cost of doing business. Unique to divorce law, lawyer fees come out of the pocket of someone who frequently has other uses for the money.

Now, add to this equation the fact that a divorce is usually the worst of economic circumstances. There is little incentive to earn or save money and plenty of incentive to spend and not work. Plus, there will be two households, with no extra money for the second household. For that matter, there probably was not enough money for the first household. Let's face it: Most people cannot afford a divorce. And now they have a lawyer or two to feed, as well.

No question, but divorce lawyers well earn their fees. The cases are difficult, both legally and emotionally. And lawyers also have families to feed.

These tips are ways to stay solvent, make an honest living, and practice divorce law at the same time.

17   **Jim Feldman** points out that divorce clients are consumers. As such, they are entitled to be treated with the utmost fairness and to have the service providers (the lawyers) work to contain fees.

18   Cash flow is a problem for any business, and **Sandra Morgan Little** suggests means of easing it for divorce lawyers by using monthly fee deposits, promissory notes, and assignments. Sandy also provides forms for doing this in an efficient and ethical manner.

19   No lawyer wants to be caught up in court over a fee dispute with a client. After all, these are the same courts that will hear our clients' cases. Arbitration clauses may be a means of avoiding going to court. **Lowell Sucherman** provides a sample form agreement for arbitrating such disputes.

20   How many times have you worked a full day or more but have been unable to account for the time in billable hours? **Joe Gitlin** suggests ways of maximizing your billable time.

21   **Joanne Wilder** has two great tips. First, she suggests some language to require a defaulting party to pay the innocent party's legal fees. Second, she discusses how using the IRS as an ally can give your client an incentive to pay, while saving the client money at the same time.

22   In certain jurisdictions, applications for fees must be made to the court. **Jim Feldman** identifies ten pitfalls to avoid when making these applications.

23   It is quite common that someone other than the client will be paying for the legal services. And often, the person writing the check expects to direct the case. Whether it is the parent, significant other, or new spouse who is standing behind the fee, the lawyer should get a fee agreement from the person writing the check, along with a signed acknowledgment that the payer is not the client. **Jennifer Rose** provides a superb form for this purpose.

24   Charging too little in fees can be as problematic as charging too much. **Bev Groner** offers practical advice on this issue and others from her years of experience as one of the country's premier matrimonial lawyers.

25   Money has a time value. **Kit Petersen** explains how to ethically charge interest and provides sample language and a disclosure statement to comply with federal consumer laws.

26   Legal fees for a contested trial can go through the ceiling. I have told clients that if they have to ask the cost, they cannot afford it. A client who does not have to pay for the trial may not try as hard to settle the case. **Sandy Morris** suggests a clause in the fee agreement stipulating that separate terms must be negotiated if the case is not settled out of court.

27   Many states allow a charging lien to secure lawyer fees. Securing such a lien, however, raises certain ethical implications that **David Walther** considers. Walther concludes that it is possible to be ethical and get paid at the same time.

28   **Sharon Corbitt** discusses how billing a client can accomplish more than simply getting paid. When detailed billing is used, the client will receive an ongoing description of the legal services being performed while the lawyer will be establishing a historical record if one is needed in the future.

29   When parties go to mediation, the role of the attorney may be different than when representing clients in a traditional divorce case. Many clients do not want the full panoply of services, but only a limited review of the proposed agreement reached in mediation. As a result, **Deborah Tate** suggests using a different fee agreement in such cases and provides a sample agreement for use when hired as review counsel.

17

Charging Legal Fees: Consumer Rights of Divorce Clients

James H. Feldman

LAWYERS, IN GENERAL, have hit a low point in public opinion. Divorce lawyers, in particular, recently have been under attack for ethical shortcomings in their dealings with clients.

- Divorce lawyers have been assailed for their fee-charging practices. One recent critique has led to a call for the regulation of the fees charged by divorce lawyers. *The Wall Street Journal* reported in March, 1992, a study sponsored by New York City's Department of Consumer Affairs of the economic relationships between divorce lawyers and their clients. The study criticizes lawyers for their coercive tactics and overcharging practices and recommends supervision of fee arrangements by the state's court administrator.
- Divorce lawyers for some time have been pilloried for sexual misconduct with clients.
- Some have called for the removal of matrimonial cases from the courts and for having them decided in mandatory arbitration.

Ironically, it is in this climate that divorce lawyers are beating their drums for finding ways to increase their fees. See Volume 7, *Journal of the American Academy of Matrimonial Lawyers* (1991).

When it comes to charging legal fees, divorce lawyers should give their foremost attention to implementing practices that help contain fees and treat clients with the utmost fairness, even exceeding the requirements of legal ethics.

These measures are necessary in response to the public's demand that divorce lawyers respect the rights of their clients who, even as consumers, are entitled to receive from their lawyer, at minimum, the following.

THE RIGHT TO RECEIVE A CLEAR EXPLANATION
OF THE TERMS OF ENGAGEMENT

Some recommendations to lawyers are:

- At the initial interview, explain your billing practices and procedures, including hourly rates, retainer, frequency of billing, timing of payment, refundability of unused retainer, responsibility for costs of experts and other expenses, and duties of other lawyers and staff on the case.
- Put the terms of engagement in writing at the outset of the representation, not later.
- Do not try to change the fee agreement in the middle of the case.

THE RIGHT TO FAIR BILLING AND
COLLECTION PRACTICES BY THE LAWYER

Some recommendations to lawyers are:

- Before billing, review the time carefully and cut your charges where you believe there has been duplication, unnecessary services, unproductive work, and the like. Tell the client you have reduced your bill when the bill is sent. Try never to send a bill that is excessive.
- Send statements regularly, and never refuse to provide a detailed itemization and/or explanation of your services.
- Never keep a retainer that has not been earned.
- Never stop work over a fee collection problem with your client until you are discharged according to court rules.
- If you are discharged as lawyer, turn over the case file promptly to the client's new counsel even if your fees have not been paid.
- Never make coercive demands on a client.

THE RIGHT TO RECEIVE COST-EFFICIENT REPRESENTATION

Some recommendations to lawyers are:
- Hire an associate and/or paralegal to work at lower hourly rates on tasks not requiring your level of expertise.
- Take the time to train associates and staff properly.
- Delegate assignments carefully and thoughtfully, considering the experience of the associate or paralegal and the difficulty of the assignment.
- Supervise closely and monitor each assignment through its various stages to keep it on track.
- Engage in practices with your opponent that can save time and expense, such as using joint appraisals, stipulating to facts, scheduling meetings to resolve disputes, and taking reasonable positions on interim matters involving discovery, temporary custody and support, and restraining orders. Disputes of this kind often distract and divert from the final resolution and cause fees to escalate out of control.

Divorce clients are entitled to have their lawyers deal fairly with them on legal fees and watch out for their pocketbooks. Divorce lawyers who actively seek to protect their clients' financial interests and keep their own fees at reasonable levels will ultimately be the most successful in getting and keeping clients. In so doing, they also are contributing to the independence of the divorce bar and possibly to the preservation of the adversarial system in divorce cases.

18

The Use of Monthly Fee Deposits and Monthly Promissory Notes and Assignments to Collect Fees

Sandra Morgan Little

MONTHLY FEE DEPOSITS

In addition to an initial deposit or retainer, we require a monthly deposit that adds to the amount the client has in trust. The monthly deposit is normally 10 percent of the initial deposit or retainer. The client is required to pay the monthly deposit throughout the case. If a client accumulates too much money in trust or a case is inactive, the monthly deposit may be waived for a time and then reinstated when the trust is drawn down or the case becomes active. The monthly deposit does several things:

- It allows the client to budget for the economic impact of the divorce.
- It educates the client that the divorce is costly and the lawyer's fees are an important part of the economic impact.
- The client owes less fees at the end of the case.

By using the monthly fee deposit, we have lowered accounts receivable substantially. For bookkeeping purposes, all monthly deposits are due the fifteenth of the month, and if a client has not made the payment, the bookkeeping department automatically sends a letter that the monthly fee deposit has not been made. If a monthly fee deposit remains unpaid for several months and satisfactory arrangements are not made, the fee agreement allows us to withdraw as lawyers.

MONTHLY PROMISSORY NOTES AND ASSIGNMENTS

Promissory notes and assignments can be used effectively on a monthly basis when fees are mounting. They are especially useful in two types of cases:

1. Those involving property that will be liquidated at the end of the case, but there is very little cash flow; and

2. Those representing the nonmoneyed spouse.

As the fee climbs each month, the client executes a promissory note and assignment. A new promissory note and assignment are mailed to the client with the monthly statement. The client signs and returns them. The client confirms that he or she is aware of the amount of fees each month and has reconfirmed an intent to pay at the end of the case. If the client refuses to sign a promissory note and assignment along the way, you are prewarned of a fee dispute. This may allow you to withdraw from the case before the account receivable becomes greater and allows time for the client to retain another lawyer.

DOMESTIC RELATIONS FEE AGREEMENT

This Agreement is by and between _____

("Client") and Little & Gilman, P.A. ("Firm").

PURPOSE: Firm will represent Client in the following matter:

_____ Review domestic relations matter

_____ Represent Client in domestic relations matter

_____ Represent Client on appeal

_____ _____

_____

FIRM PERSONNEL: Firm will assign attorneys, paralegals and staff to handle matter.

DISCLAIMER OF GUARANTEE: Nothing in this Agreement and nothing in Firm's statements to you will be construed as a promise or guarantee about the outcome of Client's matter. Firm makes no such promises or guarantees. Firm's comments about the outcome of Client's matter are expressions of opinion only.

ATTORNEY FEES: The fee for professional services will be primarily based on time expended. Some services, such as certain correspondence and pleadings, are charged at a predetermined fee. Firm retains discretion to revise fee to reflect reasonable value of services rendered, due to factors such as novelty and complexity of questions involved, skill required to render services, extraordinary time requirements, results achieved, or other significant circumstances. Hourly rates range from Thirty-five Dollars ($35) to Three Hundred ($300) for attorneys, paralegals and office staff. Hourly rates are subject to change upon

1

prior notice to Client. The New Mexico gross receipts tax is added to fees for professional services.

All litigation is expensive, and domestic relations litigation is a very significant financial event, both in terms of legal expense and property distribution. Firm policy is to attempt a reasonable settlement of your case as expeditiously as possible. However, Firm cannot control the settlement position taken by the other party.

In the past, the average legal expense for domestic relations cases has been:

1.	Modest Assets	$ 5,000 - $ 15,000
2.	Substantial Assets	$ 25,000 - $100,000
3.	Custody	$ 20,000 - $ 50,000
4.	Post Decree	$ 5,000 - $ 25,000

This estimate is illustrative only. Firm cannot guarantee your case will fall within these ranges.

COSTS AND EXPENSES: Firm is authorized to incur costs and expenses. All costs and expenses, such as filing and service fees, depositions, transcripts, fees of other professionals, photocopying, witness fees, reports, travel, long distance charges, will be paid in advance by Client, unless otherwise agreed. Costs in a dissolution of marriage proceeding, average One Thousand Five Hundred Dollars ($1,500). This estimate is illustrative only. Firm cannot guarantee the costs of Client's case will not exceed this amount.

FEE AND COST DEPOSIT: Client will pay an initial fee and cost deposit to Firm's trust account. In addition, Client will pay an additional fee deposit monthly to Firm's trust account as set forth below. The term

2

"deposits" as used below means both the initial fee and cost deposit and the additional monthly fee and cost deposits.

Part of Client's initial fee and cost deposit will be held as a cost deposit in Firm's trust account for anticipated future costs. Even though Client's trust account may show a positive balance, Client's statement may show a balance due Firm. Firm may require an additional cost deposit to meet anticipated costs. At the completion of representation, the unused balance of the cost deposit, if any, will first be applied to the outstanding attorney fees balance, if any, and the balance will then be refunded to Client.

When the balance of the fee deposits held in trust is less than One Thousand Dollars ($1,000), Client's case may be evaluated to determine the estimated cost of completion. If the estimated completion cost is greater than the balance of the fee deposits, then Firm may require either additional fee deposits or other security in order to continue Client's representation.

STATEMENTS: Firm will send Client monthly statement of attorney fees, disbursed costs, and trust balance.

DRAWS AGAINST DEPOSIT AND PAYMENTS: Firm will draw against the deposits for services rendered or costs incurred. Any total due the Firm pursuant to the statement (i.e., any fee for services in excess of fee deposits) is due when the statement is received and must be paid within thirty (30) days of receiving the statement unless prior arrangements are made. Firm may require additional security if there is any unpaid balance. Firm may withdraw from representation of Client for Client's failure to make full

3

payment, or failure to make payments or deposits as otherwise agreed to or required under this Agreement.

9. <u>LATE CHARGE</u>: If a statement has not been paid in full prior to the expiration of a thirty (30)-day period from the closing date on the statement, a LATE CHARGE of 1½%) per month (18% per annum) will be imposed on the unpaid outstanding balance. See "Your Billing Rights" and "Advice of Late Charge" which are attached to this Agreement.

10. <u>LIEN</u>: Firm has a lien on all documents, property or money in Firm's possession, to the extent of any unpaid fee. Firm has a charging lien on any property acquired through its efforts, <u>such as any assets acquired by Client by settlement agreement or court order</u>. This lien is similar to a mortgage and gives Firm an interest in the property to which it attaches. The property may be foreclosed and sold to satisfy the lien. Client will pay the costs of collecting any balance due, including Firm's time (at the applicable hourly rate) and any costs and attorney fees.

11. <u>AWARD OF FEES AND COSTS</u>: An award by the Court to Client of attorney fees and costs will <u>not</u> affect this Agreement. Client is responsible for payment. An award by the Court is an obligation of opposing party to pay Client, not Firm. Any portion of any award paid directly to Firm will be credited to Client's account.

12. <u>APPEALS AND POST-DECREE RELIEF</u>: This Agreement does not include appeals and post-decree relief, unless specifically stated. Professional services rendered after the Final Decree is entered are charged in the same manner provided by this Agreement. A separate fee deposit may be required for enforcement of the Final Decree. A separate fee deposit shall be required for an appeal.

4

13. DISPUTES AND ARBITRATION: Firm will cooperate to resolve any disputes, including fees. Client has right to submit to Firm within sixty (60) days of any disputed statement, a written notice which states what is disputed, and to have Firm review billing statement and to respond to written notice. See "Your Billing Rights" attached hereto. Such notices should be sent to Little & Gilman, P.A., Attention Bookkeeper, P.O. Box 26717, Albuquerque, NM 87125. Any unresolved fee disputes may be submitted to arbitration to a Fellow of the American Academy of Matrimonial Attorneys who is mutually agreeable to Client and Firm. Client and Firm will be bound by the results of such arbitration.

14. COMMENCEMENT OF REPRESENTATION: Representation will not commence until Firm receives a signed copy of this Agreement and the initial fee and cost deposit is paid by Client. This Agreement is void unless Firm receives a signed Agreement from Client within thirty (30) days of the date of Firm's signature.

15. TERMINATION OF REPRESENTATION: Client may discharge Firm at any time. In the event of such discharge, Firm will have an attorney lien for the work done to date, such lien to be applied to (1) the file and material contained in the case, and (2) on any judgment or settlement Client obtains after Firm's discharge. Firm shall have the right to terminate this Agreement upon Client's failure to cooperate with Firm in handling Client's case. Upon termination by either Client or Firm, all attorney's fees and costs, including New Mexico gross receipts, become due and payable in full and shall be satisfied first from the Client's fee deposits held in trust by Firm on behalf of Client, and if Client has an

5

insufficient fee deposit being held in trust by Firm, then payment in full is due upon termination.

16. CLIENT'S SIGNATURE: Client should not sign this Agreement unless Client has read, understands and voluntarily accepts each and every term of this Agreement. Client should have another attorney review this Agreement. Client's signature acknowledges the receipt of a copy of this Agreement.

INITIAL DEPOSIT $_____

MINIMUM MONTHLY
    FEE DEPOSIT $_____
        DUE THE 15th OF EACH MONTH
        COMMENCING _____

LITTLE & GILMAN, P.A.

By _____   _____
    For the Firm   CLIENT

    DATE: _____   DATE: _____

STATE OF   )
) ss.
COUNTY OF   )

     On this _____ day of _____,_____, before me personally appeared _____ , known to me to be the person described in and who executed the foregoing instrument, and acknowledged that he or she executed the same as his or her free act and deed.

My Commission Expires: _____
                                    Notary Public

_____

YOUR BILLING RIGHTS - KEEP THIS NOTICE FOR FUTURE USE

This notice contains important information about your rights and our responsibilities under the Fair Credit Billing Act.

NOTIFY US IN CASE OF ERRORS OR QUESTIONS ABOUT YOUR BILL

If you think your bill is wrong, or if you need more information about a transaction on your bill, write us at the address listed on your bill. Write to us as soon as possible. We must hear from you no later than sixty (60) days after we sent you the first bill on which the error or problem appeared. You can telephone us, but doing so will not preserve your rights.

In your letter, give us the following information:

. Your name and account number.

. The dollar amount of the suspected error.

. Describe the error and explain, if you can, why you believe there is an error. If you need more information, describe the item you are not sure about.

YOUR RIGHTS AND OUR RESPONSIBILITIES AFTER WE RECEIVE YOUR WRITTEN NOTICE.

We must acknowledge your letter within thirty (30) days unless we have corrected the error by then. Within ninety (90) days, we must either correct the error or explain why we believe the bill was correct.

After we receive your letter, we cannot try to collect any amount you question, or report you as delinquent. We can continue to bill you for the amount you question, including finance charges, and we can apply any unpaid amount from the balance of the deposit. You do not have to pay any questioned amount while we are investigating, but you are still obligated to pay the parts of your bill that are not in question.

If we find that we made a mistake on your bill, you will not have to pay any finance charges related to any questioned amount. If we did not make a mistake, you will have to pay the questioned amount and you may have to pay finance charges. In either case, we will send you a statement of the amount you owe and the date that it is due.

If you fail to pay the amount that we think you owe, we may report you as delinquent. However, if our explanation does not satisfy you and you write to us within ten days telling us that you still refuse to pay, we must tell anyone we report you to that you have a question about your bill. And, we must tell you the name of anyone we reported you to. We must tell anyone we report you to that the matter has been settled between us when it finally is.

If we don't follow these rules, we can't collect the first Fifty Dollars ($50) of the questioned amount, even if your bill was correct.

ADVICE OF LATE CHARGE

Paragraph 8. of the Domestic Relations Fee Agreement provides that if Client does not pay any outstanding balance within thirty (30) days of receiving the statement, a LATE CHARGE of 1.5% per month will be imposed on the unpaid outstanding balance. This is an ANNUAL PERCENTAGE RATE of 18% which is an effective rate of 19.56%. The LATE CHARGE will begin to accrue thirty (30) days after the date on your statement. If paid in full prior to the expiration of the thirty (30)-day period, no LATE CHARGE will be imposed. If a LATE CHARGE is imposed, Client will receive a statement as of the end of each billing period setting forth separately (a) the balance of the account at the beginning of the billing Cycle ("Balance from last statement"); (b) payments thereon ("Current payments") and credits thereto ("Adjustments") during such Billing Cycle; (c) the balance on which the LATE CHARGE is computed which is the unpaid balance (balance subject to LATE CHARGE) which is the sum of the amounts due in the aging column (i.e. thirty (30) days, sixty (60) days, etc.); (d) "Late Charge"; (e) charges for legal services incurred during the Billing Cycle ("Current fees"); (f) costs incurred during the Billing Cycle ("Current costs"); (g) the balance due on the billing date ("Total due"); (h) the monthly periodic rate of LATE CHARGE ("Periodic Rate"); (i) the ANNUAL PERCENTAGE RATE; (j) the date by which the New Balance must be paid to avoid additional LATE CHARGES; and (k) the address to be used for notice of any billing errors. The minimum payment required to be made will be not less than the minimum monthly deposit stated within the Domestic Relations Fee Agreement. Current payments shall be applied first to the payment of outstanding costs, then LATE CHARGES, and then to the fees for legal services. Firm reserves the right to amend or modify the terms and conditions set forth herein upon notice to Client in accordance with applicable law.

Date

Clara Client
Address
Albuquerque, NM

Re: Retaining Little & Gilman, P.A.

Dear Ms. Client:

This will confirm your meeting with this office regarding our representation. The following issues were discussed relating to the Fee Agreement:

1. You have retained Little & Gilman, P.A., and provided an initial deposit of $10,000;

2. You have read and understand the Fee Agreement and have had the opportunity to discuss with us any questions regarding the Fee Agreement;

3. You have received a copy of the signed Fee Agreement;

4. You first monthly deposit payment of $1,000 is due the 15th of each month;

5. You will receive a monthly statement which details the time expended on your behalf and the fees and costs incurred on your case;

6. We are to forward your monthly statements to:

    Clara Client
    Address
    Albuquerque, NM

    If your address changes, please notify this office of your new address and telephone number

7. If new issues arise, a New Fee Agreement may be required;

8. As long as there are sufficient funds in your trust account, the balance owing for legal services will be deducted from your trust account. If there are insufficient funds, the balance due Little & Gilman, P.A., must be paid upon receipt of each monthly statement.

If this is not your understanding, please contact this office with any questions.

Very truly,

Office Administrator

Date

Clara Client
Address
Albuquerque, NM

                    Re: Monthly Deposit

Dear Ms. Client:

According to our records, we have not received your monthly
deposit. Pursuant to Paragraphs 6 and 14 of the Fee Agreement,
you have agreed to make a monthly deposit on the 15th of each
month. Please mail your monthly deposit today.

If you have paid your monthly deposit, please disregard this
letter.

If you have any questions, please call.

                    Very truly,

                    Office Administrator

Date

Clara Client
Address
Albuquerque, NM

                    Re: Monthly Deposit

Dear Ms. Client:

This confirms that you need not make your monthly deposit to the
Firm this month. Because there is no activity in your case at
this time, this office waives the monthly deposit for
_____.

However, when activity begins in your case, it will be necessary
for you to make the monthly deposit as you agreed.

If you have any questions, please call.

                    Very truly,

                    Office Administrator

Date

Clara Client
Address
Albuquerque, NM

                          Re: Withdrawal of Little & Gilman, P.A.

Dear Ms. Client:

The continued representation of a client by Little & Gilman,
P.A., is based upon satisfactory financial arrangements.
Unfortunately, the financial obligations to this firm have not
been met. Therefore, we are withdrawing as your attorney.

Enclosed is an original and one copy of a Withdrawal & Entry of
Appearance Pro Se. Please sign and return the original
Withdrawal to this office. We will furnish you and the opposing
counsel with an endorsed copy of the Withdrawal.

When we have received the signed Withdrawal, we will prepare a
final accounting of your trust account and refund any unused part
of the retainer.

Should you desire names of attorneys who might be willing to
represent you, we will supply you a list of names.

If you have any questions, please call.

                          Very truly,

                          Office Administrator

19

Arbitration Clauses

Lowell H. Sucherman

USE OF ARBITRATION CLAUSES IN YOUR FEE CONTRACT

Many states will permit you to use an arbitration clause in your contract. California is an example.

SUCHERMAN & COLLINS
ATTORNEYS AT LAW
88 KEARNY STREET. SUITE 1750
SAN FRANCISCO, CA 94108-5530

TELEPHONE (415) 956-5554
FACSIMILE (415) 781-4367

LOWELL H. SUCHERMAN*
CARROLL J. COLLINS III*
MICHELENE INSALACO

*CERTIFIED SPECIALIST - FAMILY LAW
THE STATE BAR OF CALIFORNIA
BOARD OF LEGAL SPECIALIZATION

I. USE OF ARBITRATION CLAUSES IN YOUR FEE CONTRACT

Many states will permit you to use an arbitration clause in your contract. Ours is an example:

Attorney-Client Arbitration Agreement

Article 1: Agreement to Arbitrate: It is understood that any dispute as to legal malpractice, that is as to whether any legal services rendered under this contract were unnecessary or unauthorized or were improperly, negligently, or incompletely rendered, will be determined by submission to binding arbitration as provided by California law, and to the extent they do not contradict the following rules, the rules of the American Arbitration Association (herein "AAA") then in effect, and not by lawsuit or resort to court process except as California law provides for judicial review of arbitration proceedings. Both parties to this contract, by entering into it, are giving up their Constitutional right to have any such disputes decided in a court of law before a jury and instead are accepting the use of arbitration.

Article 2: All Claims Must Be Arbitrated: It is the intention of the parties that this agreement bind all parties whose claims may arise out of or relate to services provided by the attorney, including any spouse or heirs of the client and the attorney, and his or her association, corporation, partnership, employees and agents, for any claims, including without limitation, fee disputes and claims for loss of consortium, wrongful death, emotional distress, or punitive damages. This agreement is also intended to bind any children of the client whether born or unborn at the time of the occurrence giving rise to any claim.

Article 3: Procedures and Applicable Law: A demand for arbitration must be communicated in writing to all parties. Three arbitrators shall comprise the arbitration panel for the purpose of this contract. As soon as one part has notified the other of its demand for arbitration and names its arbitrator, the other party shall name its arbitrator within thirty (30) days of said notice. Both the client and Sucherman & Collins shall name an attorney at law as their respective arbitrators. Within thirty (30) days of the naming of the second arbitrator, the two arbitrators shall select a third arbitrator to be Chairperson of the panel. Should the two arbitrators not be able to agree on the choice of the third, then the AAA shall make the appointment of a person who is neutral to the parties in controversy. None of the arbitrators shall be current or former officers or current or former employees or current or former family members within the third degree of consanguinity of the parties of this contract.

Either party shall have the absolute right to bifurcate the arbitration of liability and damage issues upon written request to the Chairperson of the arbitration panel. The parties consent to the intervention and joinder in this arbitration of any person or entity which would otherwise be a proper additional party in a court action.

Each party to this contract shall submit its case with supporting documents to the arbitration panel within thirty (30) days after the appointment of the third arbitrator. However, the panel may extend this period for a reasonable time. Unless extended by the consent of the parties to this contract, the majority of the three arbitrators shall issue a written decision resolving the controversy before them within thirty (30) days of the time both parties are required to submit their case and related documentation. The arbitrator's written decision shall state the facts reviewed, conclusions reached and the reasons for these conclusions. Said decision shall be final and binding upon both parties in any court of competent jurisdiction. Each party shall pay the fees and expenses of its arbitrator, unless otherwise agreed to by the parties. The remaining costs of arbitration shall be shared equally by both parties. Arbitration shall take place in the state of California unless otherwise agreed to by both parties.

Article 4: Revocation: This agreement may be revoked by written notice delivered to the attorney within thirty (30) days of signature and if not revoked will govern all legal services received by the client after the date of this agreement.

If any provision of this arbitration agreement is held invalid or unenforceable, the remaining provisions shall remain in full force and shall not be affected by the invalidity of any other provisions.

NOTICE: BY SIGNING THIS CONTRACT YOU ARE AGREEING TO HAVE ANY ISSUE OF LEGAL MALPRACTICE DECIDED BY A NEUTRAL ARBITRATION AND YOU ARE GIVING UP YOUR RIGHT TO A JURY OR COURT TRIAL. SEE ARTICLE 1 OF THIS CONTRACT.

Dated: _____   _____

Dated: _____   _____
                                LOWELL H. SUCHERMAN

20

Maximizing Billable Time

H. Joseph Gitlin

FIRST WE LEARNED that lawyers who keep time sheets make more money. Now we are in the second generation of billable hours and are perfecting our timekeeping skills. The tips that follow will guarantee you more billable hours.

1. Put a stopwatch on your desk and use it. This will make you conscious of the fact that all of your time must be accounted for.
2. In addition to time sheets, keep a running tally of your billable time for each day. For example, if the first piece of work you do for the day takes one hour, record that on the yellow pad on your desk. If the next work is for half an hour, your next line would show 1.50 hours, and so on for the rest of the day, without identifying the client or the matter. This running tally lets you know from day to day, and from task to task, if you are meeting your goal for billable hours.
3. Make the time sheet immediately after you have completed the item of service. Almost inevitably if there is a lapse of time between the item of service and making the time sheet, the value of the services diminishes in your mind, and therefore the amount of time for the time sheet is smaller.
4. Use value billing. The reason that eight hours of time behind your desk does not produce eight billable hours is that time is lost in transition by such matters as finding the client file and putting it back, making file memos of tele-cons, reviewing correspondence from a client, reviewing a rough draft of a letter or document for the client, etc. This "lost time" must be found and billed. The easiest way to do it is to use a multiplier for work at your desk, that is, that a client is billed for more time than actually is spent on his or her case to pick up for the time spent on the case that was not "clocked."

21

Some Tips for Collecting Counsel Fees

Joanne Ross Wilder

ENFORCEMENT PROVISIONS IN PROPERTY SETTLEMENT AGREEMENTS

Most of us are careful to include a provision in the agreements that we draft to require the defaulting party to pay the legal expenses of the nondefaulting party. These clauses sometimes come back to haunt us when our nondefaulting clients want us to enforce their agreements. Naturally, these clients think that your fees should be paid by the defaulting party and that the responsibility for collecting is entirely yours or, at least, not theirs. The problem is further complicated by the fact that the court probably will not award the full amount that you bill to the client but will assess a compromise figure based on what the judge thinks a reasonable amount should be, in 1965 dollars of course.

You can alleviate this problem by drafting the agreement to provide that

the defaulting party shall reimburse the nondefaulting party for any legal fees and costs paid in any action or proceeding to compel performance hereunder.

This provision makes clear the primary obligation of the client to pay and limits the court's authority to second-guess the charges.

GIVE YOUR CLIENT A TAX BREAK

A. Counsel fees and expenses incurred in connection with the production of taxable income (alimony, alimony *pendente lite*, spousal support, and maintenance are all examples of taxable income) are deductible for federal income tax purposes IN THE YEAR PAID. Because the deduction is available only to the extent that the taxpayer's miscellaneous itemized deductions, including such things as union dues and unreimbursed employee business expenses, exceed 2 percent of that party's adjusted gross income, this is a real incentive for some clients to pay up before the end of the year. It is helpful to inform the client, in writing, of this tax-saving device early in the year, with a reminder in September or October.

B. The lawyer must keep careful records of the billing amount attributable to tax-deductible matters, because the burden is on the taxpayer to prove every claimed deduction. An easy way to keep current on this and, not incidentally, to provide clients with an incentive to pay the bill, is to include a paragraph at the end of each monthly statement along the lines of

> the amount of $_____ is attributable to the production of taxable income and/or tax advice and therefore is deductible for federal income tax purposes to the extent permitted by the Internal Revenue Code.

The client who thinks that he or she is getting a tax break is more likely to give the lawyer's bill higher priority.

C. Legal fees incurred in preserving assets or defending against a support or equitable distribution action are not deductible. Some clients, however, can capitalize a portion of their legal expenses to the extent that these expenses are attributable to the acquisition of title to capital assets. Capitalizing the legal fees means that they are added to the basis of the asset, reducing the gain on which capital gains taxes ultimately will have to be paid. Of course, the lawyer must keep careful records and provide the client with a statement detailing the amount of fees attributable to the acquisition of a particular block of stock, parcel of real estate, and so forth.

22

Fee Applications: Do Not Self-Destruct

James H. Feldman

WHEN MAKING YOUR FEE APPLICATION to the court, make sure to avoid these ten pitfalls.

1. *Do not fail to itemize your services in detail.* To calculate the lodestar, courts require accurate, contemporaneous, and detailed time records. Courts view reconstructed records as suspect and may disregard them where the lawyer has destroyed the original records.

2. *Do not ignore the "nontime" factors that go into calculating the award.* These factors include the necessity of the services; the lawyer's expertise; the customary fees in the area; the complexity, novelty, and importance of the issues; the result or benefits obtained; the financial positions of the parties; any time limitations imposed by the client or the circumstances; the nature and length of the professional relationship with the client; and the degree of responsibility. All are important in the calculation, and a lawyer who neglects them may seriously prejudice his or her application.

3. *Do not forget to prove your fee contract with the client.* The fee contract should, of course, be in writing. Beware of including a contingent fee aspect, however; contingent fees in matrimonial actions generally are prohibited. Also beware of making the fee contract with someone other than the client. Under DR 5-107(b) and Model Rule 1.8, a lawyer may accept compensation for fees from one other than the client only with the client's consent after full disclosure. Even then, however, some courts view payment by a third party as creating a potential conflict of interest between the client's interests and the wishes of the person paying the bill.

4. *Do not charge uniform hourly rates.* Courts frown on charging the same hourly rate for each lawyer who works on the case. The hourly rate must reflect the amount of experience and expertise of each lawyer, and courts therefore will not award the same fees to a junior associate as they will to a senior partner. Also, beware of charging the same amount for services rendered in your office as for

court time, for court time generally is (though often wrongly) viewed as requiring greater skill.

5. *Do not set your contractual hourly rate at a level below what you hope to recover from the other spouse.* Lawyers sometimes tell their clients that their rates are so much per hour, but will attempt to recover from the other spouses fees based on a higher hourly rate. Except in unusual cases, courts will say that the price you set with your client provides an outside limit on your recovery from the other side.

6. *Do not take jewelry or other property as security for your fee.* Under DR 5-103 and Model Rule 1.8, taking property may well constitute acquiring an interest in the litigation, if the asset or the client's right to it could be affected by the outcome of the litigation. As in the case of contingent fees, this arrangement is prohibited under most circumstances. Note that both the ABA Code and the Model Rules have special rules for obtaining literary or media rights to your client's story.

7. *Do not modify the fee contract to your advantage in the middle of the litigation.* The lawyer, standing in a fiduciary relationship to the client, is put to a heavy burden to justify the modification. Courts are wary of such modifications and are likely to disregard them if they perceive that the lawyer tried to extract more money from the client at a time when the client could not really say no.

8. *Do not merely offer your time records at trial.* Review your time records before disclosing them and be careful to take all appropriate steps to protect confidentiality and assert privileges regarding their contents. It also is important to submit summaries of time records to aid the court's understanding of the material, especially in complex or lengthy matters. Time records alone just do not tell the story.

9. *Do not fail to anticipate an attack based on duplication of effort.* A favorite defense to a fee petition is to show, for example, that two or more lawyers were at court or at meetings when one would have sufficed. Be prepared to justify the duplication.

10. *Do not refuse a good settlement offer.* A common criticism of using the lodestar to calculate lawyers' fees is that it discourages lawyers from settling. Judges often are sensitive to this criticism and often will view negatively a lawyer's rejection of what appears to have been a good settlement offer. Your fees are likely to be reduced if the outcome of the case produces benefits for the client that are not significantly better than the settlement offered.

23

When Your Client Cannot Afford You

Jennifer J. Rose

SOMETIMES THE WILLINGNESS of your family law client to sign the retainer agreement, and even pay the retainer, just is not enough to make sure that you are going to get paid. You know that your client simply does not have the financial resources to fund costly litigation such as a protracted custody case, modification, or appeal. Perhaps the client's mother, boyfriend, or new spouse promises to pay your fee. Get that promise in writing. Make sure the payor understands exactly what his or her role is in the case: The payor is a source of payment only. Have the nonclient sign a Joinder and Guarantee Agreement to ensure payment of your fee.

Joinder and Guarantee Agreement

FOR AND IN CONSIDERATION OF Jennifer J. Rose ("Lawyer") performing legal services on behalf of and extending credit to _____ ("Client"), we join and guarantee to pay Lawyer in full any indebtedness now or hereafter owing to the Lawyer, arising out of services provided for by the terms of the Retainer Agreement executed on _____(date)_____, a copy of which is attached hereto and by this reference incorporated herein. The liability of the undersigned ("Guarantors") shall be full and absolute as though the same were parties to the Retainer Agreement.

The guarantors understand and agree:

1. Liability for payment of this debt does not create a lawyer-client relationship between Lawyer and Guarantors.

2. Execution of the joinder and guarantee agreement does not entitle the Guarantors to control of litigation.

3. The Guarantors are not entitled to inspection of Lawyer's files or information concerning this case.

4. The Lawyer will act and rely on this agreement in extension of credit on behalf of the Client.

This joinder and guarantee agreement shall be immediately binding upon the Guarantors and shall continue in full force and effect until the Guarantors have given written notice to the Lawyer not to extend further credit. Delivery of notice shall operate to prevent any liability on the part of the Guarantors for future indebtedness, but the Guarantors shall remain liable on all indebtedness then existing.

DATED this _____ day of _____, _____.

_____
GUARANTOR

_____
GUARANTOR

24

Practical Aspects of Legal Fees in Matrimonial Cases

Beverly Anne Groner

THERE ARE MANY significant practical aspects to legal fees. Indeed, it is probable that they are one of the two principal subjects—poor performance is the other—that cause practicing lawyers to recall the bitter lament of King Lear when he opined, in substance, "How sharper than a serpent's tooth it is, to have a thankless [client]."

The Rules of Professional Conduct tell us that fees should be based on:

A. The time and labor required, the novelty and difficulty of the questions involved, and the skill requisite to perform the legal service properly;

B. The likelihood, if apparent to the client, that the acceptance of the particular employment will preclude other employment by the lawyer;

C. The fee customarily charged in the locality for similar legal services;

D. The amount involved and the results obtained;

E. The time limitations imposed by the client or by the circumstances;

F. The nature and length of the professional relationship with the client; and

G. The experience, reputation, and ability of the lawyer or lawyers performing the services.

When setting fees and deciding on your kind or practice, you could reasonably consider a choice between mass production, boutique, or mixture (and, if so, what mix). In so doing, you would consider the general scale of fees in your community and determine what that level is. You should decide where you reasonably fit, both in your heart and, objectively, in your head.

You also should consider and decide on your initial (exploratory) conference fee, your engagement fee, the type and nature of your retainer, your hourly rate, and any subsequent "value billing."

If you are relatively new in the profession and have not yet found or established your preferred level of practice, you still have some options when determining matters relating to fees. Often, new lawyers are reluctant to set a realistic fee, in the mistaken belief that a fee that objectively reflects the value of their services may dishearten or discourage potential clients. In fact, this writer's experience has been to the contrary. Most clients expect and accept a fair billing basis, even though it may be more than what they anticipated. Your fee is derivative from the value that you reasonably place on your time and on the quality of your services.

Of course, fees that are higher than average may not appeal to persons who are very much interested in bargain hunting. Serving clients who expect unreasonably low fees, however, should present a disheartening prospect, primarily because it circumscribes and limits the services that counsel is actually able to render and may curtail the time available, with ensuing regret by both client and counsel. A realistic assessment of the time required and the value of counsel's services, along with an assessment of the potential benefit reasonably to be anticipated by the client, should be factored into the setting of fees.

Fees that are too low sometimes are thought to be more desirable than fees that are too high. All too often I have known of counsel who, in an effort to be accommodating, have set fees that were too low to be realistic, and not only received no thanks from the client, but did receive a lack of respect. I have heard of several situations in which, as soon as the client was financially able to leave such an accommodating lawyer, the client did so, even though making the change escalated substantially the level of legal fees the client was willingly incurring.

I believe that the offering of a "free initial conference" fits into the same category as an excessively low fee, at least in client perception. Although it may be a laudable thing to offer, whether or not it is economically feasible is dubious. Furthermore, I believe that it sets an undesirable tone for the lawyer-client relationship.

We should be reminded, too, that fees that reach the higher range of customary fees in your locality often are justified by the detail of the statement of account. This should evidence the seriousness of both lawyer and client in approaching the case. On more than one occasion I have heard of a surprised spouse who was consternated at the decisive action taken by the other spouse in protecting himself or herself, particularly when the latter previously was believed to be passive and unlikely to engage in effective self-help. Sometimes, on hearing that counsel of recognized stature had been retained, with fees that appropriately reflected that stature, that other spouse has been heard to say, "I thought you'd get a Ford; instead you got a Cadillac [and I'm surprised]."

A further advantage of fees that may be higher than those you originally considered setting for your practice is that a thorough approach often requires that more time be devoted to a case than a lawyer can afford who is deluged with obligations flowing from having undertaken too many cases. A mass production practice is especially replete with emergency demands and ensuing tension. Matrimonial cases are especially likely to generate more emergencies in a law practice than other areas of specialization. Some lawyers state that they have "hundreds" of open matrimonial cases. It seems inevitable to me that those hundreds of cases will have a relatively higher quotient of client dissatisfaction than those where counsel is able to devote adequate time and substance to the representation. Not every case or every client requires substantial amounts of time all the time, but counsel must be able to recognize the situation, make appropriate recommendations, and devote the requisite time when the time is required.

Counsel's awareness of cost-effectiveness and potential benefit to the client must be predominant at all times. There always are specific actions that could be taken in a given case and that might conceivably bring ultimate benefits. Judges, when approving fee arrangements or determining spousal contributions to costs incurred, however, are observant and vocal in commenting on "excessive diligence." Due diligence is fine; excessive diligence is not. There are better ways for clients to spend their money, and for lawyers to spend their time, than in pursuing microscopic details or matters that will not have any ultimate impact on the resolution to the case. This matter should be thoroughly explored with the client, and the decision should be that of the client.

We all are aware of malpractice considerations. Just as physicians sometimes practice defensive medicine, so do many lawyers practice law defensively. Often this defensive practice of law is justified. Sometimes, however, it is not, and counsel must be alert and aware of the differences.

The benefit to counsel and to the client's experts, such as accountants who previously have worked with the client, is substantial and should not be overlooked. Although you may decide in some cases to utilize certain services of an accountant with whom you often work, it is generally the case that the better choice would be the client's own accountant. This, of course, is a decision that can be made only after you have met with the accountant and are familiar with the financial and business background of the case.

You absolutely must have a meeting of the minds with the client on the fees and expenses involved, and you must communicate to the client the terms of that agreement, both generally and specifically. It is necessary to preclude any misunderstanding between you and the client and make absolutely certain the client understands clearly the effect of relevant contingencies.

You should make certain, also, that the client agrees, with informed consent, to your various recommended decisions, for an unpleasantly surprised client is likely to be an unsatisfied and troublesome one. Reduce the fee agreement to writing, signed by both the client and yourself. Spell out clearly any provisions for refund or nonrefund of fees paid, and for your release from the case if the client fails to pay as agreed. Obviously, there are many times when you would decide to remain in the case notwithstanding your client's inability to keep current financially, but whether or not to do so should be your own decision.

With reference to receiving your fees, you must carefully determine when to bill, how to bill, how to follow up, what you should do about deadbeats, and when you should do it. Some general considerations that help to keep clients happy and up-to-date are the following:

A. Advise the client early and realistically about prospective results.
B. Reach and insist on enforcing a clear understanding that you, and not the client, will manage the case. Of course, you should be conversant with and sensitive to the client's perspective and objectives.
C. Do the work promptly and competently.
D. Keep the client informed, and currently informed, of what is going on.

Legal fees usually are viewed by clients within the perspective and framework of results achieved. We all have seen situations, however, where the client's primary reaction to the quality and cost of representation has been mainly derived from the client's perception of the degree to which counsel was truly involved in the case and sincerely took a personal, not simply a clinical, interest in it.

No lawyer can be assured that he or she never will suffer the pain of having a thankless client. But every lawyer can make sure that he or she does not deserve one.

25

Collection of Interest on Family Law Fees

Catherine Holland Petersen

COLLECTION OF FEES for most family law lawyers is a chronic headache. There are a variety of suggestions concerning methods of collection. This chapter deals with the use of interest charged on fee balances as a means of prompting faster fee payment by clients.

Family law clients are consumers within the context of the Uniform Consumer Credit Code (U.C.C.C. § 1.301 (11); 14A O.S. § 2.104). Although the code has been adopted by only eleven states and Guam in one form or another (Colorado, Idaho, Indiana, Iowa, Kansas, Maine, Oklahoma, South Carolina, Utah, Wisconsin, and Wyoming), compliance with the Code will ensure valid and effective collective efforts. Consequently, lawyers in a family law practice are well advised to comply with the credit restrictions found in the Code. To avoid the restrictions, the fee must be collected contemporaneously with each service rendered—a practical impossibility for family law lawyers. Not only can the client not be expected to pay contemporaneously for each telephone call, for example, but often a client cannot afford to pay the bill he or she receives in full immediately. The moment the family law lawyer allows the client to make a partial payment, he or she has become an extender of credit under the Code (U.C.C.C. §§ 1.301 (12)(a) and 1.301(18); 14A O.S. § 2-104(1)).

Because the collection of fees is a principal practical concern of all lawyers, one means of expediting that collection is to charge interest. If faced with limited funds, and apparently unlimited bills, many (if not most) people will pay without delay the bill that will cost them more with delay, before they will pay the bill that will be the same next month as it is this. As a consequence, assessing interest is helpful in moving the bill for lawyers' fees to the top of the stack.

Some lawyers argue that they cannot ethically charge interest on fees. There is nothing in the Rules of Professional Conduct adopted by the ABA and many of the states in one form or another that prohibits charging interest on fees. Fees must simply be reasonable. Interest charged on an unpaid fee is not a part of the fee itself, but simply a collection technique. There is nothing in the Rules to prohibit any lawful collection technique. The restrictions are in the Uniform Consumer Credit Code.

To comply with the Code, a written agreement between the lawyer and the client in which the client agrees to pay interest is required (U.C.C.C. § 3.203; 14A O.S. § 2.302(b)). The written agreement must be clear, and a copy must be provided to the client. (Appendix A shows a paragraph concerning the charge of interest to be included in a lawyer's fee contract.) The written agreement is not sufficient on its own, however. A disclosure statement that explains in detail how interest will be computed, the fee to be charged, closing dates for the statements, how to address errors about the bill, and a summary of the client's credit rights must be provided to the client (U.C.C.C. §§ 3.201–3.209; 14A O.S. §§ 2.302–2.304). (Appendix B contains a suggested disclosure statement.) Good practice and the law (U.C.C.C. § 3.203; 14A O.S. § 2.302 (1) (B)) require that the client receive a copy of the contract and the disclosure statement immediately on execution.

The final step in compliance with the Code is found in the proper billing form. The computation of interest must be recited clearly, the balance subject to finance charge (interest) must be clear, the credit of payments must be set forth, and the closing date for the bill and the date by which payments must be received to be credited against the account must be clearly stated (U.C.C.C. § 2.202; 14A O.S. § 2.310).

Even if the charge of interest does not prompt all clients to pay their bills in full each month, the collection of the interest does help compensate the lawyer for the lost use of the money he or she has earned. Assessment of interest is good business practice, both lawful and helpful.

APPENDIX A

CONTRACT FOR LEGAL SERVICES

Paragraph concerning charge of interest

The FIRM alone shall determine the fees to be charged and the time to be used. CLIENT shall pay for all services performed and costs incurred as reflected in all bills on receipt of the bill. Visa or Mastercard is an acceptable method of payment. CLIENT agrees to be assessed and to pay interest at the rate of 1.5 percent per month (18 percent per annum) on any balance outstanding for more then thirty (30) days. CLIENT hereby acknowledges receipt of a Disclosure Statement setting forth the particulars of the finance charge.

APPENDIX B

PETERSEN ASSOCIATES, INC.
P. O. Box 1243
Norman, Oklahoma 73070
(405) 329-3307

DISCLOSURE STATEMENT

This disclosure statement is submitted in compliance with the Oklahoma Uniform Consumer Credit Code, and your signature at the bottom represents your understanding and acceptance of the terms herein.

_____
Name

_____
Mailing Address

_____
City, State and Zip Code

1. PREVIOUS BALANCE for Legal Services Rendered $_____

2. PAYMENT MADE $_____

3. UNPAID BALANCE (1 minus 2) subject to
    finance charge $_____

4. **FINANCE CHARGE** on Unpaid Balance at monthly
    periodic rate of 1.5% (**ANNUAL PERCENTAGE
    RATE** of 18%) $_____

5. MINIMUM FEE CHARGED $_____

6. MINIMUM FEE PAID $_____

7. MINIMUM FEE UNPAID $_____

8. NEW BALANCE (3 plus 4 plus 7) $_____

9. CLOSING DATE for services rendered   25th of Month

10. CLOSING DATE for payments received   End of Month

11. PAYMENT DUE DATE   _____

104

METHOD OF CALCULATION OF BALANCE SUBJECT TO FINANCE CHARGE: ADJUSTED BALANCE METHOD. Apply the monthly periodic rate shown to balance owed at the end of the previous billing cycle (Previous Balance), including any unpaid finance charge from a previous billing period, and subtract any payments received during the present billing cycle. This gives the "Adjusted Balance."

IN CASE OF ERRORS ABOUT YOUR BILL: Send your inquiry in writing on a separate sheet to the address shown above so that we receive it within 60 days after the bill was mailed to you. Your inquiry should include (1) your name, (2) a description of the suspected error and why you believe it is an error, and (3) the dollar amount of the error.

THIS IS A SUMMARY OF YOUR RIGHTS. A full statement of your rights and our responsibilities under the Federal Fair Credit Billing Act will be sent to you upon request or in response to a billing error notice.

Client acknowledges receipt of a complete copy of this Disclosure Statement.

_____

Client's Signature

_____

Date

26

Trial Retainer Clause in Fee Agreements

Sandra Joan Morris

WE ALL HAVE EXPERIENCED the frustration of walking into court for a set trial, knowing that the client owes a fee that is highly unlikely ever to be paid for either the balance due or the costs of the trial. Often, the entrance to the courtroom for trial was preceded by a settlement conference at which one or both parties unreasonably frustrated a potential settlement. If the party frustrating the settlement was your client, you may for this or other reasons have lost rapport with your client, and the relationship is hardly enhanced by the failure to have your bill paid.

A solution to these problems might be the inclusion in your fee agreement of a provision requiring the client to provide a trial retainer prior to your representing the client at trial.

This clause might read, for example:

> I have agreed to represent you in your pending dissolution of marriage action by rendering services to you up to, but not including, any trial that may be had regarding your case. Should you wish to retain me as trial counsel, the terms must be separately negotiated between us and a new retainer remitted to my office no later than sixty (60) days before trial, or on the conclusion of an unsuccessful settlement conference. Absent such a new agreement, you are free to obtain other counsel as trial counsel, and I am free to decline to represent you at trial.
>
> The trial retainer will take into consideration the estimated length of trial, the number and type of witnesses expected to be called to testify, the issues involved, the complexity of the case, and the cause of any failure to settle the case at formal or informal settlement conference.

If your jurisdiction permits, you might have the client sign a substitution of lawyer with the date blank and include a provision in your agreement that the client has signed the substitution, which is to be used without the client's prior consent only at the conclusion of the contracted-for services and no later than sixty (60) days prior to the trial date. While there is no magic in the number of days, it is important to leave enough time available for your client to obtain new counsel for the trial, if that is what you both determine at the appropriate time. If your jurisdiction would not permit you to obtain a signed substitution of lawyer in advance, you must leave enough time to file a request to be removed as lawyer of record.

Some practitioners have included a provision that the fee increases if the client unreasonably fails to work toward settlement at the settlement conference. This concept can be factored into the trial retainer if you still wish to represent your client in further proceedings at trial.

Even in the best of lawyer-client relationships, there is a tendency for the client both to run out of money before trial, and to feel that a lot of money has been spent without having yet reached the trial stage. By separating the two concepts, the client is fully aware of the fact that the funds being paid are not and never were anticipated to cover the costs of trial. This separation encourages the client to make sure that all the fees are paid in a timely fashion to preserve you as trial counsel, and it protects you from being forced into representation of a client at trial with no funds available.

27

Charging Liens

David L. Walther

NEW MEXICO, LIKE MANY OTHER STATES, allows a charging lien to secure lawyers' fees, which constitute a lien on the portion of the estate recovered for the client. This is not a lien on the divisible portion of the assets, but only attaches to the portion of the estate recovered on behalf of the client. Furthermore, it does not guarantee payment of the amount charged, but merely secures such a fee as may ultimately be determined to be reasonable and proper.

Because this arrangement constitutes a business dealing with a client, the prevailing wisdom is that the client must be given the opportunity for separate representation for such a lien to be valid. In all of my fee agreements, therefore, I include a provision that the fees will be secured by a charging lien on the client's share of the recovery. But to make sure that this holds up, the first sentence of my fee agreement provides that the client should have this fee agreement reviewed by his or her regular lawyer or a business adviser if the client chooses to do so. In addition, I do not have the client sign the fee agreement in my office. I mail the fee agreement to the client, and I request that the client return a signed copy in the enclosed envelope.

Very rarely does the client take advantage of the proposal that he or she seek independent counsel. I assume the client does not want to pay an extra fee for this purpose. The only times that clients have received a separate opinion are when they have a relative or a friend who reviews the agreement, or when the agreement is reviewed by a business lawyer who has referred the case to me. I do not believe I have ever lost a case by putting this provision in the fee agreement. If I am going to have difficulty charging the client pursuant to the fee agreement, however, I want to know that before I have put substantial work into the case. Moreover, in the fee disputes that I have had, the fact that I have referred the client to outside counsel with respect to the fee agreement has been a very strong factor in favor of upholding the agreement.

Furthermore, this allows me, ethically, to file a charging lien on the real estate awarded to my client in any case where I believe payment is insecure.

I obviously do not have to file the lien in every case, but if the "red alarm" goes off with respect to payment of the fee, I file the lien every time.

I indicated that the lien does not guarantee payment but merely secures the fee that is ultimately determined to be reasonable. Invariably the lien shows up on a title report immediately prior to the sale of the piece of real estate, and the title company calls me, asking for the amount I need to release the lien together with interest. In effect, the lien works as a very effective collection device. I have received payment of five- and six-year-old receivables.

I have had several cases where the client has objected to the fees after the lien has been filed. At the very minimum, if the fee goes to arbitration or litigation, I am certain of payment from the proceeds of the lien.

I would strongly recommend this combination, because it has saved me more money than it has lost—that is, allowing the client to go to outside counsel to review the fee agreement and the filing of the charging lien.

28

Detailed Billing

Sharon L. Corbitt

ALWAYS MAKE SURE THE BILLING STATEMENTS you send to your clients not only reflect time kept contemporaneously with the billing incident but include details as well. Not only will this make it easier for you to substantiate an attorney fee request in court, but it can also serve you well if, for example, a client later says, "We never discussed . . ." or "Why didn't you tell me . . .?" A clear reference on the statement not only to the date but specifically to what was discussed, with whom it was discussed, any advice given or decision ultimately made by client, etc., will refresh not only your memory (for purposes of the attorney fee hearing) but that of your client as well (when they have a convenient memory loss).

Often I see billings that simply list entries such as telephone conference with client, office visit with client, telephone conference with expert, etc. A preferable way to bill would be something along the lines of the following: telephone conference with client concerning need for personal property appraisal, upcoming holiday visitation, change in employment status, ongoing negotiations with husband's parents concerning daycare issues.

29

Fee Agreement as Review Counsel

Deborah M. Tate

A S MEDIATION BECOMES MORE OFTEN the choice of parties who are divorcing, it is critical that we explain to clients how our roles in representing them will differ. In representing a party during the mediation process, we are not investigating the finances or facts of the marriage and divorce of the parties. Our roles are not adversarial ones. We are more like the coach on the sidelines, advising, counseling, and providing encouragement.

For this reason, it is important for the client to understand the difference, particularly in those cases when mediation has failed and now the client needs you to be an advocate.

As a result, we use a separate fee agreement for those clients who are using a mediator to resolve their case. We find that little of what is spoken during the consultation is retained. By giving clients a copy of the agreement, they have an opportunity to review it and then ask questions if necessary.

You still need to be mindful of your state's disciplinary rules before utilizing this form of agreement.

If the mediation does fail, we then give our client our standard fee agreement because the process, for the most part, is just beginning.

McINTYRE, TATE, LYNCH & HOLT

COUNSELLORS AT LAW

JERRY L. McINTYRE †
DEBORAH MILLER TATE *Δ
WILLIAM J. LYNCH
WILLIAM F. HOLT
DAVID J. STRACHMAN
ROBERT S. PARKER *

Also member
† New York Bar
* Massachusetts Bar
Δ Florida Bar

FEE AGREEMENT
AS REVIEW COUNSEL

You have asked me to provide you with individual advice concerning the mediation of your divorce and advice concerning a tentative separation agreement you have reached or are working on with your spouse as a result of the mediation conducted by _____. In contracting with me to provide this service, please understand the nature of my role.

In reviewing an unsigned draft of your proposed agreement, I will advise you as to the legal significance of each provision as it appears from the written text of the agreement in conjunction with the facts you supply to me. Prior to each mediation session, I may meet with you to review the legal issues that you may encounter in mediation and work with you to review your interests and how the law may apply to those interests.

Often, it is customary for a lawyer who represents you, and only you, to negotiate the agreement for you, to investigate all facts, and even to compel production of facts including financial information related to your case from your spouse, under oath through discovery and court proceedings. However, in asking me to serve as review counsel instead, you have informed me that you want to do without these additional steps in order to save time, professional fees and court costs, as well as to preserve a conciliatory family climate. This is acceptable to me as long as you understand that any advice I formulate without full factual information about your case could be entirely different from any advice if I were fully informed of all relevant facts.

I shall tell you what is legally advisable, but will ultimately be governed in this matter by your expressed desire that, in choosing mediation, you have consciously chosen to sacrifice or compromise the fullest advancement of your individual interests in favor of preserving a conciliatory family climate, pursuing other interests, and saving time, professional fees and court costs. My understanding is that for these reasons, you have not elected to seek adversary lawyer representation that would require full investigation of all facts and the fullest advancement of your individual interests, and at all costs.

To begin our work, please provide an immediate engagement fee of $_____ which shall be applied towards the total fee. With respect to the time portion of your bill, the current hourly rates are as follows: Jerry L. McIntyre - $290.00; Deborah M. Tate - $275.00; William J. Lynch - $250.00; William F. Holt - $250.00; Robert S. Parker - $200.00; David J. Strachman - $200.00; Virginia K. Greenwood (legal assistant) - $125.00, other legal assistant(s)-$90.00. The hourly rate is reviewed by this firm each May 1 and may be increased at that time. The increase will be reflected in your statement at such time as it becomes effective.

You will receive monthly bills which will reflect how much time has been spent on your case. You are obligated to pay the monthly bills upon receipt. To the extent that your balance exceeds $1,000 and you have not arranged for a schedule of payment, you understand that I reserve the right to terminate and withdraw from your representation upon reasonable notice, and if necessary, with court approval.

You understand that if you delay in making payment of any statement for a period in excess of thirty (30) days of receipt of the statement, we may assess a late charge of twelve (12%) per annum on the outstanding balance. In no event will the late charge be greater than permitted by any applicable law.

Any costs incurred or expended will be billed separately, including a "communications" charge of 2% of the monthly fee to cover postage, telephone and toll charges and Telecopier expenses.

You further understand that in the event your account has not been paid in full at such time as any money or assets are distributed to me as a result of any settlement or distribution of assets pursuant to any court order, you will pay all outstanding fees and costs due upon receipt of said monies or assets. Further, you authorize me to make payment of said fees and costs from any such settlement or distribution, if received by me. In any event, all fees and costs shall be paid in full prior to entry of the Final Judgment.

In the event you and your spouse have not reached an agreement in mediation or have not accepted a Memorandum of agreement, then this fee agreement shall become null and void. You will then enter into a Standard Fee Agreement and any unused portion of your engagement fee shall be applied toward the engagement fee as set forth in said Standard Fee Agreement.

To the extent there is any dispute as to the fee charged, I agree that this dispute shall be settled by the Rhode Island Bar Association Fee Arbitration Panel. I agree that the decision of the Rhode Island Bar Association Fee Arbitration Panel shall be accepted as the final determinator and binding upon both of us.

If the above coincides with your understanding of our relationship and you agree that I shall not undertake the full adversarial inquiry into your proposed separation agreement, please sign this Agreement in the space provided below.

_____   _____
Client   Date   Attorney   Date

_____
Copy Received

revised 5/01

115

PART

III

Custody

IS THERE ANY AREA OF FAMILY LAW more sensitive, difficult, or important than custody? The very title carries connotations of two people fighting over children. Yet, when parents separate, custody of the children must be dealt with.

The law on custody has changed dramatically over the years. What has not changed is that most lawyers truly want to protect the children, who are the innocent victims of divorce.

Following are tips from the experts on how to handle various custody issues in an ethical and effective manner.

30   Wisconsin law mandates appointment of guardians ad litem (GAL) in most custody cases. **Judge Francis T. Wasielewski** attaches great weight to the GAL's recommendation, recognizing that, properly handled, the GAL's role will promote settlement. Judge Wasielewski shares the salient points a GAL must keep in mind when reaching a recommendation.

31   Many times we hear the term "primary parent" as if it were a litmus test for custody. **Dr. Richard Warshak** finds the presumption meaningless and explains why it is misleading when searching for the best interests of children.

32   Nothing is more terrifying than the concept of a child being abducted overseas, where return may well be impossible. Too often the legal system seeks only to punish after the harm has occurred, rather than acting to prevent the harm in the first place. **Phil Schwartz** provides no less than fourteen tips on how to prevent this tragedy from happening.

33 Most lay witnesses do not want to get involved in testifying in custody cases. Yet, their testimony may be critical in placing important facts before the court. **Lindsey Short** shows how to prepare lay witnesses for testimony effectively and with sensitivity.

34 If a picture is worth a thousands words, a videotape is worth a million words. **Ann Haralambie** describes how to effectually use a videotape in a custody proceeding.

35 Allegations of mental disorder are common in custody cases. **Lynne Gold-Bikin** explains how to use the *Diagnostic and Statistical Manual of Mental Disorders,* 3d ed., rev. (DSM-IV-R), and provides valuable advice for using the cross-examination of a mental health expert to a client's advantage.

36 **Sandy Morris** points out that allegations of sexual abuse should be divided into questions. The first is whether molestation actually took place. It is only when that question is answered in the affirmative that the court gets to the second question of who the perpetrator is. Keeping these issues separate can be quite effective.

37 Can a test really quantify whether sexual abuse took place? Dr. Richard Gardner has developed a highly controversial Sexual Abuse Legitimacy scale that he claims can be used to distinguish between true and false accusations. **Ann Haralambie** shows how Dr. Gardner's scale can be cross-examined, using his own words to impeach him.

38 How do you assess parenting? **Ann Haralambie** provides a form to use for depositions. The form can be supplied to a mental health expert or used to set a basis for impeachment. Either way, the form is an invaluable resource.

39 **Robert Barnard** tells how to protect custody jurisdiction under the Uniform Child Custody Jurisdiction Act (UCCJA) if there was a prior custody order in a foreign court.

40 Lawyers are not trained in psychology or any child-related science. Most lawyers would not want to fight a custody case for a person who is not a good parent, but how are they to know? **Harvey Golden** suggests referring potential clients to a licensed clinical psychologist for a full Minnesota Multiphasic Personality Inventory (MMPI) *prior* to accepting the case.

41 We live in a visual society, and judges watch television as much as anyone else. Therefore, demonstrative evidence can be invaluable in court to get and keep the attention of the judge. **Phyllis Bossin** provides several creative examples of the type of demonstrative evidence that can be used in custody trials.

42 If custody cases are the most emotionally charged area of family law, the most emotionally charged type of custody case is the removal case. Unlike other issues that usually can be compromised, having a child move many miles away creates huge obstacles to an involved parent. **Ellen Effron** suggests ways a nonmoving parent can use expert testimony to educate the court regarding the emotional and cognitive development issues a child faces if the child is deprived of continual contact with a parent.

43 It's bad enough to move a child many miles away *within* the country. International custody disputes are governed by The Hague Convention, and **George Stern** and **Susan Hurst** discuss the meaning and effect of "habitual residence" under its terms.

44 **Richard Podell** goes even further, explaining the objective of The Hague Convention and describing its mechanism.

45 Many custody cases are won or lost when the social-service worker meets with the client and visits the client's home. **Lindsey Short** gives some practical suggestions on how to put the best light on the client in the eyes of a social worker.

46 Given our highly mobile society, some parents wind up being far away from the children they love. In her hot tip, **Sandra Little** provides a handout she gives clients with some practical advice on how to be an involved parent from far away.

47 Perhaps the hottest issue in family law today is the constitutionality of third-party visitation statutes. **Prof. Lewis Becker** discusses the United States Supreme Court case of *Troxel v. Granville*, which ignited the controversy.

48 Often clients allege drug or alcohol use by their spouse or ex-spouse—or deny such an allegation by the other side. **David Levy** outlines the type of screening tests that can be used to ascertain the truthfulness of these allegations.

49 If a Native American child is involved in a custody action, federal law may preempt any state laws. As a result, familiarity with the federal Indian Child Welfare Act is essential. **Ann Haralambie** gives a brief overview of the federal statute and its effects on custody, foster care, adoption cases, and more.

30

Guardian Ad Litem Recommendations in Custody Actions: A View from the Bench

Hon. Francis T. Wasielewski

THE GUARDIAN AD LITEM (GAL) represents the best interests of the children. In this role, the guardian is an advocate for the children, who generally are not able to speak for themselves.

The guardian's position is unique because no allegiance is owed to either of the contending parties. A particular party's position is favored only to the extent that it advances the ward's position. For this reason, the court usually will attach great weight to the guardian's final recommendation.

Experienced counsel for the parents generally will explain to their clients the role of a GAL and the importance of cooperating. With the parties "primed" in advance, the guardian has an excellent opportunity to gain their confidence and initiate investigation and discussion of the problem areas in the case. This often leads to settlement. Also, because the guardian does not serve at the pleasure of the parties, there is a greater measure of independence. A skilled guardian often can initiate discussion and obtain movement on issues where previous efforts of counsel may have been unavailing.

The guardian's recommendation must be based on a thorough investigation of the case. Use interviews, interrogatories, and depositions as dictated by the needs of your case. At least one visit to each party's home is a must. You also should check all records that bear on the case, including medical records, school records, juvenile court records, social-service agency records, and employment records. Be sure that you have talked to everyone who may have information. This includes teachers, counselors, school nurses, social workers, and psychologists. Conduct your investigation with the fact in mind that as a GAL you will not be able to testify as a witness.

Be prepared as you would at any other trial. You are the equivalent of trial counsel with the duty of advancing your client's interest.

Points to keep in mind in reaching a recommendation include:

1. Be sure you can prove the facts on which the recommendation is based. Think through any evidentiary problems you may have and be sure your recommendation is not based on evidence that is inadmissible at the final hearing. Be prepared to subpoena any necessary witnesses.

2. It should be based on evidence to be introduced at the final hearing. Make sure that all facts on which you will rely become part of the record.

3. Many states have a statute that enumerates specific factors to be considered by the court when determining the child's best interest. These factors typically include wishes of the child or the child's parents with respect to custody; relationship between child, parent, siblings, and anyone else who may significantly affect the child's interest; mental and physical health of the child and parents; the child's adjustment to home, school, religion, and community. If your state has such a statute, be sure to discuss the applicable factors when making your recommendation.

4. Let the chips fall where they may. The guardian's charge is to represent the best interests of the child. The guardian should not be worried about conflict between the recommendation and the opinion of others involved in the case, e.g., psychologists, lawyers, counselors, etc. The recommendation need not align consistently with the position of either party in the case.

5. The guardian is the advocate for children's interests, which are not necessarily the same as the children's desires. While you should consider the children's desires when reaching a recommendation, these should not be determinative. Make sure the children's desires are not the result of parental prompting. Remember that you are in the case because the ward lacks the sufficient age and maturity to make these decisions.

6. Sprinkle your recommendation with a healthy dose of street sense. Invariably one or both of the parties will be attempting to manipulate the child. Be aware of this and weigh carefully what you are told. Try to keep the child out of the parental crossfire.

7. Let parties know before the trial what your recommendation will be if the evidence comes in as you expect. Do not hold your recommendation to surprise them at the final hearing. Disclosure before the hearing may facilitate settlement discussions. Consider a pretrial meeting where parties, expert witnesses, and lawyers meet to discuss the case. However, do not simply align yourself with one party. New information or circumstances at the trial may change the recommendation. Make sure the parties realize this.

31

The Primary Parent Presumption: Primarily Meaningless

Richard A. Warshak, Ph.D.

THE YEAR 1993 marked the thirtieth anniversary of the publication of *The Feminine Mystique,* the book that spearheaded the drive to unlace the cultural straitjacket of rigid sex-role prescriptions. As we expanded the conventional image of women to include roles beyond those of wife, housekeeper, and mother, we encouraged men to think of themselves as more than just husbands and breadwinners. We invited them to become active partners in the delivery room, and they accepted. We required their participation in Indian Guides, and they complied. We extolled the importance of father–child bonding, trumpeted statistics linking a father's absence to juvenile delinquency, and they listened.

The problem for some divorcing women is that their husbands listened too well and took seriously the call to parenthood. They became emotionally attached to their offspring and when the marriage ended, they were unwilling to be demoted to the second string; they were unwilling to sit on the sidelines of their children's lives. Although lacking in hard data to prove the point, we have at least the perception that more men are seeking and gaining custody of their children after divorce.

Why is this a problem? Because women do not enjoy living apart from their children any more than men do. Also, most women do not want to relinquish the power that goes with custody. This has led to the ironic situation in which some of the same feminists who, in the early 1970s, denounced motherhood as "enslavement" now lead a campaign to protect motherhood from divorced fathers who want more involvement with their children. But they face a crucial dilemma. They need to resurrect the belief that women are uniquely suited to rear children and therefore the natural choice for sole custody without appearing to endorse the notions that biology is destiny and that the sexes merit unequal treatment before the law.

The solution to this dilemma is the linguistic sleight of hand known as the "primary parent presumption." This guideline would give preference to the parent who is designated "primary" in the child's life, variously defined as the parent who spends the most time with the child, is more responsible for the child's day-to-day care, or performs more of the daily repetitive maintenance tasks such as chauffeuring, shopping for clothes, preparing meals, and bathing. Although touted as a gender-neutral standard, everyone agrees that the primary parent presumption would give mothers the same advantage that they enjoyed with the tender years presumption. In fact, law professor Mary Becker advocates dropping the pretense of gender neutrality and renaming the primary parent presumption the "maternal deference standard."

Briefly, the argument is that because women are more involved in primary caretaking, they deserve custody. Fathers'-rights advocates respond that it is unfair to penalize men for reduced involvement with their children, for they are only fulfilling society's notions of the man's role as the family's breadwinner.

Neither side's argument is compelling. Both are blinded by the pre–19th-century premise that children are property to be "awarded" to the rightful owner. Both sides miss the point that a custody decision should be guided by the needs of the child, not the parents' sense of entitlement.

Some of my colleagues offer arguments in support of the primary parent presumption. They point out that a woman who has been most involved in her children's daily care already possesses the requisite skills. She has less to learn than the father and, by virtue of her experience, probably is more competent to assume the duties of sole custody. Also, because the primary parent standard appears less ambiguous than the best interests standard, parents would be less likely to litigate over custody—a distinct advantage to the family. But that may be its only advantage. Under critical appraisal, this proposal suffers many serious drawbacks.

Unless we regard custody as a reward for past deeds, the decision about the children's living arrangements should reflect a judgment about what situation will best meet their needs now and in the future. Differences in past performance are relevant only if they predict future parental competence and child adjustment. They do not.

The primary parent presumption overlooks the fact that being a single parent is a very different challenge than being one of two parents in the same home. A consensus of research reveals a predictable deterioration in the single mother's relationship with her children. After divorce, the average mother has less time and energy for her children and more problems managing their behavior. Research has also demonstrated that *despite* a mother's greater experience in daily child care, fathers who would not be considered primary caretakers during the marriage are as capable as divorced mothers in managing the responsibilities of custody. And, most important, their children fare as well as children in the custody of their mother.

A more basic problem with the proposed standard is, how do we determine who is the primary parent? Before divorce, parents think of themselves as partners in rearing their children. Whether or not they spend equal time with the children, both parents are important, and mountains of psychological research support this. Before divorce, we do not rank-order parents. Only in the heat of a custody battle do Mom and Dad begin vying for the designation "primary parent."

On what basis do we award this coveted title? We simply cannot measure the amount of time each parent spends with the child. Research has established that beyond a certain minimum the amount of time a parent spends with a child is a poor index of that parent's importance to the child, of the quality of their relationship, or of the parent's competence in child-rearing. In fact, we all know of parents who are *too* involved with their children, so-called "smothering" parents who squelch any signs of independence.

If more extensive contact does not make a primary parent, what does? Most definitions provide a list of responsibilities. The primary parent shops for food and clothes, prepares meals, changes diapers, bathes and dresses the child, takes the child to the doctor, and drives the child to school and recreational activities. Such criteria, though, ignore the overriding importance of the *quality* of parent–child relationships.

Furthermore, critics have argued that this list reflects gender bias. Shopping for food and clothes is included, but not earning the money that funds the shopping trips. Also conspicuously absent are responsibilities typically shared by fathers and in which fathers often predominate, activities such as playing, discipline, moral guidance, encouragement and assistance with schoolwork, gender socialization, coaching team sports, and—something whose significance to children is often overlooked—providing a sense of physical protection and security.

Is the primary caretaker the one who does the most to foster the child's sense of emotional security, the person to whom the child turns in times of stress—the role we most often associate with mothers? Or is it the parent who does the most to promote the child's ability to meet the demands of the world outside the family—the role we most often associate with fathers? There really is no basis for preferring one contribution over the other. Both are necessary for healthy psychological functioning.

We can say that both parents contribute distinctively to their child's welfare. And during different development stages a child may relate better to one parent than the other, or rely on one parent more than the other. But most children form strong attachments to both parents in the first year of life and maintain important ties to both parents throughout their lives. By rank-ordering the importance of parents, we dismiss children's own experiences of their parents' value, reinforce gender stereotypes, and perhaps discourage fathers from assuming more parental responsibilities.

In sum, the primary parent presumption is misinformed, misguided, misleading, and primarily meaningless.

32

Advance Tips on Preventing a Child from Being Abducted Abroad

Philip Schwartz

1. Maintain complete current medical and other records on the child: photographs (full frontal and profile as well as facial), fingerprints, identity marks, etc.
2. Teach the child his or her full name, address, telephone number; how to dial the operator, call collect, and use 911; how to avoid strangers.
3. Maintain complete current records on the spouse: photographs, passport copy, handwriting sample, employment, bank and credit card accounts, automobile license, Social Security number, data on friends and relatives, long-distance telephone records, etc.
4. Be alert to the spouse's reaction to remarriage and moving plans, ties to community and foreign countries, mobility of skills.
5. Avoid disgruntling a spouse by seeking his or her input and collaboration on major decisions affecting the child, see a mediator to resolve disputes, be flexible and cooperative on visitations.
6. Obtain a passport for the child.
7. Seek a custody order with one or more of the following provisions:
   a. Specify visitation precisely.
   b. Avoid joint custody.
   c. Only chaperoned or accompanied visitation allowed.
   d. Visitation must be in custodial parent's home only.
   e. Child is not to be removed from the area, state, or country, and violation is a crime and contempt of court punishable by imprisonment.
   f. Spouse must deposit all his or her and child's passports in his or her possession, either permanently or during visitation, and file an affidavit that no others have been applied for or issued.

g. Spouse periodically obtains official statement from his or her home country's embassy that no other passports, visas, etc., have been applied for or issued.

h. Enjoin the Bureau of Vital Statistics not to issue copies of the child's birth certificate without a court order or to flag the file to notify you if an application is received.

i. Enjoin the school from transferring the child's records.

j. Require the spouse to post a substantial bond for the return of the child or fix a daily accumulation of liquidated damages with confessed judgment.

k. Direct the spouse to file a petition in the home country for an order recognizing the court here as having exclusive jurisdiction over the child.

l. Seek a stipulation that the court has the continuing exclusive jurisdiction over the child, the spouse will not assert to the contrary in any court, and the custodial parent is the best custodian.

8. If the child was born in another state, register a decree there and seek an injunctive order against its Bureau of Vital Statistics not to release copies of the child's birth certificate or flag the file.

9. Send a copy of the decree to the embassy of the spouse's home country and request assistance.

10. Furnish the child's school with a court order, discuss with the principal and teachers, caution against releasing the child to anyone but the custodial parent, request the school and babysitter to quickly report any unexplained absence of the child.

11. Maintain notarized statements of supporting witnesses and transcripts of favorable depositions and trial testimony.

12. Keep at least five fully exemplified copies of all custody and visitation orders and other relevant court records, preferably with as many seals and ribbons as possible.

13. Have relevant orders translated into the language of the spouse's home country and have the translator append to each a sworn certificate of accuracy for possible future use.

14. Notify the State Department by telephone to flag the child's name because of the custody dispute and send an exemplified copy of the order denying removal of the child from the country; also notify U.S. embassies in Ottawa, Canada, and Mexico City, Mexico, and certain other countries that permit entry without a passport.

33

Preparing a Lay Witness in a Custody Case

J. Lindsey Short Jr.

WHEN PREPARING YOUR LAY WITNESS, I recommend that you do not have the client advise the potential witness about what he or she will be testifying about. Simply have the client contact the witness to advise him or her that a member of the law firm will contact him or her to find out some information about what has been the historical set of facts involving the parties and their child or children. The client should have previously provided the firm with a list of potential witnesses as well as what factors or circumstances he or she feels the witness has knowledge about.

The first contact from the law office should be made by a legal assistant who presents the attitude and concept that he or she is simply trying to get information about the case, not that he or she is trying to have the witness say anything bad about anyone. This approach should be made to keep a witness from crystallizing an opinion that may be detrimental or for the witness to decide he or she will not become involved. The interview should be a very general discussion of the facts of the case but with an emphasis on events and circumstances that the witness has seen. At that time, an arrangement and agreement should be made by the legal assistant to contact the witness again.

The second contact should be made a couple of weeks later. At that time, the legal assistant should have reviewed all the events and circumstances involving the particular witness and the witness's relationship with the child and the client, and an effort should be made to direct the discussion with the witness toward those areas that will aid your client in the presentation of evidence to the trier of fact. The legal assistant should remind the potential witness about those events that have occurred and that the witness has observed relating to the child. Sayings, impressions, or descriptions concerning events in the witness's own words that will be appealing to the fact finder should be written down by the legal assistant so they can be used at trial.

Because your case should involve predominantly the presentation of the positive parenting skills and the relationship between your client and the child, the legal assistant should again try to generally avoid truly negative statements about the other parent. Of course, if the witness can be prompted to mention these factors, so much the better. Obviously, because your firm is calling the witness for a second time, the potential witness should begin to feel somewhat more at ease when discussing the various situations. By this time, you probably have decided that the witness will be one of the people you would likely use at the time of the trial. The witness should be further advised at this time regarding generally when the trial is scheduled and how helpful for the best interest of the child the testimony of that particular witness would be. The witness should be assured that you respect his or her privacy and his or her time commitments and that every effort will be made to keep his or her time away from home and business to a minimum.

Finally, in the ten days preceding the date set for trial, a third contact should be made by the firm with the witness. At this time, the witness should be thoroughly familiar with speaking with members of the firm and some degree of comfort should have been achieved. A rapport should be developing. Specific facts, a reminder of sayings, impressions, and expressions, as well as a discussion of cross-examination, should be held with the witness at this time. The potential witness should be taught what formal objections by a lawyer are, who makes them, and what the witness's response should be, among other things. Now is the time to deal with the details of proper dress for court, how to get to the courthouse, parking, or other problems that could be encountered.

Working slowly and carefully, in stages, with witnesses will ensure that they are more prepared, more at ease, and more willing to assist your client with the presentation of the facts of their case.

34

Using Videotapes in Custody Cases to Show Positive and Typical Interactions

Ann M. Haralambie

IN CUSTODY CASES, sometimes the real issues become obscured by a plethora of accusations and posturing. The bottom line in all custody cases is the best interests of the child. To make a proper determination, the judge must have a sense of the child, the parties as parents, the parent–child interactions, and the child's environment. A domestic relations lawyer can demonstrate these issues with videotape evidence in the same way that a personal injury lawyer shows day-in-the-life films to juries to depict the impact of the injury on the plaintiff's daily life.

The videotape can show the child's home, room, and neighborhood at the client's home. It can show the child (who is now a person with a face and personality) as he or she interacts with the parent, siblings, and "significant others" to give the judge a feel for what the child's life with that parent would be like.

The evidentiary videotape should not be "home movies." It should include vignettes that are varied and characteristic of the child's life. Routine and even unpleasant situations should be included. It is important, for example, for the judge to see how the parent deals with prenap crankiness, mealtimes, and discipline problems.

While many hours of taping will be involved, the final exhibit should run no longer than fifteen to thirty minutes to maintain the judge's attention and willingness to view the videotape. The original tapes should be kept to protect against the charge that the sequences are not in context. Put the burden on opposing counsel to point out the unfairness by offering to allow the judge to see all of the unedited tapes. It is unlikely that a judge will want to view several hours of tapes, but if he or she does, the opposing counsel will clearly annoy the judge if no unfairness is found after the protracted viewing.

The exhibit videotape may be edited professionally or even by the client or the lawyer's staff, using two video recording machines.

Minicams and camcorders are easily available for rental and are easy to use. Many lawyers are purchasing the equipment for use in their practices. A videotaping fee can be added to the client's bill to help defray the purchase price and as the equivalent of an outside rental. It is preferable for the video camera to have date and time clock capabilities to document the time sequences.

35

Diagnosis of a Mental Disorder in a Custody Case

Lynne Z. Gold-Bikin

IN A CUSTODY CASE in which a psychiatrist or a psychologist will be used as an expert, there often will be a diagnosis of a mental disorder.

This diagnosis can be made only with the use of the *Diagnostic and Statistical Manual of Mental Disorders,* 4th ed., rev. (DSM-IV-R), and any subsequent revision to the manual. This manual is published every four years with interim manuals two years after the publication.

This publication is the official manual of mental disorders and contains a glossary of descriptions of the various diagnoses. The volume sets forth explicit criteria necessary for the physician to justify a particular diagnosis. It is extremely important for the practitioner to have a copy of the DSM-IV-R and to refer to the specific diagnosis in the manual.

Each disorder is set forth in the manual with a list of the essential features required for the diagnosis. Without the presence of a sufficient number of criteria, the diagnosis cannot stand.

When cross-examining the expert, the practitioner must not only ask him or her to describe the criteria used to make the diagnosis, but also to describe the source of the information for establishing the existence of the criteria.

When the criteria and the source of information are challenged, the entire diagnosis may fall. Also, disclaimers in the manual for each disorder often may make a diagnosis improper in a marital setting.

A good review of the manual before cross-examination and a comparison to the expert's report before cross-examination also may undermine the diagnosis.

The DSM-IV-R is a critical part of any practitioner's library and can be purchased in most medical and university bookstores.

36

Allegations of Sex Abuse in Child Custody Cases

Sandra Joan Morris

ONE OF THE DIFFICULTIES in divorce custody cases in which child sexual abuse has been raised as an allegation is getting the court to focus on whether a molestation occurred at all, rather than on whether the parent (usually the father) has committed the molestation.

The obvious anger between the parents, and the concern that the reporting parent is vindictive, creates confusion in the mind of the court, as well as in the minds of many helping professionals who deal with these matters, regarding whether the reporting parent could have either fabricated the allegation or coached the child to fabricate the allegation.

I have found that the most effective way to get the information across to the court is to ask the court for permission to bifurcate the question of whether the molestation occurred from the issue of who the perpetrator might be.

In so bifurcating the matter for trial, the court focuses first on whatever medical, testimonial, or psychological information can be marshaled to substantiate the occurrence of a molestation. If the court cannot find that a molestation occurred at all, there is no point in pitting the parents against each other by way of accusation and defense. Although there is unlikely to be much confusion regarding who the reporting parent thinks was the perpetrator of the molestation, we are all aware of how damaging the in-court testimony can be to any possibility of a future ongoing relationship as parents between the mother and father.

If, on the other hand, the evidence substantiates that a molestation has taken place, the accusing parent is taken "off the hook" for having made his or her report and is free to marshal evidence on the issue of the identity of the perpetrator without as much danger of being accused of vindictiveness. Furthermore, the court will have committed itself to a position from which it is unlikely it will retreat, despite accusations of fabrication by the alleged perpetrator.

37

Cross-Examining Richard Gardner's Sexual Abuse Legitimacy Scale with Its Own Words*

Ann M. Haralambie

ONE OF THE MOST FREQUENTLY USED "TESTS" in child sexual abuse cases arising in the divorce or postdivorce context is psychiatrist Richard Gardner's Sexual Abuse Legitimacy (SAL) scale, self-published in *The Parental Alienation Syndrome and the Differentiation between Fabricated and Genuine Child Sex Abuse* by R. Gardner (Creative Therapeutics, 1987).

The SAL scale can be cross-examined effectively by referring to Gardner's own admissions and caveats. The scale itself contains on its cover page, "**WARNING:** In order to be used in a meaningful way, this instrument *must* be used in association with the information provided in . . . chapters 3, 4, and 5. . . . The book explains how best to evaluate and score each of the items in the scale. Failure to use these guidelines may result in misleading or erroneous conclusions."

The lawyer should read through the book carefully to pull out useful impeachment information. This tip addresses only the highlights.

The SAL scale never has been standardized, validated, or accepted in a peer-reviewed journal, the means accepted in the mental health community for determining that psychological instruments are accepted in the field. Gardner recognizes that some might criticize his lack of scientific evidence to support his conclusion, saying, "I agree that I have no such studies to support my hypothesis and that my conclusions are based on my own experiences as well as colleagues in the mental health professions. . . ." *Id.* at 106. He says that examiners "are advised that the cutoff levels and their significance should be viewed as preliminary and tentative." *Id.* at 176. He also warns that evaluators "should not use this scale independently of other data." *Id.*

Adapted from Chapter 16, A. Haralambie, Handling Child Custody, Abuse, and Adoption Cases, *2d ed. New York: Shepard's/McGraw-Hill, 1993.*

With respect to his criteria for mothers, Gardner states, "What I present below are tentative conclusions, held by many who examine such mothers. We must recognize, however, that these conclusions will probably have to be modified as we gain more experience in this area." *Id.* at 124.

Gardner states that "it is dangerous for an examiner to conclude that there are typical personality patterns of the parents of sexually abused children and/or the parents of fabricators." *Id.* at 131. He continues, "The fathers who are bona fide abusers are often said to fall into certain personality categories. I believe such generalizations are dangerous." *Id.* at 132. Nevertheless, his scoring depends on these very generalizations and patterns. When dealing specifically with allegations in the divorce-related arena, Gardner says that "it would be an error for the reader to conclude that children whose parents are litigating for their custody are not likely to be sexually abused. It would also be an error to conclude that children who are suffering with parental alienation syndromes are immune from such abuse. This is not so." *Id.* at 168.

He points out: "The abuse may have taken place prior to the separation, and the child may have been fearful of divulging it because of the omnipresence of the father. A custody dispute may increase a child's animosity and thereby increase the likelihood that the abuse will be revealed. . . . Just as the divorce situation is likely to precipitate the child's divulgence of a preexisting pattern of abuse, the divorce situation may actually precipitate sex abuse on the part of a parent when it did not exist previously. Divorce is one of the more important and severe stresses of life. Under this stress some parents may regress and involve themselves in pedophilia. Contested divorces are even more stressful, and custody litigation adds even further to that stress. The child offers innocent and unconditional acceptance of a potential abuser. There is little chance of rejection. Rejected by a spouse, the parent then may turn to a child. In the context of a weekend visitation, in a one-bedroom apartment with an adoring child, the parent may be unable to resist the pedophilic urges." *Id.* at 168–69.

The scale itself says "face validity only is claimed for these items." *Id.* at 301 (Sexual Abuse Legitimacy scale, p. 3). The scale also says that the "cutoff levels and their significance should be viewed as preliminary and tentative." *Id.* at 176.

The criteria and scoring for the SAL scale were based on Gardner's review of about thirty cases in his own practice for which he had made a determination that there was or was not abuse. In his review of those cases, he decided that some bona fide abusers obtained scores in the vicinity of 30 percent to 40 percent of the maximum range, but "in order to diminish the likelihood that innocents might be falsely considered bona fide offenders, I decided to use the 50 percent level as the cutoff point. This conservative approach to the setting of the cutoff point for bona fide sex abuse is based on the American legal principle that 'it is better to let 100 guilty men go free than to convict one innocent man. . . . I have chosen to recommend a cutoff point at a level that *might* indeed exonerate bona fide perpetrators in order to protect innocents who might be falsely considered guilty." *Id.* at 175–76. Unfortunately for children, application of the criminal presumption of innocence for an accused provides no protection for the molested child. It may be conservative in the criminal area, but it is certainly not conservative for the best interests of the child, the applicable legal touchstone in the divorce and postdivorce context. By Gardner's own writing, he is deliberately slanting his scoring system to favor the accused.

A review of the weighted criteria also shows Gardner's admitted bias. Despite requiring a 50 percent or better showing to determine that the allegations are true, he admits that more than half of the available points may tend to miss actual abuse. For example, there are sixty points available for the child, of which twenty-two (47 percent) are stated in the explanatory section for those questions as possibly tending to miss actual abuse questions 1, 4, 7, 11, 14–17, and 21, and six are stated in other sections of the book but for some reason not in the questions themselves, as possibly tending to miss actual abuse questions 12 and 13. Only six points (10 percent) may falsely accuse (questions 19, 20, 22, and 23).

The accuser has twenty-seven possible points, of which twenty-two (81 percent) may tend to miss actual abuse: direct cautions appearing in questions 1, 4, 5, 9, 10, and 11, and cautions elsewhere in the book appearing for questions 2, 3, and 8. Only one point (less than 4 percent) may falsely accuse (question 11).

The accused also has twenty-seven possible points, of which twenty-five (93 percent) may tend to miss actual abuse: direct cautions appearing in questions 1, 2, 4, 5, 7, and 9–13 and cautions elsewhere in the book appearing for questions 3 and 8. Only five points (20 percent) may falsely accuse (questions 6 and 11–13). Some questions can both underinclude and overinclude, explaining why thirty points are discussed as being inaccurate.

Gardner states in the sections on each question containing direct cautions that he hopes other criteria will accurately distinguish between true and false allegations. However, with 47 percent, 81 percent, and 93 percent of the points risking missing true allegations and 10 percent, 4 percent, and 20 percent of the points risking false allegation, the usefulness of a weighted instrument, especially with its "tentative" conclusions, to the trier of fact is highly suspect.

By using Gardner's own admissions and caveats, the lawyer may be able to preclude testimony about the results of the SAL scale during *voir dire* as not meeting the foundational requirements of *Frye v. United States,* 293 F.2d 1013 (D.C. Cir. 1923). If an expert is permitted to testify about the SAL scale, the book should be used to impeach the instrument during cross-examination.

38

Parenting Assessment Discovery Form for Lawyers*

Ann M. Haralambie

PARENTING ASSESSMENT DISCOVERY FORM FOR LAWYERS

Instructions for Use

This form is meant to provide a basis for the deposition examination of parties in custody cases. The form is worded for interparent cases, but may be adapted to other situations.

The questions should be asked in a conversational manner, using the lawyer's own speech patterns, rather than being read faithfully, word by word. Where questions are inappropriate to the age of the children involved (e.g., asking if an infant has regular responsibilities around the house), they should be omitted.

Wherever possible, the names of the parties involved and their children should be used. The form is structured to start out with questions more usually asked in a deposition, and the more obvious *test-type* questions are at the end of the form. This is done deliberately to minimize the deponent's guardedness and his or her lawyer's objections.

Where appropriate, follow-up questions should be asked, and additional questions relevant to the issues in the particular case should be added. The purpose of the form is to elicit information from which a psychologist, psychiatrist, or other mental health professional can gain information concerning the parent's attitudes, knowledge, and parenting skills. Because this is not a scaled test, variations in the questions or methods of presentation do not affect its usefulness.

For maximum usefulness, both parents should be asked the questions. The lawyer's own client may answer the questions during a taped interview

---

by the lawyer, even without notice to opposing counsel, from which a transcript is made and given to the mental health professional. This will allow a direct comparison.

The form should not be subject to objection, because all of the questions relate to relevant, admissible testimony concerning the parent's custodial fitness. The speculative questions should be permitted because they will lead to relevant evidence from the mental health professional, to whom the answers are relevant and material.

The form was designed for use in depositions, and while some information may be obtained by incorporating some of the questions in interrogatories, the results will be far less probative, because the lawyer will be phrasing the answers, and the parent will have an opportunity to research answers or consult with other people before answering.

Parenting Assessment Discovery Form for Lawyers

([Y] indicates a question to be asked only concerning young children. Other questions may be omitted if the children are too young.)

What are the names and ages of your children?

Describe [each child]'s relationship to you.

Describe [each child]'s relationship to [the other parent].

How are the children reacting to the divorce/separation?

What have you said to the children about the divorce?

What was their reaction?

Do you talk to the children about [the other parent]?

What do you say?

How do you feel about your children's relationship with [the other parent]'s relatives?

Do you expect to be involved with your children continuing that relationship? How?

Who do the children go to when they're hurt? Sad?

Why do you want custody?

In what ways do you think you would be the better parent? Why?

Do you think [the other parent] is a good parent?

Do you have any objections to the way he/she parents?

Are there any areas of major disagreement between you concerning child rearing? religion? education? lifestyles? moral values?

Do you think the children have any preferences about whom they want to live with?

If you do not get sole custody, what visitation do you want?

If you do get sole custody, what visitation do you think would be appropriate for [the other parent]?

What do you think about joint custody?

Do you think it might work in your situation? Why/why not?

How do you feel about telephone contact between the children and [the other parent] when they are with you?

Are you involved with anybody who will have a lot of contact with the children when they are with you?

What is the children's relationship with him/her?

What do you think the role of a stepparent should be?

Do you see any difficulties in being a single parent?

What are your current work hours?

What are your career goals?

What child care arrangements do you have for the time you are not able to take care of the children yourself?

How do you usually discipline your children?

What do you think are the best ways of disciplining a child?

What do you think about physical punishment?

What types of behavior do you feel warrant punishment?

What do you think about the use of rewards as a way to discipline your children?

What do you think are the most important influences on children's behavior?

What do you think about parents admitting to a child he/she is wrong?

When your children are with you, what do you generally feed them?

What do you think constitutes a good daily diet for your children?

What do you do when your children won't eat what you think they need?

How do you deal with your children lying?

Why do you think children lie?

At what age should a child be willing and able to tell the truth most of the time?

What do you think a parent's responsibility is with regard to the children's education?

What are your educational goals for the children?

[Y] What do you think a parent should teach a child before he/she enters school?

What have you taught your children already?

What values do you think are important to teach a child?

How do you teach your children those values?

Have you had any parenting education?

Have you read any books on child development or parenting?

What? Do you own any of those books?

What age do you start talking to your children about sex? Have you done that yet?

What contacts have you had with your children's school?

What responsibilities do you think a [fill in ages of children involved]-year-old child should have in the home? [Repeat for each child]

How important do you think it is for children to be polite?

At what age do you think children should be able to be polite to visitors, friends, and relatives?

Are your children polite? What happens when they are not polite?

[Y] At what age should they be able to sit quietly for half an hour?

[Y] When do you think they should be able to totally dress themselves?

[Y] When do you think they should be able to bathe themselves?

[Y] When do you think they should be able to get themselves ready for bed?

[Y] At what age should a child be completely toilet-trained?

[Y] When do you think they should be able to play cooperatively with other children?

What do you consider to be good table manners?

At what age should a child have good table manners?

Do you think your children have good table manners?

[If they don't] How do you handle their poor table manners?

At what age should children show respect to their parents?

When should they be able to sympathize with their parent's feelings?

How old do you think children should be before they are expected to do routine chores without being reminded?

Do your children have any routine chores when they are with you? Do they do them?

How long can your children be left unattended during the day?

At night?

Are your children pretty responsible about staying alone?

Do you know what they do when they're alone?

How much TV do your children watch? What shows?

Do you watch TV with them? How often?

Do you think your children have any need for counseling?

[If yes] Why?

Have you been involved with any counseling with them?

Do you think [the other parent] should go to counseling with them?

What have you done with respect to your children's health care needs?

[Y] What have you done to make your home safe for your children?

39

How to "Cut the Cord" before an Interstate Custody Proceeding Is Filed

Robert J. Barnard Jr.

IF YOUR CLIENT (a parent [with or without custody], a stepparent, a grand-parent, a person acting as a parent, or a person claiming custodial or visitation rights with respect to a child, Uniform Child Custody Jurisdiction Act Sec. 15, 16, 28 U.S.C.A. § 1738A(b)(2), (6), (d) and (e)) claims a custody or visitation right to a minor child who was the subject of a custody order in a prior proceeding in a foreign court, certain procedural steps should be taken before another custody dispute arises.

1. The foreign judgment promptly should be filed (registered) in the new state under the UCCJA (Sec. 16). Attach an affidavit showing the present addresses of the child and the persons with whom the child has resided (UCCJA Sec. 9).
2. Request that a certified copy of the new state order of registry and affidavit be sent by the clerk to the prior foreign state court (UCCJA Sec. 17).
3. On any change of a current custodian or a change of address of a person with whom the child has lived, file a modified affidavit and send a certified copy to the prior court, even if a contestant no longer resides there.

If these three steps are taken before another custody dispute arises, the courts and agencies involved will be in a better position to evaluate child custody jurisdictional conflicts under the UCCJA and the Parental Kidnapping Prevention Act (27 U.S.C. § 1738A), and your client will have been responsible for providing the necessary information to both courts.

40

Use of Psychologists When Screening Prospective Custody Clients

Harvey L. Golden

AT THE INITIAL INTERVIEW, if I determine that my potential client is serious about making or defending a custody challenge, I will send that person immediately to a licensed clinical psychologist for a full-scale evaluation including the Minnesota Multiphasic Personality Inventory (MMPI) and clinical interview. This is before I accept the case.

This evaluation will establish several things:

- *First,* I find out if my potential client is a serious, realistic candidate for custody or has problems that may disqualify or adversely affect a custody claim.

- *Second,* a competent psychologist gets on board early enough to provide testimony or affidavits for the temporary hearing. This testimony also provides independent corroboration of my client's strong points and articulates his or her parenting skills.

- *Third,* by introducing a psychologist or competent mental health professional early in the case, I may be able to convince opposing counsel or the judge that this psychologist should be chosen by the court to evaluate everyone connected with the case, including both parents, the children (if old enough), grandparents, and anyone else having significant exposure to the child.

- *Fourth,* I assure myself in the best way possible that I will not be using my skills to obtain custody for a psychopath who could endanger the child. This is the most important reason of all.

41

Use of Demonstrative Evidence in Custody Cases

Phyllis G. Bossin

WHILE MATRIMONIAL LAWYERS are becoming more sophisticated when using demonstrative evidence in divorce cases generally, particularly with the use of computer-generated financial data, they still are underutilizing visual aids in contested custody litigation.

The uses of demonstrative evidence in custody litigation are almost endless. Personal injury lawyers have long made use of the professionally prepared chart and graph for use in the courtroom. These same types of professionally produced charts can be extremely effective in the custody case. Custody cases lend themselves to visual demonstration of a large number of issues. Some examples are:

- Charting a child's school progress. Report cards can be enlarged and reproduced and then graphed to show progress or decline.
- If there is a developmental problem related to parenting by one of the parents, a development chart showing the particular child's development compared to normal development at that age can be prepared in contrasting colors.
- If a psychological evaluation has been prepared and the opposing spouse demonstrates particular negative characteristics or psychological problems, certain phrases or words can be pulled out of the report and listed on a chart. This is much more cumulative and effective for the court than simply reading the report.
- If a particular syndrome is being demonstrated, such as brainwashing and programming, a list of those characteristics can be prepared and alongside it a corresponding place to demonstrate how the particular child is being affected by the syndrome, e.g., specific characteristics being displayed by the child.

- Graphs and charts to demonstrate comparative amounts of time spent by each parent with the child, broken down by days, weeks, or even hours.
- Graphs or charts to demonstrate comparative duties performed by each parent for the child.

These are just a few examples of the use of charts and graphs in the custody case. Likewise, counsel should be creative in the utilization of the day-in-the-life movie. These should not be used in every case but can be extremely effective in the right case. They can be used not only to demonstrate your client's relationship with the child in a contested custody case but can be used in postdecree litigation involving visitation situations to demonstrate the positive relationship of the child with the noncustodial parent. They also can be used to demonstrate the relationship of the children with grandparents, etc., who might be seeking independent rights of visitation. If your client's mental health is being questioned, the video can be used to show your client at work and in a number of situations to demonstrate his or her stability and normalcy.

In short, if finances permit, counsel should have charts and graphs prepared by companies that specialize in litigation graphics. The day-in-the-life movie can be produced by a video company or, if there is a university in your city, by a student at far less cost.

42

Expert Testimony in Relocation Cases

Ellen J. Effron

THE FIFTY STATES have been experimenting with removal and antiremoval statutes, while case law has shifted between delegating the greater burden to the party seeking or resisting removal. Despite window dressing that refers to constitutional rights to travel and enhanced quality of life of the custodial parent, the bottom line seems to be that courts have adopted the attitude that what works best for the mother—perhaps a new job or relationship—is heralded as in the best interests of the child.

In those states that adopt a permissive attitude regarding relocation by the child and custodial parent, the lawyer representing the noncustodial parent must overcome a substantial handicap. The custodial parent is likely to present a case with the following facts: The mother has been the primary caretaker since birth; she has a legitimate, nonvindictive motive for leaving the area; no egregious psychiatric disorders are discernible. The noncustodial parent then should introduce mental health testimony that calls attention to the child's emotional and cognitive needs, tempered by both the child's sex and the developmental stage. The focus is therefore on the child, not the mother, in those states where the best interests of the child are the controlling custodial standard. By retaining a child psychiatrist or psychologist with a background in child development, the recent psychological literature regarding the detrimental impact of relocation can be brought to the court's attention.

The concept of the noncustodial parent's availability as a buffer has been elaborated by Joan B. Kelly and Mavis Hetherington, among others. Where the custodial parent has minor or severe psychiatric disturbance, the mediating role of the noncustodial parent should not be underestimated. The door thereby is opened for the noncustodial parent's lawyer to introduce testimony on the custodial parent's limitations.

Boys in particular suffer from separation from their fathers. Separation correlates with less masculine behavior in boys, at least in the short run. A review of the literature finds deficits in cognitive functioning for children, particularly boys, from single-parent families. The importance of the father as role model after divorce is highlighted by recent data and correlated with success in school and peer relations.

The mental health expert should specifically relate the impact of relocation to the developmental state of the particular minor in question. Preschool children may believe themselves responsible for the loss or separation from their father. Some authors assess the differential damage during the oedipal and latency phases, while others note that parental loss during adolescence may disrupt identity formation and lead to disturbance in the area of autonomy struggles.

As the child cognitively matures, his or her sense of time changes radically. Not until adolescence does a child's sense of time approximate that of adults. Thus, courts that allow visitation only for several weeks during winter, spring, and summer school recesses often do not perceive time through the eyes of a six-year-old.

The psychological literature is replete with references to the principle that continuity of relationships with both parents is critical. Arrangements and structure can change over time, but visitation is best when it is frequent and routine. Children relocated by the custodial parent are placed in a vulnerable position. By introducing expert testimony focusing on the child's emotional and cognitive development as well as the possibility of future psychopathology, previously unwinnable relocation cases may be addressed and decided differently by the courts.

43

Habitual Residence =
Domicile within the Meaning
of The Hague Convention

George S. Stern
Susan A. Hurst

THE CONVENTION ON CIVIL ASPECTS of International Child Abduction held at The Hague on October 25, 1980, as implemented by the International Child Abduction Remedies Act, 42 U.S.C. § 11601, *et seq.*, "establishes legal rights and procedures for the prompt return of children who have been wrongfully removed or retained."

For The Hague Convention to be applicable in a case where a child has been removed from a foreign jurisdiction to the United States, the child must have been a habitual resident of the foreign jurisdiction.

In a 1990 case in Georgia, the habitual residence of the child was the issue before the court. According to the U.S. State Department, the habitual residence issue had not been previously litigated. In the Georgia case, the child was present in Switzerland with her mother (a Swiss citizen) for approximately three months prior to the removal. The father was present with mother and child in Switzerland for approximately six weeks prior to the removal of the child by the father to the United States.

At the hearing under The Hague Convention, the petitioner argued the following:

A. "Habitual residence," a term used in a number of Hague Conventions, "has never been defined but is understood to approximate the meaning of 'domicile' without embracing all technical implications of that term in English or American law." *Bodenheimer,* The Hague Draft Convention on International Child Abduction, 98 *Fam. L.Q.,* Vol. XIV, No. 2, 99, 104 N. 25 (1980). (Professor Bodenheimer was the U.S. delegate to The Hague Convention.)

B. Generally, habitual residence "requires physical presence in a place for a period of time, together presumably with the maintenance there of a physical place of abode." *Reece,* 14 *Am. J. Comp. L.* 692, 693 (1965–66); *see also, Philip,* Hague Draft Convention on Matrimonial Property, 24 *Am. J. Comp. L.* 308 (1976).

C. At the time of the removal of the child, the child was a domiciliary and also a habitual resident of Switzerland.
   1. Georgia law provides that the domicile of a minor child is that of the parents if the parents are domiciled in the same country;
      a. The evidence showed that the parties were domiciliaries of Switzerland at the time of the removal.
   2. Georgia law further provides that if a minor child's parents are separated, the child's domicile is that of the custodial parent.
      a. The evidence showed that the mother was a domiciliary of Switzerland at the time of the removal and the mother was lawfully the custodial parent, having obtained a Temporary Custody Order in the Swiss courts.

The respondent argued that evidence showed he was not a domiciliary of Switzerland, and that the Swiss courts had no jurisdiction to enter a Temporary Custody Order.

The opinion of the court adopted the language of domicile for determining habitual residence of the child. Finding that the evidence supported the respondent's contentions, the court stated that "[t]he father never *intended* a permanent residence in Switzerland." (Emphasis added.) Concluding that the Swiss court did not have jurisdiction, the court found that the child was not a habitual resident of Switzerland.

The court adopted the U.S. concept of domicile in determining whether the child was a habitual resident of the foreign jurisdiction. Professor Bodenheimer's article, *supra,* implies that something less than technical domicile is required to establish habitual residence within the meaning of The Hague Convention. It appears that, thus far, a Georgia court has chosen to apply a traditional interpretation of "domicile" to The Hague Convention. Clearly, the opinion would allow for habitual residence without requiring the six-month "home state" standard of the Uniform Child Custody Jurisdiction Act, but the authors assert that the requirement should be less stringent than that applied by the court in this case.

44

The Hague Convention on the Civil Aspects of International Child Abductions

Richard J. Podell

WHY WAS THAT CONVENTION ADOPTED?

Identification of Problem

1. Problem possibly results because of greater facility to travel, immigration, and international marriages;
2. Difficulty in locating the child in a foreign country;
3. Difficulty in having custody order recognized and enforced in another country—often a child is abducted when there is no custody order;
4. Difficulty in finding lawyers in a foreign country because of language and distance; and
5. The abducting parent often will try to have the courts of the country where he or she took the child grant him or her a custody order, thus obtaining some force of legitimacy for his or her action. The result is two conflicting custody orders from the courts of two states.

All those obstacles lead to delays preventing the prompt return of the abducted child.

An international solution is needed, under which states would agree to respect rights of custody and access under the law of another state and to secure the prompt return of abducted children.

A solution that would deal with civil aspects of international child abduction as opposed to criminal aspects also is needed.

WHAT ARE THE OBJECTIVES?

1. To secure the prompt return of children wrongfully removed to or retained in any contracting states; and

2. To ensure that rights of custody and of access under the law of one contracting state are effectively respected in other contracting states.

In other words, the Convention seeks to reestablish, through the obligation to promptly return the abducted child, the status quo that existed prior to the abduction.

The principle underlying the Convention is that any dispute on the right of custody is to be determined by the court of the habitual residence of the child.

The second objective, closely linked to the first objective, incorporates the need to take all necessary measures to prevent wrongful removals of children.

DESCRIPTION OF CONVENTION MECHANISM

The Convention protects custody rights and access rights. Access rights are considered corollary to custody rights.

The Convention ceases to apply when the child attains the age of sixteen years. It seems that the practice of states differs, some states having suspended procedures under the Convention when the child attains the age of sixteen, while other states have continued to apply the Convention when the child attains the age of sixteen during the procedures; in the latter case the child's views become a critical factor.

The Convention is not a convention on recognition and enforcement of custody orders. This question gave rise to lengthy debates during the drafting of the Convention. The conclusion was that procedures for recognition and enforcement could be lengthy and that in cases of child abduction time is essential and the decision on the return of the child must be taken rapidly to prevent further psychological troubles for the child.

Article 12 of the Convention prescribes that the judge must order the return of the child if there has been a wrongful removal or retention. The same article also provides that even where proceedings have commenced more than a year after the wrongful removal or retention, the judge shall order the return of the child unless it is demonstrated that the child is settled in his or her new environment.

The Convention is a convention on legal cooperation between state authorities.

States' parties to the Convention must designate a "Central Authority." These Central Authorities shall cooperate with each other and promote cooperation among the competent authorities in their respective states to secure the prompt return of children and achieve the other objects of the Convention. The United States has designated one Central Authority that is the Office of Citizens Consular Services, Department of State.

The following measures are among those that shall be taken by Central Authorities:

- Locating the child;
- Securing the voluntary return of the child;

- Exchanging information on the child;
- Providing information as to the law of their state in connection with the application of the Convention;
- Initiating or facilitating the institution of judicial or administrative proceedings for the return of the child and organizing access rights; and
- Providing or facilitating the provision of legal aid.

The petitioner should submit a request as complete as possible with all information and documents that would assist the Central Authority in finding the child or justifying his or her return. Information is needed to show that the child was wrongfully removed or retained.

There are certain exceptions to the obligations to order the return of the child:

1. If the person having the care of the person of the child was not exercising custody rights at the time of the removal or retention, or has acquiesced in the removal or retention (Article 13 a);
2. There is a grave risk that the return of the child would expose the child to physical or psychological harm (Article 13 b);
3. Where the child objects to being returned and is old and mature enough that it is appropriate to take account of his or her views (Article 13, second paragraph); or
4. If the return would not be permitted by fundamental human rights principles (Article 20).

45

The Client's Dealings with Social-Service Agencies

J. Lindsey Short Jr.

IN MOST JURISDICTIONS there will be an investigative report prepared and filed by a social-service arm of the court or county. For purposes of prioritizing potential witnesses, I refer to this expert as a quasi-expert. This investigator can be vitally important. Entire articles have been written on the subject of cross-examining these investigators, so my remarks will be brief. The lawyer should meet and get to know the investigators to become familiar with their prejudices and biases to carefully prepare his or her client for their face-to-face meeting with the agency representative. There are certain basic things that should be performed:

1. If the investigator is to visit the home, clean the house. Try to freshen the living areas and make the bedrooms look "warm."
2. Prepare a legible list of source witnesses with addresses, telephone numbers, and areas of information to give to the social worker and keep a copy for cross-examination in case they are not contacted.
3. Prepare a quiet and comfortable place for the interview to take place in the home.
4. Instruct your client to be polite, cooperative, and sincere but not to be condescending or solicitous. A staff member of the firm should practice with the client in advance of the meeting.
5. Request that a time be established when the social worker will be able to interview the child after the child has been with your client for at least a day.
6. Provide a place separate and apart from where you will be when the child is to be interviewed.
7. Prepare an outline of significant events that have occurred—for example, when the spouses met, when they were married, when the children were born, dates of medical or mental health episodes, etc.
8. Once the report is filed, obtain a copy, study it, and be prepared to keep it out of evidence if it is filled with "bootstrap hearsay" that is

detrimental to your client. Object on sound legal ground to the admissibility of the report. No matter how bad the report is, however, remember there usually are some favorable portions. Stand ready with them to make the points that you can. Remember, the investigator is overworked and understaffed and can be effectively cross-examined regarding methodology and results if the lawyer is prepared. Do not simply rehash detrimental portions and argue with the expert.

46

Help Your Long-Distance-Parent Client Stay in Touch

Sandra Morgan Little

PROVIDING INFORMATION TO YOUR CLIENTS that they can actually use without having to talk to you is practical and is one of the greatest services you can provide. Your client may not be able to hear your advice or process information correctly while he or she is in the depths of the divorce process. Provide information through handouts to which your client can refer at a later time. Not only is this helpful to your client, it is also a great marketing tool. This particular handout can make a long-distance parent's relationship with a child more rewarding. You can keep copies in your reception room and provide them to lay groups when you speak.

TEN+ EASY WAYS A LONG-DISTANCE PARENT CAN STAY IN TOUCH

1. *Read Stories on Tape.* Read a story or a book in your own voice onto a tape. Buy your child a tape player that is age-appropriate (consider earphones), teach your child how to operate the player, and send the tapes. Read from age-appropriate literature. It is an easy way for your child to hear your voice every day. You may also want to send the stories or books so your child can read along.

2. *Postcards.* You do not need to write long letters. Just a simple "I love you and I am thinking about you" is enough. Send a postcard weekly. Select scenic cards from the area in which you live, scenic cards from where you visit or take business trips, humorous cards, or cards of a particular interest to your child.

3. *Magazine Subscriptions.* Kids love getting mail addressed to them. There are many age-appropriate magazines that are reasonably priced. There are certainly magazines your child would enjoy. When the magazine arrives, your child thinks of you.

4. *Collections.* Start a collection that is unique to you and your child. It can be something your child is interested in, such as baseball

cards or animal knickknacks. Send something from places you visit, for special occasions, and "just because." It will be a special collection.

5. *Fax, E-Mail, and Computer Contact.* Many households now have fax machines, or you can set up your child's computer so you can write every day, every week, or at some regular interval. It can just be "hi," to celebrate a special event, or just to report about a normal day. It is a high-tech and easy way to stay in touch.

6. *Make Videotapes.* Send your child videotapes of your daily life, your travel, and special events. Special events are easy, but remember your child is also interested in your normal routine, the dog or cat, and just to see you and hear your voice. When your child is with you, make sure he or she knows how to run a VCR without help.

7. *Photo Album.* This is the same idea as the videotape except in still form. Buy an album and send pictures of you doing routine daily things as well as trips and special events. Take pictures when your child is with you and send them.

8. *Watch TV Shows Together.* Find a TV show that your child enjoys and "watch it together." You may be miles apart, but you each know you are "sharing" the show. When you talk on the phone, you have something in common to discuss. It may be a great ice-breaker.

9. *Provide Addressed Postcards, Stationery, and Stamped Envelopes.* Let your child stay in touch with you without having to ask for help. Give your child a supply of postcards or stationery with stamped and addressed envelopes. Your child can write you and put it in the mail.

10. *Phone Cards or 1-800 Numbers.* You can purchase phone cards for your child that have a determined number of long-distance minutes to call you without any help. 1-800 numbers are not very expensive. This will enable your child to call you whenever he or she wants to tell you something or just hear your voice.

11. *Talk to the Teacher.* Make arrangements with your child's teacher to send copies of his or her work regularly. Provide envelopes and stamps. Most teachers are happy to oblige. Also arrange a regular time to talk to your child's teacher. You'll feel much closer.

47

What Does Troxel *Mean for You?*

Lewis Becker

IN *Troxel v. Granville,* 530 U.S. 57 (2000), the U.S. Supreme Court considered the constitutionality of a Washington statute that provided that "any person may petition the court for visitation rights at any time" and that visitation could be granted if in the best interest of the child. Six Justices voted to affirm the holding of the Washington Supreme Court that the statute was unconstitutional. Four of these six Justices joined in an opinion (the "plurality opinion") authored by Justice O'Connor, which held the statute unconstitutional as applied in the circumstances of the case. The plurality opinion described the statute as "breathtakingly broad" and stated that "in practical effect . . . a court can disregard and overturn any decision by a fit custodial parent concerning visitation." The opinion stated that "the record reveals that the . . . order [granting visitation] was based on precisely the type of mere disagreement we have described and nothing more" and held that "the combination of several factors" compelled the conclusion that the statute was unconstitutional as applied:

—the grandparents had not alleged that the mother was an unfit parent and that was important because there is a presumption that fit parents act in the best interests of their children ("so long as a parent adequately cares for his or her children (i.e., is fit), there will normally be no reason for the State to inject itself into the private realm of the family to further question the ability of that parent to make the best decisions concerning the rearing of that parent's children");

—the court that granted visitation gave no special weight to the parent's determination of the children's best interests;

—there was no allegation that the parent had ever sought to cut off visitation entirely; rather, she preferred restricting visitation to one short visit per month and special holidays.

The plurality Opinion expressly did not consider whether the due process clause requires all non-parental visitation statutes to require a showing of harm or potential harm to the child as a condition precedent to granting visitation (the Washington Supreme Court had held that the due process clause did compel such a requirement).

Troxel has had an enormous impact in cases considering non-parental visitation. It is also beginning to have an impact in cases involving a sole custody battle between a parent and a non-parent. Given all this, **what does *Troxel* mean for you?**

I. Visitation cases

    A. Points for the lawyer for the non-parent

        1. If your statute or governing case law is not as broad as the Washington statute (e.g., if it limits visitation to certain grandparents such as those whose child is deceased), argue that *Troxel* should not be applied because your state's law is narrower than the statute in *Troxel*. The more limitations on visitation (e.g., that visitation can be ordered only when visitation has been unreasonably denied), the better the argument that *Troxel* is inapplicable. See, distinguishing *Troxel* on this type of basis, *Galjour v. Harris*, 2001 WL 293689 (La. Ct. App. 2001); *In re G.P.C.* (*Cabral v. Cabral*), 28 S.W.3d 357 (Mo. Ct. App. 2000).

        (i). Perhaps the best chance for distinguishing *Troxel* is where a statute or governing case law provides for a detailed and specific inquiry as a condition for granting visitation to non-parents. For an example, see Ariz. Revised Stat. Sec. 25-409, which authorizes visitation for grandparents and great-grandparents if in the best interests of the child, but which requires the court to consider specific factors including the quantity of visitation time requested and the potential adverse impact that visitation will have on the child's customary activities. The constitutionality of this statute was upheld in *Jackson v. Tangreen*, 18 P.3d 100 (Ariz. Ct. App. 2000).

        (ii). But see, refusing to distinguish *Troxel* even though the statute in question contained language that arguably made it narrower that the statute in *Troxel*, *Punsly v. Ho*, 105 Cal. Rptr.2d 139 (Cal. Ct. App. 2001); *Hertz v. Hertz*, 717 N.Y.S.2d 497 (N.Y., Supreme Court, Kings Co. 2000); *Brice v. Brice*, 754 A.2d 1132 (Md. Ct. Spec. App. 2000).

        2. Emphasize any periods in which the child lived with the non-parent in a parental type of relationship. These parental-type contacts can be crucial in overcoming the *Troxel* presumption that a fit parent makes decisions in the best interest of the child because of the emotional harm that a child may suffer by the termination of any contact with the former caregivers. Psychological evidence may be necessary to buttress the argument of harm. Even if the contacts between the non-parent and the child were not caregiving in nature, the closer the tie between the child and the non-parent, the better the chance of overcoming the presumption. The strongest fact situation is where the non-parent was the sole parental figure during the period of residence with the child, but any parental caretaking role may be significant.

    A statute that provides for visitation in these circumstances could be argued to be distinguishable from *Troxel*. Even a statute that is worded broadly could be held to be constitutional *as applied* if the non-parent has had a significant parental role. See *Rideout v. Riendeau*, 761 A.2d 291 (Me. 2000) (upholding constitutionality of statute permitting grandparent visitation if there was a "sufficient existing relationship" in a context where grandparents had in the past acted as parents for significant periods, but also stating that the trial court must consider any objection by the parents and that visitation could not be granted if it would significantly interfere with the parent–child relationship). Note, however, that some decisions have applied *Troxel* and reversed a visitation order even where the grandparents had had a prior caregiving role with the child.

3. Regarding the views of the parent to the requested non-parental visitation:

(i) If the parent refuses to consent to any visitation (as opposed to the limited visitation consented to in *Troxel*), argue that that fact distinguishes your case from *Troxel*. A court may or may not accept that distinction. For a decision holding a statute unconstitutional even though the parents opposed any visitation, see *Hertz v. Hertz*, 717 N.Y.S.2d 497 (N.Y. Supreme Court, Kings Co. 2000) (stating that where the parents opposed any visitation, court-ordered visitation would be even more of an intrusion). Note also that some courts have refused to order non-parent visitation where the parent objected to any court-ordered visitation but where the parent expressed a willingness to permit some sort of visitation if it met the parent's terms (which were not, however, spelled out): see *Punsly v. Ho*, 105 Cal. Rptr.2d 139 (Cal. Ct. App. 2001); *Brice v. Brice*, 754 A.2d 1132 (Md. Ct. Spec. App. 2000).

(ii) If the parent's reasons are based on ill feelings toward the non-parents, as opposed to what may be termed legitimate disagreements about rearing the child, argue that that fact should result in discounting the parent's decision. But see *Kyle O. v. Donald R.*, 102 Cal. Rptr.2d 476, 486–87 (Cal. App. 2000) (disregarding hostility of parent caused by grandparents' pursuit of court-ordered visitation and their refusal to deviate from scheduled visitation even when deviation was in the child's best interests; father said he'd agree to visitation, but wanted it to be "spontaneous"). In this connection, the Court, in *In re Nunn*, 14 P.3d 175 (Wash. Ct. App. 2000), stated:

> Can an otherwise fit parent be found unfit because she chooses to fight a non-parental custody petition, because she openly expresses her dislike of the side of the family that brought the custody petition, because she avoids old family friends who are supporting the other side in the custody litigation, because she doesn't trust the custody evaluators who have been brought into the litigation, and because she doesn't foster a good relationship between her child and all of those people? The answer is no.

4. Do not rely on the simple statement that grandparent contact—or other non-parental contact—can only be good for the children. This reliance on a stereotypical generalization, without any showing of application to the facts at hand, is likely to be dismissed.

5. So far as is possible, make sure that the visitation that is requested cannot be characterized as "disruptive" of the child's schedule. Be aware of the child's schedule and the effects of the requested visitation.

B. Points for the lawyer for the parent

1. The chief point is to emphasize the deference that *Troxel* requires to be given to the decision of a fit parent and to characterize the dispute about visitation as a mere disagreement about the correct way to rear the child and whom the child should be permitted to see and when.

2. The parent may want to consider granting some limited visitation to conform with the facts of *Troxel*. But note that the parent may not have to make even that concession if the parent says that the parent will agree to voluntary visitation but not court-ordered visitation: see cases discussed above. (Sam Goldwyn, the Hollywood producer, once said, "An oral contract isn't worth the paper it's written on." That sentiment could apply here.)

3. Argue that in view of the protection afforded to a parent's rights by *Troxel*, the burden of proof that a non-parent must meet in proving the lack of fitness of the parent or in overcoming the deference to the parent's decision is the "clear and convincing evidence" standard rather than the preponderance standard.

4. If the fitness of the parent is challenged, argue for a protective definition. (For example, in *Guardianship of Yushiko*, 735 N.E.2d 1260 (Mass. App. Ct. 2000), the court said: "The mere fact that the father has on occasion shown some lack of interest or involvement in the child's life clearly does not rise to the level of disinterest, abandonment, or inattentiveness which demonstrates parental unfitness. . . . Nor is there anything in the judge's findings to support a conclusion that the father is incompetent, indifferent, abusive, or incapable of performing parental obligations which would warrant a finding of unfitness."

5. If the non-parent has a strong case for visitation even under *Troxel*, argue that your state should not grant visitation unless the non-parent proves that harm will result to the child from the failure to grant visitation. The harm standard is the most pro-parent standard. Although the harm standard was not mandated by the plurality opinion in *Troxel*, some states have held that that standard was mandated by the *state* constitution. See *Neal v. Lee*, 14 P.3d 547 (Okla. 2000) (state constitution requires that harm or the threat of harm be shown before best interests can be reached in a non-parent visitation case); *Belair v. Drew*, 776 So.2d 1105 (Fla. Dist. Ct. App. 2001).

II. Sole custody [i.e., non-visitation] cases

Where a parent and a non-parent are each seeking sole custody, a few courts have applied a best-interest-of-the-child test, but most apply either a fit-parent-always-wins test or some sort of test that gives the parent an edge over a non-parent (e.g., a presumption in favor of the fit parent or a requirement that the non-parent show special circumstances which justify the application of a best-interest-of-the-child test).

A parent can try to use *Troxel* in these cases to justify (i) a requirement that whatever the test applied, the non-parent must meet a burden of proof higher than a mere preponderance of the evidence—e.g., by clear and convincing evidence—and (ii) a requirement that a court must find actual or potential harm to a child before a non-parent can be given custody (as opposed, for example, to a test that merely gives a parent the benefit of a presumption). The parent would argue that although *Troxel* concerned only visitation, the plurality opinion was premised on the recognition and protection of the interest of a fit parent and therefore that basic principle must pervade all custody disputes with a non-parent. See, applying *Troxel* in a custody case in a way that strengthens the hand of the parent, *Clark v. Wade*, 2001 WL 135672 (Ga.); *Brewer v. Brewer*, 533 S.E.2d 541 (N.C. Ct. App. 2000).

A non-parent can argue that *Troxel* is inapplicable to a sole custody case, both because the subject matter was visitation and because the opinion of the plurality in *Troxel* emphasized the need for protecting the decision-making powers of the custodial parent concerning child rearing—i.e., whom the child should be permitted to see and for how long—whereas custody does not involve decision making of the type involved in *Troxel*.

48

Everything You Wanted to Know about Drug/Alcohol Screening in Five Minutes or Less

David H. Levy

FIVE DIFFERENT WAYS TO DETECT DRUG/ALCOHOL

1. Breathalyzer
   - Used only for alcohol detection.
   - Results are instantaneous.
   - A printed readout will give you the amount of blood alcohol in a person's body.
   - Inexpensive.
2. Saliva Test
   - Used only for alcohol detection.
   - A swab collects saliva on the inside cheek of the person.
   - This acts only as a screening test.
3. Urine Analysis
   - Used only for drug detection.
   - Measures the five most common types of drugs:
     - Marijuana
     - Cocaine
     - Amphetamines
     - PCP
     - Opiates (heroin, morphine, codeine).
   - Sample is first tested for presence of drugs.
   - If there is a finding of any drugs in the urine, a second-level test called a GCMS test (gas chromatography mass spectrometry) will be used to confirm the concentration of drugs in the urine.
   - The drugs that can be detected in the urine are as follows:
     - Marijuana—three weeks to three months.
     - Cocaine—three to four days.

- Amphetamines—fourteen days.
- PCP—fourteen days.
- Opiates—fourteen days.

4. Hair Follicle Test
   - Used only for drug detection.
   - Test measures the last three inches of growth from the root.
   - Hair grows approximately one inch a month. Therefore, it will test for drugs taken in the last ninety days.
   - It tests for the same five drugs listed above.
   - It tests both for the drug itself and the metabolites of the drugs. A metabolite is the residue of the drug after it has been metabolized in the system, thereby confirming that the drug was ingested and not in the hair environmentally.
   - Cost-$500–$600.

5. Blood Test
   - This test is basically out of favor with the testing labs and is not used any longer. It is occasionally used to detect alcohol in DUI-type cases.

HELPFUL HINTS

1. When you are testing for the presence of drugs, make sure you ask for a hair follicle test. It will show the presence of drugs in the system or body longer and more accurately than any of the other tests.
2. Make sure there is a positive identification of the person taking the test.
3. Caveat: Sometimes hair dye or other hair processing treatments affect the results.
4. If you elect to use only a urine test, make sure the lab you use does a GCMS test.

If the test is positive, have the test subject be required to pay for the test.

Sample Urine Analysis Report

CLIENT INFORMATION

T329 00
TOP TECH LABS (TC)
816 SEERS DR
SCHAUMBURG, IL 60173

8901 W. Lincoln Ave.
West Allis, WI 53227-0901
Milwaukee   414-328-7900
National   800-877-7016

PRINTED: 03/23/2001 13:56	ACCESSION #
REQ. #	PATIENT ID #
DATE OF BIRTH	COMPANY NAME
AGE/SEX	COLLECTION SITE DAVID LEVY
SS #	SPECIMEN TYPE OTH

PATIENT NAME   LAB ID #

REFERRING CLIENT
TOP TECH LABS (TC)

TEST	RESULT	UNITS	REFERENCE RANGE

COLLECTED:03/22/2001 18:05   RECEIVED:03/23/2001 11:00   RESULTS TO MRO
CODES ORDERED: SE4CI   (PerfAt)

```
EIA PANEL 4-CONF
  AMPHETAMINE            NEGATIVE              [NEG]
  COCAINE METABOLITE     NEGATIVE              [NEG]
  OPIATE                 NEGATIVE              [NEG]
  PHENCYCLIDINE          NEGATIVE              [NEG]
  MARIJUANA METABOLITE   NEGATIVE              [NEG]
  CERTIFYING SCIENTIST

                         DANIEL D. BRETL, B.S.
```

MAR 2 3 2001

MRO-NEGATIVE

[signature]

MEDICAL REVIEW OFFICER

DRUG CUTOFF LEVELS (NG/ML)	EIA SCREEN	GC/MS
AMPHETAMINES	1000	500
CANNABINOIDS	50	15
COCAINE METABOLITE	300	150
OPIATES	2000	2000
PHENCYCLIDINE	25	25
BARBITURATES/BENZODIAZEPINES	200	POS/NEG
METHAQUALONE/METHADONE/DARVON	300	POS/NEG

TO THE EMPLOYER: This information CANNOT be re-
released without the specific consent of the
employee, except for reasons of litigation in a
court of law. General authorizations DO NOT qualify.
As in any screening procedure, false positives may
occur. Unconfirmed positive results do NOT meet
forensic requirements of the CAP Laboratory
Accreditation Program. Prescription drugs,
over-the-counter medications and certain foods can
be detected. WE SUGGEST THE USE OF A MEDICAL REVIEW
OFFICER TO INTERPRET THESE RESULTS.

SPECIMEN TESTED UNDER CHAIN OF CUSTODY PROTOCOLS.
Dilute Specimen

[*Indicates Critical Result] = [@, H, L, Indicates Abnormal Result]
FINAL REPORT - ALL TESTS COMPLETE
COC,PT   03/23/2001 13:56   * END OF REPORT

Sample Hair Follicle Test Report

UNITED STATES DRUG TESTING LABORATORIES
1700 S. MOUNT PROSPECT ROAD
DES PLAINES, ILLINOIS 60018
(800) 235-2367
FAX (847) 375-0775

FINAL TOXICOLOGY REPORT

03/27/1 (Tue)   *****CONFIDENTIAL*****   11:35am

Client Name   : TOP TECH LABS, INC
Contact   : ATTN: KEN STOLLER/PRESIDENT
Address   : 810 SEERS DRIVE
                 SCHAUMBURG, IL 60173
                 FAX: 847-330-0755
Date Received : 3/23/01
Date Collected : 3/22/01

SPECIMEN IDENTIFICATION

    Name
    Client Number   USDTL Lab Number:
    Analysis Requested

RESULTS:

    Cocaine   DETECTED
    Benzoylecgonine (Cocaine Metabolite)   DETECTED
    Cocaethylene (Cocaine Metabolite)   DETECTED

    The presence of Cocaine, Benzoylecgonine and Cocaethylene
    was confirmed by Gas Chromatography/Mass Spectrometry,
    which has a detection cutoff of 0.1 ng/milligram for
    Cocaine, Benzoylecgonine and Cocaethylene.

    The result was 1.08 ng/mg of Cocaine.
                   0.38 ng/mg of Benzoylecgonine.
                   1.08 ng/mg of Cocaethylene.

    Unless reported as detected, the following drugs or
    classes were screened for by immunoassay and were not
    detected at the cutoff concentrations:**

    Amphetamines   0.5 ng/milligram
    Cannabinoids   0.005 ng/milligram
    Cocaine Metabolite   0.5 ng/milligram
    (Benzoylecgonine)
    Opiates   0.2 ng/milligram
    Phencyclidine (PCP)   0.3 ng/milligram

Douglas E. Lewis
Technical Director

*Note: The amount of hair processed for analysis determines the
final sensitivity of the assays. The cutoffs described above are
based on analyzing 50 milligrams of hair. Smaller samples will
have proportionally higher cutoffs.

49

Don't Overlook the Indian Child Welfare Act

Ann M. Haralambie

THE FEDERAL INDIAN CHILD WELFARE ACT of 1978 (ICWA), 25 U.S.C. § 1901 *et seq.*, applies to a variety of family law actions, excluding custody disputes between parents incident to a divorce. The Act does apply to foster care, institutional or guardianship placements, termination of parental rights, adoption, and pre-adoptive placements involving "Indian children," except where the parent has the right to resume custody of the child upon demand. Even a step-parent adoption would be covered. Because the federal law preempts state law and involves the sovereignty of Indian tribes and Native Alaskan villages, it is important for family lawyers to be aware of its provisions—particularly, which persons and proceedings are covered.

ICWA defines an Indian child as "any unmarried person who is under age eighteen and is either (a) a member of an Indian tribe or (b) is eligible for membership in an Indian tribe and is the biological child of a member of an Indian tribe." The Indian tribe must be federally recognized in order for ICWA to apply. Where the child is not a tribal member, and neither biological parent is a tribal member, ICWA does not apply, even though the child may have Indian heritage and may be eligible for tribal membership.

It is the Indian tribe itself that is the sole arbiter of tribal membership. 44 Fed. Reg. 67584 (November 26, 1979). Whether a child is an "Indian child" is determined as of the date of the hearing, even if the proceeding was commenced prior to a determination of membership. Eligibility requirements vary greatly among tribes, with some requiring that members have at least 50 percent blood lineage of the tribe, others requiring only that a member be a lineal descendant of a member enrolled as of a particular date. It is possible, for example, for a child's ethnic heritage to be 1/32 Indian and 31/32 another ethnicity but for that child to be covered by ICWA. Therefore, an otherwise thorough family lawyer may easily overlook the applicability of

ICWA unless an inquiry is made in all non-divorce custody or adoption-related cases as to whether the child or either parent is a member of any Indian tribe or Native Alaskan village.

If ICWA applies to a case, its protections are extended to both Indian and non-Indian parents, and the tribe is also given procedural and substantive rights in the case. If the child resides or is domiciled on an Indian reservation, the tribal court will have exclusive jurisdiction over the case, with limited exceptions. Even if the child is not domiciled or residing on a reservation, the state court *must* transfer jurisdiction to the tribal court at the request of a parent, Indian custodian, or the tribe, absent good cause to the contrary, unless either parent objects or the tribal court declines the jurisdiction. "Good cause" has been narrowly construed.

If the case remains in state court, the tribe still has the right to notice and to intervene, and the state court must apply the substantive and procedural law of ICWA. For example, an indigent parent or Indian custodian may have the right to appointed counsel, even where state law does not provide for such a right. Consent to voluntary foster care or consent to adoption must be executed before a judge and must meet specific ICWA requirements. Foster care consent is revocable at any time, and the child must be returned upon request. Consent to adoption is revocable at any time until a final order of termination of parental rights or adoption is entered. Involuntary termination of parental rights must be proven beyond a reasonable doubt and must include certain findings made with the input of particular expert testimony.

Foster care and preadoptive placements must comply with ICWA placement preferences. Absent good cause to the contrary, which is narrowly construed, the court must apply preferences in placement in the following order:

Foster Care:
1. A member of the Indian's child's extended family;
2. A foster home licensed, approved, or specified by the Indian child's tribe;
3. An Indian foster home licensed or approved by an authorized non-Indian licensing authority; or
4. An institution for children approved by an Indian tribe or operated by an Indian organization that has a program suitable to meet the Indian child's needs.

Adoption:
1. A member of the child's extended family;
2. Other members of the Indian child's tribe; or
3. Other Indian families.

These placement preferences may override even the Indian parent's individual preferences, reflecting the separate interest of the child's tribe.

A "hot tip" cannot begin to cover the complexities of ICWA. [For a more complete discussion see ANN M. HARALAMBIE, 2 HANDLING CHILD

CUSTODY, ABUSE, AND ADOPTION CASES ch. 15 (2d ed., Shepard's/McGraw-Hill 1993, 1994 Supp.). The full text of the Act and the names, addresses, and telephone numbers of recognized Indian tribes and Native Alaskan villages are included in appendices.] However, it is important to be aware of the Act.

Whenever a case involves a covered proceeding, the lawyer would be well advised to ask the client whether the child or either parent is enrolled in any Indian tribe or Native Alaskan village.

IV

Malpractice Avoidance

IT USED TO BE THE GOOD OLD DAYS when lawyers were suing doctors for malpractice. Times have changed: Lawyers now are suing other lawyers. The words "legal malpractice" are enough to send chills down the spine of the most seasoned family law practitioner.

Interestingly enough, malpractice litigation is disproportionately directed at matrimonial lawyers. In fact, some insurance companies will not insure a law firm that specializes in family law.

Is it because family lawyers commit more malpractice than other lawyers? I think not. More likely, several factors are at play in a synergistic fashion. Two important ones are the degree of unresolved anger harbored by many divorce clients and the desire of clients and lawyers to cut costs because of the difficulty of paying legal fees from a dwindling estate.

Following are some ideas from the experts on ways to avoid seeing a case with your name following the word "versus."

50   The divorce is over. The client thanks you and (hopefully) pays you. The last thing the client wants is to be sued by the ex-spouse for whatever property that ex-spouse did not get in the divorce. **Bob Spector** explains how failure to negotiate a waiver clause for spousal torts can result in malpractice, and he provides examples of clauses that will bar a subsequent interspousal tort suit.

51   Before agreeing to accept property on behalf of a client, the lawyer should be aware of any potential environmental liabilities that may substantially affect the value of the property. **Louise Raggio** highlights the federal statutes of which the family lawyer needs to be aware.

52 Military divorces have unique issues that require special expertise. There are wonderful benefits available for the nonmilitary spouse, for example, but many a malpractice lawsuit has sought to secure the benefits from the divorce lawyer's insurance carrier because the lawyer did not recognize the issue. **Marshal Willick** describes five potential malpractice traps in military cases and tells how to avoid them.

53 After the divorce is (finally!) granted, there tends to be a catharsis where tying up the loose ends can be put on the back burner. As **Joy Feinberg** points out, this can be very dangerous. Under the U.S. Supreme Court case of *Egelhoff*, failure to have your client change beneficiaries on certain retirement plans after the divorce can be an invitation to a malpractice suit.

50

Malpractice Avoidance in Marital Tort Cases: The Problem of Waiver Clauses

Robert G. Spector

FAMILY LAW IS A RAPIDLY CHANGING FIELD. One of the most dramatic developments is the relationship between tort and domestic actions. The breakup of a marriage leads inexorably to acrimony between the spouses. Today this anger and frustration often lead to the filing of a tort suit. Prior to 1980 it was almost unheard of for a divorce case to involve a separate tort. During the past decade there has been an explosion of cases involving torts and the marital relationship. It is a phenomenon that all domestic practitioners must be prepared to face on a regular basis.

One of the greatest areas of uncertainty in marital tort practice concerns the ability to bring a tort action after the divorce is over. Oklahoma never has addressed this issue, although the court did indicate that the two claims can be joined. *Roesler v. Roesler,* 641 P.2d 550 (Okla. 1982). The court suggested that while divorce and tort can be joined, they should be separately docketed and tried to prevent prejudice. Cf. *Tice v. Tice,* 672 P.2d 1168 (Okla. 1983) (wife's claim of fraudulent inducement into marriage joined with divorce petition but severed for trial).

Even though joinder of claims is not compulsory, claim preclusion can arise when the basic aspects of the tort suit are considered and decided in the divorce litigation. Several cases illustrate how this may occur. In *Jackson v. Hall,* 460 So.2d 1290 (Ala. 1984), the parties' divorce settlement agreement contained the following clause:

> In full settlement of all claims between the parties, the Wife does hereby accept the sum of $2300.

> This is a full, final, and complete settlement of all property matters and other matters between the parties.

One year after the divorce, the wife sued the husband for assault and battery. The court said that whether the wife may bring the tort action depended on how the parties' settlement agreement was construed. The court held that the language of the agreement demonstrated an intent to settle all claims between the parties. "All claims means just that." The wife was therefore precluded by contract from bringing the tort claim, even though it appeared that the clause in the agreement was "boilerplate."

In *Coleman v. Coleman,* 566 So.2d 482 (Ala. 1990), the following clause was invoked in the later tort case:

> SIXTEENTH: MUTUAL RELEASE: Each party, in consideration of this Agreement, expressly releases the other party from any and all claims and demands, other than under the provisions of this Agreement, for the settlement of property rights.

Following the divorce, Ms. Coleman sued Dr. Coleman for the alleged negligent or wanton transmission of a venereal disease, condyloma acuminatum. In an affidavit she stated that she never had raised the issue of transmission of the disease in the divorce action, and that she was not awarded any damages, expenses, or funds for treatment of the disease. The trial court found that Ms. Coleman was barred from bringing the tort claim.

The Alabama Supreme Court affirmed the trial court. It noted that Ms. Coleman was aware in September of 1985 that she was infected with a sexually transmitted disease—before the divorce action was filed by Dr. Coleman on October 17, 1985. In preparation for the trial of her divorce action, she conducted medical discovery relating to whether Dr. Coleman had a venereal disease. Most important, the court said, there also were indications in correspondence between their lawyers that Ms. Coleman attempted to use the fact that she was infected with a venereal disease to increase her settlement award. The court said that to allow Ms. Coleman to use the fact that she may have been infected with a venereal disease by her husband as leverage in her divorce settlement, and then to permit her to bring a subsequent tort action, would seriously undermine the settlement of divorce actions in the future. To do so would "cause confusion and lead to fraud, potential ambush, [and] a play on words within the settlement." The court held that to preserve the tort claim the party should expressly reserve the claim from the settlement and then subsequently sue in tort.

Another clause that should be avoided in a divorce decree was illustrated in *Overberg v. Lusby,* 727 F. Supp. 1091 (E.D.Ky 1990), *aff'd* 921 F.2d 90 (6th Cir. 1990). The decree provided that:

> Each party hereby releases and discharges the other from all obligations of support and from all other claims, rights, and duties arising or growing out of said marital relationship.

The court held that the wife's tort claim against her former husband for the infliction of a sexually transmitted disease must be dismissed.

If the waiver clause is not a general clause but rather one that relates to a specific subject matter, however, the court may refuse to extend it to cover the tort claim. In *Decker v. Rightnour,* 1992 WL 20657 (Ohio App. 9 Dist. 1992) (unpublished, text in *Westlaw*), the waiver language was as follows:

ARTICLE X: DIVISION OF PROPERTY

> It is further agreed between the parties that this Separation Agreement constitutes a complete settlement of all rights to property and alimony which exist between the parties, and that neither party hereto will make any claim whatsoever against the other for any property, real or personal, except as specified herein.

The trial court's decision that the language barred a later claim for assault and battery was reversed.

Claim preclusion also can occur if one party litigates the tort issues in the divorce context. In *Weil v. Lammon,* 503 So.2d 830 (Ala. 1987), the wife sued the husband for fraud, alleging that he promised to take care of her for the rest of her life and that instead he simply married her for his sexual gratification. In the prior divorce suit, the wife's allegations concerning this fraud were the basis of her alimony claim. Although the marriage lasted only one month, the court awarded her $1,000 in alimony. In Alabama, the fault of the parties is clearly relevant to the amount of alimony. The trial court's dismissal of the fraud suit on the basis of claim preclusion was upheld by the Alabama Supreme Court. The court noted that the wife asserted the alleged fraud and misrepresentation as the basis of her claim of alimony. Therefore she could not later bring an action for damages based on the same allegations.

The same thing occurred in *Kemp v. Kemp,* 723 S.W.2d 138 (Tenn. App. 1986). In the divorce action the wife received a sum of money for past and future medical expenses and lost wages because of the husband's battery. The wife, therefore, was precluded from bringing a subsequent tort claim.

There may be occasions when it is desirable to litigate the tort aspects as part of the alimony case. In *D.C. v. J.C.,* 802 S.W.2d 535 (Mo. App. 1991), the wife had contracted the papilloma virus also known as genital warts. The court awarded periodic alimony as well as alimony in gross. The periodic alimony was linked to the wife's future medical expenses in treating the disease. The husband claimed there was insufficient evidence to indicate that he caused the venereal disease. The court responded that it did not matter. It was a "condition she contracted during marriage." If there is insufficient evidence to establish proximate cause by a preponderance of evidence in a tort suit, it still may be possible to award a sum of money for alimony. See also *McAdoo v. McAdoo,* 492 N.W.2d 66 (N.D. 1992) (trial court instructed to retain jurisdiction for purposes of awarding additional alimony should the wife subsequently be determined to have contracted genital warts from husband).

Failure to pay close attention to waiver clauses in cases involving tort liability may result in malpractice exposure. See *Aykan v. Goldzweig,* 238 N.J. Sup. 389, 569 A.2d 905 (1989) (lawyer sued for malpractice for failure to advise the client regarding the existence of a tort claim of battery).

51

Another Malpractice Trap Rears Its Ugly Head—Know the Potential Environmental Liabilities before Your Client Takes the Property

Louise B. Raggio

As a strategist in the dissolution of an economic partnership, the lawyer must be familiar with federal, state, and local environmental laws that may affect the true values of property.

Before agreeing to a property division, or trying the case, the divorce lawyer had better know the potential environmental liabilities of the businesses and real property interests. A proper environmental audit may save the lawyer from the unhappy client who is surprised, after the divorce is completed, by a hazardous waste problem. Conversely, the business owner spouse will appreciate the lawyer's wisdom when the environmental audit reveals expensive environmental liabilities that produce a lower valuation of the business.

Perhaps the most important statute is the federal Comprehensive Environmental Response, Compensation, and Liability Act, commonly called CERCLA or "Superfund." The Act, found at 42 U.S.C. § 9601 *et seq.*, was passed in 1980 and was substantially amended in 1986 (Superfund Amendments and Reauthorization Act). The Act expresses a national commitment to clean up hazardous waste sites. Federal monies are available for cleanup, and $8.5 billion has been appropriated, but public funds are to be used only when responsible private persons cannot be found to pay for the work.

CERCLA encourages the private sector to undertake cleanups by making past and present "owners" and "operators" of hazardous waste sites jointly and severally liable for cleanup costs without regard to fault. In theory, the owner of a small dry-cleaning business who disposed of one container of waste chemicals at a dump can be held responsible for cleaning up the entire site when the Environmental Protection Agency (EPA) later designates the dump as a Superfund site. This can happen even when the owner complied with all then-applicable laws when disposing of the chemicals, and even though his or her single chemical waste drum was one of thousands at the site.

Other federal statutes careful lawyers may want to read are:

- Federal Clean Air Act, 42 U.S.C.A. § 7401 *et seq.* (West 1983 & Supp. 1989), as amended.
- Federal Insecticide, Fungicide, and Rodenticide Act (FIFRA), 7 U.S.C.A. § 136 *et seq.* (West 1980 & Supp. 1989), as amended.
- Federal Water Pollution Control Act, 33 U.S.C.A. § 1251 *et seq.* (West 1986 & Supp. 1989), as amended.
- Hazardous and Solid Waste Amendments of 1984 (HSWA), Pub. L. No. 98-616 (Nov. 9, 1984).
- Noise Control Act, 42 U.S.C.A. § 4901 *et seq.* (West 1985 & Supp. 1989), as amended.
- Occupational Safety and Health Act (OSHA), 29 U.S.C.A. § 651 *et seq.* (West 1985 & Supp. 1989), as amended.
- Resource Conservation and Recovery Act (RCRA), 42 U.S.C.A. § 6901 *et seq.* (West 1983 & Supp. 1989), as amended.
- Safe Drinking Water Act, 42 U.S.C.A. § 300f *et seq.* (West 1982 & Supp. 1989), as amended.
- Toxic Substances Control Act (TSCA), 15 U.S.C.A. § 2601 *et seq.* (West 1982 & Supp. 1989), as amended.

Of course, in addition to these federal statutes, the lawyer also must consult state statutes and local ordinances.

The divorce lawyer should retain appraisers, or environmental auditors, who are sensitive to the costs of solving asbestos, hazardous waste, and other environmental problems, and who are technically equipped to find those problems and put price tags on them.

Market values can be affected. For instance, an apartment building may be worth much less than a capitalization of its net income would suggest once the costs are included of removing or encapsulating asbestos insulation, or removing a leaking underground storage tank and oil spill. Unfortunately, some real estate and business appraisers are not attuned to the high costs of solving environmental problems and generically state only that an appraised value is subject to unspecified reductions because of asbestos, underground storage tanks, hazardous materials, or other environmental problems.

An environmental audit by a competent engineer or other environmental professional is the best way to identify and quantify risks on a business or a real estate holding the client may take in a property distribution, but it should be supplemented by comprehensive interrogatories and deposition questions posed to the spouse who manages the business or real estate. A specimen interrogatory follows.

On the other side, the lawyer representing the property-managing spouse, who expects to take sole ownership of the property after the divorce, should use the potential liabilities found in a thorough environmental audit to reduce the property's distribution value.

Perhaps the best malpractice advice in this "tip" is for the lawyer either to be an expert environmentalist, or, if not, to have an exclusionary clause in transactions where clients receive property that may carry environmental liability. The lawyer would have the client acknowledge that the lawyer's advice and opinion excepts: (1) any determination of whether any hazardous or toxic materials are legally or illegally present; or contained in, under, or on the property or its waters; or if toxic or hazardous materials have contaminated the same; and (2) or if there is any violation of or noncompliance with environmental laws.

SPECIMEN INTERROGATORY

State for each item of real property and for each business that you own or possess a greater than 10 percent beneficial interest and that may be subject to division in the pending divorce action:

All information you have concerning any conditions of or on, or operations of, the real property or business that have been the subject of, or that are reasonably expected to generate, any liabilities under any federal, state, or local environmental law or regulation. "Liabilities" include, but are not limited to, any civil or criminal liabilities for violations of environmental laws and regulations. "Environmental laws and regulations" include, but are not limited to, the federal Comprehensive Environmental Response, Compensation, and Liability Act (CERCLA), the federal Resource Conservation and Recovery Act (RCRA), the state . . . , the local . . . , and the regulations promulgated thereunder.

52

Five Malpractice Traps to Avoid in Military Cases

Marshal S. Willick

REMEMBER THAT JURISDICTION IS A STRANGE, IF NOT WONDERFUL, THING IN A MILITARY CASE

To divide a military retirement as property, "federal jurisdiction" is necessary in addition to subject matter and personal jurisdiction. Subsection c(4) of the Uniformed Services Former Spouses Protection Act (USFSPA), 10 U.S.C. § 1408, divests state courts of power to divide retired pay as property unless the jurisdictional provisions of the Act are satisfied. In other words, for an order to be enforceable, the court issuing it must have exercised personal jurisdiction over the member by reason of: (1) residence in the territorial jurisdiction of the court (other than by military assignment); (2) domicile in the territorial jurisdiction of the court; or (3) consent to the jurisdiction of the court. These limitations override state long-arm rules and must be satisfied *in addition* to any state law jurisdictional requirements. *See, e.g., Kovacich v. Kovacich,* 705 S.W.2d 281 (Tex. Ct. App. 1986); *Tarvin v. Tarvin,* 232 Cal. Rptr. 13 (Cal. Ct. App. 1986).

Most courts have held that such consent may be expressed or implied (such as from a "general appearance" in the case under state law), but the circumstances in which consent will be found vary somewhat, and the case law is not consistent.

NEVER DEFAULT AN OUT-OF-STATE MILITARY DEFENDANT WHERE A PENSION IS AT ISSUE

It is extremely dangerous for a former spouse to take default against a member if the former spouse hopes to divide military retired pay as property. The availability of a default divorce judgment should be treated by the former spouse's lawyer as a malpractice trap. The short version, at least for the spouse's lawyer, is "don't." No matter which party files for divorce, however, default divorces have caused many inequitable results.

If the former spouse files, the member's opposition to any portion of the relief sought may well be construed by the state court as a "general appearance," giving the court authority to dispose of the retirement benefits because of the member's consent to jurisdiction. The member may have to choose between not opposing an adverse ruling on custody, alimony, or other property issues on the one hand, or allowing the court to dispose of the military retirement benefits on the other.

When the *member* files for divorce and a default is possible against the former spouse, the spouse is in significant danger whether or not the military retirement was listed as an asset for division. If the asset was listed, the spouse's failure to make an appearance in the action probably will preclude later challenge to the divorce court's disposition of the asset. If the military retirement was not noted as an asset for division by the divorce court, the results might be the same, because silence in a decree effectively divests the former spouse of any interest in the military retirement benefits and there may not be a right to partition of the omitted asset (depending on what states are involved).

BEWARE OF THE "TEN-YEAR RULE"

A court order that divides military retired pay as property may be enforced only by direct payment to the former spouse if the parties were married for at least ten years during which the member performed at least ten years of creditable military service. 10 U.S.C. § 1408(d)(2); 32 C.F.R. § 63.6(a)(1)–(2). This often is called the "20/10/10" rule, for "years of service needed to reach retirement/years of marriage of the parties/years of overlap between service and marriage."

The restriction is on direct payment *only* and not on the substantive right of the former spouse under state law to a portion of the retired pay as property. If the marriage lasted less than ten years during active duty, the retired pay still could be treated as marital property by the court in balancing the property awards to each spouse, but no award to the former spouse of a portion of that retired pay could be enforced by obtaining direct payment from the military pay center. The 20/10/10 rule *is not* a limitation on the subject matter jurisdiction of the state courts.

Its practical effect is often the same as a legal bar, however. A former spouse in possession of an order that does not satisfy the rule must rely on whatever enforcement mechanisms are available under state law. The only workaround for this trap is to provide for alimony, either entirely as a replacement for a property interest in the retirement, or as a reserved possibility if the retirement cannot be divided as provided in the decree or the member fails to make promised payments.

ANTICIPATE CHANGES IN STATUS

Especially for the former spouse's lawyer, reservations of jurisdiction are very useful. For example, practitioners must know that even many years after the divorce, a member may request a disability rating, obtain it, be awarded (nondivisible) disability retired pay, and waive (divisible) retired pay equal to the sum of disability pay, thus effectively reducing or eliminating the spousal share. A reservation of jurisdiction to enter an alimony award if the retired pay is ever reduced can prevent that result as to the former spouse, as can an outright indemnification for any reduction. *See In re Strassner,* 895 S.W.2d 614 (No. 65448, Mo. Ct. App., Mar. 14, 1995), 21 FLR 1246 (BNA Apr. 4, 1995); *Owen v. Owen,* 419 S.E.2d 267 (Va. Ct. App. 1992).

DO NOT FORGET ABOUT THE SURVIVOR'S BENEFITS

The Survivor's Benefit Plan (SBP) provides monthly payments of about half (or less) of the retired pay amount to a single named survivor. It can be allocated to the former spouse by the divorce court. There is a premium for coverage, and there is a way to arrange for it to be paid by the member, the spouse, or divided between them. The spouse can be named SBP beneficiary even where he or she has little or no time-rule percentage of the retired pay itself. *See Matthews v. Matthews,* 647 A.2d 812 (Md. Ct. App. No. 127, Sept. 19, 1994), 20 FLR 1552 (BNA Oct. 4, 1994).

53

Egelhoff—*The Supreme Court Speaks*

Joy M. Feinberg

ON MARCH 21, 2001, the United States Supreme Court addressed a nagging issue which all too frequently faced recently divorced couples:

If you die after divorce, without changing your beneficiary designation forms on ERISA governed retirement plans, who will get your benefits?

And, of even greater importance:

What new burdens does *Egelhoff* place on matrimonial practitioners in order to avoid claims of malpractice?

THE FACTS OF *EGELHOFF*

David and Donna Egelhoff were divorced in April 1994. This was a second divorce for David, who had children from a prior marriage. There were no children born to David and Donna. David was a Boeing executive and the parties resided in the state of Washington. Donna had been his designated beneficiary on his company-provided life insurance and retirement benefits. In July 1994, David died, never having changed his beneficiary designations on his life insurance or retirement benefits. In the divorce settlement, David had received 100 percent of his pension benefits. Donna had received other assets. It is presumed that there was some waiver of rights language in the divorce judgment.

Naturally, David's children from his first marriage assumed that they would be the beneficiaries of his life insurance and retirement benefits that were not assigned to Donna in the divorce proceedings between Donna and their father. They filed their claim for benefits after David's death. After all, they had a state statute supporting this claim and a reasonable expectation of receipt. Much to their surprise, Donna was still named as beneficiary, and she too filed a claim for proceeds from the life insurance policy as well as the retirement benefits.

The Washington Supreme Court ruled that David's children—not his pre-divorce designated beneficiary and former spouse, Donna, were entitled to the benefits, relying on the state statute and providing that this state law was not preempted by federal law, ERISA, for these reasons:

1. Family and probate matters were traditional areas of state regulation.
2. The Washington statute allowed employers to "opt out" of the statute's application.
3. The concept of federal preemption was not applicable here. After all, if this state statute was not acceptable, then "slayer statutes" (which provide that murdering heirs are not entitled to receive property as a result of their having killed their benefactor) would also be preempted. Such a result would be abhorrent to common sensibilities.

The United States Supreme Court reversed and rejected each of the arguments put forth by the Washington Supreme Court. The U.S. Supreme Court was very clear in its ruling that this state statute would be preempted by ERISA, for it stated that determining beneficiary status was a **CORE ERISA CONCERN**. The Supreme Court noted that this state statute would interfere with the uniform national administration of plans. It went on to state that the presumption against preemption in the arena of family law was overcome when family law "conflicts with ERISA or is related to ERISA plans." The issue of the remaining validity of "slayer" statutes was not decided by *Egelhoff*; however, the ruling appears to suggest that such statutes would not be preempted by ERISA because these statutes have a history predating ERISA and are relatively uniform throughout the country, which would allow for consistent plan administration nationally.

Thus, David's former spouse, Donna—not David's children—received David's life insurance proceeds and retirement benefits.

After *Egelhoff,* will state law ever be able to protect the family law practitioner against claims for failure to warn the participant to change his/her beneficiary designation? This is doubtful.

However, most divorce decrees or judgments provide for the division of assets, including retirement benefits. Most instruments provide standardized language "waiving" all other rights in or to the former spouses' property and any right to inheritance. Will these clauses protect family law practitioners against claims for failure to warn the participant to change his/her beneficiary designation? Perhaps. There is an Eighth Circuit case that alludes to such a result, if the language in the settlement agreement is "sufficiently specific to convey the intent of the parties to divest one or the other, or both, of a beneficiary interest." *Hill v. AT&T Corp.*, 125 F.3d 646 (8th Cir. 1997). Again, the validity of a pre-*Egelhoff* case is unclear.

It is this author's belief that the most fertile area of malpractice litigation in the family law arena lies in the retirement plan portion of each case. Failure to enter a Qualified Domestic Relations Order can be devastating, especially if the participant dies prior to the entry of a Domestic Relations Order at time of Judgment entry. Even entry of a "nunc pro tunc" order will not revive the benefits provided pursuant to the Judgment for Dissolution of Marriage, unless the Judgment has all of the elements of a Domestic Relations Order and, thus, can be Qualified by the plan when the participant dies. *Guzman v. Commonwealth Edison,* 2000 W.L. 1898846 (N.D. Ill., December 28, 2000); *Samaroo v. Samaroo,* 193 F.3d 185 (3d Cir. 1999).

NEW OBLIGATION FOR FAMILY LAW PRACTITIONERS PER *EGELHOFF*

It is this author's suggestion that family law practitioners may now have a new obligation—we had better tell our clients to change their beneficiary designation forms upon Judgment entry, lest we subject ourselves to potential claims of malpractice.

Need we go so far as obtaining the change of beneficiary forms ourselves and presenting them to our clients to sign in our presence and return to the plan administrator? I think not. But we had better have written instructions in our files advising our participant clients to act on this matter as soon as the divorce is final. Without this, will we be believed that we "told" our client to act deliberately to change his/her beneficiary designations? There are some questions we need not face, this being one. I have attached a suggested form that you should copy and include in your usual procedure for every divorce case you handle.

One further note: Due to the *Egelhoff* case, ERISA counsel are suggesting to their employer clients that they amend their plan documents and include a provision that would automatically revoke pre-divorce spousal beneficiary designations. Keep a watchful eye open for such changes so that in the unusual case where you negotiate to retain the about-to-be-former spouse as the beneficiary of such benefits, there is an affirmative action taken after judgment entry to retain or reaffirm that spouse as beneficiary designate.

SUGGESTED LANGUAGE TO PROVIDE TO CLIENTS

As an employee of _____ Corporation, you are entitled to various benefits including:

Life Insurance with _____ Insurance Company;

401(k) Plan Benefits with _____
administered by: _____

Defined Benefits Plan, termed, _____
administered by: _____

Possible other benefits that your human resources department can advise you about and supply you with beneficiary change forms

You also have other assets that have beneficiary designations, such as IRAs, annuity contracts, and the like.

We are now getting close to finalizing your divorce. Contact these administrators and/or the Human Resources Department of your company to obtain the forms necessary to CHANGE THE BENEFICIARY DESIGNATION on EACH of these benefits. Have the designation changes completed and delivered to the appropriate locations the DAY BEFORE your divorce is to be finalized and advise the plan administrators that your divorce will be final on the next day. Then, provide a certified copy of your Judgment to each of these Plan Administrators or appropriate persons for their files to make your beneficiary change designation(s) become effective.

NOTE: FAILURE TO CHANGE YOUR BENEFICIARY DESIGNATION PRIOR TO YOUR DEATH MAY VERY WELL CAUSE YOUR FORMER SPOUSE TO RECEIVE THESE BENEFITS INSTEAD OF THE PERSON(S) YOU INTEND TO BENEFIT.

You should also consider sending this notice as part of your closing procedure.

V

Office Practices

IF THERE IS A BUSINESS ASPECT to the profession, law school ill prepares one for it. Where in law school, after all, is it taught how to make a living? It is almost assumed that if you know how appellate courts decide cases, you will become rich.

Truth is, we cannot make a living without some knowledge of how to run a business, and a law firm is a business. Furthermore, with rapidly developing technology, it is impossible to remain state of the art.

Fortunately, many have been there first. Following are some practical, everyday tips to make a living efficiently—consider this part the "Heloise" column.

54   Do you know what a "Bates" stamp is? If you do not use one, let **Lynne Gold-Bikin** explain for you in a mere four paragraphs how to completely organize a file.

55   Unless you have a photographic memory, you must read **Phyllis Bossin**'s idea of maintaining a running record of a case through a ledger file on the computer. For that matter, even if you do have a photographic memory, this is a great idea, because your client may not be so gifted.

56   Wonder how to dazzle clients and others with computer displays? **Steve Harhai** suggests several ways of using computer displays for meetings and presentations that you can do yourself—you won't even need advice from the nearest ten-year-old.

57 The first impression potential clients form of your office is on the telephone. What impression does your office give, and is that the impression you *want* it to give? **Pat Smits** suggests a way of investigating what potential clients think of your office.

58 Well, maybe it is more of a legal practice than an office practice, but this tip is so important, I had to find someplace to put it! **Mike Murphy** routinely asks clients if they ever have given anyone a power of attorney or a right-to-die statement. If they have, he provides forms to revoke these documents.

59 We are in a true personal services business—the client wants a human being available at his or her whim. Because most lawyers cannot be in more than one place at the same time (I know a few who seem to be everywhere), **Steve Harhai** uses a legal assistant as a case manager to keep up with the files and service the clients.

60 We all have more books in our office than we can possibly read. **Gunnar Gitlin** describes the three essential books that need to be within easy reach.

61 **Sharon Corbitt** discusses the importance of maintaining a working conflict system. Failure to do so can cause loss of business and embarrassment. As Sharon points out, making such a system work requires a team effort by the entire law office.

62 No matter how good a lawyer you may be, you need to have clients! Bringing them into the office is the subject of **Twila Larkin's** hot tip on how to market your practice with a practical touch.

63 No longer do clients ask, "Do you have e-mail?" Rather, they ask, "What is your e-mail address?" With the proliferation of e-mail and cell phones, considerations of privacy and confidentiality are important. These issues are discussed in a hot tip by **Kathleen Robertson.**

54

Organizing the Deluge of Paper

Lynne Z. Gold-Bikin

ONE OF THE MOST DIFFICULT PROBLEMS in a domestic relations practice is being buried in paper. The need to collect documents, financial statements, tax returns, and appraisals, for example, creates the burden on counsel to organize the material so that it can be focused when it is needed for negotiations or trial. The logical way to handle this material is to organize it as it comes in.

Purchase a "Bates" stamp. The Bates stamp is a sequential numbering device that allows the file to reflect the number of documents collected and to locate them when needed.

Each file should contain categories for filing. These categories should include tax returns, appraisals, expert reports, pension documents, pleadings, depositions, and insurance policies, to name a few. As each document is received, it is Bates-stamped and filed under the appropriate category. As documents are shared with the other side, the cover letter includes the Bates-stamp number as well as the title of the document so that a checklist is easily kept of documents provided.

Before trial, a list of documents as numbered and categorized is printed so both client and counsel may review it. This list (a sample follows) helps counsel to produce what is needed during negotiations and trial.

Bates List

NAME:_____

    LAST NUMBER USED: _____

TRIAL NOTEBOOK

INCOME SECTION
Income and Expense Statements
Tax Returns
Pay Stubs
Financial Statements

ASSET SECTION
Bank Statements
Securities
Pensions
Real Property
Insurance Policies
Personal/Household Property

ASSET SECTION
Trusts

EXPERT REPORTS
Valuations
Appraisals (Real Estate)
Appraisals (Personal Property)
Accountant Reports

LIABILITY SECTION
Credit-Card Statements
Mortgages
Other Debts
Medical

CUSTODY
Evaluations
Evidence

CUSTODY
Pictures
Transcripts

SUPPORT

COURT DOCUMENTS
Preconference/Inventory
Interrogatories
Transcripts

RESEARCH
Memoranda
Caselaw
Statutes

HISTORY SECTION
Lawyer Notes
Court History

MISCELLANEOUS SECTION
Estate Information
Counsel Fees

MEMOS

55

Maintaining an Accurate "Running Record" of Your Case

Phyllis G. Bossin

MOST OF US ARE FAMILIAR with the concept of dictating memos to the file whenever something of particular significance happens in a case. These memos are printed and placed somewhere in the file, either with correspondence or with a separate file marked *memos*. I have refined this concept. I maintain a complete running record of the case on the computer in a subdirectory entitled "ledgers." Each client has a ledger in this directory that is begun when the file is opened.

The opening entry provides a summary of the facts of the case in some detail and then states what immediate steps are to be taken and by whom. Each time anything of significance happens in the case, an entry is made in the ledger. This includes documentation of telephone conferences with either the client or opposing counsel and the substance of the conversation and what additional action should be taken. Entries also are made after each court appearance. A summary is made of any court orders rendered, new hearing dates, proceedings, and what needs to be performed next. Because the office is on a computer network, the ledger can be accessed by lawyers, paralegals, secretaries, etc. Whoever makes an entry puts his or her initials on that entry and dates it.

The ledger details very specifically what advice was given to a client over the telephone and his or her response and what specific discussions took place between counsel. The ledger is not printed out until the case is being closed. The ledger provides two good results: It allows anyone working on a case immediate access to whatever is going on in the case, without searching through the file for memos, which often do not tell the whole picture. An associate can review the ledger and see what has occurred on the case from the beginning in the event of main counsel's unavailability. The second result is that it has been very helpful in documenting what has occurred between counsel or with the client, when counsel can indicate that a certain conversation took place, and what agreements were reached. These ledgers can be helpful when documenting fee requests or in subsequent disputes with clients over time spent on their case or over what actually occurred.

56

Use a Computer Display for Meetings and Presentations

Stephen J. Harhai

LAWYERS ARE IN THE BUSINESS of communicating. We communicate with judges, other lawyers, experts, and most important, with our clients. Most of this communication traditionally has been oral, supplemented with written material.

Businesses have a similar stake in communication, but have developed much more effective tools. The typical business presentation involves a much greater emphasis on graphics, design, and presentation than most legal presentations. Businesses do not use presentation tools simply for fun (although they often make communication more enjoyable); they use them because these tools are more effective and lead to better communication and greater profits. Communication experts find that comprehension more than doubles when a point is communicated in written and oral form simultaneously.

Why haven't lawyers used presentation tools more effectively? The primary reasons have been cost and inconvenience. Preparing slides or transparencies traditionally has been time-consuming and expensive. Even when the time and money are available, most lawyers simply do not have the design skills to create effective presentation graphics.

The situation has changed radically with the arrival of several new technological developments. Graphical user interfaces (such as Windows) have made computers easier to look at and have simplified graphic design. Software now is available to specifically create presentations. Some of the well-known titles are Lotus Freelance and Microsoft Powerpoint. A powerful newcomer is Astound from Gold Disk Software.

The presentation can be shown on a computer monitor (large ones work better), through a special adapter to a television set, or on an overhead projector with a display panel. Our office purchased a display panel during the past year, primarily for use in public-speaking engagements. We have been surprised to find that we use it almost every day in the office. Here's how.

CASE MANAGEMENT MEETINGS

We project our case management database on the wall during weekly staff meetings. We jointly review summaries of recent activity on each client and add tickler and to-do items. If questions arise about documents, we can display our document tracking software to pinpoint the exact status of every document. This function alone would have been worth the price of the equipment. Everyone is literally on the same page, focused on the same issue. We accomplish more in less time and everyone feels a much greater sense of control over our caseload.

CLIENT MEETINGS

We frequently use project outlines in client meetings involving complex issues. We can open each outline item, add elements based on the discussion, and then close it up and move to the next topic. We estimate that we get twice as much accomplished as with a traditional meeting, and the clients love it. At the end of the meeting we can print out the updated outline for the client to take along. This gives the client a concrete sense of what was accomplished and serves to instantly document the decisions that were made.

NEGOTIATION SESSIONS

We have used financial models in spreadsheets for a number of years to handle complex financial divorces. For example, we have a model that calculates net spendable income after taxes and child support and alimony transfers, and another that monitors the present value of alternative property and alimony settlements. With the computer display, we have started using these models in negotiation sessions. The results are astounding. The focus shifts to the net effect of options and the parties are more able to shift to principled negotiation and away from positional posturing.

PUBLIC PRESENTATIONS

This was our original justification for the purchase, and the display panel has exceeded our expectations. We can do more elaborate presentations more easily. Audiences find the professional-quality graphics great aids to understanding.

57

Your Office Talks—Listen to It!

Patricia Garity Smits

MARKETING A LEGAL PRACTICE is a hot topic in the twenty-first century as lawyers scramble to compete and make a living in a changing economy. Your office can be a positive or negative marketing tool. The real issue is how to make your office attractive for the market (clients) you want to attract.

These are some of the preliminary questions that must be answered:

1. What impression does your office convey?
2. Is it the impression you want people to have?
3. What impression do you want to convey to clients, lawyers, and other people?
4. Is your office helping or hindering the impression you want to convey?
5. How can you determine the impression your office has on prospective clients and other people?
6. How can you make your office convey the image you want to project?

Let's review some descriptive terms that might describe your office:

Inviting	Elegant	Sloppy
Warm	Opulent	Tacky
Organized	Tasteful	Disorganized
Efficient	Light and airy	Unprofessional
Professional	Low-key	Tasteless
Relaxed	Bustling	Loud
Formal	Feminine	Noisy
Friendly	Masculine	Cutesy
Casual	Macho	Dark
Comfortable	Antiseptic	Messy
Quiet	Barren	Smoky
Private	Intimidating	Smelly
Discreet	Chaotic	Dirty

The first step of the process is to determine the impression your office conveys to other people. Then you can decide if you want to make any changes. It is difficult to make the assessment yourself. My tip is a simple suggestion for anyone interested in the impression that his or her office has on prospective clients and other people.

1. Select another person to give you a candid evaluation. You can ask a perceptive friend who can really be honest or a Realtor® who is successful at marketing homes. Realtors® need to be able to see houses through the eyes of prospective buyers and help owners make any changes that will improve the impression of the property.

2. Have the evaluator call the office for an initial consultation. Do not inform your staff that the person is evaluating the office—and do not clean up your office or make other changes before the appointment.

3. Treat the evaluator as any prospective client is treated. Give the evaluator enough time before you see him or her (actually better to repeat the process with both a female and a male evaluator) to form an impression of your reception and waiting area.

4. Meet with the evaluator in the location where you normally conduct initial interviews. Make sure the evaluator spends time in your office if you meet somewhere other than your office. Also give him or her the opportunity to spend time in other offices.

5. Make sure that the evaluator keeps notes of all his or her impressions—from the first telephone call until he or she leaves the office.

6. Discuss the evaluator's impressions. Share the information with your staff and get their input.

7. Use the information to create the impression you want to create.

58

Do Not Leave an Assault Weapon in Your Divorce File

Michael T. Murphy

MOST OF US WOULD NEVER knowingly create complications for ourselves in the divorce case—especially the acrimonious ones. However, how many of us routinely ask our clients these questions in the initial interview:

Have you ever given anyone a power of attorney?

Do you have a right-to-die statement (living will)?

Naturally, most of us would answer this inquiry in the negative—primarily because we view ourselves as divorce lawyers, not estate planners. Failure to make these inquiries, however, and to act appropriately may cause your client to suffer serious disadvantage and may cause you a gigantic headache.

In most states the filing of the divorce does not terminate outstanding powers of attorney between spouses. Likewise, the filing of such proceedings does not disqualify the estranged spouse from exercising health-care decisions for your client in the event of incapacity or terminal illness.

By inquiring if your client has given any power of attorney that may be outstanding, you can take steps to cancel it (see the sample form titled Revocation of Recorded Power of Attorney on page 207). Also, if your client has no power of attorney, you will have the opportunity to prepare a durable power of attorney (either presently effective or of a "springing-power" type) to deal with the client's affairs in the event of incapacity (see the sample form titled Durable Power of Attorney on pages 208–11). Not all jurisdictions allow "springing powers," so check your local statutes. Also, health-care concerns can be addressed by power of attorney in many states. The existence of this document may well be exactly the ammunition you need to defeat a claim of the estranged spouse that he or she should be the person to manage the affairs of your incapacitated client, by virtue of the marital relationship, notwithstanding a pending divorce.

Likewise, the right-to-die document will, in most jurisdictions, effectively cut off the estranged spouse's right to dictate medical treatment, or the lack thereof, for the terminally ill client (see the sample form titled Right to Die on pages 212–14).

The use of these documents protects your client's interests in the event of unforeseen circumstances, and my clients uniformly have expressed their appreciation for my having recognized the potential problem.

Some lawyers charge an additional modest flat-rate fee for the preparation of these documents. Some lawyers treat them as a lagniappe.

REVOCATION OF RECORDED POWER OF ATTORNEY

I, _____(name)_____, of _____(address)_____, _____(city)_____, County, ___(state)___, by written power of attorney executed on ___(date)___, appointed _____, of _____(address)_____, _____(city)_____, County, ___(state)___, my true and lawful attorney-in-fact for the purposes and with the powers set forth, as more fully appears by reference to the power of attorney, or to its record, made and filed on ___(date)___, in Volume _____, ____(name of records)____, Page _____, in the office of __(the County Clerk _or_ the County Recorder _or as the case may be_)__ of _____ County, ___(state)___.

Notice is now given that I, _____(name)_____, by this instrument, revoke such power of attorney, and all power and authority given, or intended to be given, by the power of attorney, to named attorney-in-fact.

In witness whereof, I have signed this instrument on ___(date)___, _____.

_____
(Name)

STATE OF _____   )
) ss.
COUNTY OF _____   )

The foregoing instrument was acknowledged before me by _____(name)_____ this _____ day of _____, _____.

_____
Notary Public

My Commission Expires:

_____

DURABLE POWER OF ATTORNEY

NAME ("principal") does hereby appoint, make, constitute and designate *ATTORNEY* ("attorney") as the principal's attorney, or, in the event said person cannot or will not serve as attorney for any reason, then Principal does hereby appoint, make, constitute and designate *SECOND ATTORNEY* ("attorney") as the principal's attorney for the principal and in the principal's name, to handle any and all transactions pertaining to the principal's affairs, both business and personal, and any other matter in which the principal may have an interest, granting and giving unto the attorney full power and authority to do and perform any and all acts and omissions whatsoever concerning the principal's affairs with the same force, effect, intent and purposes as the principal might or could do if present, with full power of substitution and revocation. The principal does hereby ratify and confirm all that the attorney shall lawfully do or cause to be done by virtue of this power of attorney. The attorney is hereby granted the power and authority to exercise and perform any act, power, duty, right and obligation whatsoever that the principal now has, or hereafter acquires, the legal right, power or capacity to exercise or perform in connection with, arising from, or relating to any person, item, transaction, thing, business property, real or personal, tangible or intangible, or matter whatsoever.

****

[ALTERNATIVE 1]

This power of attorney shall be effective only upon the disability of the principa   Accordingly, the opening phrase in this power, "does hereby appoint, make, constitute and designate," likewis shall be interpreted to be effective only upon the disability of the principal.

The question of whether or not the principal is "disabled" or "incapacitated" within the contemplation of this power of attorney shall be determined in the sole, absolute and determinative discretion of the principal's attending physician. A certification in writing by such physician that the principal is disabled or incapacitated within the contemplation of this power of attorney (i) shall be binding, determinative and conclusive on all parties and entities, and (ii) shall continue to be conclusive proof of disability and incapacity until a decertification in writing by a physician of the termination of the disability or incapacity is presented personally to the attorney, and no attempted revocation of this power by the principal shall be effective until such delivery of the declaration to the attorney.

****

[ALTERNATIVE 2]

This power of attorney shall be affective immediately upon its execution.

****

This power of attorney shall remain in full force and effect until terminated by written revocation by the principal.

Without in any way diminishing the scope and power of authority granted under this general and durable power of attorney, the principal hereby grants by way of explanation and not by way of limitation the following powers to the attorney:

(1)   Collection of Accounts: to collect, recover and receive all moneys, debts, accounts, legacies, inheritances, dividends, coupons, annuities and demands whatsoever as are now or shall hereafter become due and payable or belonging to the principal, and to use such lawful means as may be necessary for the recovery thereof; and

(2)   General Contracts: to contract, buy, sell, mortgage and in any and every way deal with the principal's personal property, chooses in action, and real estate and other property which the principal owns or in which the principal may have an interest; and

208

(3)   Real Estate: to lease, sell, convey, mortgage and hypothecate lands, tenements and hereditaments; and to sign, seal, execute and deliver and acknowledge deeds, leases, assignments, covenants, agreements, mortgages, releases, and instruments (both negotiable and non-negotiable); and

(4)   Powers of Collection and Payment; to forgive, request, demand, sue for, recover, collect, receive, hold all such sums of money, debts, dues, commercial paper, checks, drafts, accounts, deposits, legacies, bequests, devises, notes, interest, stock certificates, bonds, dividends, certificates of deposit, annuities, pensions, profit sharing, retirement, Social Security, insurance and other contractual benefits and proceeds, all documents of title, all property, real or personal, intangible and tangible property and property rights, and demands whatsoever, liquidated or unliquidated, now or hereafter owned by, or due, owing, payable or belonging to me, or in which I have or may hereafter acquire an interest; to have, use and take all lawful means and equitable and legal remedies and proceedings in my name for the collection and recover thereof, and to adjust, sell, compromise, and agree for the same, and to execute and deliver for me, on my behalf, and in my name, all endorsements, releases, receipts, or other sufficient discharges for the same; and

(5)   Banking: to make deposits in any banks or financial institutions, and to draw upon any savings or drawing accounts in said banks or financial institutions in the principal's name; and to make such transfers of deposits from savings to drawing accounts and from drawing to savings accounts as the attorney deems necessary or advisable, endorsing for the principal and on the principal's behalf and name Social Security checks and payments, retirement checks, checks or payments from any branch of the armed services of the United States, and any other government checks which may be made payable to the principal; and to have access and entry to any safe deposit box which the principal may have, together with the right to remove therefrom or place therein any and all items; and

(6)   Borrowing Money: to borrow money upon such terms as the attorney may think advisable, using as security any of the principal's property, real, personal or mixed; and to execute, acknowledge and delivery promissory notes, mortgages, security agreements, financing statements and all other documents which the attorney deems necessary or convenient in connection therewith; and

(7)   Litigation: to commence, prosecute, defend and oppose all actions, suits or legal proceedings to which the principal is now or may hereafter become a party, and to compromise and settle claims, whether by litigation or otherwise, and submit the same to judgment or other conclusion; and

(8)   Insurance Transactions: to demand, collect and sue for all amounts owing either to the principal or to the principal's beneficiaries designated by the principal under any life insurance policy, health and accident insurance policy, medical or hospitalization insurance policy, automobile or motor vehicle insurance policy of any kind, and any and all other insurance policies of any kind whatsoever; and

(9)   Taxing Authorities: to execute any and all additional powers of attorney to any and all taxing authorities, including the Internal Revenue Service, for any purpose whatsoever, including the right to endorse and collect checks in payment of any refund of Internal Revenue taxes, penalties, or interest; to execute waivers (including offers of waivers) or restrictions on assessment or collection of deficiencies in tax and waivers of notice of disallowance of a claim for credit or refund; to execute consents extending the statutory period for assessment or collection of taxes; to execute closing agreements under Section 7121 of the Internal Revenue Code; and to delegate authority or to substitute another representative; and

(10)   Management Powers: to maintain, repair, improve, invest, manage, insure, rent, lease, encumber, and in any manner deal with any real or personal property, tangible or intangible, or any interest therein, that I now own or may hereafter acquire in my name and for my benefit, upon such terms and conditions as my agent shall deem proper; and

(11)   Motor Vehicles: to apply for a Certificate of Title upon, and endorse and transfer title thereto, for any automobile, truck, pickup, van, motorcycle or other motor vehicle, and to represent in such transfer assignment that the title to said motor vehicle is free and clear of all liens and encumbrances except those specifically set forth in such transfer assignment; and

(12)   Business Interests: to conduct or participate in any lawful business of whatever nature for me and in my name; execute partnership agreements and amendments thereto; incorporate, reorganize, merge, consolidate, recapitalize, sell, liquidate or dissolve any business; elect or employ officers, directors and agents; carry out the

provisions of any agreement for the sale of any business interest or the stock therein; and exercise voting rights with respect to stock, either in person or by proxy, and exercise stock options.

[Alternative 1]

****

(13)   Health care: It is my hope that I live and enjoy life for as long as possible, but I do not want to ever receive futile medical treatment, which I define as any treatment that will provide no benefit for me with regard to recovery and which will only serve to prolong my inevitable death or irreversible coma. I demand that my wishes be carried out through the authority given to my attorney-in-fact by this document despite any feelings to the contrary held by any member of my family or by my relatives and friends. In exercise of my attorney-in-fact's authority as granted herein, my attorney-in-fact should try to discuss with me the specifics of any proposed decision regarding my medical care and treatment if I am able to communicate with my attorney-in-fact, even if only by blinking my eyes. My attorney-in-fact is further instructed that if I am unable to give any informed consent to any proposed medical treatment then, in that event, my attorney-in-fact shall give or withhold such consent for me based upon instructions I may have expressed to my attorney-in-fact while competent, whether in this instrument or otherwise. If my attorney-in-fact can not determine the treatment that I would want given, then my attorney-in-fact shall make such choice for me based upon what my attorney-in-fact believes to be in accordance with my desires. Without limiting the above and foregoing I hereby specifically authorize my attorney-in-fact to act in the following manner:

(A)   To give or withhold consent for any medical care or treatment; to revoke or change any consent previously given or implied by law for any medical care or treatment; and to arrange for my placement in or removal from any hospital, convalescent home, hospice or other facility;

(B)   To require that medical treatment which will only serve to prolong the inevitable moment of my death or irreversible coma (including by way of example only, such treatment as cardiopulmonary resuscitation, surgery, dialysis, the use of a respirator, blood transfusions, antibiotics, and any other type of drug without limitation) not be instituted or, if previously instituted, to require that it be discontinued;

(C)   To require that procedures used to provide me with nourishment and hydration (including, for example, parenteral feedings, misting, endotracheal or nasogastric tube use) not be instituted or, if previously instituted, to require that they be discontinued but only if my attending physician shall also have determined that I will not experience pain as a result of the withdrawal of nourishment or hydration; and

(D)   To the extent allowed by the law, I hereby authorize my attorney-in-fact to execute or revoke in my behalf a statement under the **New Mexico Right to Die Act (being §24-7-2, N.M.S.A., 1978)** as it now exists or may be hereinafter amended or any similar statement under the laws of any other jurisdiction, specifically including any releases of liability required by any health care provider.

****

[Alternative 2]

****

(13)   Health care: I state that I desire to live as long as possible and therefore wish to receive any and all medical treatment of every kind and nature that will extend my life and postpone my death. Accordingly, if I am unable to give informed consent to medical treatment, it is my intention to establish with this document the means by which my attorney-in-fact shall be able to direct that my life be extended and my death postponed to the maximum extent possible and to object to any effort on the part of any person whatsoever to discontinue any further medical treatment that my attorney-in-fact believes will extend my life and postpone my death. I direct that my wishes in this regard be carried out through the authority given my attorney-in-fact despite any contrary feelings, beliefs or opinions by or of any member of my family, any relative or friend. Accordingly, my attorney-in-fact is authorized to exercise all the powers granted in this Power of Attorney and all powers that I possess, to give my

210

consent to any medical treatment that will extend my life and postpone my death, including the rendering of maximum medical and surgical care available which is likely to have the effect of prolonging my life and postponing the actual moment of my death without regard to financial cost, and my attorney-in-fact is directed to object to and contest any "no-code" medical order, the withdrawal of any life support system, and the failure or refusal to provide me with medical care, surgery, sustenance or fluids, tests, drugs, care and treatment designed to prolong my life and postpone the actual moment of my death.

****

(14)   If any of the provisions of this Power of Attorney shall contravene, or be invalid, under the laws of the State of New Mexico, such contravention or invalidity shall not invalidate the entire Power of Attorney, but it shall be construed as if not containing the particular provision or provisions held to be invalid.

This Power of Attorney is and shall be a durable power of attorney and shall not be affected by my incapacity but will remain valid until my death, unless I have revoked it. If I intend to revoke this Power of Attorney, I will do so in writing and will deliver a copy of that revocation to the attorney(s)-in-fact named herein.

****

[USE **ONLY** IF ALTERNATIVE 1 CHOSEN FOR: (13) HEALTH CARE]

CERTIFICATION

I HEREBY CERTIFY THAT I HAVE READ AND UNDERSTAND THE PROVISIONS OF THIS POWER OF ATTORNEY AUTHORIZING MY ATTORNEY-IN-FACT TO REFUSE MEDICAL TREATMENT FOR ME AND THAT SUCH PROVISIONS HAVE BEEN EXPLAINED TO ME IN DETAIL TO MY SATISFACTION AND THAT SUCH PROVISIONS ABSOLUTELY AND CORRECTLY STATE MY WISHES AND DEMANDS.

****

[ALTERNATIVE 1]
****

EXECUTED on the ____ day of _____, ____

****

[ALTERNATIVE 2]

EXECUTED on the ____ day of _____, ____, the principal directing that photocopies of this Power shall have the same force and effect as an original.

****

_____
NAME

STATE OF NEW MEXICO   )
) ss.
COUNTY OF DONA ANA   )

The foregoing instrument was acknowledged before me this ____ day of _____, ____.

_____
NOTARY PUBLIC

My commission expires:

_____

211

RIGHT TO DIE

TO: MY FAMILY, MY PHYSICIAN, MY LAWYER, MY CLERGYMAN, ANY MEDICAL FACILITY IN WHOSE CARE I HAPPEN TO BE, AND ANY INDIVIDUAL WHO MAY BECOME RESPONSIBLE FOR MY HEALTH, WELFARE OR AFFAIRS

I, *Name*, of Las Cruces, Dona Ana County, New Mexico, being of sound mind and being over eighteen (18) years of age, do hereby execute this document pursuant to the New Mexico Right To Die Act (Sections 24-7-1 through 10, N.M.S.A., 1978), and hereby revoke all other and former documents made by me in conflict with this document.

I direct that if I am ever certified under the Right to Die Act, or similar law, to be suffering from a terminal illness or being in an irreversible coma, then maintenance medical treatment shall not be utilized for the prolongation of my life. I intend that the term maintenance medical treatment shall include hydration and nourishment and I do hereby authorize its withdrawal.

I am executing this instrument because I have a far greater fear of the indignity of deterioration, dependence upon others, loss of personal independence and hopeless pain and suffering, than I have fear of death itself. With this in mind, I ask that medication be mercifully administered to me as treatment for suffering resulting from any terminal illness, even if it could conceivably hasten the actual moment of my death.

Without intending to give an instruction that may be contrary to the law, I intend that my physician and my family honor this document as the final expression of my right to refuse medical or surgical treatment. I knowingly accept the consequences of this refusal of treatment.

I am aware that many other states have passed Right To Die Act. I am also aware that many states do not have such statutory law. I request that if I am ever suffering from a terminal illness or am in an irreversible coma, then maintenance medical treatment not be utilized for the prolongation of my life, even if I am not domiciled in New Mexico, not a resident of New Mexico, or not actually located in New Mexico. I request that states other than New Mexico interpret this document favorably under their similar laws or procedures so that my intent shall be carried out wherever I may be found to be in need of this document.

If any portion of this document shall be declared illegal, unlawful or unenforceable by any court of competent jurisdiction, the remaining portions of this document shall be considered separate, apart, and severable from those portions or paragraphs declared to be illegal and shall remain valid and binding.

IN WITNESS WHEREOF, I have signed my name and publish and declare this to be my declaration in the presence of the persons witnessing it at my request this ____ day of _____, ____.

_____
Name

ATTESTATION

The foregoing instrument was subscribed by *Name*, the declarant named therein, in the City of Las Cruces, County of Dona Ana, New Mexico, on the ____ day of _____, _____, in the sight and presence of us both. At the time of the declarant subscribing the same, the declarant acknowledged and declared to us that these are the declarant's instructions regarding medical treatment in the event of terminal illness, or irreversible coma, and thereupon we, at declarant's request, within the declarant's sight and presence, and within the sight and presence of each other, have subscribed our names as witnesses thereto.

_____
Witness, Las Cruces, New Mexico

_____
Witness, Las Cruces, New Mexico

STATE OF NEW MEXICO   )
) ss.
COUNTY OF DONA ANA   )

We, *Name*, _____ _____ and _____, the declarant and the witnesses, respectively, whose names are signed to the attached or foregoing document, being first duly sworn, do hereby declare to the undersigned authority that the declarant signed and executed the document as declarant's document under the Right To Die Act and that the declarant signed and executed the document willingly, and that the declarant executed it as the declarant's free and voluntary act for the purposes therein expressed; and that each of the witnesses saw the declarant sign this document, and in the presence of the declarant and in the presence of each other, signed the document as witness and that to the best of each witness' knowledge the declarant had reached the age of majority, was of sound mind, and was under no constraint or undue influence.

_____

Name

_____

WITNESS

_____

WITNESS

SUBSCRIBED AND SWORN TO, and acknowledged before me by *Name*, the declarant, and subscribed and sworn to before me by _____ and _____, the witnesses, this _____ day of _____, _____.

_____

NOTARY PUBLIC

My commission expires:

_____

59

Using Legal Assistants as Case Managers

Stephen J. Harhai

WOULD YOU LIKE TO REDUCE THE STRESS in your life, improve the quality of your work, and create a richer work environment for your staff? This is what we have effectuated by implementing a case manager system in our office.

This system benefits our clients by providing quality service at lower cost. Our legal assistants enjoy more responsibility and creativity in their work. I am able to focus my energy on the key issues that provide the greatest value to the client.

The first contact with our office is with a case manager. After checking our conflict-of-interest database, the case manager gathers key information about the case such as names, addresses, telephone numbers, children, assets, liabilities, and a history of the case. This initial interview saves time in the first lawyer meeting and saves the client time and expense when drafting documents because our intake form is geared toward drafting family law pleadings.

The client establishes a rapport with the case manager from the first telephone call. From that time on, the client will be in continuous contact with the case manager, who becomes a principal contact person with our office. We have found this works well because the case manager is virtually always available, can return calls quickly, and knows the goals and background of the case. The case manager is trained to know what kind of information is needed when a client calls and can prepare a detailed e-mail message for the lawyer. While it might appear that it would be simpler to have the lawyer speak directly to the client, the case manager method actually is quicker and less expensive for the client. Because the lawyer is less available because of court appearances, meetings, etc., a telephone call usually is delayed by "telephone tag." The case manager not only responds more quickly, but distills the call to the essential points for the lawyer and reduces the more expensive lawyer time required to solve the problem.

When a problem requires direct contact with the lawyer, the case manager schedules a meeting or telephone conference, prepares the necessary documents or materials for review, and often attends the meeting to prepare notes and lists generated by the meeting. The case manager then can immediately perform the tasks with minimal additional lawyer supervision.

We hold a weekly staff meeting to review the calendar and each case. Our networked calendar allows everyone in the office to make and modify appointments with the changes appearing immediately at every computer workstation. Our weekly collective review of the calendar allows us to review deadlines or scheduling issues and organize our resources accordingly. The case manager assigned to the case is responsible for calendaring deadlines, hearings, and meetings and updating the case status before the staff meeting. We go through each case, discuss the current status and what needs to be accomplished, and send tasks to lawyer or case manager to-do lists on our computer workstations. We specifically calendar our negotiation and hearing preparation so that we can devote an appropriate amount of time to each important phase of the case.

Because I travel a great deal, we have organized our systems so that all of the information regarding pending cases is available to me on the road or at home. Our electronic case files are akin to medical charts because every action or contact is recorded in the file and immediately available to everyone working on the case. Any location with a telephone line can instantly become an office where I can review any case file, review all the latest developments, send e-mail to the staff, and receive case updates and inquiries from case managers and associates. Having the case manager on location in our Denver office is the key to making this "work-anywhere" strategy effective.

We constantly review and improve our systems to provide better service. We currently are analyzing the work flow of the tasks we perform to reduce bottlenecks, speed turnaround times, and reduce costs.

The case-manager system, especially when coupled with an effective information-sharing system, is an effective tool to stay on top of a busy caseload.

60

Family Lawyers' Short Reference List

Gunnar J. Gitlin

BESIDES THE STATUTORY AND CASE LAW, if my library were limited to three books, they would be:

1. *Divorce Taxation* by Marjorie A. O'Connell. Published by Warren, Gorham, & Lamont, 31 St. James Avenue, Boston, MA 02116. Ph. 800/950-1205. Subscription rate $465 per year; or
   A. *Divorce Taxation Handbook: A Practical Guide to Lawyers and Judges* by Mel Frumkes. Order directly from Melvyn B. Frumkes, 100 N. Biscayne Boulevard, Suite 1607, Miami FL 33132-2380. Cost $129.95 plus postage and handling.
2. *Valuing a Business: The Analysis and Appraisal of Closely Held Companies,* Third Edition, by Shannon P. Pratt, Robert F. Reilly, and Robert P. Schweihs, Erwin Professional Publishing, which may be ordered directly from Willamette Management Associates, 111 S.W. Fifth Avenue, Suite 2150, Portland, Or 97204. Ph. 503/243-7511 Fax 503/222-7392. Cost $95 plus $3.50 postage and handling.
3. *MMPI-II: Assessing Personality and Psychopathology,* Second Edition, by John R. Graham, Oxford University Press. Ph. 800/451-7556 Fax 919/617-1303. Price $39.50 plus $3.00 shipping and handling.

Divorce Taxation: The most expensive of these publications is *Divorce Taxation.* A less expensive and excellent publication is Mel Frumkes's *Divorce Taxation Handbook: A Practical Guide to Lawyers and Judges.* While there are a number of other treatises dealing with divorce taxation, these are the best. Especially invaluable is the in-depth treatment regarding various divorce tax issues.

Valuing a Business: With growing frequency, one of the most significant issues in divorce cases is valuation of a business. Generally, the lawyer will hire an expert and rely upon his or her knowledge of the field. *Valuing a Business* is **the** authoritative treatise dealing with business valuations. The family lawyer should have this within easy reach.

MMPI-II: Most lawyers dealing with custody cases know that the critical textbook to have in their library is DSM-IV by the American Psychiatric Association. A familiarity with DSM-IV is an important reference for custody litigation. Personality tests are used in custody evaluations even though none of these tests were developed for custody litigation. The base groups upon which the data was drawn were not people undergoing the stress of a divorce or custody fight.

The standard test is the MMPI-II. The authoritative text explaining this test is *MMPI-II: Assessing Personality and Psychopathology, Second Edition.* This book explains the testing results and the interpretation of the results so that a family lawyer can understand them.

There can be two uses for knowledge of how the MMPI-II works. The first use is so the lawyer may have psychological testing of his own client when dealing with complex psychological issues, as is often the case in custody litigation. Often, a knowledge of the client's personality may assist the lawyer in working with the client.

A good example is a significant elevation on the scale 4, which is often called the psychopathic deviate scale. While an elevation on this scale may be explained by a party having an antisocial personality, it can also be explained if there is a significant amount of family discord that is strongly felt by one of the parties. Often, a custody evaluator may not have sufficient knowledge of the test interpretation to be able to accurately apply the testing in a divorce situation.

61

Making Your Conflict System Work

Sharon L. Corbitt

THE KEY TO A SUCCESSFUL OFFICE SYSTEM that avoids potential client conflicts lies not in the software nor even necessarily in the diligence of the attorneys within the firm. A successful conflict check starts with the initial interview of firm *employees,* not clients. It then maintains its viability only if religiously employed by every person within the firm.

None of us is immune to conflict, even solo practitioners, inasmuch as individuals change names, return to maiden or former names, marry former clients, and then want a divorce, etc. The larger the firm, obviously the riper the field becomes for conflict.

When interviewing potential employees for your law firm, the individual conducting the interview should provide information to prospective employees about the importance of conflict avoidance. Our employment interview not only includes general information about the importance of maintaining confidentiality about client files, but also stresses the importance of maintaining confidentiality about individuals who may have simply contacted our firm. In addition, prospective employees are told that we utilize a conflict system that must be implemented at the time of an initial telephone contact to our office, regardless of the person to whom that initial contact is made.

1. *Initial Contact by Former/Potential Client.* When an initial contact for potential representation is made to a firm, the individual to whom the initial contact is made (whether lawyer or staff person) should make inquiries of that individual concerning whether he or she is an existing or former client. The name of the adverse party should be determined as well. Third, if either party has had different last names, an inquiry should be made in that regard as well.
2. *Running the Conflict Check.* Each office should have some type of system (preferably computerized) that allows a check of the individual in question as well as the opposing party to make certain that no

individual within the firm has represented the other side or has any other type of potential conflict. In our office, we developed our own conflict check within WordPerfect.

3. *Written Memorandum.* Assuming it is preliminarily determined that no conflict exists, the lawyer who ultimately talks with the potential client, whether by telephone or in person, should complete a written memorandum of that contact. Again, the form is not important. What is important is that the names of the parties and the type of case are disseminated to all lawyers within the firm. This provides a visual "double check." Surprisingly, this "second look" sometimes turns up either conflicts that were not caught at the outset or names that for some reason never made it into the conflicts system. It is important that this written memorandum be completed and disseminated *immediately* after the initial contact. In a firm that does nothing but family practice, it is not uncommon for both sides of a lawsuit to seek out individuals within the same firm. Obviously, if two different lawyers saw opposing sides unknowingly, then the representation of either would be impossible. Not catching a conflict at the outset might result in fees having to be refunded, even if earned.

4. *Problem Areas.*

   A. If a computerized conflict system is used, lawyers within the office who are not computer literate may not be able to check the system if a call is received from an initial client during other than working hours. Accordingly, it becomes imperative that no lawyer provides information or legal advice except to existing clients until such time as a conflict check may be run.

   B. Sometimes the very practice of assuring that a conflict does not exist requires telling a caller that you are not at liberty to schedule with that person. Even if you disclose nothing other than the fact a conflict exists, this obviously may cause that party to recognize that his or her spouse has already contacted your firm. This can be problematic if the person who previously saw someone in your office may not have wanted anyone to know he or she was seeing an attorney. I personally deal with this by telling individuals at the initial interview about the conflicts check and the possibility that we would have to subsequently reveal to someone that a conflict exists.

Finally, as alluded to above, the system works only if all parts of it work. It is important to detail in office procedures exactly what is expected of everyone in the office. Everyone within the office should be aware of how critical an effective conflict check is.

CLIENT/POTENTIAL CLIENT/CONFLICT LIST

POTENTIAL CLIENT	OPPOSING PARTY	ATTY CONTACTED	DATE OF CONTACT
Adams, John	Mary Adams	SLC	06/02/92
Adams, see Smith			
Alexander, Barry	Kathy Alexander	NSJ	06/25/93
Alexander, Jackie	Paul Alexander	NSJ	01/31/95
Allen, Mark	Susan Moore	SLC	12/15/94
Anderson, Lisa	Joe Keifer	SLC	03/30/92
Anderson, see Morris			
Anderson, Scott	Lori Lake	HVR	07/29/92
Andrews, Carl, Jr.	Marcia Andrews	CMZ	01/18/94
Bailey, Donna	Bob Bailey	HVR	09/23/92
Baker, Mike	Connie Baker	HVR	08/18/94
Baker, Sandra	Doug Baker	WGL	11/08/94
Barnes, Kyle	Sharon Barnes	SLC	12/31/91
Bates, See Rich			
Bell, Dana	Steve Bell	NSJ	02/04/94
Bell, Jennifer	Jack Bell	SLC	04/21/93
Berry, Cathy	Chuck Berry	CMZ	09/01/93
Boggs, Nancy	Mark Boggs	SLC	05/12/94
Boyd, Tracy	Renea Boyd	CMZ	07/17/92
Brown, Carl		CMZ	12/02/91
Brown, Pamela	Reese Brown	NSJ	01/31/94
Brown, Cynthia	Wayne Brown	HVR	11/11/91
Brown, see Kite			
Bryant, James	Luna Pete	SLC	02/07/94
Burris, Lucy	Adam Burris	SLC	07/07/94
Carpenter, Shonda	Jim Carpenter	CMZ	02/04/94
Carpenter, Steve	Janice Carpenter	NSJ	10/13/92
Chambers, See Lord			
Chapman, June	Richard Chapman	HVR	10/30/92
Christian, Tammy	Tom Jones	SLC	09/22/91
Clark, Meg	Doug Clark	SLC	12/21/92

(continued)

POTENTIAL CLIENT	OPPOSING PARTY	ATTY CONTACTED	DATE OF CONTACT
Clark, Suzie	Kent Clark	HVR	07/20/92
Collins, Rachel	Jeff Collins	CMZ	10/31/94
Collins, Joan	Tom Collins	SLC	09/10/92
Cooper, Gary	Mary Cooper	SLC	07/15/93
Cox, Wilma	Harry Cox	HVR	10/13/93
Davis, Ann	Mac Davis	NSJ	01/12/95
Davis, Nora	John Davis	SLC	11/02/92
Douglas, Diane	Kirk Douglas	CMZ	07/13/93
Edwards, Joyce	Steve Edwards	CMZ	07/16/93
Edwards, see Hood			
Evans, Donna	Bobby Evans	CMZ	04/10/92
Ford, Glenn	Francis Ford	HVR	11/04/93
George, Martha	Frank George	HVR	03/22/95
Gordon, Teresa	Evan Gordon	SLC	01/24/95
Grant, Paige	Lou Smith	HVR	09/12/94
Green, Tommy	Gail Green	HVR	04/02/92

CONFLICTS MEMORANDUM

TO: ALL ATTORNEYS

FROM: _____

DATE: _____

NAME OF CLIENT: _____

NAME OF OPPOSING PARTY: _____

TYPE OF ACTION: _____

FIRM'S PREVIOUS INVOLVEMENT (if any): _____

REFERRED BY: _____

RETAINER FEE QUOTED: _____

FIRM RETAINED: YES/NO (circle)

ADDITIONAL INFORMATION: _____

62

How to Market Your Practice with a Personal Touch

Twila B. Larkin

WE'VE ALL BEEN INVOLVED in marketing activities such as working on state bar committees, speaking at seminars, and writing articles. The list of activities in which one can become involved is endless. I submit to you that the marketing efforts that really work are those that have a personal touch. I want to suggest some ways that you can market your practice with a personal touch and to share with you some of the marketing efforts that have worked in our domestic relations practice.

As one of your first steps in focusing your marketing efforts, you need to identify your actual or potential referral sources. If you are just starting out in practice or perhaps changing areas of practice, you must give serious thought to how potential clients will come across your name. This also requires you to give serious thought to the type of practice you want and what type of clients you want. For this paper, we are going to assume that you have established a practice, but you need to bring some focus to your marketing efforts.

The easy way to identify your actual referral sources is to begin to ask potential clients when they make initial contact with your office. Develop an intake form that your paralegal or secretary can use to gather some basic information from the potential client so that you can properly evaluate the case before scheduling an appointment. One of the questions on the intake form is how they heard of you or your firm or who referred them to you. Then that information can be retrieved from the intake sheet and tracked on a spreadsheet according to the following categories: estate planning lawyer, business lawyer, other types of lawyer, accountant, psychologist, friend, former client, etc.

Beginning to track your referral sources according to category provides you with invaluable information. For instance, we have found that most of our referrals come from estate planning lawyers and former clients. Even when we had a large Yellow Pages advertisement, it did not affect our referrals. We saved several thousand dollars per year by reducing our Yellow Pages advertising to a very small advertisement.

Don't forget to send a thank-you note or letter to the actual referral source. Your secretary can have a standard letter prepared for your signature.

Now give your marketing a personal touch by taking your referral sources out to lunch. Have your secretary begin to compile a list of the actual people who have referred cases to you, and have your secretary schedule at least one lunch a week with one of your referral sources. You can begin to rotate through your list of referrals with weekly lunches.

By tracking the categories of your referral sources, you can begin to identify new possible sources of referrals. For instance, once we identified that most of our referrals were coming from estate planning lawyers, then we could begin to schedule lunches with estate planning lawyers who had not previously referred cases to us.

Once you get your weekly lunch program working, you can then begin to focus on groups in which you find your category of referral sources. They may have monthly luncheons or dinners. They may have periodic section meetings or educational seminars. You can find out by talking to your referral sources if there are meetings that you can attend. You can volunteer to speak at these meetings, or even organize lunch-and-learn seminars for small groups of your referral sources.

Finally, you can continue to add to the people you know by attending local bar luncheons and seminars. Everywhere you go, try to meet at least one person you can then call the next day or week and take out to lunch. In this way, you may develop a new category of referral sources.

In short, the way to market your practice with a personal touch is to take a person out to lunch!

63

Using Cell Phones and E-Mail to Communicate Confidential Information to Clients

Kathleen Robertson

THERE IS A DANGER of unintended disclosure of confidential client information if you engage in confidential communications with your client via e-mail or cellular and cordless telephones. No one can guarantee the security of a cellular telephone or electronic mail. While the danger may be remote, some practitioners are concerned enough to implement a policy that requires use of encryption methods in their office, and encourage or require that their client also employ encryption methods.

Review your state's Rules of Professional Conduct opinion regarding the use of e-mail and cellular and cordless telephones to communicate confidential information to clients. The prevalent view of most states is that communications by e-mail and digital cordless or cellular phones, like those by mail and conventional corded telephones, generally are considered secure. Interception involves intent, expertise, and violation of federal law.

Some states have required client consent or encryption for the use of e-mail, but the majority of recent state ethics opinions sanction the use of e-mail without such requirements. *Note that analog cordless or cellular telephones are generally not secure. They can be intercepted intentionally or inadvertently with relatively unsophisticated and readily available equipment.*

Do we, as practitioners, have a duty to inform our clients of the confidentiality risks associated with inadvertent interception? Should we adopt office policies that require client consent to communicate confidential information via e-mail or cellular phones? I believe the answer to both questions is yes.

As lawyers, we are charged with the ethical duty to protect a confidence or secret of a client, as well as exercise care to prevent the unintended disclosure of the confidence or secret. Unless your state has already made a determination regarding the use of e-mail and cellular telephones in a professional responsibility opinion, and has approved the use of e-mail without encryption and the use of digital cordless and cellular telephones for confidential communications with clients, you may violate your ethical duty to your clients if you do not inform them of the potential problems and obtain their consent. Even if your state has taken the position that e-mail and digital cordless and cellular telephones are secure for purposes of confidential communication, I believe it is good practice to advise your clients of the risk of interception.

I include the following language regarding the use of e-mail and cellular phones in my retention letter that is signed by the client upon retaining our firm:

Warning Regarding the Use of E-Mail and Cellular Telephones

No one can guarantee the confidentiality or security of e-mail or cellular and cordless telephones. If you choose to communicate with me, or any of my staff, via e-mail or cellular and cordless telephones, your communication may be overheard or intercepted. If overheard or intercepted, the communication may lose protection as a privileged communication within the attorney-client privilege. I will not e-mail confidential information to you or communicate confidential information via cell phone unless you have instructed me to do so. Norris & Rossi, LLP does not employ any encryption methods or protect e-mail communications with passwords. Do not use an analog cordless or cellular phone when calling me. Analog cordless and cellular phones are not secure and can be easily intercepted with readily available inexpensive equipment. By signing this retention letter, you are acknowledging the risks of communicating confidential information via e-mail or cellular and cordless telephones.

I further suggest that you provide your client with your written policy regarding e-mail communications, with the hope that you and your staff will have fewer problems with e-mail communications, including timeliness of response, appropriate content, and avoidance of inadvertent dissemination. We provide our policy at the time our client retains us:

1. No one can guarantee the security of e-mail communications. We do not employ encryption methods. Any use of e-mail is at your own risk.

2. Do not send an e-mail from an address where you do not want a reply to be sent. We assume that, if we receive an e-mail communication from you, it is safe to send a reply message back to that address.

3. Do not rely upon e-mail for urgent matters. Please use the telephone to transmit urgent messages.

4. When the attorney working on your case is in court or unavailable, your e-mails may not be reviewed until the attorney returns to the office. Again, do not rely upon e-mail for urgent matters.

5. You may e-mail my secretary, Paulette, for scheduling of appointments or to obtain other general information regarding your case.

6. You are billed for attorney and/or paralegal time for reviewing and responding to e-mails.

7. Do not e-mail particularly sensitive, confidential, or potentially embarrassing information. There is a risk, however slight, that your e-mail could be intercepted. There is also a risk that your e-mail could be misdirected, inadvertently disseminated, and read by others.

PART
VI

Discovery

THERE IS AN ODD TWIST IN FAMILY LAW. In almost every other area of law, the litigants are total, or almost total, strangers. Unique to family law, the litigants know each other as intimately as two human beings can know each other. Yet the same discovery devices available to two strangers who collide at a red light are also available to family law litigants.

Certainly, some of discovery has little to do with the knowledge of each other, such as discovery related to trial tactics. Other discovery may be related to areas where one spouse has little knowledge, such as a business. Courts frequently turn a deaf ear to discovery disputes in family law, however, rationalizing that these people must have intimate knowledge of each other.

The following tips are designed for the necessary discovery in family law without running up huge uncollectible receivables and without triggering a response that ends up before an uncaring court.

64   A good place to start is with a general review of discovery tools available to matrimonial lawyers. **Elaine Rudnick-Sheps** provides such a review, stressing their use with minimum expense for maximum effect.

65   The most cost-effective discovery device is the Request for Admission. It is easy to do (no court reporters) and narrows, rather than increases, the issues for settlement and trial. **Judge Howard Lipsey** explains its effectiveness and provides several examples.

66   **Michael Albano** agrees that Requests for Admission are extremely effective and economical, and he provides an example of a Request for Admission. I don't know if it comes from a real case, but you don't have to see the answers to know that you will be glad you did not represent the petitioner.

67 While depositions can be quite costly, they are sometime indispensable. **Ira Lurvey** gives not one but ten tips on how to take a deposition effectively and efficiently.

68 Some assets are less obvious than others. Bank accounts and retirement plans, for example, are relatively easy to find and value. In her hot tip, **Phyllis Bossin** discusses some assets which are less apparent, but may have substantial value.

64

Discovery: Road to Victory

Elaine Rudnick-Sheps

As JON A. DEMAY STATED, in his excellent volume *Discovery: How to Win Your Case without Trial*, the purpose in utilizing various discovery procedures is to get your case in such condition that you can try it well or settle it on terms favorable to your client.

While the purpose of discovery is for information, to shorten trials, and encourage settlement, it also must be accomplished with minimum expense yet achieve maximum effect.

The following discovery devices are particularly applicable to matrimonial trial.

THE DEPOSITION

The deposition is one of the most powerful discovery tools, but it must be utilized wisely and strategically.

The lawyer always must be in control of a deposition. Counsel must avoid conviviality and conversation. Counsel must "take charge." As the deposition is a minitrial, counsel must be fully prepared. An outline is essential. Write out important questions if you want to make certain they are asked. Know the purpose and objective of your case and know the proof required.

Save your devastating questions for the latter part of the deposition when the toughest questioning should be forged. Be blunt, direct, and *never back off.*

If you are uncertain of your grounds or your case, do not test it in the choppy waters of the deposition.

REQUESTS FOR ADMISSION

While a Request for Admission cannot win a case, it is a superb vehicle for admission of facts. It is particularly appropriate in matrimonial cases where it is necessary to obtain admissions relating, e.g., to bank accounts, purchase cost of property, reported earnings, deposits, financial contributions to separate property, and facts that one cannot quarrel with and that have documents to back up the proper answer.

The Request for Admission goes to the heart of the case. Each request must be answered. Most lawyers will not allow a client to lie.

When a litigant is confronted with the facts, that litigant may have no alternative but to admit them. Sometimes the opposing side will know "the game is over" when lawyer and client sit down and prepare answers to an admission request.

Interrogatories must be crafted with care. If the interrogatory is clear but the answers are evasive, however, a motion can bring the case to the door of settlement. Most judges can read between the lines; and where a question is clear and the answer is "a masterpiece of subterfuge," your opponent will be compelled to file a new and proper answer.

Use interrogatories as investigative tools. Ask more questions than less. Force your opponent to answer directly at all times.

While it is difficult to win a matrimonial case solely on discovery, effective use of discovery devices can, in most instances, result in extremely favorable settlements and impress the client with counsel's organizational skills, comprehension of fact, and thoroughness of preparation.

Discovery devices are invaluable tools that the matrimonial lawyer should use to maximum advantage for stunning results.

Requests for Admission also can establish authenticity of records, which can be a great timesaver in matrimonial trials where numerous documents have to be admitted in evidence and you want the other side to admit their authenticity. It also is helpful when you want to establish certain facts that you believe to be uncontested but that would be laborious to prove at the trial. Caveat: Do not waste time requesting admissions concerning opinions or judgment. This is not the purpose of a Request for Admission.

INTERROGATORIES

The preparation of interrogatories is hard work. If you are enticed by forms, stay away from interrogatories.

Interrogatories should be expressly designed for the individual case from scratch. This does not mean you cannot prepare your own set of forms for certain valuations, e.g., medical practice, law practice, etc. However, the forms cannot be "blunderbuss." You also must determine the desirability of utilizing interrogatories in lieu of a deposition. The basic consideration is the cost factor. The deposition may not always be worth the expense and the interrogatories can, at times, produce a comparable result.

65

Immediate Use of Request for Admission

Hon. Howard I. Lipsey

THE TRIAL TECHNIQUES of a domestic relations case often can be based on those procedures we have learned in the course of our tort practices. A familiarity with the rules of discovery can greatly assist in the positive use of techniques that can propel you into most advantageous positions on behalf of your client.

In the usual course of a domestic relations case, we fall into a routine of filing a set of interrogatories and then a request for production of documents. We know that the answers to the interrogatories will be prepared and edited by opposing counsel. In those jurisdictions where "fault" or "conduct" is an issue with respect to either spousal support or equitable assignment of property, obtaining information adverse to the other party at the earliest possible time during the proceedings can be invaluable. It often can lead to immediate "cooperation" with the disclosure of assets and income as well as early settlement overtures.

In the appropriate case, therefore, start your discovery process immediately by filing a Request for Admission of facts under Federal Rule 36 or your jurisdiction's equivalent rule. While the equivalent to Federal Rule 33 (interrogatories) usually allows forty days for a response and usually is extended beyond that, a Rule 36 request ordinarily is required to be answered ten days after service.

While you may not have all the specifics available regarding "fault or conduct," you may have enough information to frame some broad requests that will suffice for this technique. For example:

1. The defendant has had sexual relations with a woman not his wife since his marriage to the plaintiff.
2. The defendant has had sexual relations with a woman not his wife between the date of marriage and prior to the date of separation.

3. The defendant has had sexual relations with a woman not his wife between the date of the separation and the present time.

The other party will immediately be placed in the dilemma of either answering in the affirmative, not answering—which will be deemed an admission under the Rule—or denying the requests in a sworn statement.

In any event, the pressure is on the other party through the legitimate use of a discovery technique that is both simple in its use, inexpensive in its application, and potentially devastating to the other party in its effect.

66

Requests for and Effect of Admission

Michael J. Albano

REQUESTS FOR ADMISSION seem to have become a lost art in domestic cases. I find this to be a surprising development, for admissions can be used successfully in most cases.

Any party to a divorce action can serve on the other party a written Request for Admission of the genuineness of any relevant documents described in and exhibited with the request. The written request also may ask the other party to admit the truth of any relevant and material matters of fact set forth in the request.

Usually, any matter admitted is conclusively established unless the court permits withdrawal or amendment of the admission on motion of the other party.

I have found the use of Requests for Admission extremely beneficial. For instance, they make it very difficult for the other party to change his or her story at the time of trial. In addition, they tend to:

1. Reduce the length of the trial;
2. Reduce the number of controverted issues;
3. Reduce and/or eliminate unnecessary impeachment tactics during the trial; and
4. Bring about settlements.

My paralegal outlines every deposition taken in the case. She also identifies every helpful admission made by the other party. I then prepare the Request for Admission for the other spouse. This usually is accomplished within ten days after the deposition is transcribed.

I also have used the admissions during opening statements and closing arguments. On most occasions, I read the admissions into the record as additional evidence on my client's behalf as "admissions against interest" on the part of the opposing party.

I have provided an example of a Request for Admission for your review. I sincerely hope that it will be of some assistance to you in your practice.

IN THE CIRCUIT COURT OF JACKSON COUNTY, MISSOURI
AT KANSAS CITY

IN RE THE MARRIAGE OF:)
)
)
)
        Petitioner,   )
)
and   ) Case No. _____
)
)
        Respondent.   )

RESPONDENT'S REQUEST FOR ADMISSION

COMES NOW the Respondent, by and through his attorney of record, and requests that within twenty (20) days of service of this request that Petitioner make the following admissions for the purpose of this action only and subject to all pertinent objections to admissibility which may be interposed at the trial:

A. That each of the following statements is true:

1. That Petitioner is and has been a resident of the State of Missouri for at least ninety (90) days immediately preceding the filing of her Petition for Legal Separation.

2. That Petitioner now resides at _____.

3. That Petitioner and Respondent were married on the _____ day of _____ in _____, _____ County, State.

4. That there were two (2) children born of the marriage and that both children are now emancipated.

5. That Petitioner is not pregnant at this time.

1

6.   That Petitioner is unemployed.

7.   That Petitioner's Social Security Number is:_____.

8.   That Respondent is presently employed at _____.

9.   That Respondent's Social Security Number is:_____.

10.   That neither Petitioner nor Respondent is now on active duty with the Armed Forces of the United States of American or any of its allies.

11.   That there is no reasonable likelihood that the marriage of Petitioner and Respondent can be preserved and, therefore, the marriage is irretrievably broken.

12.   That Petitioner established a trust account document which was drafted by _____.

13.   That Petitioner assets that said original trust document has been altered.

14.   That Petitioner sent a letter of complaint to the _____.

15.   That Petitioner initially refused to pay _____.

16.   That Petitioner has written a letter of complaint to _____ regarding carpentry work.

17.   That Petitioner has refused to pay _____ for services rendered.

18.   That Petitioner has written a letter of complaint to _____ regarding plumbing work.

19.   That Petitioner initially refused to pay said _____ for services rendered.

20.   That Petitioner wrote a letter of complaint to _____ regarding poor installation and replacement of glass.

21.   That Petitioner wrote a letter to _____ complaining about poor alterations.

22.   That Petitioner has written a letter of complaint to _____.

23.   That Petitioner believes that someone has been entering her home and altering and/or damaging her clothing.

24.   That Petitioner believes that as of _____, _____,_____, someone was still coming into her home and damaging and/or altering her clothing.

25.   That Petitioner believes that it is possible that someone has changed the locks on her home without her knowledge.

26.   That Petitioner has sent a letter of complaint to _____ regarding jewelry which has been altered without her consent or knowledge.

27.   That Petitioner believes that her shoes, while in the home, have been altered or damaged, to-wit:

      (a)   Heels have been slashed;

      (b)   The sizes have been changed.

28.   That the Petitioner believes that her jewelry has been altered or damaged, to-wit:

      (a)   Pieces have been copied;

      (b)   Pieces have been reduced;

      (c)   Lesser stones have been placed in said jewelry.

3

29.   That Petitioner believes that Respondent may be hiring someone to damage and/or alter Petitioner's possessions.

30.   That Petitioner believes that it is within the realm of possibility that some is hypnotizing Petitioner and directing her to alter and/or damage her personal belongings.

31.   That Petitioner utilized a knife to damage a portion of three or four walls within the marital home.

32.   That Petitioner scratched the dining room table.

33.   That Petitioner made three or four scratches, each of less than four inches long, on the buffet.

34.   That Petitioner has damaged her own clothing, to-wit:

(a) Petitioner has torn the seams out of her clothing.

35.   That Petitioner has used a knife to cut holes in the Respondent's suit.

36.   That Petitioner has used a knife to place two or three slashes on Respondent's shoes.

37.   That Petitioner utilized a screwdriver to place a three foot scratch on Respondent's car.

38.   That Petitioner has sought psychiatric treatment only upon the initiation of Respondent.

39.   That Petitioner has seen the following psychologists and/or psychiatrists:

_____ and a psychiatrist and/or psychologist at the _____ while in _____ at the _____.

4

40.   That Petitioner has written letters asserting that someone is getting into her home and cutting her hair, damaging her teeth, putting plastic underneath her fingernails.

41.   That Petitioner utilized either a knife or a screwdriver to make five or six inch long scratches on Respondent's computer.

42.   That Petitioner has utilized either a knife or a screwdriver to make a five or six inch scratch on Respondent's desk.

43.   That Petitioner has utilized an instrument to scratch a chair of Respondent's.

44.   That Petitioner has found small scratches on furniture throughout her home.

45.   That Petitioner has given away essentially brand-new clothing as she perceives said clothing to be damaged.

46.   That Petitioner has ripped up new clothing as the seams were not symmetrical and therefore said clothing were impossible to wear.

47.   That Petitioner has never thrown a fur coat out in the front yard.

48.   That since Respondent and Petitioner's separation, Petitioner has told Respondent that he is an honest man of good integrity.

49.   That Petitioner believes that someone has come into her home and tampered with her legal papers.

50.   That Petitioner believes that someone has come into her home and destroyed her files.

51.   That Petitioner has failed to file an income tax return for the year _____.

52.   That Petitioner believes that someone comes into her home and cuts her hair without her knowledge and/or consent.

53.   That Petitioner has sought the services of the following attorneys regarding the present cause:

      (a)
      (b)
      (c)

54.   That Petitioner has been sued by the following attorneys:

      (a)
      (b)
      (c)

55.   That Petitioner has refused to pay _____ for services rendered.

56.   That Petitioner has filed complaints regarding _____ and

_____.

57.   That Petitioner has seen the following dentists or periodontists:

      (a) Dr.
      (b) Dr.
      (c) Dr.
      (d) Dr.

58.   That Petitioner has failed and refused to pay the following dentists:

      (a) Dr.
      (b) Dr.
      (c) Dr.
      (d) Dr.

59.   That Petitioner has complained, either by letter or by telephone call, to the following organizations regarding improper dental and/or periodontal treatment:

(a)

(b)

(c)

60.   That Petitioner has personally removed filings from her own teeth.

61.   That Petitioner has visited doctors using a fictitious name in both

_____ and _____.

62.   That Petitioner believes that dentists have fraudulently drilled on her teeth

63.   That Petitioner believes and has indicated to others that there is a dental

conspiracy against the Petitioner.

64.   That Petitioner retained the _____ income tax refund for the year

_____.

65.   That Petitioner deposited said _____ in an account in her name

only or an account in Petitioner's name and the name of her children and/or

grandchildren.

66.   That Petitioner placed _____ in an account in her name only or an

account in Petitioner's name and the name of her children and/or grandchildren.

67.   That Petitioner has utilized said sums to purchase stock which is held in

her name only.

68.   That Petitioner believes that "gremlins" enter her home without her

knowledge and:

(a)   damage her plastic belongings;
(b)   alter her clothing;
(c)   cut her hair;
(d)   put plastic under her fingernails; and
(e)   alter and/or destroy documents.

69.   Petitioner sent the attached letter on _____, _____, to

_____, (See attachment market Exhibit "A").

70.   Since _____, ____, Petitioner has taken a trip to Europe traveling to countries of England, France, Switzerland, and West Germany.

71.   Petitioner has been sued by _____, Inc., for her refusal to pay said company for a security system installed at her home.

72.   Petitioner has refused to take the advice of the _____ that she be hospitalized for her present mental condition.

73.   Petitioner has refused to take medication prescribed for her mental condition.

74.   Petitioner has in her possession and control marital and non-marital assets including but not limited to, stock, and cash.

WELCH, MARTIN, ALBANO & MANNERS, P.C.

BY:_____
            MICHAEL J. ALBANO #20288
            311 W. Kansas
            Independence, Missouri 64050
            Telephone: (816) 836-8000
            Facsimile: (816) 836-8953

            ATTORNEYS FOR RESPONDENT

67

Ten Tips toward a Better Deposition

Ira Lurvey

PERHAPS THE MOST OVERUSED but underrated legal procedure in family law is the deposition upon oral examination. Properly prepared and executed, it can be as forceful as a trial. Wisely considered, it can prompt instant settlement. Artfully handled, it can be devastatingly efficient.

Ten tips toward a more effective deposition in family law cases might be summarized as follows:

TIP ONE—Prepare Fully. If a Deposition Is Worth Taking, It's Worth Taking Well. In real estate, the three most important considerations are "location, location, and location." In the taking of depositions, the three most important acts are "preparation, preparation, and preparation." Considering the currently increasing costs of court reporters' time, deposition transcribing fees, and, of course, the time for the lawyers' preparing and taking of the session, a deposition is not a procedural vehicle to be used lightly. Once the decision to notice a deposition is made, however, the energies and attentions directed to the deposition should rival those devoted to a full trial. A deposition is not something to be sloughed off or ad-libbed.

So, how does one prepare for taking a deposition?

1. Understand the nature of a deposition. A deposition has only two central purposes: (1) to learn material facts and circumstances relevant to the case of which facts you, as taker of the deposition, have not previously been aware; and (2) to establish clearly for the record the assertions and position of the opposing party on the key issues.
2. Understand what are the material facts and issues in the case. A deposition is not when you are supposed to learn for the first time what the case is all about. You should come into the deposition already knowing almost all of the facts and issues that exist regarding the case, and understanding the precise relationship that these controlling facts have to the issues you need to establish to prevail on behalf of your client.

3. Understand how to present questions. Lightning mainly strikes on golf courses. Depositions usually are taken in offices. Thus, lightning generally does not strike inside a deposition. Only in scripted play-acting does a confession suddenly emerge on interrogation to conclusively solve a dispute. In real life and real time, questions and answers come and go in a more plodding fashion. In taking a deposition, questions generally should be phrased so that the deponent is forced to use his or her own words in presenting an answer. Occasionally a question can be phrased so that it calls for only a simple "yes" or "no" answer, but if you insist on asking questions in so rigid a form, be prepared to receive limited answers, or even less. Thus, instead of framing your question to ask, "Didn't you cross the street at noon yesterday?" ask, "What did you do with respect to crossing the street?" and "When did you do it?"

4. Understand the evidence you already have in hand. Examine all the documents and exhibits you have already gathered that are material to the case. Use the deposition as a vehicle to authenticate the legitimacy of these writings, to establish the circumstances in which the writings came into being, and to learn, or confirm, what was said between the parties incident to signing or delivering these key papers.

TIP TWO—Use a Deposition Notebook. Once the deposition begins, questions and answers fly with rapidity. You cannot make up the key questions as you go along. Therefore, prepare in advance a series of questions constituting more or less of an outline of all that you hope to get as a minimum from the deposition. Then set those questions down in writing, about three to five questions to a page on ordinary 8½x11 notepaper, hole-punched for use in a three-ring binder (or two-ring special binder for large amounts of paper). That will give you your deposition notebook. The advantage of using a loose-leaf notebook over simply a pad of paper or loose papers is that you have the flexibility of turning from page to page and can insert later questions into the area where they are most relevant, without having to sacrifice space or creating a jumble of writing so crowded together that it becomes indecipherable.

TIP THREE—Know Your Court Reporter. The transcript to be prepared for the deposition depends in large part upon a competent transcriber, i.e., the court reporter. Little is more unnerving than a court reporter who interjects himself or herself into the process, either by oversolicitude or by uncaring. [War story: I once had a court reporter who insisted that he had to go to the bathroom at times during the deposition when the questioning was getting close to eliciting material admissions from the opponent witness. Then there was the reporter who, when a particularly intense exchange began between lawyers, put down her machine and said her health was such that she could not stand tension in the workplace, and unless the lawyers calmed down, she would call for a replacement.] Then there are the reporters who stop the flow of questioning by demanding that names or words they do not immediately understand be spelled out for them instantly. The ideal court reporter is someone who for all practical purposes is invisible throughout the deposition. He or she is there but so unintrusive that your deposition continues unimpaired. The solution is to develop a rapport with one or more reporters, and engage these reporters, whom you know and trust, to perform deposition services whenever you have the opportunity to choose the reporter.

TIP FOUR—Use a Practical Room for the Deposition. To be efficient, a deposition usually should be in a room that will accommodate a large, usually oblong, table where you as deposing attorney can sit opposite the deponent, and the court reporter can sit between you, at right angles to each of you. Thus the court reporter is at a right angle to each of the persons who will do most of the speaking and you are seated directly across the table from the person you are questioning. The oblong table also affords you the length of table to your right (or left, if you so choose) on which to lay out your papers and exhibits. In contrast, taking a deposition from behind your desk while the deponent sits on a couch across the room or in some other location, and the court reporter more or less squats some other place in the room, seems both out of symmetry and confusing. You as questioner want relative control of the room to facilitate taking of the deposition. You want a facility that permits you to maximize that convenience and have mastery of the space at hand.

TIP FIVE—Orally Record or Videotape the Deposition. In most jurisdictions, it is permitted upon proper advance notice to use a mechanical recording device along with the court reporter for transcribing the deposition. The advantage of inserting even a small, household variety of sound tape recorder is that an instant audiotape can be had of the day's proceedings, for you to review as soon as that evening; and to share with your client or other counsel who may not be present at the deposition. The client will then hear the actual dynamics of the deposition, beyond simply reading the more sterile two-dimensional transcript. Moreover, in certain instances, simply having the oral transcribing may prove sufficient. You may not even need to have the proceeding transcribed in writing. There can be a substantial cost saving to your client in that instance, especially where the case is settled shortly after the deposition, with your client having to pay only the attendance fee of the court reporter rather than the more extensive full transcribing fee. In addition, in the event that you believe the written transcribing is incorrect, you have at least a homemade tape recording against which to check its accuracy.

TIP SIX—Use Pre-printed Explanations. The two forms of Deposition Explanations appended to the end of this summary are examples of avoiding the need to give an oral explanation of deposition proceedings at the outset of each deposition. By simply referencing these written explanations, which the witness and opposing attorney sign and the witness initials on each page, there is dispelled the issue of assuring that the witness/deponent does not later disclaim any testimony on grounds that he or she did not understand the nature of a deposition. There can be no misunderstanding the import of the explanation. It is a quick, efficient, and less costly way of giving the proper explanation rather than reciting the same litany orally before each deposition. The witness and opposing counsel usually examine and sign off on the explanation before the deposition record even opens, and it then is marked as Exhibit 1 to the proceedings to reflect that the witness has been given a full explanation and signed off; and you can open by asking if, in view of such signing off, the deponent has any questions about the nature of the deposition process. Invariably, the answer will be, "no," and you can proceed accordingly.

TIP SEVEN—Have Your Exhibits in a Bellows or Similar Folder Ready for Use in Sequence. The writings that you want to discuss as material portions of evidence during the deposition should be stored in a bellows or other segregating file so that they may be pulled out for you on instant reference when that aspect of the questioning comes up in the deposition. In your deposition notebook, whenever you intend to call upon a new exhibit, the exhibit should be noted and circled, so that when you are reading your deposition notebook during the deposition, whenever you come to a circle, you know it is time to reach into your bellows and introduce another exhibit.

TIP EIGHT—Segregate Your Questions So That You Follow through with a Complete Topic before Shifting to Another; "Read" Your Transcript as You Are Creating It. Just as the better trial lawyers always try their cases with one eye out for the appellate record, in taking a deposition, keep a ready ear for how a turn of phrase or response will read at time of trial when you are using this portion of the deposition in lieu of live evidence from a party, or to impeach an unfriendly witness. Understand that items do not always read the same way they sound. Try and keep your questions short and pointed. Listen for a very good answer and visualize how that can be used to your advantage at trial.

TIP NINE—Don't Be a Pig; When You Get a Good Answer, Don't Push for a Perfect One. A favorite saying of mine is that little piggies are cute but big hogs get slaughtered. When you get what you believe to be a good answer to a question, do not push on for an even better answer. More times than not, the response you get back will weaken or destroy the good answer you already had.

TIP TEN—Be Polite. Civil law is called that for a reason. You can obtain the same benefit and information from a deposition conducted civilly and professionally as from one managed as if a neighborhood street fight was in session. (War story: I once had a witness hop up on the table and begin eating an apple, to imply he was mentally unbalanced and try and halt the deposition. After we reseated him, he began hiding under the table. We adjourned and got a court order and sanctions that the deposition proceed to conclusion before a referee at the deponent's sole expense. That calmed him down appreciably.) If opposing counsel or the witness makes conducting a gentlewomanly proceeding impossible, then adjourn to request court protective orders or the employment of an outside referee to monitor the proceedings. In those circumstances, you also might want to consider using a videotape recording process to supplement all other forms of recording, so you ultimately can show the court just what was going on; but be mindful that videotaping of depositions usually just has a stable camera focusing only on a head shot of the deponent.

Those are ten "hot tips." Have fun.

EXPLANATION OF DEPOSITION PROCEEDINGS

(Witness and Attorney)

TO THE WITNESS _____ :

    PLEASE READ THIS CAREFULLY. IT IS IMPORTANT TO YOU.

    This proceeding in which you are about to give testimony here today is known as a "deposition." Your attorney is being handed this written explanation to read and review with you before your deposition even begins, so as best to inform you of the nature and effect of this proceeding and to save all of us the time and expense of orally reciting this explanation to you on the record after the deposition begins.

    If after reading this Explanation, you still have any questions about the nature of deposition proceedings, please ask them of your attorney before the proceeding begins.

    Our purpose in taking your deposition is to obtain facts and information within your knowledge related to matters involved in this lawsuit or proceeding. We do not seek to trick or trap you. We do not wish to cause you discomfort.

    The person transcribing the deposition is a Certified Shorthand Reporter.

    At the outset, you will be placed under oath. You then will be asked questions which you are expected to answer fully and truthfully, under oath.

    Please do not guess. We request your best present recollection of the facts and events about which you will be questioned. We will presume therefore that whatever you testify today is your best present recollection and not a guess.

INITIAL HERE: _____

Although this deposition is being held in the informality of these law offices, and coffee and soft drinks are available throughout as our courtesy to you, this deposition does have all the solemnity of courtroom testimony. Since you are under oath, your testimony here today will have the same force and effect and be subject to the same penalties as if you were testifying in a courtroom before a judge.

Among such penalties to which you are subject is the penalty of perjury. Perjury is defined as "willfully, and contrary to an oath administered, stating as true any material fact which one knows to be false." Perjury is a crime. The penalties for perjury are set forth in the California Penal Code.

Everything said during your deposition will be taken down and transcribed by the Court Reporter. Every question we ask every answer or comment you give everything said by your attorney, all will be duly transcribed.

It therefore is vital that if, at any time, you do not hear or do not understand any question, you tell us at once, so that we may have the opportunity immediately to repeat or rephrase our question to you. Obviously, if you do not promptly tell us otherwise, we will have no choice but to presume that you did clearly hear and understand each question, and that your answer to each question is based upon such complete and full understanding by you.

Please remember that the Court Reporter is only able to transcribe audible responses, so do not nod or shake your head, or grunt "uh huh" or "uh uh".

INITIAL HERE: _____   Page 2 of 4

251

Please also remember that the Court Reporter can record the words of only one person speaking at a time, so allow time for the question fully to be completed before you begin to respond. If you inadvertently are interrupted before you finish your answer, please tell me immediately. Otherwise we must presume that your answer as recorded was complete and you had nothing further to say on the subject.

At the conclusion of this session, the Court Reporter will transcribe what has been said into booklet form. You will have an opportunity to read that booklet and make any changes in the form or substance of the answer to any question that you feel necessary. Be advised that at time of trial we will question you before the Judge as to why you made any such changes, and we will take the position that your memory and recollections here today are as good or better than at any later time.

For your convenience we are prepared upon the signing of this acknowledgment and stipulation now by you and your attorney, to waive the requirement set forth in subparagraph (q)(1) of Section 2025 of the Code of Civil Procedure that you directly contact the deposition officer to arrange for the reading and signing of your deposition. Instead, your and your attorney's signing of this writing will constitute both of your express representations to us that within _____ days after delivery by the deposition officer of the transcript to your attorney at his office of record, you will make any changes and sign the original of the transcript under penalty of perjury and deliver it to us, Lurvey & Shapiro, 2121 Avenue of the Stars, Suite 1550, Los Angeles, California 90067. If we do not receive the signed transcript within

INITIAL HERE: _____   Page 3 of 4

252

the allotted period, a copy of the deposition shall be given the same effect as though duly and timely signed without any changes, and may be used for all purposes accordingly.

Your initials placed on pages 1, 2 and 3 of this explanation and Stipulation, and your signature and that of your attorney placed below on this final page, 4, will reflect your acknowledgment that you have read and understand all of the foregoing, and that you enter into the Stipulation for direct delivery of your deposition transcript to your attorney in accordance with the terms above.

DATED: _____   _____
                                   Signature of Deponent

                                   _____
                                   Signature of Attorney for Deponent

Page 4 of 4

253

EXPLANATION OF DEPOSITION PROCEEDINGS

(Witness in Pro Per)

TO THE WITNESS _____ :

    PLEASE READ THIS CAREFULLY. IT IS IMPORTANT TO YOU.

    This proceeding in which you are about to give testimony here today is known as a "deposition." You have advised us that you are appearing here without an attorney and that it is your free will and desire so to proceed. You are being handed this written explanation to read and review before your deposition even begins, so as best to inform you of the nature and effect of this proceeding and to save all of us the time and expense of orally reciting this explanation to you on the record after the deposition begins.

    If after reading this Explanation, you still have any questions about the nature of deposition proceedings, please ask them before the proceeding begins.

    Our purpose in taking your deposition is to obtain facts and information within your knowledge related to matters involved in this lawsuit or proceeding. We do not seek to trick or trap you. We do not wish to cause you discomfort.

    The person transcribing the deposition is a Certified Shorthand Reporter.

    At the outset, you will be placed under oath. You then will be asked questions which you are expected to answer fully and truthfully, under oath.

    Please do not guess. We request your best present recollection of the facts and events about which you will

INITIAL HERE: _____   Page 1 of 4

254

be questioned. We will presume therefore that whatever you testify

today is your best present recollection and not a guess.

Although this deposition is being held in the informal-

ity of these law offices, and coffee and soft drinks are available

throughout as our courtesy to you, this deposition does have all

the solemnity of courtroom testimony. Since you are under oath,

your testimony here today will have the same force and effect

and be subject to the same penalties as if you were testifying

in a courtroom before a judge.

Among such penalties to which you are subject is the

penalty of perjury. Perjury is defined as "willfully, and con-

trary to an oath administered, stating as true any material fact

which one knows to be false." Perjury is a crime. The penal-

ties for perjury are set forth in the California Penal Code.

Everything said during your deposition will be taken

down and transcribed by the Court Reporter. Every question we

ask, every answer or comment you give, all will be duly transcribed.

It therefore is vital that if, at any time, you do not

hear or do not understand any question, you tell us at once, so

that we may have the opportunity immediately to repeat or rephrase

our question to you. Obviously, if you do not promptly tell us

otherwise, we will have no choice but to presume that you did

clearly hear and understand each question, and that your answer

to each question is based upon such complete and full understanding

by you.

Please remember that the Court Reporter is only able to

transcribe audible responses, so do not nod or shake your head,

or grunt "uh huh" or "uh uh".

INITIAL HERE: _____   Page 2 of 4

1   Please also remember that the Court Reporter can record
2   the words of only one person speaking at a time, so allow time for
3   the question fully to be completed before you begin to respond. If
4   you inadvertently are interrupted before you can finish your
5   answer, please tell me immediately. Otherwise, we must presume that
6   your answer as recorded was complete and you had nothing further to
7   say on the subject.

8   At the conclusion of this session, the Court Reporter
9   will transcribe what has been said into booklet form. You will have
10 an opportunity to read that booklet and make and changes in the
11 form or substance of the answer to any question that you feel
12 necessary. Be advised that at time of trial we w: l question you
13 before the Judge as to why you made any such cha.ges and we will
14 take the position that your memory and recollections here today are
15 as good or better than at any later time.

16   For your convenience we are prepared upon the signing of
17 this acknowledgment and stipulation now by you to waive the
18 requirement set forth in subparagraph (q)(1) of Section 2025 of the
19 Code of Civil Procedure that you directly contact the deposition
20 officer to arrange for the reading and signing of your deposition.
21 Instead, your signing of this writing will constitute your express
22 representations to us that within ____ days after delivery by the
23 deposition officer of the transcript to you at the address written
24 below, you will make any changes and sign the original of the
25 transcript under penalty of perjury and deliver it to us, Lurvey &
26 Shapiro, 2121 Avenue of the Stars, Suite 1550, Los Angeles,
27 California 90067. If we do not receive the signed transcript within
28

INITIAL HERE: _____   Page 3 of 4

256

1 | the alloted period, a copy of the deposition shall be given the
2 | same effect as though duly and timely signed without any changes,
3 | and may be used for all purposes accordingly.

4 | Your initials placed on pages 1, 2 and 3 of this
5 | explanation and Stipulation, and your signature placed below on
6 | this final page, 4, will reflect your acknowledgment that you have
7 | read and understand all of the foregoing, and that you freely,
8 | voluntarily and knowingly enter into the Stipulation for direct
9 | delivery of your deposition transcript to you in accordance with
10 | the terms above.

11 |
12 | DATED:_____.   _____
                                         (Signature of Deponent)
13 |
14 | _____
15 | (Address to which Transcript
                                          Is to Be Sent. Please print)
16 |
17 |
18 |
19 |
20 |
21 |
22 |
23 |
24 |
25 |
26 |
27 |
28 |

68

Don't Forget the Hidden "Bonus" Assets

Phyllis G. Bossin

OFTEN WHEN WE ARE ENGAGING in the discovery process in preparation for trial and/or settlement, we look for the obvious assets and it is easy to overlook some assets that may have substantial value. A discussion of just some of these will follow:

1. Frequent-flyer points. Accumulated miles in airline mileage programs can have substantial value. As such, they should be deemed to be a marital asset and subject to equitable distribution to the extent that they are earned during the marriage. Most companies do not "own" the points earned by the employee nor do they require the employee to use such miles when traveling on business. They are a perk of business travel. When a spouse travels frequently on business, particularly to Europe or the Far East, which occurs more and more frequently, he or she can accumulate literally hundreds of thousands of miles. These are a valuable asset. Counsel must determine the marital number of miles, whether one spouse has diminished the mileage balance during separation and should be charged with receiving an asset of value, and how the miles will be divided. Certain airlines, in the case of divorce, allow the actual transfer of the miles to a spouse's account. Other airlines permit redemption, but not transfer, of the miles. In such cases, the decree or separation agreement should recite the number of miles that are marital, require the spouse owning the miles to maintain a minimum number of miles in the account, which number is the other spouse's one-half interest in the program, and set forth the procedure by which the spouse owning the miles will redeem them for the other spouse. The alternative method of valuing the miles would be to determine the number of miles needed to redeem a coach ticket anywhere in the United States and determine the average ticket price, thus putting a dollar value on the miles owned by the spouse. Most spouses would probably prefer to have access to the miles.

2. Hotel programs. Most major hotel chains now have programs whereby a member of the "club" can accumulate points, which can then be transferred to a participating airline or left in the program for certain benefits. Upon the accumulation of a certain number of points, the member is entitled to not only hotel upgrades but free trips. For example, the Westin Premier Club, upon accumulation of a certain level of points, awards free hotel stays at varying levels of its resorts. Such points clearly have value for purposes of equitable distribution.

3. Credit card point systems. In addition to the points earned directly with an airline, certain credit cards accumulate points which the members can use for various purposes. For example, American Express has the Membership Rewards Program, which allows the participant to transfer points to a mileage program but also permits the member to purchase products using the points. Such points have value.

4. Bank credit cards. Certain banks have credit cards that accumulate points on their own rather than transferring them directly to an airline account. (We all know that Citibank Visa points go directly to the American Airlines Advantage Program.) For example, Key Bank allows participating members in the Skymiles Program to accumulate points and then purchase an airline ticket on the airline of their choice. Such points also obviously have value.

5. Exclusive department stores. Some department stores allow certain card-holders, or all cardholders, to accumulate points which can then be used for hotel upgrades or other purposes. Nieman Marcus, for example, has such a program. Other department stores offer a direct financial reward for certain cardholders. For example, Saks Fifth Avenue has the Saks First Program, whereby members of the program accumulate points for every dollar they spend. At the end of the year, they actually receive a gift check, which is a percentage of their points, to be spent at Saks. This clearly has a value.

6. Bonds for swim clubs. A family that joins an organization such as a swim club is usually required to purchase a "bond," which is in addition to the annual dues. The parties may have held this asset for many years and have forgotten completely about it. However, it does have value and should be offset to the party receiving the membership.

7. Country club memberships and initiation fees. Such fees can be very substantial, particularly at exclusive clubs. The membership has in effect been purchased with the initiation fee, which is also in addition to the annual dues. This membership clearly has a value. Since often a wife is excluded from country club membership if her husband is the primary member, she can argue that she should receive credit for the value of the membership or that he should purchase a membership for her of equal value.

8. Built-up equity in an automobile lease. Many people assume that a leased car has no value whatsoever. However, depending upon the terms of the lease agreement, there may be some built-up equity. For example,

if the car is turned in prior to the expiration of the lease for the purpose of obtaining another leased car, and if the actual value of the car at the time it is turned in exceeds the predetermined residual value, a larger credit may be obtained as a down payment on the new leased vehicle. Furthermore, many lease companies require a deposit that is held until the end of the lease.

9. Season tickets to sporting events, theater, etc. These clearly have a value, even though it costs to renew them each year. They should be equitably divided between the parties. The decree or separation agreement should provide a method for dividing the actual tickets, with the parties alternating selecting. In addition, however, since generally only one of the parties "owns" the tickets, the other spouse should be given the right of first refusal to purchase the tickets if the other spouse no longer wishes to own them. This process is often overlooked by counsel.

Counsel thus needs to explore with his or her client at the time of the initial interview or during the financial information-gathering process all memberships that may potentially have value. Many clients do not understand that such assets are considered marital and thus will not volunteer this information. Client questionnaires should be revised to determine the existence of such "hidden" bonus assets.

VII

Premarital Agreements

AMONG THE ODDITIES of family law practice, negotiating premarital agreements has to be right up there on the list. We can handle legal representation between two people who regard each other with a degree of disgust normally reserved for warring countries. But how about legal representation for two people who pledge, often before God, their eternal love and loyalty? How long is "eternal"?

Truth is, many marriages are made to be broken and the lawyer must treat "eternal" as ending sooner or later. The pitfalls in pretending that divorce never will happen have haunted many spouses, and sometimes their lawyers as well.

Drafting premarital agreements has lots of pitfalls. Not only are the two "litigants" in love (at least, hopefully so), but no one knows when, if at all, the agreement will be needed. In fact, the paying parties are hoping that it never will be used. Sort of like a life insurance policy.

69 Let's face it, no one in his or her right mind (that excludes a lot of lawyers I know) drafts any agreement from scratch. A good place to start this part on premarital agreements is, therefore, with a form, and **William Mulloy** provides a good one.

70 Certain basic rules of thumb exist and **Ira Lurvey** provides some important do's and don'ts that everyone should know and remember.

71 One of the drawbacks in negotiating premarital agreements is the possibility of becoming a witness. If you think the attorney–client privilege rule prevents that, consider very carefully the tip from **Dan**

Jaffe and **David Luboff** regarding the lawyer's certification to these agreements and the possibility that such certification can constitute a waiver of the privilege.

72 Frequently, premarital agreements attempt to waive spousal rights under the Employee Retirement Income Security Act of 1974 (ERISA). **Kathleen Robertson** points out that several cases have held that these rights cannot be waived in a premarital agreement because the waiving party is not yet a spouse. Kathleen warns lawyers who draft prenuptial agreements to include ERISA waiver language and includes several possible variations.

69

Antenuptial Agreement

William P. Mulloy Sr.

ANTENUPTIAL AGREEMENT

THIS ANTENUPTIAL AGREEMENT (the "Agreement"), made and entered into this ___ day of _____, _____, by and between _____ of _____ County, _____, and _____ of _____ County, _____,

<u>WITNESSETH</u>:

WHEREAS, a marriage is contemplated between the parties hereto and said parties wish to establish their respective rights in and to their own and each other's property; and

WHEREAS, each party hereto desires to waive all rights he or she may have, after the consummation of said marriage, as husband, or wife, surviving spouse, heir of the other, or otherwise, in all real and personal property and all other assets which the other party now has or may acquire in the future.

NOW, THEREFORE, in consideration of the sum of One Dollar ($1.00), the receipt of which is hereby acknowledged, for the mutual promises contained herein, and for the further consideration of the solemnization of the proposed marriage between the parties hereto, the parties represent, warrant, covenant, and agree as follows:

1. Each party hereby waives, releases and relinquishes any and all claims and rights of every kind, nature or description that he or she may acquire by reason of the marriage as husband or wife, surviving spouse, heir of the other or otherwise in the party's property or estate under the present or future laws and statutes of the _____ of _____ or any other jurisdiction, including but not limited to:

   (a) Distributive share in the event of intestacy;

   (b) Right of election to take against the other's will;

   (c) Dower;

   (d) Curtesy;

   (e) Widow's or widower's allowance;

   (f) Homestead or residue in the other's dwelling house;

   (g) Right to act as, or nominate, the personal representative of the other's estate;

   (h) Support, maintenance, and the right to an equitable division of marital property and attorney's fees in a dissolution proceeding;

(i)   Inheritance;

(j)   Allowance for property existing from administration; and

(k)   All rights whatsoever which he or she might hereafter otherwise acquire (whether as husband or wife, surviving spouse, heir of the other, or otherwise) in all property of every nature that the other party now owns or may hereafter (including during the said marriage) own, become seized of or acquire.

2.   (a)   Each party hereby acknowledges that the other party has made a full disclosure of the nature, extent, and value of each party's separate estate and financial condition, as of the date of this Agreement. Each party further acknowledges that each has been afforded full and adequate opportunity to verify and to seek and receive independent advice concerning all such representations each party has made to the other party, the rights each party has in the property of the other party, the rights, which by the terms hereof, each party is relinquishing in the property of the other party, including, without being limited to, the marital rights to which each party is entitled and the marital rights which each party is surrendering hereunder.

(b)   Specifically, the parties hereto are aware that a surviving spouse is entitled under _____ law to renounce the terms of a decedent spouse's will, and in such event, the surviving spouse is entitled to the following property: (i) The right to one-third (1/3) of the decedent's surplus real property, of which he or she was seized at death, in fee simple; (ii) The right to one-third (1/3) of the decedent's real property, of which he or she was seized during the marriage but not at death, for life; and (iii) The right to one-half (1/2) of the decedent's surplus personal property, which is left by the decedent at death, absolutely and in fee simple. The parties hereby realize, acknowledge, and understand that such rights and entitlements under _____ law may change and be different at the death of either or both of the parties hereto. The parties also realize, acknowledge, and understand that either or both of them may not be _____ residents at death, that either or both of them may own property which does not pass pursuant to Kentucky law, and that either or both of them may die intestate.

(c)   Specifically, the parties hereto are aware of the following dower rights upon the death of a spouse intestate under _____ law: (i) The right to one-half (1/2) of the decedent's surplus real property, of which he or she was seized at death, in fee simple; (ii) The right to one-third (1/3) of the decedent's real property, of which he or she was seized during the marriage but not at death, for life; and (iii) The right to one-half (1/2) of the decedent's surplus real property left by the decedent at death, absolutely and in fee simple. The parties hereby realize, acknowledge and understand such rights and entitlements under _____ law may change and be different at the death of either or both of them. The parties also realize, acknowledge, and understand that either or both of them may not be _____ residents at death, that either or both of them may own property which does not pass pursuant to _____ law, and that either or both of them may die testate.

(d)   Specifically, the parties hereto realize, acknowledge, and understand that <u>each of them has no obligation whatsoever, either under law or as a prerequisite to marriage, to enter into this Agreement or to waive any of the marital rights waived hereunder.</u>

3.   Both parties have obtained independent legal consultation and advice concerning all matters herein set forth or referred to including the nature, purpose, and effect of this Agreement.

4.   Each party has exhibited to the other a schedule of his or her individual assets as of the date hereof, and said schedules have been fully reviewed and executed by the parties hereto, and have been attached hereto and made a part hereof as Exhibit A. These schedules identify substantially the nature, extent and value of all of the independent and separate property owned by each party as of the date of this Agreement, and each party realizes, acknowledges and accepts such values and the methods by which such values were obtained.

5.   Each party shall have the exclusive right to use, control, sell, give, devise, bequeath or dispose of all property, real, personal or otherwise, which either of them now own or may hereafter own, acquire or become seized of, free and clear of any claim of the other party, and each party shall request of the other party, his or her executors, administrators and assigns, make, execute, acknowledge and deliver all instruments of writing relating to any of said property and shall do all things that may be reasonably required of him or her to carry into effect the intent and provisions of this Agreement; and each waives, discharges and releases any right, title or interest whatsoever which he or she may acquire in the property of the other at the time hereafter by reason of the marriage, either during marriage or at the death of the other.

6.   _____ hereby consents to (i) _____ election to waive, (ii) his election, if any, to revoke such waiver, and (iii) any election by him to subsequently waive, a qualified joint and survivor annuity form of benefit under any plan of deferred compensation to which Section 401 (a)(11) of the Internal Revenue Code of 1954 (the "Code") or Section 205 of the Employee Retirement Income Security Act of 1974 ("ERISA") shall apply in which _____ currently or hereinafter be deemed a vested participant within the meaning of Section 417 (f)(1) of the Code and Section 205 (h)(1) of ERISA. _____ herein acknowledges that as a result of such consent, she may not be entitled to a death benefit under such

plans. In the event of a dissolution of her marriage to
_____, _____ hereby waives
any and all rights she may have had as a spouse to
_____ benefit under any plans subject to Section
401 (a) of the Code or Part 2 of Subtitle B of Title I of ERISA.

7. This Agreement contains the entire understanding of the
parties. There are no representations, warranties or promises
other than those expressly set forth herein.

8. This Agreement shall inure to the benefit of, and shall
be binding upon, the heirs, executors and administrators of the
parties, and shall be governed by and construed pursuant to, the
laws of the State of _____.

9. Nothing herein shall prevent any party from voluntarily
transferring property to the other, by Last Will and Testament or
otherwise.

10. Should any portion of this Agreement for any reason be
declared invalid or contrary to law, the remaining portions hereto
shall be binding upon the parties.

11. This Agreement is entered into between the parties in the
expectation that the marriage of the parties shall continue during
their joint lives. The parties have inserted in this Agreement
provisions with regard to a possible divorce or judicial
separation, although they do not contemplate such an event. The
provisions with regard to divorce or judicial separation have been
inserted in the hope that applicable state law will permit the
parties to contract as to property rights (and relinquishment
thereof) in the event of a divorce, since the agreement is not
entered into solely or primarily in expectation of a divorce or
judicial separation. If after the consummation of the marriage
either party hereto finds for cause or otherwise that he or she is
unable or unwilling to continue the marriage relationship, or if
either party hereto violates the bonds, obligations and duties of
matrimony, then neither party hereto shall have or take any right,
title or interest in or to the property of the other. If
_____ and _____ do not
marry, this Agreement shall be null and void.

12. The parties hereto agree (i) that this Agreement may be
recorded at any time by either party hereto, but only if the
Exhibits hereto are first removed and not put to record; and (ii)
either party may at any time put a Memorandum of Antenuptial
Agreement to record evidencing the primary terms hereof (but only
so long as the assets and liabilities of the parties are not
described or summarized) in lieu of recording this Antenuptial
Agreement itself.

IN WITNESS WHEREOF, the parties hereto have executed and acknowledged this Agreement as of the date first above written.

_____

_____

STATE OF _____   )
) SS:
COUNTY OF _____)

I, the undersigned, a Notary Public, do hereby certify that on the ___ day of _____, _____, the above and foregoing Instrument of writing was acknowledged and delivered before me by _____, a party hereto, to be his free and voluntary act and deed for the purposes therein set forth.

My commission expires:_____.

_____
NOTARY PUBLIC

STATE OF _____   )
) SS:
COUNTY OF_____   )

I, the undersigned a Notary Public, do hereby certify that on the ___ day of _____, _____, the above and foregoing Instrument of writing was acknowledged and delivered before me by _____, a party hereto, to be her free and voluntary act and deed for the purposes therein set forth.

My commission expires:_____.

_____
NOTARY PUBLIC

We certify that we prepared
the foregoing Antenuptial
Agreement this ___ day of
_____, _____.

_____

Counsel for _____

_____

Counsel for _____

70

Do's and Don'ts for Premarital Agreements

Ira Lurvey

INTRODUCTION

Changing attitudes toward divorce and the reduction in court resources available for disputes have given new impetus to enforcing premarital agreements to lessen the likelihood of litigation over property and related issues at the time of dissolution.

DRAFTING

A. When to use a premarital agreement; how to decide whether to enter into a premarital agreement;
   1. The party with the greater assets;
   2. The party with the greater desire for marriage.
B. Whom a party should look to for drafting a premarital agreement; and
C. What considerations should go into determining what to draft in a premarital agreement.

CONSIDER THE UNIFORM ACT

Premarital agreements now have reached the stage of legitimacy in which they are embodied within a Uniform Act. The terms and provisions of the Uniform Act are instructive regarding the present nature and scope of premarital agreements. The Uniform Act should be carefully considered in light of your particular state's adoption of it. In particular, the relevance of public policy in your state should be examined.

HOW TO GO ABOUT CONSIDERING THE TERMS

A. What are the real objectives you seek to obtain;
B. Compare what is available at law without need for a premarital agreement;

1. Listing of existing properties at time of marriage; what your state law provides;
2. Understanding the rules regarding commingling.
C. The static line: from agreement to marriage;
D. Property protections versus support considerations; and
E. Use of elections: do they really make a contribution;
   1. Compare the use of elections in probate;
   2. Do elections soften the underlying rules by implying that there is a question of enforceability.

DO'S AND DON'TS IN THE FINAL ANALYSIS

Treat the matter seriously, disdain "standard" clauses but rely on prior law for guidance, know what everything means, and say what you intend with utmost clarity. At the same time, document the full nature and extent of negotiations and all phases. Remember, there is no substitute for hard work and no shortcut for time spent. Do not simply walk away from disputes because that seems the easiest way. At the same time, do not ever underestimate the importance of separate, independent representation.

NEW CONCEPTS: PREMARITAL DECLARATORY RELIEF

Is it time for a fixed procedure by which parties to a premarital agreement can obtain an express judicial blessing on their pact before the marriage begins, thus removing for all time any postmarital challenge to the validity of the agreement? What about forms on the back of marriage licenses?

CONCLUSION

Premarital agreements may well be the instruments of control within the years to come. The New Century and the New Family may encircle the new understanding that entry into marriage no longer is simply the first chapter of entry into litigation on divorce. Clear knowledge of terms and conditions of termination at the time of inception may be the answer.

71

Lawyer Certifications to Prenuptial and Marital Settlement Agreements May Waive the Attorney–Client and Work–Product Privileges

Daniel J. Jaffe
David M. Luboff

MOST MARITAL SETTLEMENT AGREEMENTS and virtually all prenuptial agreements contain a variation of the following clause in the body of and at the end of the agreement:

> I am a lawyer licensed to practice in the state of X. I am a member of Smith & Jones. I have been retained by John Doe in connection with the negotiation and drafting of the foregoing prenuptial/marital settlement agreement. I have explained each of the terms of the agreement to him. He has acknowledged that he has read the agreement in its entirety and that he understands each of its terms. I have explained the legal effect of this agreement and the effect that it has on his rights and obligations otherwise obtaining as a matter of law. After being duly advised by the undersigned, he acknowledged that he executed this agreement voluntarily, free from any duress or undue influence, in the presence of the undersigned.

The purpose of this clause is to document the fact that each party to the agreement has been advised by counsel concerning the contents of the document and that the document, as signed, accurately sets forth the agreement that was reached between the parties and counsel.

ISSUE

By including the language quoted previously in the settlement or prenuptial agreement, has the client waived the attorney–client privilege? Can the opposing counsel, when the agreement is attacked in a later proceeding, depose the attacking party's lawyer at the time of the negotiating and drafting of the agreement?

The answer may depend on the type of challenge to the agreement. Some examples include:

1. "My lawyer never told me that . . ."
2. "My lawyer told me that . . ."
3. "I didn't understand that . . ."
4. "I was forced to sign because my spouse said he or she would . . ."
5. "My spouse (fiancé or fiancée) said, 'Don't worry about that. I'll never enforce' . . ."
6. "That provision is illegal and I didn't know . . ."
7. "My spouse (fiancé or fiancée) did not disclose that . . ."
8. "I was so emotionally upset I would have signed . . ."
9. "I didn't know I could have appraised . . . or discovered . . ."
10. "My lawyer was incompetent. He or she didn't . . ."
11. "I didn't have enough time to think about . . . examine . . ."
12. "The agreement is unconscionable. I don't get . . ."

The attorney–client privilege is of singular importance. Unfortunately, existing judicial precedents are of little assistance in determining whether there has been a waiver of the attorney–client privilege. Subject to certain exceptions, it applies to every confidential communication between a client and a lawyer. The privilege normally would protect all written and oral communications between the lawyer and the client. The defender of the validity of the agreement would like nothing more than to introduce into evidence:

A. Letter from client to lawyer: "My spouse (fiancé or fiancée) does not know that . . . , and that's why I am signing the agreement against your advice."
B. Letter from lawyer to client (known as CYA letter): "I have advised you that you are waiving:
    1. Your right to acquire an interest in marital property;
    2. Rights to support (in many states);
    3. An equal (or equitable) share of property on divorce;
    4. Probate and similar rights;
    5. Etc."

All of this evidence would negate the claim of an uninformed consent to an agreement.

In similar circumstances, courts have found that there has been a waiver of the attorney–client privilege or of the lawyer work-product privilege. In *Jarvis v. Jarvis* (1988), 141 Misc. 2d 207, 533 N.Y.S.2d 207, a commission was obtained in a Pennsylvania divorce action to secure the deposition of the New York lawyer who had advised the wife regarding her prenuptial agreement.

At the deposition, the wife's divorce lawyer asked questions of her prior lawyer concerning communications that he had with the wife outside of the husband's presence. The prior lawyer declined to answer certain questions that were posed by the husband's divorce lawyer.

The husband petitioned the New York court to compel the wife's prior lawyer to answer questions at the deposition and to produce his client file. The deposition questions related to the then-pending amendment to New York's Domestic Relations Law to provide for the equitable distribution of marital property. The lawyer was asked about how he had advised his client concerning this amendment. He was asked whether he had advised his client to expedite the signing of the prenuptial agreement.

The court stated that Pennsylvania law should be applied to determine the nature of the attorney–client privilege and to determine whether the privilege had been waived. The court stated that any effort to limit disclosure should be directed to the Pennsylvania court. Apparently, no request for a protective order was made to the Pennsylvania court.

The New York court concluded by ordering disclosure:

> Unless the information sought is irrelevant to the issues of the pending action, palpably improper, or unfair, disclosure procedure should be liberally construed in favor of eliciting the information sought. *Jarvis v. Jarvis, supra,* 533 N.Y.S.2d at 207.

In California, a lawyer was ordered to submit to his deposition after he had given a declaration in a dissolution proceeding. *In re Marriage of Niklas* (1989), 211 Cal. App. 3d 28, 258 *Cal. Rptr.* 921. Although his declaration did not relate to advice given regarding a prenuptial agreement or marital settlement agreement, the wife's lawyer gave a detailed statement concerning the husband's business, his income and assets, and the assets of the community. The lawyer claimed that he had personal knowledge of these matters. The trial court found that this amounted to a waiver of the attorney–client and lawyer work-product privileges. The court ordered the lawyer to answer questions at his deposition. Although he had announced his intention to do so, the lawyer never applied for an extraordinary writ to test the validity of the order.

When the lawyer did not provide satisfactory answers at his deposition, the trial court imposed sanctions. On appeal, the lawyer claimed that the original order requiring him to answer questions was erroneous and unenforceable by sanctions. The court of appeal disagreed, holding that so long as the order was merely erroneous and not in excess of the court's jurisdiction or unconstitutional, the lawyer was obligated to obey it.

The appellate court assumed (but did not decide) that the trial court was correct in its initial determination that the lawyer had waived the privileges by giving his declaration:

> The court below was within its jurisdiction in ruling that the protections of the work-product doctrine and the attorney–client privilege had been waived and ordering [the lawyer] and his client to comply with discovery, [the lawyer] and his client having failed to avail themselves of the opportunity to obtain appellate review. *Even if the trial court had erred* in issuing the discovery orders, sanctions could be imposed for the willful violation of the court's orders." *In re Marriage of Niklas, supra,* 211 Cal. App. 3d at 36, 258 *Cal. Rptr.* at 926. [Citations omitted; emphasis supplied.]

For other cases considering waiver of the attorney–client privilege, see *Weingarten v. Weingarten* (1989), 234 N.J. Super. 318, 560 A.2d 1243 (in a proceeding to set aside a marital settlement agreement, the wife who submitted declaration relating to confidential communications with her lawyer was held to have waived the attorney–client privilege with respect to issues raised in the declaration), and *Ostrin v. Ostrin* (1982), 86 App. Div. 655, 446 N.Y.S.2d 405 (the husband who at his deposition repeatedly referred the wife to his lawyer for information was held to have waived the privilege). The standard lawyer certifications attached to prenuptial agreements and marital settlement agreements have the potential to effect a waiver of the attorney–client and the lawyer work-product privileges. The most probable result is a waiver of the privileges, but only regarding the issues subsumed within the certifications. Some courts, however, may find that there has been a broader waiver of the privilege encompassing all communications between the lawyer and the client.

TIP

If you represent the monied party in the drafting of a prenuptial or marital settlement agreement and you wish to obtain maximum protection against later claims that the agreement is invalid, you should attempt to obtain maximum certification by a lawyer.

If you represent the nonmonied party and you wish to protect the CYA letter or other attorney–client communications that would show that your client had knowledge of and understood the adverse provisions of the agreement, you should sign the document as "approved as to form only." Try to avoid giving a certification, or if you must give a certification, include a specific provision in the text of the agreement that the attached certifications do not constitute a waiver of the attorney–client or lawyer work-product privileges.

72

Prenuptial Agreements and ERISA: Can Your Client Waive Rights to an ERISA-Qualified Retirement Plan in a Prenuptial Agreement?

Kathleen Robertson

THE EMPLOYEE RETIREMENT INCOME SECURITY ACT (ERISA), 29 U.S.C. § 1001 *et seq.*, presents special problems in the context of prenuptial agreements. ERISA contains an anti-alienation clause that prevents transfer or invasion of ERISA pension assets. Because of the ERISA anti-alienation provisions and the federal preemption of state law regarding ERISA-regulated retirement benefits, family law courts have only one way to assign ERISA-regulated retirement benefits. A Qualified Domestic Relations Order is required.

What if you are presented with a client who wants to waive any and all rights to an ERISA-regulated retirement plan in a prenuptial agreement?

As a family law practitioner, you should be aware that an attempt to waive survivor benefits derived from an ERISA-regulated retirement plan via a prenuptial agreement will fail. The only way to waive ERISA survivor benefits is to follow the strict requirements of 29 U.S.C. §1055(c)(1) and (2). Since the parties signing the prenuptial agreement are not yet married, they cannot meet the first criterion of an ERISA survivor benefit waiver: a spouse must make the waiver.

As highlighted by the recent decision in *Hagwood v. Newton*, No. 01-1909 (U.S. Court of Appeals, 4th Circuit, February 26, 2002), a premarital agreement standing alone does not meet the waiver requirements of 29 U.S.C. § 1055(c).

One month before their marriage, Toni Odom and Charles Newton signed a premarital agreement. The premarital agreement was clear regarding the parties' intent. It provided that "all separately owned property and the income from it belonging to each of them at the commencement of the marriage or obtained by either of them during the marriage shall remain his or her separate property." The agreement referred to stocks, bonds, and employee savings and retirement accounts. In addition, Newton explicitly waived any rights that he had in Odom's "employee savings and security plans and retirement accounts." Newton also explicitly waived all rights to a distributive share of Odom's estate. Two years after the marriage, Odom died, and Odom's estate sought to enforce the premarital agreement against Newton's survivor rights in Odom's ERISA-regulated retirement plans.

The court was asked to decide whether an otherwise valid premarital agreement could operate as a waiver of a spouse's right to survivor benefits under an ERISA-regulated retirement plan. The court concluded that the premarital agreement in that case did not meet the ERISA waiver requirements, *and* that premarital agreements *in general* would not be able to meet these requirements. The *Hagwood* court noted that 29 U.S.C. § 1055(c)(2)(A) provides that benefits may be waived only if "(i) the spouse of the participant consents in writing to such election [to waive], (ii) such election designates a beneficiary (or a form of benefits) which may not be changed without spousal consent (or the consent of the spouse expressly permits designation by the participant without any requirement of further consent of the spouse), and (iii) the spouse's consent acknowledges the effect of such election [to waive] and is witnessed by a plan representative or a notary public." *Hagwood* at p.4.

It is unclear whether a prenuptial agreement will be sufficient to waive other ERISA retirement rights. Some jurisdictions have found that only ERISA survivor benefits are restricted from waiver by prenuptial agreements under the theory that 29 U.S.C. §1055 pertains solely to a spouse's right to waive rights to qualified joint and survivor annuities.

Other jurisdictions find no distinction between survivor benefits and other ERISA-regulated rights and have held that no ERISA-regulated rights may be waived in a premarital agreement. Know your jurisdiction's position on this issue!

Can the family law practitioner draft around the ERISA waiver predicament? That is, by including a provision that requires each party to execute and deliver all necessary documents to accomplish the ERISA waiver *after* the parties are married?

The *Hagwood* decision answered this question in the affirmative. The premarital agreement in *Hagwood* contained a provision that provided that "each of the parties to this Agreement shall execute, acknowledge, and deliver all documents and instruments that may be deemed necessary to accomplish the terms of this Agreement." Despite the fact that the prenuptial agreement did not specifically require the parties to execute and deliver all documents required to effect the waiver of ERISA rights, the *Hagwood* court found that Odom could have compelled Newton to execute a waiver of his survivor benefits (after marriage) that met the requirements of § 1055(c), but never did so. *Hagwood, supra,* at p. 5.

Family law practitioners are well advised to include specific language regarding the waiver of ERISA-regulated rights when drafting prenuptial agreements. Advise your clients, in writing, that it is essential that he/she provide the necessary waiver documents to their new spouse.

Variations of typical ERISA waiver paragraphs follow:

EXAMPLE 1

Immediately after the marriage of the parties or at any other time thereafter upon request, each party shall execute, acknowledge, and deliver any documents necessary to effectuate the terms of this agreement. More specifically, each party shall, upon request of the other party and upon being provided with the necessary documents, execute all necessary documents to execute a waiver of any and all rights to ERISA-regulated retirement plans, or benefits derived there from including survivor benefits, in accordance with 29 U.S.C. § 1055.

EXAMPLE 2

Immediately upon solemnization of the marriage and at any other time thereafter upon request, the parties shall execute waivers of their respective rights in each other's pension, profit sharing, 401(k), Keogh, individual retirement account, or any other retirement and/or deferred account plan or benefit plans consistent with the provisions of this Agreement.

EXAMPLE 3

The parties shall execute waivers of their respective rights in each other's pension, profit sharing, 401(k), individual retirement account, or any other retirement and/or deferred account plan or benefit plans consistent with the provisions of this Agreement immediately after their marriage and at any other time thereafter upon the request of the other party. The parties acknowledge that their attorneys have explained that they cannot waive ERISA rights without executing additional documents and that ERISA waivers must be executed after they are married to be effective.

EXAMPLE 4

Without limiting the generality of the other provisions of this Agreement, including the other provisions of this Article, _____ and _____ each (a) waives, as between them, any rights he or she may now or hereafter have to a qualified pre-retirement survivor annuity or to a qualified joint and survivor annuity from the other party's employee benefit plans, systems, or trusts, or, with respect to a defined benefit or defined contribution plan or other plans referred to in this Section ____ to the other party's vested account balance (collectively, "Annuities, Plans, and Trusts"), (b) consents to any beneficiary designation, form of distribution, withdrawal, or benefit distribution made at any time by or on behalf of the other party (collectively "Designation or Distribution"). The parties agree that to implement this provision, it shall be necessary to sign waivers after the marriage. Each agrees to promptly execute consents, waivers, or other documents reasonably required by the other party, including any which may be required by such Annuities, Plans, or Trusts or under law at any time in order to effectuate any waiver of the rights which the other party may now or hereafter have in such Annuities, Plans, or Trusts or other employment-related or deferred compensation plan (including to any vested account balance) as well as any consent to any Designation or Distribution. The employee benefit plans in which _____ currently participates are included in Exhibit ___.

VIII

Taxes

BEING A CAPABLE LITIGATOR and an armchair psychologist (as divergent as those roles are) is not sufficient to be a quality family law practitioner. One also needs to be an accountant—or at least to have a good familiarity with tax law.

Properly used, the tax law is a family lawyer's best friend. The tax code can be used to make payments more palatable to the payor. By using different tax brackets, the tax code can be used to benefit both parties and their children—a kind of government subsidy. The tax code also can take some of the bite out of paying legal fees.

Unfortunately, the tax-code labyrinth can haunt a family law practitioner, as well. The many details one needs to keep in mind can easily be forgotten, and the result can be disastrous to a client.

In this part, our experts give their ideas on how to receive the blessings of a complicated tax law and avoid the curses.

73   The tax law requires every wage employee to receive a W-2 form. It's about one-third of a page in size. What can you learn from such a short, standard document? You'd be surprised. **Peggy Podell** dissects a W-2, and the wealth of information she uncovers is remarkable.

74   Clients do not like paying lawyers' fees—after all, the same money can be used for other far more enjoyable things. Making all or a portion of lawyers' fees tax-deductible takes some of the sting out of paying—as well as encourages the payment of fees in the first place. **Ian McLachlan** provides examples of when lawyers' fees in divorce actions might be deductible and the IRS becomes your best friend.

75 Some assets carry tax attributes with them. Where these attributes are positive, such as a loss carryforward, it is a good thing for the client receiving the asset. Where these attributes are negative, well, the word "malpractice" raises its ugly head. The point is, the matrimonial lawyers need to know *before* the final award. **Roseanna Purzycki** discusses the tax attributes, both good and bad, that follow assets after the divorce.

76 The rules for qualifying as an innocent spouse are very narrow. When you represent the economically dependent spouse, it is not a good idea to count on the mercy of the IRS if tax audits and delinquencies arise following the divorce from jointly filed returns. **Marshall Wolf** provides a sample form tax indemnification agreement designed to protect the economically dependent spouse.

77 Now for the dark side—what the court gives, the IRS can take away. To avoid unpleasant surprises, **Sam Schoonmaker** warns of the "secret lien" and suggests means for avoiding it.

78 While alimony deduction is a great means of using the tax code to both parties' advantages, it cannot be used to disguise a property transfer. **David Hopkins** discusses the alimony recapture rule, giving its history and mechanics and an easy-to-follow schedule for avoiding recapture problems. David includes sample language to adjust payments in the event of an unintended recapture.

79 OK, so you think you know all the tax rules for property transfer in a divorce. Well, do you know that there are different rules if one of the parties is a nonresident alien? If you did not know that, you need to read **Marjorie O'Connell**'s tip on this subject.

80 Almost every divorce involves the issue of the implication of filing joint tax returns. Also, many divorces involve the issue of the sale of a home. The combination of these issues is of critical importance, and **Peggy Podell** navigates these dangerous waters.

81 Any tip that begins with the word "inexpensive" catches my attention. **Barbara Kahn Stark** tells how to get some valuable tax information for free or at a minimal cost.

82 **Peggy Podell** discusses IRS rules for waiving the dependency exemption for minor children and how to handle cases where a party does not cooperate in signing the necessary forms.

83 Typically, spousal support payments are tax deductible to the payer and taxable to the recipient. However, according to **Melvyn Frumkes**, author of *Frumkes on Divorce Taxation*, this does not have to be the case. Rather, as is explained in this hot tip, the court may have the authority to designate spousal support to be nontaxable payments.

84   Dividing nonqualified deferred compensation plans and nonstatutory stock options in a divorce is a pain in the you-know-where and
rife with potential tax issues. Recently, however, the IRS issued *Revenue Ruling 2002-22,* which discusses the tax consequences for these
types of assets. In his hot tip, **Don Schiller** describes the revenue ruling and its impact and provides some sample language for settlement
agreements.

73

What Can You Learn from a W-2?

*Peggy L. Podell**

A REVIEW OF AN INDIVIDUAL'S W-2 FORM can help you develop lines of financial inquiry:

A. Many times the only financial documents you have at the commencement of an action are the parties' tax returns and W-2 forms.

B. Sometimes W-2 forms are glossed over in the race to review "more important" financial documents. Deceptively simple, the W-2 can give you an idea of what has occurred, and is occurring, financially.

C. Following is a W-2 form.

a Control number	22222	Void ☐	For Official Use Only ▶ OMB No. 1545-0008		
b Employer identification number				1 Wages, tips, other compensation $	2 Federal income tax withheld $
c Employer's name, address, and ZIP code				3 Social security wages $	4 Social security tax withheld $
				5 Medicare wages and tips $	6 Medicare tax withheld $
				7 Social security tips $	8 Allocated tips $
d Employee's social security number				9 Advance EIC payment $	10 Dependent care benefits $
e Employee's first name and initial	Last name			11 Nonqualified plans $	12a See instructions for box 12 $
				13 Statutory employee ☐ Retirement plan ☐ Third-party sick pay ☐	12b $
				14 Other	12c $
					12d $
f Employee's address and ZIP code					

15 State	Employer's state ID number	16 State wages, tips, etc. $	17 State income tax $	18 Local wages, tips, etc. $	19 Local income tax $	20 Locality name
		$	$	$	$	

Form **W-2** **Wage and Tax Statement** (99)   **2002**   Department of the Treasury—Internal Revenue Service
For Privacy Act and Paperwork Reduction Act Notice, see separate instructions.

Copy A For Social Security Administration—Send this entire page with Form W-3 to the Social Security Administration; photocopies are **not** acceptable.   Cat. No. 10134D

Do Not Cut, Fold, or Staple Forms on This Page — Do Not Cut, Fold, or Staple Forms on This Page

---

*The author would like to thank David M. Franklin, CPA, Milwaukee, Wisconsin, for his assistance in preparing this outline.

Employers are required to check various boxes on the employee's W-2 form to alert the taxing authorities to certain financial information. This information also can be used to develop a discovery plan by the lawyer representing the other spouse.

A. Box 13 contains a number of other boxes that are to be checked if applicable. Some of these may be of interest to you.

   1. Statutory employee. This box is checked if the employee's earnings are not subject to federal income tax withholding. The earnings still would be subject to Social Security and Medicare taxes.

   2. Retirement plan. This box is checked if the employee was an active participant (i.e., a contribution made during the year in question) in a retirement plan maintained by the employer (i.e., a qualified pension, profit-sharing, or stock bonus plan described in IRC 401, including a 401(k) plan; an annuity plan, annuity contract or custodial account described in IRC 403(b), a simplified employee pension (SEP); a SIMPLE retirement account; a trust described in IRC 501(c)(18); or a plan for Federal, state, or local government employees). If contributions were made to a non-qualified plan or an s. 457 plan, this box would not be checked.

   3. Third-party sick pay. This box is checked only if the individual or entity preparing the form is a third-party sick pay payer filing the form for the insured's employee or is an employer reporting sick pay payments that were made by a third party.

B. Box 9, Advance EIC payment, is used to show the total amount paid to the employee as advance earned-income credit payments.

C. Box 1. Wages, tips, other compensation. The amount shown in this box, before any payroll deductions, includes the following:

   1. Total wages and tips paid.

   2. Total prizes and awards paid.

   3. Total noncash payments, including fringe benefits.

   4. Certain business expense reimbursements.

   5. Taxable benefits from an s. 125 (cafeteria) plan.

   6. Under certain circumstances the cost of accident and health insurance, group life insurance, and qualified long-term care services.

   7. All other compensation including items such as certain scholarships and fellowship grants and moving expense payments.

   8. This figure in Box 1 excludes elective deferrals except s. 501(c)(18) contributions.

D. Box 11. Nonqualified plans. The total amount of any distribution from a nonqualified plan or s. 457 plan is shown in this box. The amount also is included in Box 1.

E. Box 12. This box is used for entries covering a variety of categories. Code letters are used to identify the category. Some examples include the following:

1. If the employer provided more than $50,000 of group–term life insurance to the employee, the cost of the coverage over $50,000 is shown in Box 12 preceded by the letter "c." This amount also is included in Boxes 1, 3 (up to the Social Security wage base), and 5.

2. The amount of the elective deferral made to an s. 401(k), 403(b), 408(k)(6), 457(b), or 501(c)(18)(D) plan is reported in this box preceded by the letter code corresponding to the type of plan.

   a. The letter codes are: D—s. 401(k); E—s. 403(b); F—s. 408(k)(6); G—s. 457(b); and H—s. 501(c)(18)(D).

   b. The amount reported is only the portion of the employee's salary or other compensation not received because of the deferral.

   c. Nonelective contributions made by the employer on behalf of the employee are not elective deferrals and are not reported in Box 12.

   d. Box 12 codes are as follows:

      1) A—Uncollected Social Security or RRTA tax on tips;

      2) B—Uncollected Medicare tax on tips;

      3) C—Cost of group–term life insurance over $50,000;

      4) D—Elective deferrals to an s. 401(k) cash or deferred arrangement;

      5) E—Elective deferrals under an s. 403(b) salary reduction agreement;

      6) F—Elective deferrals to an s. 408(k)(6) salary reduction SEP;

      7) G—Elective deferrals and employer contributions to an s. 457(b) deferred compensation plan;

      8) H—Elective deferrals to an s. 501(c)(18)(D) tax-exempt organization plan;

      9) J—Nontaxable sick pay;

      10) K—20 percent excise tax on excess golden parachute payments;

      11) L—Substantiated employee business expense reimbursements;

      12) M—Uncollected Social Security tax or RRTA tax on cost of group–term life insurance over $50,000 (for former employees);

      13) N—Uncollected Medicare tax on cost of group–term life insurance over $50,000 (for former employees);

      14) P—Excludable moving expense reimbursements paid directly to employee;

      15) Q—Military employee basic housing, subsistence, and combat zone compensation;

      16) R—Employer contributions to an Archer MSA;

17) S—Employee salary reduction contributions under a s. 408(p) SIMPLE;

18) T—Adoption benefits:

19) V—Income from the exercise of nonstatutory stock options(s).

g. Only four items can be entered in Box 12. If additional items need to be reported, a separate form W-2 is to be used to report the additional items.

F. Box 14. Other. This box can be used by the employer to provide information to the employee on various topics. These include the lease value of a vehicle provided to the employee, educational assistance payments, union dues, and health insurance premiums deducted.

G. Box 10. Dependent care benefits. The total amount of dependent care benefits under s. 129 that are paid for or incurred by the employer for the benefit of the employee are to be reported in this box. If it is employer-provided or -sponsored day care, the employer is to report the fair market value of these services. Also to be reported are amounts paid or incurred in an s. 125 (cafeteria) plan. The total reported should include any amount in excess of the exclusion.

For more information, see the IRS's Instructions for Form W-2 Wage and Tax Statement which can be accessed at the IRS's website.

74

Are Lawyers' Fees Deductible?

C. Ian McLachlan

GENERALLY, LAWYERS' FEES for personal representation are not deductible. *United States v. Gilmore*, 372 U.S. 53, 1963. However, lawyers' fees for the production or collection of sums includable in gross income and for the management, conservation, or maintenance of *income-producing* property and for advice related to the determination of taxes or tax due are deductible. § 212 Internal Revenue Code.

Examples include:

1. Production or collection of income;
   A. Alimony. *R. K. Wild*, 42 TC 706.
   B. Arrearages (including interest). *D. Buckley Est.*, 37 TC 664.
   C. Alimony payor not entitled to deductions. *T. A. O'Loughlin*, 61-1 TC 9366.
2. Management, conservation, or maintenance of property held for production of income;
   A. Expenses relating to establishing ownership rights in income-producing property in divorce not deductible but fees related to possession of or participation in income from property already owned deductible. *G. M. Hahn*, 35 TCM 509. Note: *Gilmore* "Origin of Litigation."
3. In connection with determination, collection or refund of tax. *W. K. Carpenter*, 338 F.2d 366.

Limits on deductibility: Lawyers' fees are miscellaneous deductions to individuals. Miscellaneous deductions are subject to the 2 percent limitation. Miscellaneous deductions are subject to "phase out." Miscellaneous deductions are not excludable in determining the Alternative Minimum Tax.

Other alternatives include:

- A portion of lawyers' fees may be added to the acquisition cost of real estate or other property. *Gilmore.*
- Separate bills may be rendered for related discrete services, i.e., real estate, estate planning, etc.

- A corporation could properly deduct fees paid by it to defend a lawsuit brought against it by a spouse to preserve marital assets where costs incurred to resist action that interfered with business account of corporation. *U.S. v. R. Dolese,* 605 F.2d 1146 (10th Cir. 1979), *cert. den.* 446 U.S. 961.

75

Tax Attributes—
Who Gets Them after a Divorce?

Roseanna L. Purzycki

CARRYOVER BASIS IN PROPERTY TRANSFERRED

Because no gain or loss is recognized on the property transfer pursuant to Section 1041, the transferee will acquire a carryover basis in the property received (even when liabilities exceed basis).

The holding period also carries over.

The basis rule applies even when there has been a bona fide sale between spouses or former spouses. The transferee cannot declare a step up in basis regardless of the consideration given. Thus, the taxation on the property's appreciation is conveyed from the transferor to the transferee.

SUSPENDED LOSSES FROM PASSIVE ACTIVITIES

IRC § 469(h)(5) provides: "In determining whether a taxpayer materially participates, the participation of the spouse of the taxpayer shall be taken into account." Reg. § 1.469-5T(f)(3) clarifies that this is true without regard to whether the spouses file a joint return for the taxable year. Note that the legal status of the marriage is important because it could affect the classification of the activity to the nonparticipating spouse when the other spouse is a material or active participant in the activity.

For tax years after December 31, 1993, individuals engaged in real property trades and businesses will be allowed to take passive activity losses against nonpassive income if certain requirements are met. They are:

1. More than 50 percent of the individual's personal services during the tax year are performed in real property trades or businesses in which the individual materially participates; and
2. The individual performs more than 750 hours of service in the real property trades or businesses in which the individual materially participates. On a Married Filing Jointly return, one spouse must separately satisfy both requirements.

When passive activity losses (PAL) and credits are disallowed for a taxable year, the disallowed items must be identified by property and carried forward under IRC § 469(b). Reg. § 1.469-1T(j)(3) states:

If an individual:

1. Does not file a joint return for the taxable year; and
2. Filed a joint return for the immediately preceding taxable year; then the passive activity deductions and credits allocable to such individual's activities for the taxable year under Reg. § 1.469-1T(f)(4) shall be determined by taking into account the items of deduction and credit attributable to the individual's interests in passive activities for the immediately preceding taxable year.

Although the regulations do not provide rules for determining a spouse's proper share of the deductions shown on a joint return, this determination presumably should be made by reference to each spouse's legal interest in items of income and expense reflected on the joint return.

When there is a complete disposition of passive activity property by sale, any overall loss from the activity is recognized and allowed against all types of income. The suspended losses are allowed in full as a deduction on the disposition. (IRC § 469(g)(1))

IRC § 469(j)(6) provides a special rule for disposition by *gift* by which the "basis of such interest immediately before the transfer shall be increased by the amount of any passive activity losses allocable to such interest with respect to which a deduction has not been allowed." Thus, in gift dispositions, suspended losses are not triggered to the transferor but added to the basis of the transferred property in the hands of the transferee.

When there is a transfer of a passive activity between spouses during marriage, suspended losses are not triggered because the transfer is between related parties. (IRC § 469(g)(1)(B)) Related parties are defined by IRC § 267(b) or IRC § 707(b)(1). The family of an individual shall include only brothers and sisters, spouse, ancestors, and lineal descendants.

When IRC § 1041 applies to a transfer of a passive activity interest to a spouse or former spouse, the recipient treats the transfer as a gift. Thus, the suspended losses are added to the basis of the property.

The increase in basis if it is a transfer of the actual asset (i.e., apartment building) allows the recipient spouse to take additional depreciation deductions. Depreciation is computed according to the rules for property acquired by gift. Property acquired by gift after 1986 is subject to the Modified Accelerated Cost Recovery System depreciation and recovery rules. If the transfer is of a partnership interest, then the suspended losses added to the basis are not depreciable.

If the transferor of the passive activity wants to recognize the suspended losses, then the property must be sold to a third party.

CAPITAL LOSS CARRYFORWARD

The amount of capital loss from a joint return that is carried forward to separate returns is determined by identifying which sales and other dispositions caused the loss. Then the capital assets sold must be classified as community property or separate property of one of the spouses. If the loss resulted from a community property asset, then the loss is split evenly. If the loss is from one spouse's separate property, then that capital loss is a tax attribute of and follows that particular spouse.

CHARITABLE CONTRIBUTIONS CARRYOVERS

When there are unused charitable contribution carryovers from a joint return and the taxpayers file separate returns during the carryover period, then the taxpayers must allocate the contribution carryover in accordance with rules outlined in Reg. § 1.170A-10(d)(4)(i). Basically, the taxpayers must allocate the contribution carryover as if they had filed separate tax returns instead of joint returns.

NET OPERATING LOSS (NOL)

NOL carryforward from a joint return to separate returns. Reg § 1.172-7(d) proscribes rules for determining the separate NOL carryover that each spouse is allocated from a joint return that is eligible to be reported on a subsequent separate return. The purpose of the method is to divide income and deductions reported on a joint return between the two spouses in a manner that reflects the actual allocation that would have occurred had separate returns been filed.

NOL carryback from a separate return to a joint return. The IRS has issued Rev. Rul. 86-57, 1986-1 CB 362, where a divorced spouse with an NOL must share the refund with the former spouse with whom he or she filed the prior joint return. If a divorcing taxpayer anticipates an NOL in a subsequent year, the taxpayer should consider an election to forgo the carryback period (that includes a joint return year) or should include a clause in the marital settlement agreement that allocates the expected refund to the taxpayer with the NOL.

NOL carryforward from a separate return to a joint return. An NOL incurred by one spouse before the marriage cannot be used to offset the other spouse's income on a joint return (*Calvin v. U.S.* (CA-10, 1965), 354 F.2d 202). The NOL can be applied only against the taxpayer's separate taxable income.

Carryover period. A taxpayer with an NOL in the current year may carry the loss back three years and then forward for fifteen years. This presents problems when the taxpayers with the NOL have a different filing status from year to year. The taxpayer with the NOL may make an election to forgo the three-year carryback period.

76

Form Tax Indemnification Agreement for Economically Dependent Spouse Regarding Income Tax Returns

Marshall J. Wolf

<u>TAX INDEMNIFICATION AGREEMENT</u>

This agreement entered into this _____ day of

_____, _____ by and between [NAME]˜ and [NAME]˜,

hereinafter referred to respectively as husband and wife.

W I T N E S S E T H :

WHEREAS [NAME]˜ and [NAME]˜ are husband and wife living

separate and apart; and

WHEREAS the parties have previously filed joint federal and

state tax returns and husband desires to have wife join with him

in filing joint returns for [YEAR]˜; and

WHEREAS husband has provided the information for and

procured the preparation of all such returns including the

returns for [YEAR]˜; and

WHEREAS wife has relied and continues to rely upon the

representations of husband regarding the preparation and

statements contained within said returns; and

WHEREAS in consideration of wife agreeing to join in signing

joint returns for [YEAR]˜, husband agrees to assume certain

responsibilities and warrant the information contained in said

returns, including specifically the returns for [YEAR]˜.

NOW, THEREFORE, in consideration of the mutual promises hereinafter set forth, the parties agree as follows:

I. <u>Joint Returns for [YEAR]˜</u>.

Wife agrees to join with husband in filing joint federal and state income tax returns for [YEAR]˜. Husband shall be responsible for the preparation and filing of said returns.

II. <u>Payment of Amounts Due</u>.

Husband shall be solely responsible for and shall pay any and all payments due, whether for taxes, interest, penalties, deficiency claims, assessments or otherwise in connection with the joint federal and state income tax returns for the year [YEAR]˜ and all previous years wherein joint returns were filed by the parties.

III. <u>Warranties as to Accuracy</u>.

A. Husband warrants that the federal and state joint returns for [YEAR]˜ attached hereto as Exhibits A and B are true, accurate and complete copies of such returns as filed with the Federal Income Revenue Service and Treasurer of the State of Ohio.

B. Husband warrants and represents that the representations and statements including specifically his personal or business income and expenses on the [YEAR]˜ returns and all prior joint returns are true and accurate.

2

C. Husband warrants that he shall not cause any amended return to be filed without the express written agreement of wife.

IV. Indemnification and Hold Harmless Protection.

A. Husband shall indemnify and hold wife harmless from any and all financial responsibility or sums found to be due arising out of the filing of the [YEAR]˜ joint returns or for any later imposed tax payments, interest, penalties, assessments or deficiency claims on said returns or any joint returns previously filed by the parties.

B. In the event that wife retains counsel to represent her interests due to any audit, deficiency assessment or other proceeding related to the [YEAR]˜ joint returns or any joint returns heretofore filed by the parties, any costs incurred by her for such purpose shall be assumed and paid by the husband who hereby indemnifies and holds the wife harmless from the payment of any such costs.

V. Full Cooperation.

Husband and wife agree to fully cooperate in the signing of any and all powers of attorney or other documents which may be necessary for them or their authorized agents to defend against deficiency claims, claims for deficiency, penalty or interest assessment and/or papers required to complete any tax audits. The parties shall extend the same full cooperation as expressed

3

in the foregoing sentence to any papers compromising or settling any disputes which may arise with regard to previously filed joint tax returns.

VI. Revocable Power of Attorney.

On request of the husband or his authorized representatives, the wife shall sign a revocable power of attorney to designate husband or his designated agent as her attorney-in-fact to sign her name on any papers related to tax audits or asserted claims for tax deficiency, penalties or interest. The husband or his representatives shall inform the wife when the revocable power of attorney is used by the husband or the designated agent. Copies shall be provided to the wife or her counsel. Such power of attorney provided for in this Article shall be limited to matters arising out of filed joint tax returns.

VII. Amendments.

If deemed appropriate, joint returns may be amended and the husband or his designated agent shall have the right to file such amended returns, after first submitting same to wife. The Full Cooperation and Revocable Power of Attorney articles of this agreement shall apply equally to any amended return so filed. All provisions of the Indemnification and Hold Harmless Protection article shall apply to any amended returns so filed. If any refunds are generated by amended returns, the parties shall be entitled to same equally.

4

Both parties represent and acknowledge that they have sought and received the benefit of independent legal counsel before signing this agreement.

IN WITNESS WHEREOF the parties have signed and acknowledged this indemnification agreement in four counterparts, each of which shall constitute an original.

_____   _____
WITNESS

_____   _____
WITNESS

5

77

Beware the Secret Lien

Samuel V. Schoonmaker III

FACTS

During their marriage, Mr. and Mrs. Jones filed separate federal income tax returns. During 2000, Mr. Jones filed his tax return but failed to pay the tax.

The parties entered into a separation agreement and their marriage was dissolved on December 19, 2001. Pursuant to the agreement and decree, the husband transferred his entire interest in the family home by quitclaim deed to the wife. The wife recorded that quitclaim deed on December 30, 2001, after conducting a rundown search that showed no liens on the property other than a first mortgage.

On December 2, 2001, seventeen days before the divorce and twenty-eight days before the quitclaim deed was recorded, the IRS made an assessment of federal income tax against Mr. Jones for the unpaid taxes on his 1984 return.

In consideration for the transfer of title, Mrs. Jones assumed responsibility for the outstanding principal balance on the first mortgage and paid Mr. Jones $60,000 in cash.

Prior to recording the quitclaim deed on December 30, 2001, neither Mr. nor Mrs. Jones had any knowledge whatsoever of the federal tax assessment.

Almost one year later, specifically on November 22, 2002, the IRS filed a tax lien against Mr. Jones's interest in the real estate. The IRS claims that the lien is superior to the rights of Mrs. Jones pursuant to the quitclaim deed.

THE LAW

Section 6321 of the IRC of 1986 provides for the existence of a lien in favor of the United States to secure the payment of taxes that attaches to all property belonging to the taxpayer. Section 6322 states that the lien arises at the time of the *assessment of the tax* and continues until the tax liability is discharged.

Under § 6322, the lien against Mrs. Jones's property arose on December 2, 2001, the date on which the income tax assessment against Mr. Jones was made somewhere within the IRS bureaucracy. The making of the assessment was in all respects secret and not known to anyone except the IRS. To avoid the burden of the lien, Mrs. Jones must prove that she purchased the property from Mr. Jones to qualify her as a "purchaser" under Code § 6323(a). If she can prove she is a purchaser, her lien will be superior to the IRS's. Otherwise, Mr. Jones was the owner of the property when the assessment was made, and the tax lien is superior to the interest of Mrs. Jones.

A purchaser is defined under the statute as "a person who for adequate and full consideration in money or money's worth acquires an interest in property that is valid under local law against subsequent purchasers without actual notice," § 6323(h)(6). Under treasury regulations, the relinquishment of the interest of one spouse in the estate of the other, or of "other marital rights," is explicitly not considered a transfer for "money's worth."

Third parties, or even Mrs. Jones, who pay adequate and full consideration in money or money's worth for property subject to a federal tax lien are protected against the lien prior to the date on which the lien is recorded.

Pursuant to the separation agreement and decree, Mrs. Jones exchanged three elements of value for Mr. Jones's interest in the property: $60,000 of cash, a waiver of periodic alimony, and the release of her right of contribution from Mr. Jones for his share of the mortgage obligation secured by the property. The cash payment clearly constitutes consideration paid by Mrs. Jones for the property. On the other hand, the release of alimony rights apparently does not constitute consideration under the regulations. It is unclear whether Mrs. Jones's release of her rights of contribution constitutes consideration, for this right may be too speculative to be reducible to a money value as required by the regulations.

THE PEARL

Avoid wrestling with problems such as this. If the opposing party has filed a separate tax return, make sure you review each such return and determine whether the amount shown due has been paid. To obtain complete comfort, it would be necessary to call the IRS and at least try to determine whether any secret assessment has been made before accepting the property transfer. Obviously, the inquiry to the IRS could stir up trouble, but if the inquiry is not made, your client takes a risk.

78

Alimony Recapture: Its Origins and Operation

David H. Hopkins

INTRODUCTION

Alimony recapture is all too often criticized by litigants and lawyers alike for a host of reasons. This criticism, however, generally overlooks the provisions of prior law that recapture replaced, provisions that produced much confusion, uncertainty, and controversy. Alimony recapture is mechanical, lends itself to effective tax-planning, and is undeserving of the "bad rap" that it often receives.

The recapture rule, as first enacted in 1984, at the behest of the House/Senate Conference Committee, focused on a six-year period, as well as entailed great complexity and draconian results in some cases. Fortunately, the six-year rule was overhauled in 1986, with the original three-year approach to recapture contemplated by the 1984 House bill being adopted. This version of the recapture rule, applicable since 1987, basically provides that if alimony payments in the first year exceed the average of payments in the second year and third year by more than $15,000, and/or if alimony payments in the second year exceed third-year payments by more than $15,000, these excess payments are recaptured in the third year. Correspondingly, the alimony recipient is entitled to a correlative deduction.

The rationale for the recapture rule was to establish a system that reasonably blocked "property settlement" payments from being structured as alimony. *See* H.R. Rep. No. 432, Part II, 98th Cong. 2d Sess. at 1496 (1984). In 1984, alimony recapture was deemed especially important in light of the elimination of three subjective rules of prior law, as follows. As a practical matter, alimony recapture can be understood only if the elimination of the foregoing rules is taken into account.

SUBJECTIVE PRE-1985 RULES THAT WERE ELIMINATED

Rule #1: Support Test

One of the least understood areas of pre-1985 law had been the so-called support test, established by the regulations interpreting "old" § 71. The confusion was due, in part, to the fact that "support" was a subjective concept, which, generally speaking, limited the right to alimony treatment only for periodic payments made in discharge of a local law obligation of support. *See* old Treas. Reg. § 1.71-1(b). This support requirement had been a prolific source of litigation with respect to the "alimony/property" distinction—i.e., are the payments that are being made in "periodic form" ones being made for support of the recipient, or are the payments actually intended to compensate the recipient for a release or transfer of property? In the 1970s and early 1980s, the problems in this area increased in direct relation to adoption by various states of the "equitable distribution" doctrine. Notably, by the early 1980s, the tax court began to address the plethora of § 71 cases, as well as the need for reform, with increasingly blunt statements. For example, in a footnote to a memorandum decision filed on June 30, 1981, Judge Cynthia Hall stated as follows:

> When Congress first enacted sections 71 and 215, it did not anticipate the litigation which has arisen over whether certain payments were made in discharge of a legal obligation arising out of a marital or family relationship. It is time for Congress to reconsider this statute and perhaps supply taxpayers with a safe harbor in this area. *Schatz v. Commissioner*, 42 T.C.M. (CCH) 292, 296 n. 10 (1981).

Similarly, in the text of his opinion in *Beard v. Commissioner*, 77 T.C. 1275 (1981), Judge Howard Dawson reiterated the point set out in *Schatz*, as follows:

> It is well settled that the determination of whether payments are in the nature of support or part of a property settlement does not turn on the labels assigned to the payments by the court in the divorce decree or by the parties in their agreement. [Citations omitted.] The issue is a factual one and requires an examination of all the surrounding facts and circumstances. [Citations omitted.] Unfortunately, because of the vexing problems which frequently arise in determining the nature and extent of a spouse's property rights under State law, this supposedly factual inquiry has all too often taken on a metaphysical aura as the courts have struggled to classify a particular payment as either support or property settlement, when, in reality, the payment possesses a hybrid nature sharing characteristics of both. In the process, similarly situated taxpayers have occasionally been accorded disparate treatment merely because of differences in State marital property laws. For this reason, and because the confusion in this area has spawned a relentless stream of litigation, it would appear that legislative reform is warranted. As we stated in *Schatz v. Commissioner*, T.C. Memo 1981-341, note 10, some sort of safe harbor is needed so that taxpayers and divorce courts can predict with confidence the income-tax consequences stemming from periodic payments occa-

sioned by divorce. Until such legislation is enacted, however, we are left with no alternative but to plunge into the morass of the decided cases, many of them irreconcilable, and resolve this issue as best we can by applying the various factors which have been identified in prior decisions. 77 T.C. at 1283–1284.

As noted, in 1984, the support requirement of § 71 was eliminated except, under § 71(b)(2)(C), in the context of a temporary order. The Temporary Regulations make this change in the law explicit, as follows:

> Q-3. In order to be treated as alimony or separate maintenance payments, must the payments be "periodic" as that term was defined prior to enactment of the Tax Reform Act of 1984 or be made in discharge of a legal obligation of the payor to support the payee arising out of a marital or family relationship?

> A-3. No. The Tax Reform Act of 1984 replaces the old requirements with the requirements described in A-2 above. Thus, the requirements that alimony or separate maintenance payments be "periodic" and be made in discharge of a legal obligation to support arising out of a marital or family relationship have been eliminated. Temp. Treas. Reg. § 1.71-1T(a), Q&A 3.

Rule #2: Periodicity Rule

As noted previously, the pre-1985 requirement that a stream of payments be "periodic" was eliminated completely in 1984. This rule had served in the past to preclude a one-shot payment from qualifying as alimony and had caused uncertainty in cases of payments over short periods (i.e., less than one year).

Rule #3: Netting Principle

Under prior law, a so-called netting rule operated in the alimony area (as generally noted in the *Beard* case, cited previously). This rule served to preclude alimony treatment when a stream of payments (otherwise structured as alimony) was, in reality, consideration for an asset titled in the name of and being transferred from the alimony recipient to the alimony payor. For example, if an alimony recipient transferred $100,000 in securities to the alimony payor under the property division section of a marital settlement agreement, while the alimony payor was responsible for paying $300,000 in alimony to the recipient over a period of years, under the "netting" rule, the first $100,000 of purported alimony would have been treated as the purchase of the securities. Thus, the first $100,000 in claimed alimony deductions would have been disallowed. As indicated, this rule was eliminated in 1984, and the effect is that a payment or stream of payments, otherwise meeting alimony requirements of § 71, will not be disallowed, even if there is property being transferred from the alimony recipient or, alternatively, claims to property remaining with the payor are being relinquished by the alimony recipient.

In sum, alimony recapture was intended to be a mechanical replacement for the previously mentioned three subjective rules of prior law. For planning purposes, litigants are far better off with the alimony recapture rules than the predecessor rules, particularly in terms of achieving certainty; and, altogether, alimony recapture is a small price to have paid in exchange for the elimination of the previously described subjectivity of pre-1985 law.

MECHANICS OF RECAPTURE

The three-year recapture rule, effective since 1987, is a bit tedious in its operation. Unlike the original six-year rule, though, it entails a single computation as of the end of the third year. The steps for computing recapture at any given time—which are the steps that should be used at the planning stage—can be summarized as follows:

Step 1: Determine second-year recapture by adding $15,000 to third-year alimony payments and subtracting the result from second-year alimony payments.

Step 2: Determine adjusted second-year alimony by reducing actual alimony payments by amount of second-year recapture (as determined under Step 1).

Step 3: Determine the average of (i) second-year alimony (as adjusted under Step 2) and (ii) third-year alimony; and then increase the average by $15,000.

Step 4: Determine first-year recapture by subtracting the amount determined under Step 3 from first-year alimony.

Step 5: Determine total recapture by adding the previously determined amounts of second- and first-year recapture (i.e., amounts determined under Steps 1 and 4).

Apart from the mechanics, a review of a number of hypothetical situations underscores various planning parameters. Most important, it should be understood that despite the repeated references to recapture being a three-year rule, all applicable recapture requirements can be met in a period as short as twelve months and two days. The three-year element relates to three calendar years; and, except with respect to percentage payments, it does not necessitate a stretch-out of payments over a thirty-six-month period. Further review of the following illustrative examples demonstrates that the starting time in the calendar year of the first year is quite often very significant.

EXAMPLE 1: A "One-shotter"

Alimony: Year 1—$50,000
           Year 2—   0
           Year 3—   0

Recapture Computation:
Step 1: $0 − ($0 + $15,000)   = $ 0
Step 2:   N/A
Step 3:   ($0 + $0) divided by 2 + $15,000 = $15,000
Step 4: $50,000 − $15,000   = $35,000
Step 5: $0 + $35,000   = $35,000 (Recapture)

COMMENT: This example illustrates the classic front-end loading situation—i.e., a substantial one-shot payment.

EXAMPLE 2: *Alimony in Only Two Years*

Alimony:	Year 1—	$50,000
	Year 2—	$20,000
	Year 3—	-0-

Recapture Computation:

Step 1:	$20,000 − ($0 + $15,000)	= $ 5,000
Step 2:	$20,000 − $5,000	= $15,000
Step 3:	($15,000 + $0) divided by 2 + $15,000	= $22,500
Step 4:	$50,000 − $22,500	= $27,500
Step 5:	$5,000 + $27,500	= $32,500 (Recapture)

COMMENT: This example also illustrates the results for the type of excess front-end loading at which the recapture rules are primarily aimed.

EXAMPLE 3: *Heavily "Front-End Loaded"*

Alimony:	Year 1—	$50,000
	Year 2—	$15,000
	Year 3—	$ 5,000

Recapture Computation:

Step 1:	$15,000 − ($5,000 + $15,000)	= $ 0
Step 2:	N/A	
Step 3:	($15,000 + $5,000) divided by 2 + $15,000	= $25,000
Step 4:	$50,000 − $25,000	= $25,000
Step 5:	$0 + $25,000	= $25,000 (Recapture)

COMMENT: It should be noted that, as compared with EXAMPLE 2, the mere shift of $5,000 in alimony from Year 2 to Year 3 reduces recapture by $7,500.

EXAMPLE 4: *Alimony over Thirty Months, Starting in a January*

Alimony:	Year 1—	$36,000
	Year 2—	$36,000
	Year 3—	$18,000

Recapture Computation:

Step 1:	$36,000 − ($18,000 + $15,000)	= $ 3,000
Step 2:	$36,000 − $3,000	= $33,000
Step 3:	($33,000 + $18,000) divided by 2 + $15,000	= $40,500
Step 4:	$36,000 − $40,500	= $ 0
Step 5:	$3,000 + $0	= $ 3,000 (Recapture)

COMMENT: While recapture ensues from the above rateable approach for two and a half years, the amount is relatively small.

EXAMPLE 5: Alimony over Thirty Months, Starting in a February

Alimony: Year 1— $33,000
          Year 2— $36,000
          Year 3— $21,000

Recapture Computation:

Step 1:	$36,000 − ($21,000 + $15,000)	= $ 0
Step 2:	N/A	
Step 3:	($36,000 + $21,000) divided by 2 + $15,000	= $43,500
Step 4:	$33,000 − $43,500	= $ 0
Step 5:	$0 + $0	= $ 0 (Recapture)

COMMENT: By merely starting payments one month later than in EXAMPLE 4, all recapture is precluded.

EXAMPLE 6: Alimony over Twenty Months, Starting in a December

Alimony: Year 1— $ 3,000
          Year 2— $36,000
          Year 3— $21,000

Recapture Computation:

Step 1:	$36,000 − ($21,000 + $15,000)	= $ 0
Step 2:	N/A	
Step 3:	($36,000 + $21,000) divided by 2 + $15,000	= $43,500
Step 4:	$3,000 − $43,500	= $ 0
Step 5:	$0 + $0	= $ 0 (Recapture)

COMMENT: The example illustrates how short the critical period may actually be in a particular case. The fact that the first year entails only one monthly payment (for December of such year) should be underscored. In many cases, various planning possibilities will pivot on the point in time in any particular calendar year the first payment is made.

Apart from these operational parameters, it should be noted that recapture is not triggered if alimony payments cease because of the death of either party or the remarriage of the recipient, as is expressly set out in § 71(f)(5)(A). Termination of alimony because of cohabitation, however, can present problems in some cases. Similarly, an arrearage payment in Year 2 could bunch Year 1 and Year 2 alimony together, causing a problem. Payments pursuant to a predivorce temporary support order, within the scope of new § 71(b) (2)(C), also are exempt from recapture. In addition, under § 71(f)(5)(C), payments constituting a fixed portion of income from a business or property or from compensation for employment or self-employment, if required to be made for at least three years, also are excepted.

CERTAIN PLANNING PARAMETERS: SHIFTING THE BURDEN AND "REINSTATEMENT ALIMONY"

As noted previously, to the extent there is alimony recapture triggered for the alimony payor, there is a correlative deduction available to the alimony recipient. Thus, corresponding benefits and burdens arise whenever recapture actually occurs. In this regard, it is perfectly permissible for the parties to make monetary adjustments between themselves that shift the ultimate cost of recapture, in whole or in part. For example, it is perfectly permissible, if there is a premature termination of alimony because of an ex-wife's cohabitation, for the entire recapture burden to be shifted to the cohabiting ex-wife. (If the recapture cost for the alimony payor is less than the cost of the extinguished payments, perhaps the payor should not be complaining.) In all events, reallocation of a recapture burden is a matter that is subject to negotiation. Following is an illustrative clause that provides for an equal allocation of the ultimate cost:

> **Recapture Adjustments.** The parties also acknowledge their intent to preclude any future reduction during 1994–1996 in the payments required under paragraph ____, above, that would lead to the Husband realizing "recapture income" and the Wife realizing a "recapture deduction" under § 71(f)(2) of the Internal Revenue Code. They further agree that if any "recapture" occurs for any reason, as to each recapture year the Wife's "benefit" and the Husband's "burden" shall be netted, and that the Wife shall make a payment to the Husband in such amount as will allocate the overall cost of recapture for that year equally between themselves. For purposes of computing in any year the Wife's "recapture benefit" and the Husband's "recapture burden," the appropriate party's tax returns shall be prepared taking into account the requisite recapture amount, as well as prepared excluding that amount, and the total federal and state tax liability shown on one set of returns shall be subtracted from the total liability shown on the other set of returns. As to any payment from the Wife to the Husband required hereunder (and in accordance with § 71(b)(1)(B) of the Internal Revenue Code), the parties expressly agree to designate, and herewith do designate, each such payment as an excludable/nondeductible payment for purposes of §§ 71 and 215 of the Code, respectively.

A concept that is relatively new to matrimonial law relates primarily to situations in which spousal support is appropriate for a fairly long period and a complete or partial "ride-through" of remarriage cannot be agreed on. In many of these situations, an alimony recipient does hope to remarry, which would ordinarily terminate all rights to alimony from the first husband under local law. In some situations, the possible "forfeiture" may virtually ensure that an ex-spouse will not remarry or, alternatively, may make a new matrimonial venture a very risky proposition, economically speaking. Such a prospect may make a negotiated settlement very difficult to attain. A new concept, sometimes utilized in these situations, generally is referred to as "reinstatement alimony," entailing a negotiated "tolling" of alimony during a subsequent marriage of the alimony recipient, with the further result that, if the second marriage fails, there will be, in whole or in part, a reinstatement of the original alimony arrangement. Alimony payors are remarkably unresistant to this approach, often recognizing that reinstatement alimony may encourage remarriage, thus perhaps reducing the alimony payor's ultimate overall cost. Whether alimony treatment for reinstated payments could have been achieved under pre-1985 tax law is unclear (as such an arrangement might have been viewed as flying in the face of the "support requirement" of prior law). In all events, under current tax law, reinstatement alimony is entirely permissible, and implementation of one approach to this alimony is illustrated by the following clause:

> **Termination and/or Reduction.** In the event of the Wife's death, the Husband's obligation to the Wife under this Article III shall terminate. These obligations, however, shall not immediately terminate in the event of the Husband's death; and payments of Basic and Supplemental Maintenance pursuant to subparagraphs _____, above, shall be made to the Wife by the Husband's executor, trustee, or other successor until such a date on which the full amount of insurance proceeds and/or payment in lieu of those proceeds from his successor, as required under subparagraph ___, below, is actually paid to the Wife, at which time the Husband's obligations under subparagraph _____ shall terminate. In the event of the Wife's remarriage (or her cohabitation with another person on a resident, continuing, conjugal basis, within the scope of Section 510(c) of the Illinois Marriage and Dissolution of Marriage Act, which shall not be deemed to occur any earlier than the date on which the Husband files a petition for termination), the Husband's obligation to pay Basic and Supplemental Maintenance shall be tolled—i.e., he shall have no obligation to make and shall stop making the payments, but his obligations under this subparagraph _____ shall remain, subject to reinstatement, in whole or in part, as provided below. Specifically, if the Wife remarries or cohabits (so that the Husband's obligations respecting Basic and Supplemental Maintenance are tolled) and thereafter she is divorced and/or the cohabitation ceases, then, effective as of the date of such divorce or cessation, the Husband's tolled obligation shall be reinstated, except that as of that date and thereafter the amount(s) of Basic and Supplemental Maintenance shall be reduced by twenty percent (20%) for each full year of tolling. (Thus, for example, if the Wife is remarried for five full years and then divorced, no reinstatement of any of the Basic and Supplemental Maintenance shall be effectuated.) If after a reinstatement hereunder, the Wife again remarries or cohabits, tolling in terms of Basic and Supplemental Maintenance shall again be in effect.

CONCLUSION

As noted previously, alimony recapture has all too frequently in the past been severely criticized—i.e., given a bad rap—to an extent that is not deserved. Much of the perspective of practitioners in the matrimonial field, of course, surely traces back to the draconian version of alimony recapture first enacted in 1984. This initial venture into alimony recapture, however, now has been relegated to a historical footnote, and, as a practical matter, the reality is that the present alimony recapture rule—as something of a hedge against property settlement payments being structured as alimony—is a remarkable improvement over the subjective rules of pre-1985 law. Moreover, any review of the mechanics of recapture plainly demonstrates that most bona fide arrangements can easily run the gamut of the rules, particularly because the three-year element of the rules ordinarily can be met in a period that is far less than thirty-six months. In all events, the elimination of the old subjective rules opens the door to considerable planning possibilities, ones with far greater certainty in terms of attainment.

79

Property Transfers Involving Nonresident Aliens

Marjorie A. O'Connell

MOST PROPERTY TRANSFERS between spouses or former spouses are not the occasion for the imposition of federal income, estate, or gift taxes. The tax rules may be different when a nonresident alien is involved as either the transferor or recipient of the property.

An alien is any person who is not a citizen, but does not include persons with dual citizenship in the United States and a foreign country. The first statutory definition of a nonresident alien was adopted in § 7701(b) in 1985. While the statute has numerous special rules, in general there are two tests to determine when an alien is a resident of the United States.

First, an alien is a resident alien if he or she can lawfully reside permanently in the United States, usually evidenced by holding a Bureau of Immigration "green card." The second test measures the amount of the time that the alien spends in the United States. The alien must be present in the United States thirty-one days or more during the current calendar year and a total of 183 "deemed" days during the current year and the two prior years.

IRC § 1041 provides that most transfers of property between spouses or former spouses incident to a divorce are not taxable events. For § 1041 transfers, the transferor does not pay income tax and the recipient takes a carryover basis in the property. One of the few exceptions to § 1041 is for transfers from an individual to his or her spouse who is a nonresident alien. This exception to § 1041 can be avoided easily in most cases to prevent the transferor from paying taxes.

GIFT DURING MARRIAGE IS NOT A TAXABLE EVENT

The first way to avoid this restriction is a transfer during marriage. Section 1041 applies when the transferor otherwise would recognize gain because the recipient provides some consideration to the transferor. The classic example is a *Davis** exchange where the recipient gives up marital rights for

---

*U.S. v. Davis, 370 U.S. 65 (1982).

the property. Section 1041 applies if the recipient's consideration is money or the transfer of other property to the transferor. If the recipient does not give any consideration, then the transfer is a gift by the transferor. For a true gift, the transferor does not have to recognize any gain or loss on the transfer (IRC § 1001). Therefore, a gift during marriage is not a taxable event, even if § 1041 does not apply. (The gift tax aspects of this transaction are as follows.)

TRANSFER TO FORMER SPOUSE IS NOT A TAXABLE EVENT

When the parties are involved in a divorce, the § 1041 exception can be avoided by a second method. The § 1041 exception applies only to transfers to a nonresident alien "spouse." The statute distinguishes between a spouse and a former spouse. If the transfer is made after the divorce to a non-spouse, the transferor does not recognize gain or loss because the § 1041 nonrecognition rule applies. While the policy for this distinction between spouses and former spouses is unclear, the statutory language is clear.

Section 1041 applies separately to each property transferred. Therefore, a transferor could select those properties that would produce a loss and transfer them to the nonresident alien spouse prior to the divorce. The transferor would recognize the loss. After the divorce, all gain property could be transferred and no gain would be recognized. If the nonresident alien has no U.S. income, the carryover basis of the property that would apply to the recipient on any later sale may be meaningless.

ESTATE AND GIFT TAXES USE A
DIFFERENT DEFINITION OF NONRESIDENT ALIEN

Estate and gift taxes (transfer taxes) do not use the income tax definition of resident and nonresident alien. Transfer taxes apply generally to any person who is "domiciled" in the United States (IRC § 2501). Domicile generally is defined as where a person is living with no definite present intention of moving from that place. Residence with an intention to remain indefinitely creates domicile. Therefore, transfer taxes may not apply to resident aliens who are subject to income taxation because of their presence in the United States for a sufficient number of days. U.S. transfer taxes generally do not apply to any nonresident alien, with the exception of former citizens who are found to have given up their citizenship for tax purposes.

When a U.S. domiciliary transfers property to a nonresident alien spouse, that transfer is subject to federal transfer taxes that are imposed on the U.S. transferor. The unlimited marital deduction for transfers to a spouse applies when the transferee spouse is a nonresident alien (IRC §§ 2523 and 2056). Therefore, if a transfer were treated as a gift, not subject to § 1041, the federal unlimited marital deduction would apply and no gift tax would be owed.

For transfers incident to a divorce, § 2516 provides an exception from gift taxation for transfers between spouses made pursuant to a written instrument that is executed within a three-year period beginning one year before and ending two years after the date of divorce. This gift tax exception applies to transfers made to a nonresident spouse or former spouse. Therefore, a U.S. domiciliary should not be subject to a gift tax for any transfer to a spouse or former spouse.

For estate tax purposes, the same provisions apply as for gift taxes. The federal estate tax unlimited marital deduction in § 2056 and the estate exception for transfers that qualify under § 2516 apply if the property transfers are made by the estate of the transferor (IRC §§ 2056 and 2043(b)).

80

Joint Returns and Section 1034: A Sometimes Dangerous Journey through Tax Land

Peggy L. Podell

LIABILITY ON A JOINT RETURN

Liability is joint and several for individuals filing joint returns:

1. "[E]ach spouse is jointly and severally liable for the full amount of tax penalties and interest arising out of their joint return." 33 *Am. Jur.* (2d) Federal Taxation ¶ 1671, at 696, *citing* IRC § 6013(d)(3) (hereinafter cited as Federal Taxation).
   A. IRC § 6013(d)(3) states that: "If a joint return is made, the tax shall be computed on the aggregate income and the liability with respect to the tax shall be joint and several."
   B. Items within the innocent spouse rule are an exception to this general rule. Federal Taxation ¶ 1671 at 696; *see also*, IRC § 6013(e).
2. The amount of a party's separate taxable income is not relevant when a joint return is filed. Federal Taxation ¶ 1671 at 696.

All of the tax liability can be collected from one of the parties who signed the joint return.

1. Penalties and interest also can be collected from either party with the exception of civil fraud penalties. *Id.*
2. The IRS is not required to collect the amount owed to it equally from both parties.
   A. One spouse cannot insist that the IRS pursue the other before seeking the funds from him or her. *Brown v. U.S.*, 272 F.2d 215 (5th Cir. 1959).
   B. The IRS "usually collects unpaid tax due on a joint return from the spouse having the most accessible assets." Federal Taxation ¶ 1671 at 696.

The taxing authorities are not bound by the terms of an agreement between the parties. Therefore, indemnification clauses will not prevent them from pursuing either or both parties. If party A agrees to pay party B's tax liability, this does not prevent the IRS from collecting the tax from party B. *Ballenger, Mildred,* TC Memo 1955-171.

HOW LONG ARE YOU ON THE HOOK FOR A JOINT RETURN? IT DEPENDS.

Unless provided otherwise, "the amount of any tax imposed by this title shall be assessed within three years after the return was filed (whether or not such return was filed on or after the date prescribed)." IRC § 6501(a). For purposes of § 6501, a return filed prior to the last day prescribed by law or by regulation shall be considered as filed on such last day. § 6501(b)(1) (Early Return).

"In the case of a false or fraudulent return with the intent to evade tax, the tax may be assessed, or a proceeding in court from collection of such tax may be begun without assessment, at any time." § 6501(c)(1) (False Return).

"In the case of a willful attempt in any manner to defeat or evade tax imposed by this title . . . the tax may be assessed, or a proceeding in court for the collection of such tax may be begun without assessment, at any time." § 6501(c)(2) (Willful Attempt to Evade Tax).

"In the case of failure to file a return, the tax may be assessed, or a proceeding in court for the collection of such tax may be begun without assessment, at any time." § 6501(c)(3) (No Return).

The time within which an assessment can be made can be extended by agreement between the IRS and the taxpayer. § 6501(c)(4) (Extension by Agreement).

HOW ARE CAPITAL GAINS USUALLY TAXED TO INDIVIDUALS WHO JOINTLY OWN ASSETS?

Income from property ordinarily follows ownership. Cotenants ordinarily will be taxed on income from property in accordance with their respective interests therein. (CCH-Standard Federal Tax Reports ¶ 2250.011.)

To report it any other way may result in income shifting that is impermissible.

CAPITAL GAINS + JOINT RETURN = A POTENTIALLY FINANCIALLY DEADLY DUO

Taxpayers ordinarily are required to treat gains realized on the sale of property as taxable during the year of sale.

An exception to this general rule is contained in IRC § 1034, "Rollover of Gain on Sale of Principal Residence."

"The nonrecognition provisions of § 1034(a) of the IRC of 1954 apply separately to the gains realized by the husband and by the wife from the sale of their principal residence." Rev. Rul. 74–250.

1. The husband and the wife purchased a residence in 1960 and held the property as tenants by the entirety. The property was used solely as their residence thereafter. In July of 1972 they agreed to live apart, entered a contract to sell the property, but continued to reside there until the sale was completed in September of 1972. Each was entitled to one half of the proceeds pursuant to state law. On this basis, both realized a gain from the sale of the residence.

2. Between July and September of 1972, each executed purchase contracts for separate residences. The cost of each exceeded their respective shares of the adjusted sales price of the old residence. Each new residence was purchased and occupied prior to the end of 1972.

Hall v. Commissioner, 35 TC Memo 1976-311, 35 T.C.M. 1399, 1407, *rev'd.* on another issue, 595 F.2d 1059 (5th Cir. 1979), held that where the individual was entitled to one half of the sale proceeds of the residence, he would be liable for the tax only to the extent that he did not reinvest his one-half share within the time period of § 1034. In this case the residence was sold in the year of divorce.

Filing a joint return in the year of the sale can alter the result drastically.

If the capital-gains tax is incurred and the parties file a joint return, either party could be responsible for the entire tax. *See Murphy v. Commissioner,* 103 TC 8 (filed 8/2/94).

POOR MR. MURPHY!

Holding: Mr. Murphy was jointly and severally liable under § 6013(d)(3) for the tax attributable to Mrs. Murphy's allocable one-half share of realized gain, all of which was immediately taxable, because she had failed to purchase a replacement residence within the time permitted under § 1034. In addition, he also was subject to additions to tax under §§ 6653 and 6661 for negligence and substantial understatement of income tax.

1. A gain was realized on the sale of the parties' jointly owned residence in December of 1988. They filed a joint return (Mr. Murphy's financially fatal mistake) and deferred the gain pursuant to § 1034 by indicating their intention on Form 2119 to purchase another residence within the two-year period.
   A. The home located in Illinois was sold for $465,000.
   B. A total gain of $185,629 was realized.

2. The Murphys were separated in December of 1989 and divorced in May of 1991.

3. Subsequent to the separation but within the two-year period permitted by § 1034, Mr. Murphy purchased a personal residence for himself. He filed an amended 1988 joint return that Mrs. Murphy refused to sign. In the amended return Mr. Murphy reported additional income from the sale of the joint residence to the extent that his one-half allocable share of the proceeds was not reinvested in his new residence.

     A. Mr. Murphy purchased a home in Arizona for $199,704.

     B. Mr. Murphy filed an amended joint return pursuant to Rev. Rul. 80-5, reporting $37,506 in additional gross income that was calculated on his allocable portion of the gain from the sale of the marital residence and paid the tax appropriately for his one-half of the gain. Mr. Murphy calculated his gain as follows: $237,210 (one-half of the difference between the original selling price and the original expenses of sale) minus $199,704 (the purchase price of his new residence) equals $37,506.

4. Mrs. Murphy did not purchase a new residence for herself during the two-year period provided for in § 1034.

5. The deficiency notice was based on a computation that took into account the entire proceeds of sale, not just Mr. Murphy's one-half allocable share. The IRS contended that $148,123 was to be restored to Mr. Murphy as gross income, not $37,506. This figure was based on the original gain ($185,629) minus the amount already reported as gain by Mr. Murphy ($37,506).

81

Inexpensive Tax Information at Your Fingertips

Barbara Kahn Stark

Y OU CAN HAVE DETAILED, easily accessed tax information readily available without investing in an expensive tax library.

FREE PUBLICATIONS FROM THE IRS

The IRS publishes circulars on a variety of tax issues that arise in working with divorce clients. The circulars, which are listed in the table that follows, are free and are quick sources of technical tax information.

Form 504, *Divorced or Separated Individuals,* contains a complete and comprehensible discussion of a variety of divorce tax issues. I give every litigation and mediation client a copy of this circular. Divorce clients must be familiar with tax issues to educate them to make tax- and financial-planning decisions.

When working with clients to calculate taxes for determining net income for alimony and child-support purposes, and in the analysis of property-division options, tax questions come up frequently. The IRS provides a tremendous amount of helpful information in a variety of specific tax issues. I maintain a three-ring binder in my office that contains the following IRS circulars.

IRS circulars are available at your local IRS office, or to order five copies by mail, call 800-TAX-FORM.

DIVORCE PLANNER

Many matrimonial lawyers regularly use the computer program *Divorce Planner* to calculate net income, the tax consequences of various alimony orders, and other calculations. Once in the program, you can access explanatory tax information with a push of a button. The program provides details about taxable income and explanations of various tax deductions. The disk provides federal and Social Security tax tables and informative tax tips (with supporting tax-regulation cites) in several areas, including alimony, child support, filing status, dependency exemptions, housing costs and taxes on sale, property settlements, gift tax, innocent spouse rules, Social Security, etc.

For information about *Divorce Planner,* contact Fin Plan at (800) 777–2108.

IRS CIRCULARS

Publication Number	Publication Title
504	Divorced or Separated Individuals
501	Exemptions, Standard Deduction, and Filing Information
523	Selling Your Home
463	Travel, Entertainment, and Gift Expenses
502	Child and Dependent Care Expenses
505	Tax and Withholding and Estimated Tax
521	Moving Expenses
508	Educational Expenses
525	Taxable and Nontaxable Income
527	Residential Rental Property (Including Rental of Vacation Homes)
529	Miscellaneous Deductions
530	Tax Information for First-Time Homeowners
533	Self-Employment Tax
534	Depreciation
535	Business Expenses
550	Investment Income and Expenses
575	Pension and Annuity Income (Including Simplified General Rule)
583	Taxpayers Starting a Business
917	Business Use of Your Car
587	Business Use of Your Home
915	Social Security Benefits and Equivalent Railroad Retirement Benefits

82

Waiver of the Dependency Exemption and Form 8332

Peggy L. Podell

A. The dependency exemption under IRC § 152(e).
   1. Rules for allocating the dependency exemption where parents are divorced or separated are provided in IRC § 152(e).
   2. In order for IRC § 152(e) to apply, certain conditions must exist.
      a. One or both parents provide more than half the support for the child. IRC § 152(e)(1)(A). Support received from a parent's spouse is considered to have been received from the parent. IRC § 152(e)(5).
      b. The parents must be (i) divorced or legally separated under a decree of divorce or separate maintenance, (ii) separated under a written separation agreement, or (iii) have lived apart the last six months of the year in question. IRC §§ 152(e)(1)(A)(i), (ii), (iii).
      c. One or both parents must have custody of the child for more than half the year. IRC § 152(e)(1)(B).
   3. If the decree or agreement is post-1984, the general rule is that the custodian gets the exemption for the child absent a waiver. The parent who has custody of the child for the greater portion of the year is considered the custodial parent. Treas. Reg. § 1.152-4T(a) (26 C.F.R.), Q-1; IRC § 152(e)(1).
B. Under provisions of § 152(e), the non-custodial parent is entitled to take the exemption if the custodial parent waives his/her right to do so. I.R.C. § 152(e)2.
   1. The release is to take the form of a "written declaration" from the custodial parent stating that he/she will not claim the child as a dependent for that taxable year. Treas. Reg. (26 C.F.R.) § 1.152-4T(a), Q&A 3.
   2. IRS Form 8332 is the form designated by the IRS to be used for the purpose of releasing the dependency exemption. The form is to be completed and attached to the non-custodial parent's tax return.

3. If Form 8332 is not used, "any declaration made other than on the official form [Form 8332] shall conform to the substance of such form." Treas. Reg. (26 C.F.R.) § 1.152-4T(a), Q&A 3.

4. Form 8332 "requires a taxpayer to furnish (1) the names of the children for which exemption claims were released, (2) the years for which the claims were released, (3) the signature of the custodial parent confirming his or her consent, (4) the Social Security number of the custodial parent confirming his or her consent, (4) the Social Security number of the custodial parent, (5) the date of the custodial parent's signature, and (6) the name and the Social Security number of the parent claiming the exemption." *Miller v. Commissioner,* 114 T.C. No. 13 (Filed 3/24/00).

C. *Cheryl Miller & John Lovejoy v. Commissioner,* 114 T.C. No. 13.

1. After a contested trial, a Colorado court ordered that the non-custodial parent was unconditionally allowed to claim the exemptions for the children. The "Permanent Orders," which included the award of the exemptions to the non-custodial parent, were executed by the state court judge and signed by the custodial parent's attorney approving the order "as to form." The non-custodial parent did not ask the custodial parent to sign Form 8332, he attached portions of the Permanent Orders to his return in lieu of Form 8332, and claimed the exemptions.

2. Tax Court held that the "Permanent Orders" did not qualify as a written declaration, did not satisfy the requirements of § 152(e)(2), and the non-custodial parent was not entitled to claim the dependency exemptions.

   a. The orders could not substitute for Form 8332 because it did not, among other requirements, contain the signature of the custodial parent. "Satisfying the signature requirement is critical to the successful release of the dependency exemption within the meaning of section 152 (e)(2). . . . By signing the document, the custodial parent affirmatively consents to the release of the dependency exemption to the non-custodial parent." *Miller v. Commissioner.*

      1) *Neal v. Commissioner,* T.C. Memo. 1999-97. Held that an unsigned Form 8332 was not effective to give the exemption to the non-custodial parent.

      2) *White v. Commissioner,* T.C. Memo. 1996-438. Held that a letter signed by the custodial spouse restating that the divorce decree entitled the non-custodial spouse to the exemptions did not conform to the substance of a Form 8332.

      3) *Paulson v. Commissioner,* T.C. Memo. 1996-560. Held that the non-custodial spouse was not entitled to the exemption where nothing was attached to the return and the award was a conditional one.

   b. The Tax Court in *Miller* also pointed out that in addition to lacking the signature of the custodial parent and the date of that signature, the Permanent Orders lacked other information which is included on Form 8332 including the years for which the claims were released and Social Security numbers.

    c. The Tax Court further held that the signature of the custodial parent's attorney approving the Orders as to form was not sufficient but specifically stated that they were not deciding "whether there are any circumstances under which the signature of a custodial parent's attorney can ever satisfy the signature requirement of sec. 152(3)(2)." *Miller v. Commissioner,* n. 8.

    d. As to the effect of having the state court grant the non-custodial parent the right to claim the exemptions, the Tax Court stated that "a State court cannot determine issues of Federal tax law." *Miller v. Commissioner* (citation omitted).

    e. The Tax Court in *Miller* discussed the weight to be given to IRS publications and stated that the fact that an IRS publication is inaccurate or unclear is no defense, "taxpayers rely on such publications at their peril . . . [a]dministrative guidance contained in IRS publications is not binding on the Government, nor can it change the plain meaning of tax statutes." The Tax Court further stated that the "authoritative sources of Federal tax law are the statutes, regulations, and judicial decisions; they do not include informal IRS publications." *Miller v. Commissioner.*

D. Non-custodial parent's relief option.

    1. If the custodial parent refuses to sign Form 8332, the only remedy appears to be a motion for contempt in state court to enforce the state court's order.

    2. Provisions regarding the signing and delivery of Form 8332 along with remedies in the event those provisions are not complied with should be included in your settlement agreement, or argue to the court for specific provisions in contested matters.

Form **8332**

(Rev. December 2000)

Department of the Treasury
Internal Revenue Service

Release of Claim to Exemption
for Child of Divorced or Separated Parents

▶ **Attach** to noncustodial parent's return **each year** exemption is claimed.
Caution: *Do not use this form if you were never married.*

OMB No. 1545-0915

Attachment
Sequence No. **115**

Name of noncustodial parent claiming exemption	Noncustodial parent's social security number (SSN) ▶		

Part I Release of Claim to Exemption for Current Year

I agree not to claim an exemption for _____
Name(s) of child (or children)

for the tax year 20_____ .

_____   _____   _____
Signature of custodial parent releasing claim to exemption   Custodial parent's SSN   Date

Note: *If you choose not to claim an exemption for this child (or children) for future tax years, also complete Part II.*

Part II Release of Claim to Exemption for Future Years (If completed, see **Noncustodial parent** below.)

I agree not to claim an exemption for _____
Name(s) of child (or children)

for the tax year(s) _____ .
(Specify. See instructions.)

_____   _____   _____
Signature of custodial parent releasing claim to exemption   Custodial parent's SSN   Date

General Instructions

Purpose of form. If you are a **custodial parent** and you were ever married to the child's **noncustodial parent,** you may use this form to release your claim to your child's exemption. To do so, complete this form (or a similar statement containing the same information required by this form) and give it to the noncustodial parent who will claim the child's exemption. The noncustodial parent must attach this form or similar statement to his or her tax return **each year** the exemption is claimed.

You are the **custodial parent** if you had custody of the child for most of the year. You are the **noncustodial parent** if you had custody for a shorter period of time or did not have custody at all. For the definition of custody, see **Pub. 501,** Exemptions, Standard Deduction, and Filing Information.

Support test for children of divorced or separated parents. Generally, the custodial parent is treated as having provided over half of the child's support if:

● The child received over half of his or her total support for the year from one or both of the parents **and**

● The child was in the custody of one or both of the parents for more than half of the year.

Note: *Public assistance payments, such as Temporary Assistance for Needy Families (TANF), are not support provided by the parents.*

For this support test to apply, the parents must be one of the following:

● Divorced or legally separated under a decree of divorce or separate maintenance,

● Separated under a written separation agreement, **or**

● Living apart at all times during the last 6 months of the year.

Caution: *This support test does not apply to parents who never married each other.*

If the support test applies, and the other four dependency tests in your tax return

instruction booklet are also met, the custodial parent can claim the child's exemption.

Exception. The custodial parent will not be treated as having provided over half of the child's support if **any** of the following apply.

● The custodial parent agrees not to claim the child's exemption by signing this form or similar statement.

● The child is treated as having received over half of his or her total support from a person under a multiple support agreement (**Form 2120,** Multiple Support Declaration).

● A pre-1985 divorce decree or written separation agreement states that the noncustodial parent can claim the child as a dependent. But the noncustodial parent must provide at least $600 for the child's support during the year. This rule does not apply if the decree or agreement was changed after 1984 to say that the noncustodial parent cannot claim the child as a dependent.

Additional information. For more details, see **Pub. 504,** Divorced or Separated Individuals.

Specific Instructions

Custodial parent. You may agree to release your claim to the child's exemption for the current tax year or for future years, or both.

● Complete **Part I** if you agree to release your claim to the child's exemption for the current tax year.

● Complete **Part II** if you agree to release your claim to the child's exemption for any or all future years. If you do, write the specific future year(s) or "all future years" in the space provided in Part II.

 To help ensure future support, you may not want to release your claim to the child's exemption for future years.

Noncustodial parent. Attach this form or similar statement to your tax return for **each year** you claim the child's exemption. You may claim the exemption **only** if the other four dependency tests in your tax return instruction booklet are met.

Note: *If the custodial parent released his or her claim to the child's exemption for any future year, you* **must** *attach a copy of this form or similar statement to your tax return for each future year that you claim the exemption.* **Keep a copy for your records.**

Paperwork Reduction Act Notice. We ask for the information on this form to carry out the Internal Revenue laws of the United States. You are required to give us the information. We need it to ensure that you are complying with these laws and to allow us to figure and collect the right amount of tax.

You are not required to provide the information requested on a form that is subject to the Paperwork Reduction Act unless the form displays a valid OMB control number. Books or records relating to a form or its instructions must be retained as long as their contents may become material in the administration of any Internal Revenue law. Generally, tax returns and return information are confidential, as required by Internal Revenue Code section 6103.

The time needed to complete and file this form will vary depending on individual circumstances. The estimated average time is:

Recordkeeping . . . . 7 min.

Learning about the law or the form . . . . 5 min.

Preparing the form . . . . . . 7 min.

Copying, assembling, and sending the form to the IRS . . 14 min.

If you have comments concerning the accuracy of these time estimates or suggestions for making this form simpler, we would be happy to hear from you. You can write to the Tax Forms Committee, Western Area Distribution Center, Rancho Cordova, CA 95743-0001. **Do not** send the form to this address. Instead, see the Instructions for Form 1040 or Form 1040A.

Cat. No. 13910F

Form **8332** (Rev. 12-2000)

83

Alimony Nontaxable/Nondeductible[1]

Melvyn B. Frumkes

DESIGNATION OF SUPPORT AS NONTAXABLE, NONDEDUCTIBLE

Under the alimony provisions of the Code,[2] a stream of payments paid under a divorce or separation instrument[3] which is cash to or on behalf of a spouse[4] the obligation for which ceases upon the death of the payee[5] for spouses living in separate households where the status of the marriage has changed,[6] and not fixed as child support[7] will be taxable to the payee[8] and deductible to the payor[9] so long as the divorce or separation instrument "does not designate such payment. . . . [as] not includable in gross income under [the alimony section of the Code § 71] and not allowable as a deduction under Section 215."

There are three types of divorce or separation instruments. The term "divorce or separation instrument" is defined in I.R.C. § 71(b)(2) as:

(A) a decree of divorce or separate maintenance or a written instrument incident to such a decree,

(B) a written separation agreement, or

(C) a decree (not described in subparagraph (A)) requiring a spouse to make payments for the support or maintenance of the other spouse.[10]

---

1. The following are excerpts from *Frumkes on Divorce Taxation*, Third Edition, by Melvyn B. Frumkes and published by the James Publishing, Inc., 3505 Cadillac Avenue, Suite H, Costa Mesa, California, toll-free telephone number 1-800-394-2626, website http://www .jamespublishing.com.
2. I.R.C. § 71.
3. I.R.C. § 71(b)(1)(A).
4. Including a former spouse.
5. I.R.C. § 71(b)(1)(D).
6. I.R.C. § 71(b)(1)(C).
7. I.R.C. § 71(c).
8. I.R.C. § 71(a).
9. I.R.C. § 215.
10. I.R.C. § 71(b)(2).

The court in *Richardson v. Commissioner,* 125 F.2d 551, 556 (7th Cir. 1997), in footnote 3, observed:

> Surprisingly, the Commissioner has not promulgated any regulations describing what a divorce or separation instrument must say, or what a divorce court must do, to "designate" the tax treatment to be afforded inter-spousal payments.

In *Richardson,* the court stated that in common usage, the term designate means "to make known directly" (quoting from *Webster's Third New International Dictionary*) and "to mark out and make known; to point out; to name; indicate" (quoting from *Black's Law Dictionary*).

An election can therefore be made to keep the payments out of "alimony" treatment under the Code and thus be nontaxable to the payee and nondeductible to the payor. A designation that payments are taxable/deductible is meaningless as the payments will be taxable/deductible only if the criteria of the Code are met, not if designated as such.[11]

Language in an order, decree, or agreement that the payor "shall be responsible for income taxes due" on the payments was held in *Jaffe v. Commissioner,* 77 T.C.M. 2167 (1999) that it "does not suffice to constitute a designation" of nontaxability/nondeductibility. Thus, the payee, Ms. Jaffe, was required to include payments to her as taxable income.

Since a court should take into consideration the net after-tax amount of alimony to a payee spouse, *Lutgert v. Lutgert,* 362 So. 2d 58 (Fla. 2d DCA 1978), thought should be given to designating the payments as nontaxable to the payee and nondeductible to the payor. Such a designation could accomplish the court's purpose of providing for all of the impecunious spouse's needs, which needs may not be fully met unless the amount of taxes on the alimony are taken into consideration in determining that amount.

Under the Domestic Relations provisions of the Tax Reform Act of 1984, separate streams of payment under a judgment, agreement, or order for support can have a different tax effect; that is, one stream of payment can comply with the alimony rules and qualify as deductible/taxable while another stream of payments can be designated as nondeductible and nontaxable.

A copy of the instrument containing the designation of payments as not alimony or separate maintenance payments must be attached to the payee's tax return (Form 1040) for each year in which the designation applies.[12]

DESIGNATION BY THE PARTIES

The designation of nontaxability/nondeductibility must be made pursuant to a divorce or separation instrument one of which, by its definition, is a written separation agreement. This, of course, is an agreement between the parties.[13]

Temp. Treas. Reg. § 1.71-1T, Q-8 inquires: "How may spouses designate that payments otherwise qualifying as alimony or separate maintenance

---

11. *McKelvey v. McKelvey,* 534 So. 2d 801 (Fla. 3d DCA 1988).
12. Temp. Treas. Reg. § 1.71-1T A8.
13. See § 3.4.2 of *Frumkes on Divorce Taxation* for a discussion of "a written separation agreement."

payments shall be excludible from the gross income of the payee and nondeductible by the payor?"

The answer in A-8 is: "The spouses may designate that payments otherwise qualifying as alimony or separate maintenance payments shall be nondeductible by the payor and excludible from gross income by the payee by so providing in a divorce or separation instrument (as defined in section 71(b)(2)). If the spouses have executed a written separation agreement (as described in section 71(b)(2)(B)), any writing signed by both spouses which designates otherwise qualifying alimony or separate maintenance payments as nondeductible and excludible and which refers to the written separation agreement will be treated as a written separation agreement (and thus a divorce or separation instrument) for purposes of the preceding sentence."

TEMPORARY SUPPORT ORDER, DESIGNATION BY COURT

An order for temporary support is a "(C)" type of divorce or separation instrument; i.e., "a decree [not a decree of divorce or separate maintenance] requiring a spouse to make payments for the support or maintenance of the other spouse."

Thus, the designation of nontaxability/nondeductibility can be made in an order or decree for temporary or *pendente lite* support or maintenance. Temp. Treas. Reg. § 1.71-1T A-8 so contemplates when it articulates that "If the spouses are subject to temporary support orders (as described in section 71(b)(2)(C)), the designation of otherwise qualifying alimony or separate payments as nondeductible and excludible must be made in the original or a subsequent temporary support order."[14]

FINAL DECREE OF DIVORCE OR
SEPARATE MAINTENANCE, DESIGNATION BY COURT

A final decree of divorce or separate maintenance also comes within the definition of a divorce or separation instrument in which the designation of nontaxability/nondeductibility can be made.

I.R.C. § 71(b)(2) uses the connective "or" in listing three types of divorce or separation instrument. Since the word "or" is a conjunctive "used to express a choice or a difference or to connect words or group of words of equal importance,"[15,16] there should be little doubt that a trial judge in the final decree or judgment of a divorce or dissolution of the marriage has the right to make the designation of a stream of payments as being nontaxable, nondeductible.

Many courts so recognize. In *Lowe v. Lowe*, 622 N.Y.S.2d 26 (App.Div. 1st Dept. 1995) it was held that "It is within the sound discretion of the

---

14. See also *McKelvey v. McKelvey*, 534 So. 2d 801 (Fla. 3d DCA 1988).

15. *The World Book Dictionary*, page 1050.

16. *Black's Law Dictionary* defines the word "or" as "a disjunctive particle used to express an alternative or to give a choice of one among two or more things."

court, pursuant to I.R.C. § 71(b)(1)(B), to provide in its order that the maintenance payments be neither income to the plaintiff [wife] nor deductible to the defendant [husband]."

An Ohio appellate decision has recognized that the trial court, even over the objection of one of the parties, can designate a stream of payments as "nontaxable spousal support."[17] In *Roddy v. Roddy*, 1999 WL 22589 (Ohio 4th Dist. 1999) the court said

> Not all court-ordered alimony and separate maintenance payments, however, fall within the federal statutory definition of "alimony or separate maintenance payment". . . . Pursuant to [I.R.C. § 71(b)(1)(A)] if a court designates a payment as not includible in the payee's gross income pursuant to Section 71 and not deductible from the payor's gross income pursuant to Section 215, then the payment, by definition, is not "alimony or separate maintenance."

A Virginia trial court in *Hamilton v. Hamilton*, 19 Va.Cir. 241, 1990 WL 751116 (Cir. Ct. of Va. 1990), in answering the question of whether the court may order a party, over his objection, to allocate the tax burden to him held that I.R.C. § 71 contains no prohibition of such court action "and no conflict between state and federal law would be created."

In *Almodovar v. Almodovar*, 754 So. 2d 861 (Fla. 3d DCA 2000), the appellate court observed:

> The usual treatment of alimony is to make the alimony taxable to the recipient and deductible by the payor. If the trial court wanted to avoid burdening the former wife with the tax consequences of the alimony payments the court has the discretion to provide that "the payor [former husband] will not deduct the alimony payments so that the payee [former wife] may then exclude the payments from gross income."

However, as in many family law cases, there is a holding to the contrary. Accordingly, notwithstanding the *Almodovar* decision of another district court, the 5th District Court of Appeal in Florida held in *Rykiel v. Rykiel*, 795 So. 2d 90 (Fla. 5th DCA 2000) that a trial court cannot make a designation in the final judgment that a stream of support payments be nontaxable without the agreement of the parties. In *Rykiel* the appellate court held that the trial court erred by designating an award of permanent periodic alimony as nontaxable to the receiving party because "there is no legal authority which would permit such practice. Permanent alimony is taxable to the recipient under federal tax law. Its taxability cannot be changed by a state court order."

On rehearing, the *Rykiel* court's rationale for its holding is that I.R.C. § 71 "was rewritten to clarify when a continuing stream of payments were to be characterized as maintenance and thereby taxable, or a property

---

17. The payments that were designated as nontaxable/nondeductible were an award of attorney's fees as "nontaxable spousal support." The fees were ordered to be paid in three equal monthly installments.

distribution, which is nontaxable."[18] In fact, the court opined that Temp. Treas. Reg. § 1.71-1T, A-8,[19] specifically provides that "the spouses may designate that separate maintenance payments are nondeductible by the payor and excludible from the gross income of the payee." The opinion went on, stating that "a reading of 26 U.S.C. § 71 and 26 C.F.R. § 1.71-1T, as a whole, convinces us that only the parties may agree to this in a written document, or on the record before the trial judge, which would be reduced to judgment."

Nevertheless, this author believes that the *Rykiel* opinion is wrong. It is this writer's firm opinion that a divorce court can designate in the final judgment that a stream of payments is nontaxable to the recipient and that the agreement of the parties is just another method of making such designation.

I.R.C. § 71 (b)(1)(B) provides that the payments will be taxable/deductible if not designated as nontaxable/nondeductible in "the divorce or separation instrument." The term "divorce or separation instrument" includes not only "a written separation agreement" (I.R.C. § 71 (b)(2)(B)), (thus, the "agreement by the parties"), but also a "decree of divorce" (I.R.C. § 71(b) (2)(A)), (which is solely for the court to enter).

When the *Rykiel* court adds that for the divorce decree to have a valid designation of nontaxability/nondeductibility it must be pursuant to an agreement of the parties "on the record before the trial judge," it adds to the Code an element that is just not there.

This writer believes that the Court based its thinking on the Q & A-8 of the Temporary Regulations 1.71-1T. The Temporary Regulation does not address the question of whether or not a trial court in its final judgment can designate payments as nontaxable/nondeductible. Q-8 of § 1.71-1T deals only with the question of "how may spouses designate that payments otherwise qualifying as alimony or separate maintenance payments shall be excludable from the gross income of the payee and nondeductible by the payor?" Q-8 does not ask how a court could make that designation.

It is also written in the introductory section, entitled "Supplementary Information," of the Temporary Regulations, that "no inference, however, should be drawn regarding questions not expressly raised and answered."

---

18. This author believes the *Rykiel* court misunderstood the 1984 Act that promulgated the current laws dealing with the taxability of alimony. The Code in § 71 makes no distinction of whether the payments are characterized as maintenance or property distribution.

In *Nelson v. Commissioner,* T.C. Memo 1998-268 (U.S. Tax Ct. 1998), the court agreed with the taxpayer's argument that "because the payments fit within the definition of alimony for federal income tax purposes, the intended purpose for the payments is of no consequence." It held "the possibility that the payments might have represented a division of marital property, makes no difference."

Likewise, in *Hopkinson v. Commissioner,* T.C. Memo 1999-154 (U.S. Tax Ct. 1999), the taxpayer unsuccessfully argued that she properly excluded the payments in issue from her gross income because they were intended by the parties to be a property settlement and not alimony.

19. The Temporary Regulations on Domestic Relations Tax Reform Act.

While the *Rykiel* case is now "on the books" in Florida (at least for those in the area of the Fifth District Court of Appeal) this writer believes the opinion is just plain wrong and should not be followed. This view is bolstered by a Florida decision handed down subsequent to *Rykiel*. In *Rashotsky v. Rashotsky*, 782 So. 2d 542 (Fla. 3d DCA 2001) the Court repeated what it pronounced in *Almodovar, supra*.

84

Taxation of Nonstatutory Stock Options and Deferred Compensation

Donald C. Schiller

WE HAVE ALL UNDERSTOOD that if an employee spouse transfers a portion of his or her stock options and retirement benefits upon divorce, the employee spouse is making a Section 1041 transfer to his or her former spouse. The former spouse then takes the employee spouse's basis for tax purposes, and there is no tax on the transfer to the former spouse. When the options are sold or exercised, the transferee/former spouse must declare the income.

Now, *Revenue Ruling* 2002-22 confirms our understanding, but creates a distinction between vested and unvested stock options and deferred compensation rights.

The issues discussed in the *Revenue Ruling* are as follows:

1. Is a taxpayer who transfers interests in nonstatutory stock options and nonqualified deferred compensation plans to the taxpayer's former spouse incident to divorce required to include the amounts in gross income at the time of the transfer?
2. Is the taxpayer or the former spouse required to include an amount in gross income when the former spouse exercises the stock options or when the deferred compensation is paid or made available to the former spouse?

The facts in the *Revenue Ruling* involved an employee who was given nonstatutory stock options by his employer. The options did not have a readily ascertainable fair market value within the meaning of Section 1.83-7(b) of the *Income Tax Regulations* at the time the options were granted. As a result, nothing was included in the employee spouse's gross income with respect to the options at the time of the grant.

The employee spouse also maintained two unfunded, nonqualified deferred compensation plans which gave the employee spouse the right to receive post-employment payments. The employee spouse's contractual rights to the deferred compensation benefits under his two plans were not contingent on his performance of future services for the company.

Under the law of the state where the parties lived, stock options and unfunded deferred compensation rights earned by a spouse during the marriage were marital property subject to equitable division between the spouses. Pursuant to the property settlement incorporated in the 2002 divorce judgment, the employee spouse transferred one-third of the non-statutory stock options and the right to receive portions of the deferred compensation payments to the non-employee spouse. The *Revenue Ruling* then assumed that: in 2006, the non-employee spouse exercised all of the stock options and received stock with a fair market value in excess of the exercised price of the options; and in 2011, the employee spouse terminated employment and the non-employee spouse therefore received payments from both of the deferred compensation plans.

The *Revenue Ruling* discusses the fact that Section 1041(a) provides that no gain or loss is recognized on a transfer of property to a former spouse incident to divorce. Section 1041(b) provides that the property transferred is treated as acquired by the receiving spouse by gift such that the receiving spouse's basis in the property is the unfunded deferred compensation rights or other future income rights to the extent such options or rights are unvested at the time of transfer or to the extent that the transferor's rights to such income are subject to substantial contingencies at the time of the transfer. *See Kochansky v. Commissioner,* 92 F.3d 957 (9th Cir. 1996). Although transfers of certain types of property incident to divorce whose tax consequences are governed by a specific provision of the code or regulations will not be affected by this ruling, there are other types of unvested or contingent rights that may constitute marital property which the courts divide on an "if, as and when received" basis. These types of assets would be taxed to the transferor spouse under application of this *Revenue Ruling.*

The Hot Tip is that if there are unvested benefits of any kind or other future income rights that are subject to contingencies at the time of transfer, include provisions in your marital settlement agreement specifically indicating how the spouses will treat these items for purposes of federal and state income taxation. The following is my suggested sample language:

> **Tax Treatment of Non-Statutory Stock Options/Unfunded Deferred Compensation/Other Future Income Rights Transferred Incident to Divorce.** In the event that all or any part of the property and/or income to be earned and received pursuant to Paragraph _____ of this marital settlement agreement is not so includible by the (name of transferee spouse) and is deemed taxable to the (transferor spouse), whether by Internal Revenue Service interpretation, amendment or repeal of existing revenue statutes, by case law or otherwise, then the (transferee spouse) shall pay to the (transferor spouse) an amount equal to the transferor's spouse's tax detriment as a result of tax treatment not intended by this marital settlement agreement.

PART

IX

Retirement Plans

NO OFFENSE TO EMPLOYEE BENEFIT LAWYERS intended, but family lawyers are people people. They do not tend to stay in a closed office all day reading fine print in IRS regulations. This suits family lawyers well in meeting with clients and in settlement. But retirement-plan analysis requires being familiar with lots of small print.

The problem is that almost every divorce requires familiarity with retirement-plan issues. In our debt-ridden consumer society, the retirement plan is frequently the only asset that can be leveraged or spent. As a result, these plans play a great role in our cases. After all, when you get to property division in a case, it is nice to have some property to divide.

So these matters are complicated and technical yet incredibly important. Time to turn to our experts for their tips and ideas on how to handle them.

85 Not all pensions are going to be divided equally. Sometimes, there is less than full vesting at the time of divorce, or not all of the pension was earned during the marriage. Calculating the spousal share is necessary to determine an equitable outcome, and **David Zaumeyer** gives some simple suggestions for those of us who are "arithmetic-challenged."

86 QDROs are great for qualified plans, but nonqualified plans can be worth substantial money. **Dan Jaffe** provides examples of plans to look for that are not subject to ERISA.

87 Many times, securing approval of the QDRO takes longer than the divorce itself. Sometimes the process seems to take longer than the parties were married. **Terry Kapp** suggests some practical and easy ways to speed up the process.

88 If you never have tried to divide a military pension, do not assume that they are like other retirement plans. They are not. **William Darrah** discusses the intricacies of military retirement benefits as they apply in divorce.

89 While retirement assets are frequently the major asset (and sometimes the only asset) of a marital estate in divorce, many clients face a cash crunch because of the financial disadvantages of being divorced. Removing the funds early from the retirement plan triggers a 10 percent penalty, but the money is needed now, not years later at retirement. **Dan Jaffe** reveals a means of avoiding the 10 percent premature distribution penalty and includes several sample scenarios.

90 Some retirement plans are more difficult to divide than others. Federal civil service plans are particularly tricky, and **Susan Wolfson** explains some of the dangers and how to avoid them.

91 **Joanne Ross Wilder** notes that the manner in which the QDRO is drafted is of great importance. She discusses some of the potential problems and provides a sample form with options to choose to fit the individual circumstances of each case.

92 While there are various forms available for dividing retirement plans, there is still great room for creativity. By negotiating specific clauses and drafting clauses appropriately, lawyers can provide great service to their clients. **Joy Feinberg's** hot tip lists certain benefits that can be gained by careful drafting and provides sample language.

93 Did you know that a QDRO can be used not only to divide a retirement plan, but to enforce spousal and child support as well? **Laura Morgan** explains how, including examining the tricky tax issues involved and giving citations to a number of cases from around the country.

85

Pension Arithmetic Made Easier: Calculating the Spousal Share

David J. Zaumeyer, Ph.D., CPA

INTRODUCTION

Family law practitioners and the courts have struggled with computing the share of employee spouse's pension distributable to the nonemployee spouse ever since it was decided that pensions are marital property. The "share" calculation has some potentially difficult aspects that can be made somewhat easier using the following simple suggestions.

HOW MUCH OF THE PENSION IS MARITAL?

Because lawyers are inevitably dealing with unmatured pensions (vested or not), pension valuators calculate the value of the **accrued** (accumulated) benefit as of a particular date. So the first task is to identify how much (i.e., what percentage) of the value of this accrued benefit accumulated **during the marriage**. The calculation employs the following fraction:

$$\frac{\text{Years in Pension Plan While Married}}{\text{Total Years in Pension Plan to Calculation Date}} = \underline{\hspace{1cm}}\%$$

A couple married in 1970 commencing a divorce action in 1988 with the employee spouse in the pension plan since 1970 (or any time thereafter) should have 100 percent of the accrued benefit deemed marital, while only 90 percent would be deemed marital if the employee spouse joined the plan in 1968.

HOW MUCH OF THE PENSION DEEMED MARITAL IS DISTRIBUTABLE?

When unmatured pensions are not collectible until normal retirement age, a second calculation should be used to determine the distributive share. This calculation would reflect the fact that the nonemployee spouse shared in only a *portion* of the total employment period required to reach collectible status. In other words, where the employee spouse must stay employed and perhaps fulfill other obligations as well beyond the divorce until the designated retirement date for the pension to have *realizable value,* a calculation, such as what follows, might be used to find the distributable share:

$$\frac{\text{Years in Pension Plan While Married}}{\text{Total Years in Pension Plan Until Normal Retirement}} = \underline{\qquad}\%$$

For example, a couple married in 1970, commencing a divorce action in 1988 with the employee spouse in the plan since 1970 who must wait nine more years until age fifty-five (or in the year 1997) to collect anything, would split 2/3 (18/27) of the total present value of the accrued benefit. Under the most equitable situations, the maximum a nonemployee spouse would be entitled to is 50 percent of the distributable share, or approximately 33⅓ percent. If the present value of the accrued benefit is $100,000, $66,667 is distributable and $33,334 is the nonemployee spouse's share.

HOW MUCH IS THE DISTRIBUTABLE SHARE OF THE ACCRUED PENSION BENEFIT REALLY WORTH?

If the nonemployee spouse is to be given a share of the accrued pension benefit calculated as of a particular point in time (e.g., the commencement of the divorce action or actual separation), some allowance for the time value of money (i.e., interest) might be conceded if the distributable share is not paid until the date of divorce.

There are at least three alternative calculations that can be performed to remove perceived inequity because of "waiting time":

1. Calculate the interest that might otherwise have been earned on the distributive share if it had been paid out at the calculation date. From the previous example, the nonemployee's share was $33,334. If three years elapsed between calculation (say in 1988) and divorce/payout (in say 1991), the value of this share would grow to approximately $38,600 at 5 percent interest.

2. Recalculate the previous "distributable share" fraction, increasing the numerator of the fraction by the amount of "waiting time"; multiply the resultant adjusted percentage by the benefit value. Again using the previous example, the distributive share percentage now would be 77.8 percent (21/27), the distributive share of $100,000 would amount to $77,800, and a fifty-fifty distribution would give the nonemployee spouse $38,850.

3. Recalculate the value of the pension as of the divorce (or trial) date (let's say that now it is $135,000) and recalculate the distributive share fraction increasing the denominator to 21 for the "waiting time" (three years) and leaving the numerator unchanged at 18, which yields the fraction 18/21, or 86 percent. Using this data, the nonemployee spouse's share would be $38,700 ($135,000 × 86 percent × 66.7 percent × 50 percent).

HOW MUCH SHOULD THE EMPLOYED SPOUSE PAY OUT?

Once the distributive share value has been determined, there remains the question of how much to actually pay out or exchange in kind. This arithmetic is complicated by two factors:

1. Income tax considerations and
2. Present value considerations.

A realistic position by the payer spouse may be to reduce the value of the distributive share by the appropriate marginal tax rate if this share were to be paid in cash. If the share were to be exchanged for another asset or the right to a share of this asset, then the appropriate tax rates on each should be calculated and netted one against the other.

If the original commencement date is to be considered the distribution date even if the actual divorce will occur some time in the future (as in the previous example), some discounting to present value (from the divorce or trial date to the original commencement date) may be in order. This discounting simply recognizes the time value of money in favor of the payer spouse.

NOTE: Consult with your pension expert before applying any of the formulas suggested previously. Each pension plan must be evaluated uniquely, for vesting provisions, funding requirements, and other plan attributes can differ significantly.

86

Do Not Miss the Nonqualified Deferred Compensation Plans

Daniel J. Jaffe

MOST LAWYERS NOW KNOW about and do not miss the normal ERISA-qualified deferred compensation plans when handling dissolution matters. They discover, evaluate, and divide:

A. Defined benefit plans;
B. Defined contribution plans;
C. Keogh plans;
D. 401(k) plans;
E. Incentive stock options; and
F. IRAs.

Most lawyers do not know about and consequently do not discover, evaluate, and divide deferred compensation plans normally established for the highly compensated executive.

New nonqualified deferred compensation plans are being developed for the following reasons:

A. Tax laws have changed that have decreased the benefits of most defined benefit plans as follows:
    1. Decrease in amount of yearly benefits;
    2. Vesting rules include more employees making plans more expensive; and
    3. Penalties and excise taxes on overfunded plans.
B. Decrease in tax rates includes:
    1. Less benefit to employee to defer receipt of benefit when rates may increase; and
    2. Cost to employer increases with reduction in tax rates.
C. Leveraged buyouts and hostile takeovers create methods to protect the executive:
    1. "Golden Parachutes" and
    2. "Silver Seatbelts."
D. Shifting of executives from company to company creates the need for vehicles to attract and keep highly compensated individuals.

Nonqualified compensation plans are difficult to locate and may be missed:

A. Do not appear on "employee benefits" line of corporate tax return; and

B. Are not pension plans, and improperly phrased interrogatories or deposition questions will miss.

The New Executive Benefit Plans include:

A. "Excess Benefit Plans":
    1. Provide benefits in excess of limits on contributions and benefits of tax-qualified plans;
    2. Can discriminate in favor of highly compensated executive; and
    3. Contribution nondeductible to company until the executive has constructive receipt of benefit.

B. Supplemental Executive Retirement Plans (SERPs):
    1. Provide benefits in excess of $200,000 compensation limit;
    2. Provide for employee pretax deferrals in excess of $7,000 limits on 401(k) plan;
    3. Replace benefits for employee hired away;
    4. Benefits enhanced for early retirement; and
    5. Avoid 15 percent excise tax on annual distributions of more than $150,000.

C. "Top-Hat" Plans (ERISA 201(2), 301(A)(3), 401(A)(1)):
    1. Must exist for SERP to avoid ERISA restrictions for funding, vesting; and
    2. Must be unfunded and maintained for providing deferred compensation for select or "highly compensated" employees (top 2 percent or three times Social Security base—$135,000)

D. Rabbi Trusts:
    1. Irrevocable grantor trust to hold assets for deferred compensation or supplemental retirement benefits;
    2. Trust remains subject to the creditors of employer or insolvency;
    3. Secure employee benefits against changes in management;
    4. IRS has approved since 1984 (PLR 8113107; GCM 39230); and
    5. Sometimes funded with life insurance policies or annuities.

E. Springing Rabbi Trusts:
    1. Funded on the occurrence of a specific event; and
    2. Sometimes used to fund in event of a hostile takeover.

F. Secular Trusts and Annuities:
    1. Irrevocable trust where assets are not subject to claims of creditors;
    2. Higher immediate funding costs; if used with "Top-Hat" Plan, must comply with ERISA requirements; early reversions to employer not permitted if overfunded; and
    3. Generally tax-deductible to employer when made and taxable to employee who usually receives gross-up bonus to cover.

87

A Quicker Way to Obtain Approval of Your Qualified Domestic Relations Order

C. Terrence Kapp

AS WE ALL ARE AWARE under § 414(p)(6)(A)(ii) of the IRC, the plan administrator has a reasonable time in which to approve a QDRO. Here is a tip regarding what I have done and do regularly in my practice to expedite the obtaining of that approval.

When I first become aware that a QDRO may be issued, I immediately determine the name and address of the plan administrator. I then telephone the plan administrator and advise the administrator there may be a QDRO issued regarding one of the participants in the plan. I then inquire whether or not the company uses a standard format. Many companies do. If they do, I ask for a copy. When the time comes to prepare the QDRO, I use as much of the plan administrator's language as possible.

I then take it one step further and again telephone the plan administrator and advise the administrator that I will be sending a draft of the QDRO to the administrator to review. At this point, you will be told the plan administrator cannot preapprove the QDRO by looking at a draft. No approval can be given until the actual QDRO is received. However, by advising the plan administrator that you are totally aware of this, and that all you are looking to do at this stage is to determine whether the draft is satisfactory, you can correct any possible problems in advance.

I have found that most plan administrators actually are delighted to work with you. They find that it saves them work because most problems can be solved in advance. In fact, I find that they become very cooperative and want to help.

Even if you find a company that does not use a standard format, you still can use this approach. It still is an excellent idea to establish a relationship with the plan administrator. Get to know him or her on a first-name basis. It is wise to send a draft of the QDRO to the plan administrator for review to determine if there are any problems. Again, you will be advised that in no way does this imply any approval whatsoever. However, this process almost assures the approval of your plan and also expedites its approval.

88

Military Issues in Divorce

William C. Darrah

THOSE ISSUES THAT TYPICALLY ARISE in a divorce involving a military member are as follows:

A. Division of military retirement as and for property division;
B. Military retirement as a source for alimony and/or child support;
C. Benefits under the military Survivor Benefit Plan;
D. Medical, commissary, and exchange privileges;
E. Champus, Medicare, and group health insurance for those not qualifying for military medical care;
F. ID cards for spouses, former spouses, and children;
G. Tax aspects of division of military benefits; and
H. Social Security benefits.

MILITARY RETIREMENT

The Uniform Services Former Spouses Protection Act of 1982 (USFSPA) authorizes state divorce courts to divide military retirement pay for alimony, child support, or property division. Where the parties were married for at least ten years while the member was on active duty, USFSPA provides for direct payment from the military.

Where the divorce was final before November 14, 1986, the retirement pay of a member retired for disability under Chapter 61 of Title 10 of the U.S. Code is exempt. A portion of the retirement pay of a disabled member who retired after November 14, 1986, is divisible.

Under USFSPA, payment to a former spouse is to be either in a dollar amount or as a percentage of "disposable retired or retainer pay." Disposable retired or retainer pay is gross pay less deductions for amounts owed to the United States for fines, etc., withholding for federal, state, or local income taxes, and withholding for Survivor Benefit Plan (SBP) premiums if the former spouse is a beneficiary. Direct payment to a former spouse cannot exceed 50 percent of the member's disposable retired or retainer pay. Payment of up to an additional 15 percent of disposable retired pay is authorized to honor garnishment orders for child support and/or alimony, and garnishment orders for nonpayment of property settlement other than division of retired pay.

Where more than one former spouse is entitled to a share of the member's retirement, their respective claims will be honored on a "first come, first served" basis.

Federal taxes are withheld on the entire amount of a military member's retirement without regard to amounts paid to the former spouse. The member therefore withholds for both parties. When the member receives his W-2P at the end of each year, withholding is allocated between the member and the former spouse in proportion to the division of gross retirement, and each party reports its gross retirement as income on his or her separate tax return.

SURVIVOR BENEFIT PLAN

Membership in the military (SBP) entitles the beneficiary to annuity benefits following the death of the member. A military member may elect SBP coverage for a qualified beneficiary at the time of his or her retirement. If the member elects SBP coverage, a monthly premium is deducted from retired pay following retirement.

If a former spouse was an SBP beneficiary before the divorce, he or she may be reinstated if both parties so agree in writing and their agreement is incorporated into their divorce decree or if the court so orders.

If the member has not retired at the time of the divorce, the parties may make a binding agreement obligating the member to designate his or her former spouse as an SBP beneficiary at the time of retirement or the court may so order.

In any event, a qualified ex-spouse must make application for coverage within one year of the date of the divorce, or within one year of the member's date of retirement following the divorce, whichever comes later. Failure to do so will cause a loss of coverage, notwithstanding existing court orders.

MEDICAL, COMMISSARY, AND EXCHANGE PRIVILEGES

A former spouse who was married to a military member for at least twenty years while the member was on active duty is entitled to full medical, commissary, and exchange privileges. Such former spouses are referred to as being in the "20-20-20" group.

Former spouses divorced before April 1, 1985, who were married to a military member for at least twenty years, fifteen years of which coincided with the member's active duty career, are entitled to continued medical privileges. They are not entitled to commissary or exchange privileges. These former spouses are referred to as being in the "20-20-15" group.

Former spouses in the "20-20-15" group divorced after April 1, 1985, retain medical privileges for one year from the date of the divorce. Thereafter, they may join the so-called Uniform Services Voluntary Insurance Plan established by Mutual of Omaha at the direction of the Department of Defense.

In all cases, a former spouse is entitled to receive medical benefits only if he or she does not have medical insurance through his or her own employment. If employment is lost, a former spouse may reapply for military benefits. Furthermore, all benefits cease if a former spouse remarries. Commissary and exchange privileges will be reinstated if the subsequent marriage ends by death or divorce, but medical privileges are not reinstated.

CHAMPUS AND MEDICARE

Former spouses in the "20-20-20" group lose their Champus medical coverage when they reach age sixty-five and are automatically enrolled in Medicare. However, they are still eligible to use military facilities for inpatient or outpatient care. Those who reside near military facilities may not wish to pay the extra cost for the so-called Medicare supplement, although it also is important to remember that military facilities will treat former spouses, as well as retirees and their dependents, only on a space-available basis.

APPLYING FOR NEW ID CARDS

Former spouses who are entitled to medical and/or commissary or exchange privileges are entitled to new ID cards. Application should be made to a facility of the former spouse's branch of service. Certified copies of the marriage certificate and divorce decree are required.

Those who do not reside near a facility of their former spouse's branch of service may communicate to the following to obtain a new ID card.

Army:	U.S. Army Reserve
	Component Personnel
	& Administration Center
	Attn: DARC-PSE-VC
	9700 Page Boulevard
	St. Louis, Missouri 63132-5200
Air Force:	Headquarters AFMPC/MPCDO
	Randolph Air Force Base
	San Antonio, Texas 78150-6001
Navy:	Commander
	Navy Military Personnel Command
	(NMPC-121)
	Navy Department
	Washington, D.C. 20370-5121
Marine Corps:	Commandant
	U.S. Marine Corps
	Headquarters U.S. Marine Corps
	Code MMSR-6
	Washington, D.C. 20380-0001
Coast Guard:	Commandant (G-PS-1)
	U.S. Coast Guard
	Washington, D.C. 20593

Nondivorced spouses and their children who are legally or physically separated from a military member are eligible for medical, commissary, and exchange privileges, and are entitled to ID cards. Children age eleven and over of former spouses in the "20-20-20" group also are entitled to commissary and exchange privileges, and ID cards. Children of all other divorced military members are eligible for medical care regardless of the status of the spouse.

QUESTIONS ABOUT MILITARY BENEFITS

Questions concerning divorce-related military issues should be addressed to the following:

Army:
Commander
Army Finance and Accounting Center
Attn: FINCL-G
Indianapolis, Indiana 46249
(317) 546-9211

Navy:
Director
Defense Finance and Accounting Services
Federal Building
Cleveland, Ohio 44199
(216) 522-5301
(216) 522-5985

Air Force:
Commander
Air Force Accounting and Finance Center
Attn: JA
Denver, Colorado 80279-5000
(303) 676-7417
1 (800) 531-7502
1 (800) 321-1080

Marine Corps:
Commanding Officer
Marine Corps Finance Center
(Code DG)
Kansas City, Missouri 64197
(816) 926-7103

Coast Guard:
Commanding Officer, Retired CSCG
Pay & Personnel Center
444 S.E. Quincy Street
Topeka, Kansas 66683-3591
(913) 357-3415

89

Avoiding the 10 Percent Penalty for Early Distributions from Retirement Plans

Daniel J. Jaffe

A 10 PERCENT PENALTY is imposed on early withdrawals from qualified retirement plans, including IRAs. The plans subject to this penalty include a plan described in section[1] 401(a), including a trust exempt from tax under section 501(a); an annuity plan described in section 403(a); an annuity contract described in section 403(b); an individual retirement account described in section 408(a); and an individual retirement annuity described in section 408(b). **See** IRC § 4974. Early withdrawal is considered withdrawal before the employee reaches the age of fifty-nine and a half.

Where the 10 percent penalty applies, the employee's income tax is increased by an amount equal to 10 percent of the amount of the premature distribution includable in gross income. The penalty is reported on Form 5329.

IRC § 72(t) provides certain limited exceptions to the rule imposing this 10 percent penalty. These exceptions include distributions:

A. Made to a beneficiary (or to the estate of the employee) on or after the death of the employee;
B. Attributable to the employee's being disabled within the meaning of subsection (m)(7);
C. Part of a series of substantially equal periodic payments (not less frequently than annually) made for the life (or life expectancy) of the employee or the joint lives (or joint life expectancies) of the employee and his or her designated beneficiary;
D. Made to an employee after separation from service after attaining the age of fifty-five;

---

1. All code references are to the Internal Revenue Code.

E. Dividends paid with respect to stock of a corporation that are described in section 404(k);

F. Medical expenses; and

G. Payments to alternative payees pursuant to qualified domestic relations orders or any distribution to an alternate payee pursuant to a qualified domestic relations order (within the meaning of § 414(p)(1)).

There are limitations to these exceptions. For example, exceptions "D," "F," and "G" do not apply to distributions from an IRA. Thus, distributions from an IRA are not payable pursuant to a QDRO and remain subject to the 10 percent penalty on early distributions. Also, periodic payments under qualified plans must begin after separation from employment. Section "C" does not apply to any amount paid from a trust described in section 401(a) that is exempt from tax under section 501(a) or from a contract described in section 72(e)(5)(D)(ii)[2] unless the series of payments begins after the employee separates from service.

TIP

When using § 408(d)(6) to divide IRA funds between divorcing spouses, remember section "C" (IRC § 72(t)(2)(1)(A)(iv)) and annuitize the distribution. Making substantially equal periodic payments will allow the supported spouse to maintain IRA funds while earning tax-free interest. With principal and interest withdrawn on a penalty-free basis, the need for spousal support will be decreased.

The following scenarios illustrate different ways $370,000 worth of IRA funds can be distributed to the supported spouse without penalty.

---

2. Section 72(e)(5)(D)(ii) states: "from a contract—(I) purchased by a trust described in clause (i), (II) purchased as part of a plan described in section 403(a), (III) described in section 403(b), or (IV) provided by employees of a life insurance company under a plan described in section 818(a)(3) . . ."

Scenario #1

Level Payments for 5 Years Then
Payments over Remaining Lifetime Starting at Age 62
Projection of Distributions & Account Balances
Based on a 6% Net Rate of Return

Data & Assumptions Utilized

Name of Payee: Donna Divorcee	Date of Birth: Aug. 9, 1937
Asset Value: $370,000	Date Valued: Dec. 31, 1993
State & Fed. Income Tax Rate: 40.0000%	1st Payment: Sep. 1, 1997
Investment Yield: 6.00%	Payment Frequency: Monthly

Projection of Distributions & Balances

Year Ending Dec. 31	Age	Invest. Income	Annuity Payments	Income Taxes	Net Payout	Balance End Year
1994	57	22,200	14,508	5,803	8,705	377,692
1995	58	22,662	34,818	13,927	20,891	365,536
1996	59	21,932	34,818	13,927	20,891	352,650
1997	60	21,159	34,818	13,927	20,891	338,991
1998	61	20,339	34,818	13,927	20,891	324,512
1999	62	19,471	26,375	10,550	15,825	317,608
2000	63	19,056	26,375	10,550	15,825	310,289
2001	64	18,617	26,375	10,550	15,825	302,532
2002	65	18,152	26,375	10,550	15,825	294,309
2003	66	17,659	26,375	10,550	15,825	285,592
2004	67	17,136	26,375	10,550	15,825	276,353
2005	68	16,581	26,375	10,550	15,825	266,559
2006	69	15,994	26,375	10,550	15,825	256,177
2007	70	15,371	26,375	10,550	15,825	245,173
2008	71	14,710	26,375	10,550	15,825	233,508
SUBTOTALS		281,039	417,530	167,011	250,519	

Scenario #1

Level Payments for 5 Years Then
Payments over Remaining Lifetime Starting at Age 62
Projection of Distributions & Account Balances
Based on a 6% Net Rate of Return

Projection of Distributions & Balances

Year Ending Dec. 31	Age	Invest. Income	Annuity Payments	Income Taxes	Net Payout	Balance End Year
2009	72	14,010	26,375	10,550	15,825	221,144
2010	73	13,269	26,375	10,550	15,825	208,037
2011	74	12,482	26,375	10,550	15,825	194,145
2012	75	11,649	26,375	10,550	15,825	179,418
2013	76	10,765	26,375	10,550	15,825	163,808
2014	77	9,829	26,375	10,550	15,825	147,262
2015	78	8,836	26,375	10,550	15,825	129,723
2016	79	7,783	26,375	10,550	15,825	111,131
2017	80	6,668	26,375	10,550	15,825	91,424
2018	81	5,485	26,375	10,550	15,825	70,534
2019	82	4,232	26,375	10,550	15,825	48,391
2020	83	2,903	26,375	10,550	15,825	24,920
2021	84	1,495	26,375	10,550	15,825	40
SUBTOTALS		109,406	342,875	137,150	205,725	
TOTALS		390,445	760,405	304,161	456,244	

Scenario #2

Level Payments for 5 Years Then
Payments over Remaining Lifetime Starting at Age 62
Projection of Distributions & Account Balances Based
on an 8% Net Rate of Return

Data & Assumptions Utilized

Name of Payee: Donna Divorcee		Date of Birth:	Aug. 9, 1937
Asset Value: $370,000		Date Valued:	Dec. 31, 1993
State & Fed. Income Tax Rate: 40.0000%		1st Payment:	Sep. 1, 1997
Investment Yield: 8.00%		Payment Frequency:	Monthly

Projection of Distributions & Balances

Year Ending Dec. 31	Age	Invest. Income	Annuity Payments	Income Taxes	Net Payout	Balance End Year
1994	57	29,600	14,508	5,803	8,705	385,092
1995	58	30,807	34,818	13,927	20,891	381,081
1996	59	30,487	34,818	13,927	20,891	376,750
1997	60	30,140	34,818	13,927	20,891	372,072
1998	61	29,766	34,818	13,927	20,891	367,020
1999	62	29,362	35,385	14,154	21,231	360,996
2000	63	28,880	35,385	14,154	21,231	354,491
2001	64	28,359	35,385	14,154	21,231	347,465
2002	65	27,797	35,385	14,154	21,231	339,877
2003	66	27,190	35,385	14,154	21,231	331,683
2004	67	26,535	35,385	14,154	21,231	322,832
2005	68	25,827	35,385	14,154	21,231	313,274
2006	69	25,062	35,385	14,154	21,231	302,951
2007	70	24,236	35,385	14,154	21,231	291,802
2008	71	23,344	35,385	14,154	21,231	279,761
SUBTOTALS		417,392	507,630	203,051	304,579	

Scenario #2

Level Payments for 5 Years Then
Payments over Remaining Lifetime Starting at Age 62
Projection of Distributions & Account Balances Based
on an 8% Net Rate of Return

Projection of Distributions & Balances

Year Ending Dec. 31	Age	Invest. Income	Annuity Payments	Income Taxes	Net Payout	Balance End Year
2009	72	22,381	35,385	14,154	21,231	266,757
2010	73	21,341	35,385	14,154	21,231	252,712
2011	74	20,217	35,385	14,154	21,231	237,544
2012	75	19,004	35,385	14,154	21,231	221,163
2013	76	17,693	35,385	14,154	21,231	203,471
2014	77	16,278	35,385	14,154	21,231	184,363
2015	78	14,749	35,385	14,154	21,231	163,727
2016	79	13,098	35,385	14,154	21,231	141,441
2017	80	11,315	35,385	14,154	21,231	117,371
2018	81	9,390	35,385	14,154	21,231	91,376
2019	82	7,310	35,385	14,154	21,231	63,301
2020	83	5,064	35,385	14,154	21,231	32,980
2021	84	2,638	35,385	14,154	21,231	233
SUBTOTALS		180,478	460,005	184,002	276,003	
TOTALS		597,870	967,635	387,053	580,582	

Scenario #3

Payments over Remaining Lifetime Starting at Age 60
Projection of Distributions & Account Balances Based
on a 6% Net Rate of Return

Data & Assumptions Utilized

Name of Payee: Donna Divorcee	Date of Birth: Aug. 9, 1937
Asset Value: $370,000	Date Valued: Dec. 31, 1993
State & Fed. Income Tax Rate: 40.0000%	1st Payment: Sep. 1, 1997
Investment Yield: 6.00%	Payment Frequency: Monthly

Projection of Distributions & Balances

Year Ending Dec. 31	Age	Invest. Income	Annuity Payments	Income Taxes	Net Payout	Balance End Year
1994	57	22,200	0	0	0	392,200
1995	58	23,532	0	0	0	415,732
1996	59	24,944	0	0	0	440,676
1997	60	26,441	34,470	13,788	20,682	432,646
1998	61	25,959	34,470	13,788	20,682	424,135
1999	62	25,448	34,470	13,788	20,682	415,113
2000	63	24,907	34,470	13,788	20,682	405,550
2001	64	24,333	34,470	13,788	20,682	395,413
2002	65	23,725	34,470	13,788	20,682	384,668
2003	66	23,080	34,470	13,788	20,682	373,278
2004	67	22,397	34,470	13,788	20,682	361,205
2005	68	21,672	34,470	13,788	20,682	348,407
2006	69	20,904	34,470	13,788	20,682	334,841
2007	70	20,090	34,470	13,788	20,682	320,462
2008	71	19,228	34,470	13,788	20,682	305,220
SUBTOTALS		348,860	413,640	165,456	248,184	

Scenario #3

Payments over Remaining Lifetime Starting at Age 60
Projection of Distributions & Account Balances Based
on a 6% Net Rate of Return

Projection of Distributions & Balances

Year Ending Dec. 31	Age	Invest. Income	Annuity Payments	Income Taxes	Net Payout	Balance End Year
2009	72	18,313	34,470	13,788	20,682	289,063
2010	73	17,344	34,470	13,788	20,682	271,937
2011	74	16,316	34,470	13,788	20,682	253,783
2012	75	15,227	34,470	13,788	20,682	234,540
2013	76	14,072	34,470	13,788	20,682	214,142
2014	77	12,849	34,470	13,788	20,682	192,521
2015	78	11,551	34,470	13,788	20,682	169,602
2016	79	10,176	34,470	13,788	20,682	145,308
2017	80	8,718	34,470	13,788	20,682	119,557
2018	81	7,173	34,470	13,788	20,682	92,260
2019	82	5,536	34,470	13,788	20,682	63,326
2020	83	3,800	34,470	13,788	20,682	32,655
2021	84	1,959	34,470	13,788	20,682	144
SUBTOTALS		143,034	448,110	179,244	268,866	
TOTALS		491,894	861,750	344,700	517,050	

Scenario #4

Payments over Remaining Lifetime Starting at Age 60
Projection of Distributions & Account Balances Based
on an 8% Net Rate of Return

Data & Assumptions Utilized

Name of Payee: Donna Divorcee	Date of Birth: Aug. 9, 1937
Asset Value: $370,000	Date Valued: Dec. 31, 1993
State & Fed. Income Tax Rate: 40.0000%	1st Payment: Sep. 1, 1997
Investment Yield: 8.00%	Payment Frequency: Monthly

Projection of Distributions & Balances

Year Ending Dec. 31	Age	Invest. Income	Annuity Payments	Income Taxes	Net Payout	Balance End Year
1994	57	29,600	0	0	0	399,600
1995	58	31,968	0	0	0	431,568
1996	59	34,525	0	0	0	466,093
1997	60	37,287	43,660	17,464	26,196	459,721
1998	61	36,778	43,660	17,464	26,196	452,839
1999	62	36,227	43,660	17,464	26,196	445,406
2000	63	35,632	43,660	17,464	26,196	437,378
2001	64	34,990	43,660	17,464	26,196	428,708
2002	65	34,297	43,660	17,464	26,196	419,345
2003	66	33,548	43,660	17,464	26,196	409,233
2004	67	32,739	43,660	17,464	26,196	398,311
2005	68	31,865	43,660	17,464	26,196	386,516
2006	69	30,921	43,660	17,464	26,196	373,777
2007	70	29,902	43,660	17,464	26,196	360,020
2008	71	28,802	43,660	17,464	26,196	345,161
SUBTOTALS		499,081	523,920	209,568	314,352	

Scenario #4

Payments over Remaining Lifetime Starting at Age 60
Projection of Distributions & Account Balances Based
on an 8% Net Rate of Return

Projection of Distributions & Balances

Year Ending Dec. 31	Age	Invest. Income	Annuity Payments	Income Taxes	Net Payout	Balance End Year
2009	72	27,613	43,660	17,464	26,196	329,114
2010	73	26,329	43,660	17,464	26,196	311,783
2011	74	24,943	43,660	17,464	26,196	293,066
2012	75	23,445	43,660	17,464	26,196	272,851
2013	76	21,828	43,660	17,464	26,196	251,019
2014	77	20,082	43,660	17,464	26,196	227,441
2015	78	18,195	43,660	17,464	26,196	201,976
2016	79	16,158	43,660	17,464	26,196	174,474
2017	80	13,958	43,660	17,464	26,196	144,772
2018	81	11,582	43,660	17,464	26,196	112,694
2019	82	9,016	43,660	17,464	26,196	78,049
2020	83	6,244	43,660	17,464	26,196	40,633
2021	84	3,251	43,660	17,464	26,196	224
SUBTOTALS		222,643	567,580	227,032	340,548	
TOTALS		721,724	1,091,500	436,600	654,900	

90

Dealing with the Civil Service and Federal Employees Retirement Systems in Divorce

Susan W. Wolfson

GIVEN THE GRAYING OF AMERICANS in general and, consequently, often the graying of our divorce practices, it is important for attorneys representing older clients to understand the rights and responsibilities of both employees and spouses under the two federal retirement systems. These systems offer benefits different in some ways from private retirement plans, and also require specific procedures which are peculiar to these programs.

A court can make an award to a spouse of a share of the employee's future retirement annuity, and can direct the Office of Personnel Management (OPM) to pay that share directly to the spouse. A court order also can specify that a spouse receive a former spouse survivor annuity on the death of the employee. These orders can be made whether the employee is still working or retired. A former spouse survivor annuity begins when the divorced employee dies, and continues for life, unless the recipient spouse remarries before age 55. Such a remarriage terminates the right to a former spouse survivor annuity. However, an insurable interest annuity can be elected instead of the former spouse survivor annuity, and the right to this would not terminate upon remarriage before age 55. This is more expensive to the employee, however, and the annuity is smaller.

Even if there is no court order re a former spouse survivor annuity, the employee can voluntarily elect to name his former spouse to such an annuity at the time the employee applies for his/her own retirement annuity. This election can be made after retirement, but must be made within two years of the divorce, and must be done in a form acceptable to OPM.

U.S. Code of Federal Regulations, Title 5, Section 838.101(a)(1), states that the OPM must comply with court orders in connection with divorces, annulments of marriage, or legal separations of employees, members, or retirees of the Civil Service Retirement System (CSRS) or the Federal

Employees Retirement System (FERS), which award a portion of the former employee's or member's retirement benefits or a survivor annuity to a former spouse. OPM determines whether or not a court order is acceptable. Appendix A, Section 702 to Subpart 1 of Part 838, dictates the proper language to award a former spouse a survivor annuity equal to the amount that the former spouse would have received if the marriage had never been terminated by divorce. That language is:

> Under Section 8341(h)(1) of title 5, United States Code, (former spouse) is awarded a former spouse survivor annuity under the Civil Service Retirement System in the same amount to which (former spouse) would have been entitled if the divorce had not occurred.

A Qualified Domestic Relations Order is not applicable here.

I recently was involved in a case in which husband and wife were in their 80s, and the husband was a civil service retiree. I was concerned about the sufficiency of an order, especially since the advanced age of the husband might have made it difficult to amend or correct the order. I made direct contact with the OPM, Retirement Operations Center in Boyers, Pa., in order to obtain approval of our specific order before requesting that the judge sign it. I drafted the order, had it approved by OPM, had the judge sign it, then obtained a certified copy of the order in addition to a certified copy of the Judgment of Divorce. We learned that, once the documents are reviewed by the Retirement Operations Center, they are sent to the Adjudication Branch in Washington, D.C., which actually issues the former spouse survivor annuity benefit, and the former spouse, rather than his or her attorney, will receive confirmation from that office. In my matter, we mailed the signed documents in November of 1995, and we received confirmation that they were sent to the Adjudication Branch in January 1996. As of the end of February 1996, our client still had not received notification of the award. We have been assured by OPM that the benefits take effect on the date of the court order, regardless of receipt of the documents, and that, even if the notification has not been received upon the death of the former employee, a proper court order will suffice.

BIG CAVEAT: If the federal worker leaves federal employment and dies before retirement, no survivor annuity will be paid. The only benefit to be paid would be a refund of contributions, and that goes to the person named as beneficiary. If no beneficiary is named, close relatives rather than a former spouse would be eligible for the lump sum payment. If you represent the spouse of a federal worker who has not retired, you should make some provision for this possibility; otherwise, your client may lose a benefit on which you may have relied in valuing the case.

91

Pensions and QDROs

Joanne Ross Wilder

The manner in which a domestic relations order is drafted can significantly enhance—or diminish—the benefits actually received by the parties. The lawyer should address these issues:

- Should the alternate payee receive a proportionate share of post-separation increases that result from the efforts of the participant, such as post-separation pay increases or contributions to the plan?
- Should the alternate payee receive a proportionate share of post-separation increases in the value of the plan where these enhancements do not directly relate to the efforts of the participant; for example, upgrades to the plan or changes in the benefit formula?
- Should the alternate payee receive a proportionate share of any early retirement incentives?

The recommended QDRO forms supplied by plan administrators almost never address such issues. They are, however, options that are consistent with federal law provided that no attempt is made to grant the alternate payee greater benefits than those available to the participant under the plan.

In the Court of Common Pleas of Allegheny County, Pennsylvania
Family Division

XX,

            Plaintiff

     vs.

XX,

            Defendant

)
)
)
)
)
)
)
)
)
)
)

No. FD xx

Domestic Relations Order

And Now, this ____ day of _____, xx, it appearing to the Court that:

A.   The parties hereto are husband and wife and a divorce action is presently pending in this Court at the above number; [or] the parties hereto were formerly husband and wife having been divorced on xx by this Court at the above number;

B.   xx, Social Security #xx, hereinafter referred to as "xx" or "Participant", is employed by xx and is a participant in the xx Retirement Plan;

C.   xx, Social Security #xx, hereinafter referred to as "xx" or "Alternate Payee", has raised claims for, *inter alia*, equitable distribution of marital property pursuant to the *Pennsylvania Domestic Relations Act*, 23 Pa. C.S.A. §3101, *et seq.*;

D.   xx's current and last known mailing address is xx.

E.   xx's current and last known mailing address is xx.

F.   The balance of the aforementioned account(s) on xx, xx was $xx.

It is Ordered, Adjudged and Decreed as follows:

360

1. A portion of the aforementioned xx account(s) is marital property subject to distribution by this Court.

[Option 1]

2. The marital property component of the Retirement Plan is xx/ of the projected estimated monthly income. The portion to be segregated for the Alternate Payee, xx, is xx% x xx/ x the Participant's projected benefit at age 65, or the appropriate actuarial equivalent if either party elects earlier retirement, plus xx *pro rata* share of any early retirement incentives that might become available to the Participant if xx elects early retirement.

[Option 2]

3. The sum of $xx from the account(s), plus actual interest, dividends and unrealized appreciation or depreciation earned on this sum from xx to the date that the retirement benefit is in pay status is awarded to the Alternate Payee, xx, and is to be segregated to an account in her name. The Participant, xx, is awarded the remainder, plus interest, dividends and unrealized appreciation or depreciation earned on the remainder.

4. The Alternate Payee shall have the same option as the Participant to elect to obtain benefits at the Participant's retirement age, and benefits shall be payable to the Alternate Payee on or after the date on which the Participant attains or would have attained the earliest retirement age, as if the Participant had retired on that date even if the Participant has not actually retired or separated from service.

[Option 1]

5. The term of said payments is for the life of the Alternate Payee, a number of years certain, or a lump sum payment, the term to be as selected by the Alternate Payee from any payment option available to her from the Plan at the time the retirement benefit is in pay

status. Payments are to commence at the retirement date chosen by the Alternate Payee but in no event earlier than the earliest retirement date provided under the Plan or, in the case of a defined contribution plan, a date which is not more than 10 years before the normal retirement age under the Plan.

[Option 2]

6. The term of said payments is for the life of the Alternate Payee, with payments to commence at the retirement date chosen by the Alternate Payee but in no event earlier than the earliest retirement date provided under the Plan.

7. The Plan to which this Order applies is the xx [retirement/annuity plan or any successor plan].

8. The Alternate Payee, xx, shall have the same rights with regard to xx portion of the account as are available to the Participant, xx, with regard to xx remaining portion of the account. These rights include but are not limited to the right to designate a beneficiary of retirement benefits, the right to elect from the existing retirement dates and payment options, and the right to such increases in value in the account as might occur as a result of general upgrading of the plan, plan amendments, earned interest, profitability of plan investments, etc., but not from increases in value which result from future increases in the Participant's compensation or his future contributions to the plan. In no event shall the Alternate Payee have greater rights than those that are available to the Participant. The Alternate Payee is not entitled to any benefit not otherwise provided under the Plan and is not entitled to any benefit specifically prohibited by the Retirement Equity Act of 1984.

9. In the event that actuarial computation is necessary to determine "actuarial equivalents" and/or the difference between benefits actuarially accrued, nonsubsidized

benefits, or employer subsidized benefits, for the purpose of the earliest retirement age option by the Alternate Payee, or otherwise, the Plan Administrator shall obtain the services of any actuary who is enrolled under subtitle C of Title III of the Employment Retirement Security Act of 1974.

10. Any reasonable costs incurred by the Plan Administrator to effectuate the terms and provisions of this Qualified Domestic Relations Order shall be assessed against the parties such that the Alternate Payee pays xx/ or xx% of the costs and the Participant pays the balance of the costs.

11. The parties shall promptly notify the xx Plan Administrator of any change in their addresses from those set forth above in this Order.

12. The parties shall promptly submit this Order to the xx Plan Administrator for determination of its status as a Qualified Domestic Relations Order.

13. Neither party shall encumber, transfer, pledge, or in any way dispose of any portion of this pension plan until such time as the Plan Administrator has qualified this Order after which each party shall be entitled to take such actions as he or she deems appropriate with regard to his or her share, free of any claim by the other.

14.   It is intended that this Order shall qualify as a Qualified Domestic Relations Order under the Retirement Equity Act of 1984. The Court retains jurisdiction to amend this order as might be necessary to establish or maintain its status as a Qualified Domestic Relations Order under the Retirement Equity Act of 1984, to effect the intent of the parties, and to enforce an award of benefits to the Alternate Payee.

BY THE COURT:

_____J

92

QDRO Clauses to Remember

Joy M. Feinberg

With all of our experience drafting QDROs since the 1984 enactment of the Retirement Equity Act (REA), I have seen too many QDRO's come across my desk recently that lack such basics as surviving spouse protection. Here are a few clauses to remember:

SURVIVING SPOUSE PROTECTION

Under the REA, defined benefit pension plans must automatically offer joint and survivor annuities to married plan participants who go into pay status or commence benefit payments. Additionally, there is a protection available to all vested participants for benefits that become payable if the participant dies *before* retiring, known as the *Pre-Retirement Surviving Spouse Annuity.* Thus, all QDROs should be written to protect the alternate payee's right to such coverage. If this coverage is not protected by inclusion in the QDRO and the participant dies before benefits commence, the alternate payee receives nothing! If the participant dies during benefit payment and no joint and survivor annuity coverage exists, then the benefits to the alternate payee also cease. These omissions should send a shiver of "malpractice" claims running up and down your spine.

Pre-Retirement Survivor Annuity Benefits
{Defined Benefit Plan}

During the period beginning with the entry of this Order and continuing until such time as {FOR A DEFINED CONTRIBUTION PLAN}: all sums awarded to Alternate Payee are transferred to her designated account, Alternate Payee shall be treated as the surviving spouse and sole beneficiary of that portion of the pre-retirement death benefits equal to her portion of Participant's interest in the specified PLAN.

{FOR A DEFINED BENEFIT PLAN}: . . . the Alternate Payee begins receiving benefits under the benefit election selected by her, shall be designated and treated as the "Surviving Spouse" of the Participant for purposes of establishing Alternate Payee's entitlement to and right to receive the PRE-RETIREMENT death benefits available to Participant {that are attributable to the Marital Portion of the Participant's accrued benefits.}[1] Any future spouse of Participant shall not be treated as the "Surviving Spouse" of the Participant for {the marital portion of}[2] such benefits payable monthly or otherwise.

SEGREGATING DEFINED CONTRIBUTION ASSETS AND PROTECTING AGAINST EARNINGS OR LOSSES UNTIL DISTRIBUTION

In defined contribution plans where an "account balance" exists for the participant, consider placing a clause in your MSA and the QDRO requiring the plan administrator to immediately segregate and separately maintain the alternate payee's benefits so that the participant cannot precariously invest or otherwise endanger the investment of these funds prior to distribution to the alternate payee.

If a segregation of account balances occurs prior to distribution to the alternate payee and while the plan determines if the QDRO is qualified, does the alternate payee's share earn interest or suffer losses equivalent to the participant's share? The answer to this question could be beneficial to the attorney before action is taken. In any event, be certain to negotiate and add to your MSA and QDRO language protecting the alternate payee so that he/she receives their share of the account balance *plus all interest, earnings, or losses accruing on that portion* until time of distribution.

USING A QDRO TO PAY CHILD SUPPORT—TAX CONSEQUENCES

When a QDRO is used to pay child support, the "distributee" parent or the parent receiving the "child support" will be charged with the income taxes due on the amounts distributed. Consider one of these alternatives:

- Make the distributee of current or delinquent child support payments the child so that Section 402(a)(9) treatment is avoided and the delinquent/non-paying participant is charged with the taxes.
- Tag on an additional lump sum to each payment to cover the cost of the taxes and/or penalty payments incurred by the parent receiving the "child support."

CONSIDER OTHER BENEFIT "BONUS" PROVISIONS

Don't forget that defined benefit plans may have special benefits, such as:

A. COLAs—cost-of-living adjustments;
B. Early retirement subsidies;
C. Alternate payee's contingent beneficiary designation rights; Disability coverage and commencement.

---

1. Consider adding this clause when representing the participant.
2. Same comment as footnote 1.

COLA CLAUSE: {Add to the clause on the Alternate Payee's assigned portion of the Participant's accrued benefits.} Additionally, Alternate Payee shall receive a pro rata share of any post-retirement cost of living adjustment(s) or other economic improvements made to the Participant's benefits on or after the date of his retirement. Such pro rata share shall be calculated in the same ratio as the Alternate Payee's share of the total benefits accrued by the Participant is calculated.

Add this *Disability clause* to your Commencement/Form of Payment Provision:

In the event that the Participant's benefits become payable at an earlier time under the Plan's Disability Retirement provisions, if any, the alternate payee may elect to commence her share of the benefits payable to participant at such earlier time as the disability benefits are available to participant.

Include all of these rights discussed above in your negotiations, marital settlement Agreements, and QDROs.

REDUCTIONS

Various "reductions" exist when defined benefit plans are divided, such as Early Commencement Reductions, Joint Survivor Annuity Reductions, Pre-Retirement Joint Survivor Annuity Reductions, and Actuarial Equivalent Reductions.

Election of PRE-RETIREMENT Survivorship Coverage: In the event that the costs associated with providing Pre-Retirement death benefit coverage are not fully subsidized by Participant's employer, then Participant shall be required and must affirmatively elect such Pre-Retirement death benefit coverage in a timely manner in accordance with the employer's election procedures.

Early Commencement Reduction: In the event that an early commencement reduction is necessary due to the Alternate Payee commencing her benefits prior to the Participant reaching his Normal Retirement Date, then such reduction shall be applied solely to Alternate Payee's benefits in accordance with the applicable provisions of the Plan.

Actuarial Adjustment: Any actuarial adjustment which might be necessary to convert the Alternate Payee's benefits to another form based on the Alternate Payee's lifetime should be applied to the Alternate Payee's benefits.[3]

IMPORTANT NOTE: Even more important, be certain to specify the alternate payee's right to receive all of these rights in the marital separation agreement. If you enter the QDRO after entry of the Judgment for Dissolution of Marriage, your MSA demonstrates your client's right to receive such benefits.

---

3. Remember that the "younger" alternate payee will receive a lesser monthly benefit, *but not less money altogether.* Because the money is being paid over a longer time period, and assuming good health for both people, the total amount paid to the alternate payee is equal to or greater than the *total* of the "monthly" benefits paid to the participant.

If the plan charges for actuarial calculations, DEFINE and NEGOTI-ATE who will be charged for this cost.

PLAN TERMINATION PROTECTION: Always include coverage for the alternate payee's right to receive his/her portion of the participant's benefits in the event that the plan is terminated prior to distribution (defined contribution plan) or benefit commencement (defined benefit plan).

PBCG PROTECTION EXTENDED TO THE ALTERNATE PAYEE:

In the event the Plan is terminated, whether on a voluntary or involuntary basis, and the Participant's benefits become guaranteed by the Pension Benefit Guaranty Corporation, (PBGC), the Alternate Payee's benefits, as stipulated herein, shall also be guaranteed to the same extent in accordance with the Plan's termination rules and in the same ratio as the Participant's benefits are guaranteed by the PBCG.

PARTICIPANT ACTION PROTECTION: Always include a paragraph that protects the alternate payee from actions taken by the participant that diminish, defeat, or eliminate the rights of the alternate payee. {N.B.: If you represent the participant, this clause is too broadly drafted to be accepted.}

The participant shall not take any actions, affirmative or otherwise, that circumvent the terms and provisions of this Qualified Domestic Relations Order, or that diminish or extinguish the rights and entitlements of the Alternate Payee as set forth in the provisions of this Order. In the event that the Participant takes any action or inaction to the detriment of the Alternate Payee, he shall be required to make equivalent tax adjusted (based on the tax rates of the Alternate Payee) payments directly to the Alternate Payee to the extent necessary to neutralize the effects of his actions or inactions against the full entitlements of Alternate Payee's rights and benefits hereunder as well as all attorneys' fees, accountant and/or actuary fees and other costs associated with Alternate Payee's expenses and other losses in establishing and enforcing such rights.

93

Using QDRO to Enforce Spousal and Child Support

Laura W. Morgan

ERISA'S QDRO PROVISIONS

In 1974, Congress passed the Employee Retirement Income Security Act of 1974 (P.L. 93-406, 88 Stat. 829) (ERISA) to provide better protection for beneficiaries of employee pension and welfare benefit plans in the private workplace. ERISA imposed a number of requirements on these plans relating to reporting and disclosure, vesting, funding, discontinuance, and payment of benefits. These requirements were imposed through amendments to both the Federal labor code (Title 29 U.S.C.) and the Internal Revenue Code (Title 26 U.S.C.). Some of the new statutory language was added to only one or the other of those codes; some was added to both codes to ensure that employers would not receive the tax benefits accorded by "qualified" plans unless those plans met the requirements imposed principally as a matter of Federal labor policy.

One of the provisions added to both codes was an anti-alienation requirement, a "spendthrift" provision precluding plan participants from assigning or alienating their benefits under pension plans subject to the Act. ERISA § 206(d)(1) added § 1056(d)(1) to Title 29 U.S.C., requiring that "[e]ach pension plan shall provide that benefits provided under the plan may not be assigned or alienated." ERISA § 1021(c) added a similar provision to the Internal Revenue Code. To the definition of "qualified trusts," it added the requirement that "[a] trust shall not constitute a qualified trust under this section unless the plan of which such trust is a part provides that benefits provided under the plan may not be assigned or alienated." 26 U.S.C. § 401(a)(13).

In both instances, ERISA allowed a limited exception to this provision, permitting employees actually receiving benefits under a plan voluntarily to assign up to 10 percent of the benefits for purposes other than defraying plan administration costs. See 29 U.S.C. § 1056(d)(2); 26 U.S.C. § 401(a)(13). The anti-alienation provisions apply to pension plans in particular; there is no similar provision applicable to other kinds of employee benefit plans subject to ERISA. *See Mackey v. Lanier Collections Agency & Service,* 486 U.S. 825, 108 S.Ct. 2182 (1988).

ERISA § 514, which became part of the labor code (29 U.S.C. § 1144), and to which no counterpart was added to the Internal Revenue Code, provided, with exceptions not relevant here, that the basic requirements of ERISA (including the anti-alienation requirement) "shall supersede any and all State laws insofar as they may now or hereafter relate to any employee benefit plan [subject to the ERISA requirements]." The term "State law," for purposes of § 514, includes "all laws, decisions, rules, regulations, or other State action having the effect of law, of any State." ERISA § 514(c)(1); 29 U.S.C. § 1144(c)(1). The preemption provision of ERISA has been regarded by the Supreme Court as "deliberately expansive, and designed to 'establish pension plan regulation as exclusively a federal concern.'" *Pilot Life Ins. Co. v. Dedeaux,* 481 U.S. 41, 46, 107 S.Ct. 1549 (1987) (quoting in part from *Alessi v. Raybestos-Manhattan, Inc.,* 451 U.S. 504, 523, 101 S.Ct. 1895, 1906 (1981)). *See also Shaw v. Delta Air Lines, Inc.,* 463 U.S. 85, 103 S.Ct. 2890 (1983).

The combination of the anti-alienation provision in both codes and the preemption provision of ERISA § 14 eventually raised a question, apparently not anticipated by Congress, as to the validity of orders entered in State domestic relations proceedings requiring that pension benefits be paid to a person other than the plan beneficiary. The question arose in two principal contexts: attachments served on plan administrators designed to enforce previously entered orders for child or spousal support, and orders entered pursuant to State community property or equitable distribution laws actually transferring pension rights.

Although the courts and the Internal Revenue Service apparently had little problem in giving effect to the first kind of order, there was more uncertainty about the second. While considering what eventually became the Retirement Equity Act of 1984 (P.L. 98-397, 98 Stat. 1433, hereinafter referred to as REA), however, Congress decided to clarify both aspects. The Congressional concern was clearly reflected in the various House and Senate Committee Reports on the REA. The House Ways and Means Committee Report noted the uncertainty caused by the anti-alienation and preemption provisions and stated, at 18:

> Your committee believes that the spendthrift rules should be clarified by creating a limited exception that permits benefits under a qualified plan to be divided under certain circumstances. In order to provide rational rules for plan administrators, your committee believes it is necessary to establish guidelines for determining whether the exception to the spendthrift rules applies. In addition, your committee believes that conforming changes to the ERISA preemption provision are necessary to ensure that only those orders that are excepted from the spendthrift provisions are not preempted by ERISA.

The device created to achieve these ends is the QDRO. As further explained in both the House Ways and Means and Senate Finance Committee Reports:

> The bill clarifies the spendthrift provisions of the Internal Revenue Code by providing new rules for the treatment of certain domestic relations orders. The bill creates an exception to the ERISA preemption provision with respect to these orders. The bill provides procedures to be followed by a plan administrator and an alternate payee (a child, spouse, or former spouse of a participant) with respect to domestic relations orders.
>
> Under the bill, if a domestic relations order requires the distribution of all or a part of a participant's benefits under a qualified plan to an alternate payee, then the creation, recognition, or assignment of the alternate payee's right to the benefits is not considered an assignment or alienation of benefits under the plan if and only if the order is a qualified domestic relations order. Because rights created, recognized, or assigned by a qualified domestic relations order, and benefit payments pursuant to such an order, are specifically permitted under the bill, State law providing for these rights and payments under a qualified domestic relations order will continue to be exempt from Federal preemption under ERISA.

H.Rep. No. 655 at 18; S.Rep. No. 575 at 19, U.S.Code Cong. & Admin.News 1984, pp. 2547, 2565.

The House Education and Labor Committee Report reflects same purpose, though naturally it was directed more toward the labor code amendments. At 39, the Committee stated:

> The Committee believes that ERISA should not preempt state domestic relations law to the extent that "qualified domestic relations orders" are issued under such State law. The bill therefore makes clear that neither the anti-attachment provisions found in section 206 of ERISA and section 40(a) of the Internal Revenue Code of 1954, nor the preemption provisions found in section 514 of ERISA, apply to qualified domestic relations orders. It is the Committee's intent to remove the confusion that now exists in this area. While ERISA should not be a barrier to recovery of alimony, child support, and property settlements, the bill makes clear that the orders have to meet specific requirements if they are to be honored by the plan. This will minimize the burden on the plan and eliminate confusion over what the court is ordering. While the order must meet specific requirements in order to be qualified, the general policy underlying the bill's provisions is that the domestic relations court is the appropriate forum to balance the equities between the parties and settle all controversies.

Because the anti-alienation requirement was part of both the labor and the tax codes, Congress amended both codes to provide for this limited exception. See REA § 104 (amending 29 U.S.C. § 1056(d)); REA § 204 (amending 26 U.S.C. §§ 401, 414). Both provisions begin with the statement that the anti-alienation requirement "shall apply to the creation, assignment, or recognition of a right to any benefit payable with respect to a participant pursuant to a domestic relations order, except that [it] shall not apply if the order is determined to be a qualified domestic relations order."

The law then defines a "qualified domestic relations order" as a domestic relations order that meets certain requirements set forth in the statute. It must first be a "domestic relations order," i.e., "any judgment, decree, or order (including approval of a property settlement agreement) which: (i) relates to the provision of child support, alimony payments, or marital property rights to a spouse, child, or other dependent of a participant, and (ii) is made pursuant to a State domestic relations law (including a community property law)."

REA §§ 104, 204; 29 U.S.C. § 1056(d)(3)(B)(ii); 26 U.S.C. § 414(p)(1)(B).

It must then meet three other requirements: (1) It must create or recognize the existence of an alternate payee's right to, or assign to an alternate payee the right to, receive all or a portion of the benefits payable with respect to a participant under a plan, 29 U.S.C. § 1056(d)(3)(B)(i); 26 U.S.C. § 414(p)(1)(A); (2) It must clearly specify: (i) the name and the last known mailing address (if any) of the participant and the name and mailing address of each alternate payee covered by the order, (ii) the amount or percentage of the participant's benefits to be paid by the plan to each such alternate payee, or the manner in which such amount or percentage is to be determined, (iii) the number of payments or period to which such order applies, and (iv) each plan to which such order applies. 29 U.S.C. § 1056(d)(3)(C); 26 U.S.C. § 414(p)(2); and (3) It: (i) does not require a plan to provide any type or form of benefit, or any option, not otherwise provided under the plan, (ii) does not require the plan to provide increased benefits (determined on the basis of actuarial value), and (iii) does not require the payment of benefits to an alternate payee which are required to be paid to another alternate payee under another order previously determined to be a qualified domestic relations order. 29 U.S.C. § 1056(d)(3)(D); 26 U.S.C. § 414(p)(3).

The law requires each plan to establish "reasonable procedures to determine the qualified status of domestic relations orders and to administer distributions under such qualified orders." 29 U.S.C. § 1056(d)(3)(G)(ii); 26 U.S.C. § 414(p)(6)(B). Upon receipt of a domestic relations order, the plan administrator must notify the participant and the alternate payee of the receipt of the order and the plan's procedures for determining its qualified status. The administrator has "a reasonable period" of up to 18 months in which to determine that status and inform the parties of the decision. See 29 U.S.C. § 1056(d)(3)(G)–(H); 26 U.S.C. § 414(p)(6)–(7).

Clearly, the QDRO has become an order of high significance in State domestic relations practice. An attempt to cause pension plan benefits payable to one party to be paid to an alternate payee, whether through an attachment in aid of a support obligation or pursuant to the disposition of marital property, can succeed only through the mechanism of a QDRO. *See Fox Valley & Vicinity Const. Workers v. Brown*, 879 F.2d 249, 252 (7th Cir.1989) ("[E]RISA preempts any attempt to alienate or assign benefits by a domestic relations order if that order is not a QDRO.") Absent such a qualified order, not only will the pension plan administrator refuse to implement the court's decision, but, given the anti-alienation provisions extant in both the labor and tax codes, coupled with the preemption provision of ERISA § 514 (29 U.S.C. § 1144), there is at least a reasonable argument that a nonqualified order may be invalid even as between the parties.

USING QDROS TO ENFORCE SPOUSAL AND CHILD SUPPORT

Even before ERISA was amended to provide for QDROs, there was general acceptance that a pension could be attached to enforce spousal and child support. The House Education and Labor Committee report stated that ERISA was not a barrier to recovery of alimony, child support, and property settlements, but the REA amendments were needed to clarify the specific requirements an order needed if it was to be honored by a plan. The amendments themselves then define a domestic relations order as "any judgment, decree, or order (including approval of a property settlement agreement) which: (i) relates to the provision of child support, alimony payments, or marital property rights to a spouse, child, or other dependent of a participant, and (ii) is made pursuant to a State domestic relations law (including a community property law)."

QDROs Not Available to Enforce Support Obligations

Despite the absolute clarity of the law that a QDRO may be used to enforce spousal or child support, a few cases have held that a QDRO may *not* be used to enforce support arrears, because that would be tantamount to a post-divorce modification of the property division.

In *Hoy v. Hoy,* 29 Va. App. 115, 510 S.E.2d 253 (1999), at the time of the divorce, the husband had no interest in a pension plan. The decree awarded the wife alimony. After the husband fell behind $84,000 in his alimony, the wife sought a QDRO on the husband's pension plan, at which time he did have an interest in the plan. The appellate court held that the post-divorce order awarding the wife $84,000 from the pension was not enforcement of a spousal support order via a QDRO, but was instead an improper attempt to reopen and modify the divorce decree. 510 S.E.2d at 254. A QDRO, the court held, must be consistent with the substantive provisions of the original decree, and that statutory exception does not empower the trial court to make substantive modification of the final decree.

The *Hoy* decision is flat-out wrong. A spouse is entitled to attach a pension for the enforcement of support, and doing so does not make the enforcement a new property division. Under the court's reasoning, placing a lien on the husband's bank accounts or other assets would also be an improper modification of the divorce decree, thereby rendering any attempt at enforcement impossible. It is especially perplexing that the Virginia court reached this conclusion in light of the line of cases holding that a pension is both an asset for division and a source of income available for support. *Moreno v. Moreno,* 24 Va. App. 190, 480 S.E.2d 792 (1997).

Hoy should be contrasted with *DeSantis v. DeSantis*, 714 So. 2d 638 (Fla. DCA 1998). In this case, the divorce judgment had awarded the husband his pension plan, and had awarded the wife her pension plan. After the wife failed to make a court-ordered cash payment to the husband, the trial court entered a QDRO to attach assets on the wife's pension plan. The appellate court reversed, holding that were the court to grant a QDRO attaching the wife's pension in favor of the husband, this would be tantamount to granting the husband an interest in an asset that he was not entitled to, that the final judgment had extinguished. The court of appeals, like the court in *Hoy*, held that this would be an impermissible modification of the final adjudication of property rights in the divorce case. *Cf. Hayden v. Hayden*, 662 So. 2d 713 (1995) (QDRO may be used to enforce support obligations). *DeSantis* is defensible, because the cash payment was not support, but part of the property division. *See also In re Marriage of Marshall*, 36 Cal. App. 4th 1170, 43 Cal. Rtpr. 2d 38 (1995) (QDRO cannot be used to enforce a collateral, contingent tax liability in a dissolution action).

QDROs Available to Enforce Support Obligations

Fortunately, most courts have not fallen into the trap of thinking that attaching a pension via a QDRO for enforcement of support is somehow an impermissible ex post facto modification of the property division. Indeed, most courts have accepted the premise with little discussion. *See Cody v. Cody*, 594 F.2d 314 (2d Cir. 1979); *Merry v. Merry*, 592 F.2d 118 (2d Cir. 1979); *Sippe v. Sippe*, 101 N.C. app. 194, 398 S.E.2d 895 (1991).

Recently, in *Hogle v. Hogle*, 732 N.E.2d 1278 (Ind. 2000), the husband was ordered to pay $1,000 a month in child support under a 1979 California decree. By 1979, his arrearage had reached over $375,000. The wife reduced the arrears to money judgments by writs of attachment, and she then sought enforcement of the writs in Indiana. The Indiana court held that the writs satisfied the technical requirements of a QDRO. ERISA, the court reasoned, does not require a QDRO to be part of the judgment in the case, but a QDRO can be used to garnish a retirement plan to satisfy past due support obligations.

Rife v. Rife, 529 N.W.2d 280 (Iowa 1995), reached the same result. There, in a 1982 divorce, the wife was awarded $500 a month in alimony. The husband made two payments in the next twelve years. In 1993, the wife obtained a QDRO that ordered the arrearage of $12,000 be satisfied by means of a garnishment of the corpus of the husband's pension plan. The Iowa court upheld the order, noting that ERISA was not intended to be a vehicle for the avoidance of family support obligations. "We see nothing in the federal statute that prohibits invasion of the corpus." 529 N.W.2d at 281.

In re Marriage of Bruns, 535 N.W.2d 157 (Iowa Ct. App. 1995), specifically disavowed the reasoning employed in *Hoy*. In this case, the court held that attachment by means of a QDRO of a former spouse's pension plan does not amount to an improper modification of the final adjudication of property rights, even when there has been an adjudication establishing that the creditor spouse has no interest in the debtor spouse's pension. The court held that the wife was not seeking to redistribute property previously awarded in the divorce decree, but was instead seeking to enforce an alimony provision through garnishment or attachment. 535 N.W.2d at 161.

Likewise, in *Baird v. Baird,* 843 S.W.2d 388 (Mo. Ct. App. 1992), the wife sought a lump sum distribution from the pension plan's current balance to cover past due spousal and child support. The trial court denied the request, noting that the divorce decree had awarded the husband his pension. The trial court, like the court in *Hoy,* held that a QDRO entered 11 years after the divorce would be an unlawful modification of the property division portion of the divorce decree. The court of appeals reversed, holding that a QDRO could be used to enforce the delinquent support payments.

Stinner v. Stinner, 520 Pa. 374, 554 A.2d 45 (1989), also allowed a quasi-QDRO for enforcement of support. In that case, the Stinners were married in 1956 and divorced in 1977. They entered into a property settlement agreement prior to the divorce that provided that the husband would pay alimony to the wife. After 18 months, the husband ceased payments. The wife brought an action in assumpsit for breach of the agreement, and a complaint in equity to enforce the agreement. Six years later, the wife filed two writs of execution to garnish the husband's Bethlehem Steel pension. The plan administrator refused to comply with the writ of execution on the grounds that it was not a QDRO. The trial court agreed.

The appellate court, however, reversed, and held that the pension could be attached to enforce the alimony agreement, and although the writ of execution itself was not a QDRO, a 1980 judgment enforcing the alimony agreement was a QDRO. The 1980 judgment satisfied the requirements of a QDRO in that it was related to alimony payments for a former spouse, it was made pursuant to Pennsylvania domestic relations law, it specified the amount of the participant's benefits to be paid and a period to which the order applied, and it named the plan participant and the alternate payee.

CONCLUSION

Congress has made it clear that QDROs may be used to enforce spousal and child support obligations. To do so is not an impermissible modification of a property division award, but only a means of enforcement of an obligation. It is time Virginia reversed the *Hoy* decision and got with the program.

PART

X

Valuation

FREQUENTLY, CLIENTS WILL ASK why they need a lawyer if the law requires equal division. Part of the answer is that equal division does not mean taking a chain saw to the house and its furnishings, although that approach has been tried. Therefore, ensuring a fair shake in a divorce requires valuation of certain assets.

Some assets, such as bank accounts, are easy to value. Others, such as real estate, are assessed with some difficulty, but usually not too much. And some, such as closely held corporations, require a great deal of care and skill.

In this part, the experts give their ideas on valuing different types of assets.

94   Different forms of property are valued in different manners. **Harriet Cohen** provides examples of various forms of property and methods of valuing them.

95   Often, the most difficult and most important asset is a family business or other closely held corporation. **Ira Lurvey** provides an invaluable summary of the basics a family lawyer needs to know about valuing this form of asset.

96   Want to be creative? Not all assets are bank accounts and furniture. **David Zaumeyer** discusses certain "hedonic" attributes of divorce that might be valued. Be careful; Zaumeyer is not talking about your run-of-the-mill house appraisal. Consideration of his approach is not for the faint of spirit.

97   Previously, we discussed the fact that many clients want top-quality representation and reduced costs at the same time. But top-quality lawyers will not cut corners. Nonetheless, **Harriet Cohen** discusses how we can use "rules of thumb" in valuation to save our clients substantial costs without sacrificing the quality of professional advice we are rendering. Included is a list of rules of thumb for various businesses. This list is worth a special place in your office.

98   Stock options were once an exotic employee benefit. Today they are relatively common. As a result, they arise in divorce cases on a frequent basis. **Don Schiller** describes some practical issues that are sometimes overlooked in dividing stock options in divorce.

94

*Valuation**

Harriet N. Cohen

THE DETERMINATION OF VALUATION is not incidental to a matrimonial action, but at its very heart. What property, when valued (separation, summons, trial, or some other date), who values (partisan appraisers—one for each side, neutral appraisers, the party himself or herself), method used (one year's net, book, fair market, investment value, and the like), how paid: All are substantive in effect, although, on the surface, procedural.

In most jurisdictions, the total value of *all* marital property must be articulated before the pot can be apportioned. The practitioner can help shape the written findings on how the values were determined by providing the court with proposed detailed findings. This will avoid conclusory valuation that appellate courts overturn.

BURDEN OF PROOF

Although the presumption in equitable distribution jurisdictions is that property is marital, and the "titled spouse" presumably has the greater knowledge of the value of the assets in dispute, the party seeking equitable distribution ordinarily has the burden of valuing the assets claimed to be marital property. Practitioners who fail to provide valuation evidence also run the risk of remittal to the trial court for another trial. One Indiana court held that it was not required *sua sponte* to fill the evidentiary void when the parties failed to provide valuation evidence. *Showley,* 454 N.E.2d 1230 (Ind. App. 1983). While preferable to no rights at all, the financial and time cost exhaust the needy spouse and make an inadequate financial settlement more likely. At the same time, the titled spouse's failure to provide the court with information needed to value a business coupled with stonewalling may result in the acceptance of an incomplete valuation submitted by the nonowner spouse. *Marriage of Moffatt,* 279 N.W.2d 15 (Sup. Ct. Iowa 1979); *Riemenschneider,* 239 Iowa 617, 30 N.W.2d 769 (1948). So the titled spouse's lawyer should understand the pitfalls in following such a hazardous course.

---

* This article is excerpted from XXIII *ABA Family Law Quarterly* 2, "Valuation of Property in Marital Dissolutions," at 339–81, by Harriet N. Cohen and Patricia Hennessey.

At least two New York appellate courts have substituted annual earnings of the husband as the net worth figure of his business in the absence of evidence presented to establish its net worth. *Ward,* 94 A.D. 2d 908, 463 N.Y.S.2d 634 (3d Dep't 1983); *Griffin,* 115 A.D.2d 587, 496 N.Y.S.2d 249 (2d Dep't 1985). This may be acceptable in certain situations, but it seems more like a rule of thumb than a sophisticated analysis.

The court may find as sufficient valuation a party's own out-of-court admissions. The husband's statement on a loan application, at odds with his later court testimony, set the value of real property in *Capasso,* 119 A.D.2d 268, 506 N.Y.S.2d 686 (1st Dep't 1986). The husband's assessment on his official form net worth statement in the matrimonial action, valuing a painting at $5,000, set that as the value of the painting in question in *Nehorayoff,* 108 Mis. 2d 311, 437 N.Y.S.2d 584 (Nassau Co., 1981). An insurance proposal prepared by a husband that placed a value on his business that he later disavowed became the value adopted by the court as the business's worth in *Patton,* 78 N.C. App. 247, 337 S.E.2d 607 (1985), *rev'd in part, remand to trial court for explanation of findings,* 318 N.C. 404, 348 S.E.2d 593 (1986), *aff'd as modified,* 88 N.C. App. 715, 364 S.E.2d 700 (1988). The message is clear: The lawyer must be intimately familiar with every piece of paper in the case and must not permit a sloppily prepared document to be submitted to court. The client will live with the error until the end of the case.

Expert testimony may be deemed unnecessary and costs held down where the court awards an equal share of all of the parties' marital assets (e.g., residence, stock, pension) to each party by an actual split of the assets themselves. *Van Housen,* 114 A.D.2d 411, 494 N.Y.S.2d 135 (2d Dep't 1985) (although no expert testimony was presented on value of marital assets, court's award of one-half value to each party upheld as effectuating the intent of equitable distribution). Particularly in a long marriage, the practitioner should ascertain in as early a court conference as possible whether this will be the court's approach. This may result in a negotiated settlement and the end of the case. The court may allow a layperson, competent as a result of having knowledge on the subject, to testify to the value of property where a proper foundation has been laid. This commonly applies to household furniture, furnishings, and personality. There is no reason it cannot also apply to art and antiques in the appropriate case.

At least one New York appellate court has held that splitting the difference, useful at the negotiation table, may not be utilized by the trial court to arrive at a valuation. In *Gainer,* 111 A.D.2d 308, 489 N.Y.S.2d 297 (2d Dep't 1985), *modifying and aff'g,* 100 A.D.2d 533, 473 N.Y.S.2d 233 (2d Dep't 1984), the trial court had averaged the appraisals of the two sides' expert witnesses to arrive at the value of real property. The appellate court rejected that approach on the basis that the trial judge had not articulated any reasons for its determination. Conversely, a Minnesota court has approved such an averaging, while cautioning that this method should be used only when the two values are not too widely divergent. *Balogh,* 356 N.W.2d 307 (Minn. Ct. App. 1984), *aff'd as modified,* 376 N.W.2d 752 (Minn. Ct. App. 1985).

COURT-APPOINTED AND JOINT EXPERTS

There is only limited experience in the use of court-appointed neutral experts. To the extent that the appointment of a court-appointed expert reduces stonewalling and promotes fair evaluation, it is an attractive option for the nontitled spouse. But will who pays for the court's expert have a bearing on the result? If so, the practitioner will urge the client (monied spouse) to agree to pay the fees. Will the expert be swayed by the judge's attitude about the rights, equal or otherwise, of the other spouse? If so, the practitioner may wish to say no to such an appointment, depending on which side of the table he or she is on, and insist on the opportunity to use only hired experts. Is there such a thing as a neutral appraiser anyway? Will the "neutral" expert be so wary of lawsuits by the disappointed litigant that the results will be affected? Other concerns include whether the appointment of a "neutral" expert will reduce the source of expert fees from which the court might otherwise order the financially able spouse to pay to the expert for the less able spouse.

The practitioner also will be faced with requests by the other side to agree to abide by the valuation of a jointly selected (not a court-appointed) expert or his or her expert. This, too, gives rise to concerns, including that the range of acceptable valuations may be wide, and a joint expert may lean to the wrong end of the scale. The practitioner may surrender the ability to advocate meaningfully regarding the results desired for his or her client.

NEW FORMS OF PROPERTY

Goodwill

Goodwill is a form of property (a thing of value) in many jurisdictions. (There is a split among the states about whether goodwill in a professional practice should be valued in marital dissolution.) The practitioner should know that the determination of goodwill is a question of fact and not of law. *Levy,* 164 N.J. Super. 542, 397 A.2d 374 (1978). Expert opinion is helpful but not binding. "Excess earnings" of an enterprise that are attributable to its goodwill are measured. They are derived by deducting from average earnings whatever amounts are appropriate to compensate for a proper return on capital, the reasonable value of the personal services, or both. What is being measured is, in reality, the capacity of repeat patronage and a certain immunity to competition to produce earnings beyond the average for that kind of business. The multiple to be applied will vary inversely with the amount and intensity of competitiveness in the line of business being appraised. Goodwill may be measured by using an accounting formula. Capitalization of excess earnings is a formula used frequently. Rev. Rul. 68-609. The practitioner also should be thoroughly familiar with Rev. Rul. 59–60.

Celebrity Status

Celebrity status is an emerging form of property in states like New Jersey and New York. Joe Piscopo's celebrity status, which provided him with an excess earning capacity, was judged an asset capable of distribution. *Piscopo,* 231 N.J. Super. 576, 555 A.2d 1190 (Ch. Div., 1988), *aff'd in part, rev'd in part,* 232 N.J. Super. 559, 557 A.2d 1040, No. A-35-88-T5F (App. Ct. May 1, 1989). Remuneration commanded and received for commercials was deemed directly related to computing the value of his celebrity status. The practitioner will find the same factors relevant to valuing professional goodwill equally applicable to determining the existence and value of celebrity goodwill. *Golub,* 139 Misc. 2d 440, 527 N.Y.S.2d 946 (Sup. Ct. 1988), contains an interesting discussion of the practitioner's burden in proving the value of "enhanced earning ability." There, actress Marisa Berenson's lawyer husband, Richard Golub, did not meet that burden of proof.

The practitioner for the celebrity will contend, among other things, that the celebrity's excess earnings are susceptible to attenuation by illness and other negative factors. The spouse's lawyer will counter that the linchpin of goodwill is objective as measured by past earnings capacity and the probability, not the possibility, that it will continue. Accepted accounting methodology in the entertainment field accommodates the difference between entertainment and other professions by applying a discount rather than a multiple to excess earnings to reach the capitalization factor. Spousal deprivation of what could be the most significant asset of the marriage in this most lucrative of industries thus is avoided.

While the entertainment business is the ultimate personal service industry that in totality generates billions of dollars, as do law and medicine (*U.S. Bureau of the Census Statistical Abstract of the United States,* 108 ed. 1987, at 746–47), the principles enunciated in *Piscopo* and *Golub* are equally applicable to earnings ability from any employment. Because earnings ability, if included in the definition of marital property, will be the single largest asset in most households, practitioners should become familiar with the methods of proving their value. Guidance and valuation tables are available in the wrongful death area of the law as well as in pension valuations. Pocket calculators are available on the commercial market that are programmed to perform present value computations. An alternative to present valuing the income stream would be to allocate the future earnings to the two post-divorce households on a cash-flow basis, as in pension distributions, if, as, and when the earnings actually are generated. The practitioner will have to show the court that the earnings are the result of the marriage partnership to achieve such an allocation for the homemaker spouse.

Professional Licenses

In economic terms, the value of a professional degree is the present discounted value of the difference between what the professional person will earn with the degree and what he or she would have earned without it. Blumberg, "Intangible Assets Recognition and Valuation," in *Valuation and Distribution of Marital Property* (Rutkin, *et al.* eds.). Only New York expressly recognizes a professional license, without a practice, as marital property subject to valuation and distribution. *O'Brien,* 66 N.Y.2d 576, 498 N.Y.S.2d 743, 489 N.E.2d 712 (1985). All states, including New York, agree that when the license has merged into a practice or business, only the practice or business should be valued.

The practitioner will value the medical degree in the same manner as calculations are made to determine damages in a wrongful death action (using the U.S. Department of the Census Survey on Earnings). The annual survey on physicians' earnings published by *Medical Economics* is helpful.

While the method of reducing a future income stream to present value is a standard forensic technique, there are choices made by the expert in performing the calculation that merit special attention for both the proponent and the opponent of the valuation. Are the surveys used (to project the college graduate's income and the physician's income) truly comparable to the party in the case? There is a certain speculativeness inherent in this valuation exercise, but the problems presented are no more difficult than computing tort damages for wrongful death or diminished earnings capacity resulting from injury. They differ only in degree from problems presented when valuing a professional practice—a subject not covered in this chapter.

Valuation issues have become increasingly sophisticated, giving rise to the application in the matrimonial context of principles developed in the fields of taxation, wrongful death, antitrust, and business litigation. While valuation appears at first to be a daunting task, the practitioner can master the concepts. Study of the relevant and constantly developing law of the particular jurisdiction and the other jurisdictions will lead to an effective and efficient trial (and negotiation) presentation. Retention of careful and knowledgeable experts also is essential. That does not substitute, however, for matrimonial lawyers themselves being fully familiar with accounting methods and concepts, such as Rev. Rul. 59–60 (valuing of stock in closely held corporations), 68-609 (the formula approach to the capitalization of excess earnings), 74-456 (valuing patient lists), the capitalization of earnings method and understanding the ramifications of buy/sell agreements, "book value," "investment value," "fair market value," discounting for key-man marketability, applying a premium for control, and present valuing of future income streams, among others.

Courts should not hesitate to recognize new forms of property, such as enhanced earnings capacity, celebrity goodwill, and licenses because of the misperception that the valuation process is insurmountable. Techniques for valuing such property already exist (e.g., present valuing of future income streams and capitalization of excess earnings methods) and have been applied in other contexts (wrongful death cases). Nor should courts make imprecise and inaccurate valuations of traditional forms of property, such as close corporations, because of an unfamiliarity with or unwillingness to apply appropriate valuation techniques.

In sum, there is no reason for the valuation process to frustrate the underlying purposes of the divorce reforms. With willingness on the part of the divorce courts to fashion fair distributions based on accurate valuations, litigants who use the courts will be able to predict the outcome and, thus, negotiate more readily to an out-of-court settlement.

95

Valuing Closely Held Corporations: Some Tips for the Preliminaries

Ira Lurvey

DETERMINING THE VALUE of closely held shares in a corporation, whether it is in a professional corporation such as a doctor's or lawyer's practice, or in a nonservice business or industry owned by a family or a few friends or associates, often is the most complex property issue in resolving a divorce.

What follows are some preliminary tips to try to get a general overview at the beginning of such a valuation. It need not be so difficult as it sometimes seems.

THE THRESHOLD: THE THREE BASIC APPROACHES

Essentially, there are three generally accepted basic approaches to the valuation of closely held shares:

- *Capitalization of earnings:* In this method, used primarily to calculate the value of earnings in the closely held practice or entity, the "normal earnings" of the corporation are multiplied by a "capitalization rate" that is supposed to reflect the stability of the past income of the entity and the predictability of the future corporate earnings. *See* O'Neal, "Restrictions on Transfer of Stock in Closely Held Corporations: Planning and Drafting" (1952), 65 *Harv. L. Rev.* 773, 802–803.

- *Capitalization of dividends:* In this approach, the procedure is to determine the dividend-paying (or profit-paying) capacity of the corporation as a method of its value. This method follows essentially the same schedule as the capitalization of earnings concept, except that it focuses on dividends rather than earnings. Critics of this method contend that it should not be given material consideration because dividend payments really are nothing more than a direct function of a corporation's earnings, and thus a method that combined earnings value and dividend payments could be said to be double-dipping in its "capitalization" of the closely held corporation.

- *Book value:* This method of valuation, sometimes also called "net asset value," involves determining the value of the corporation by taking the value of its underlying assets as shown by the company's balance sheet and prorating this underlying value to the number of outstanding shares. The value is determined by first adjusting the balance-sheet accounts, the technical "book value," as of the date of valuation to reflect the actual economic worth of the assets and the real liabilities of the business, and then deducting the actual liabilities from the actual assets. This then gives you the so-called net asset value, which then is divided by the number of shares of stock outstanding to get the price per share.

FINDING "FAIR MARKET VALUE"

The problem often arises when a confrontation arises between "investment value" of the closely held shares, as is determined by the three basic methods, *supra,* and "fair market value" as of the date of trial, which is the generally accepted method of valuing the closely held shares on divorce. The "fair market value" may be quite something else again.

Because by its very definition, closely held stock is not actively traded on an exchange or over the counter, the general marketplace cannot be looked to for unimpeachable verification of the actual price and worth. A *hypothetical* market thus must be created. It is in the creation of this hypothetical marketplace that most of the troubles arise.

THE HYPOTHETICAL MARKET: ITS CREATION AND EFFECT

Recent Specific Sales

It obviously is easiest to create a hypothetical market when a real market existed at some time previously. Thus, where you can show recent sales of the unlisted closely held stock made in good faith and at arm's length, this may suffice for the divorce valuation.

Price–Earnings Ratio

Another method for creating the hypothetical market is to multiply the price–earnings ratios of comparable actively traded corporations that are listed on exchanges, with the earnings per share of the closely held company. Sophisticated courts, however, recognize that there may be classic differences between a publicly traded company and a closely held one, even if the companies otherwise are comparable in almost every other respect. Relying solely on price–earnings ratios of comparable companies across the publicly traded barrier is thus a generally disfavored way to proceed.

Rev. Rul. 59–60: Is This the Answer?

As if clairvoyant, the IRS in 1959 promulgated a Revenue Ruling (1959-1 Cum. Bull. 237) that recites that in properly valuing the worth of closely held shares, one should take into consideration eight separate factors, no single one of which may be controlling. The eight are as follows:

1. The nature of the business and the history of the enterprise from its inception;
2. The economic outlook in general and the condition and outlook of the specific industry in particular;
3. The book value of the stock and the financial condition of the business;
4. The earning capacity of the company;
5. The dividend-paying capacity of the company;
6. Whether or not the enterprise has goodwill or other intangible value;
7. Sales of stock and the size of the block of stock to be valued; and
8. The market price of the stocks of corporations engaged in the same or a similar line of business having their stocks actively traded in a free and open market, either on an exchange or over the counter.

THE BUY–SELL AGREEMENT

Further complicating the valuation of a closely held business often is the existence of a buy–sell agreement between the shareholders, or other agreements, purporting expressly to fix the price at which the closely held shares can be traded. The issue then becomes whether these agreements are controlling as between the divorcing spouses, especially where one of the spouses may not even have signed or even been aware of the agreement.

There is no hard-and-fast rule for dealing with buy–sell agreements. Generally, however, the more factual evidence that can be introduced showing that the buy–sell agreement was entered at arm's length outside of the control of the party who seeks to assert it and completely separate and apart from any interspousal or divorce considerations, the more likely it is that the court will accept the agreement as controlling.

CONCLUSION

When determining the value of shares of a closely held corporation, whether a professional corporation or a nonservice business, the procedures may not be so complicated and intimidating as they at first appear. The catchword may be to avoid being limited to only one criterion for the valuation and to understand the interplay between the various criteria often referred to by accountants and the court.

Rev. Rul. 59–60 seems invaluable for this purpose. Common sense and the use of an experienced forensic accountant as a consultant will not hurt either.

96

Hedonic Values in Divorce Litigation: Where and How Lawyers Can Use Them in Equitable Distribution

David J. Zaumeyer, Ph.D., CPA

DIVORCE LITIGATION IS ENSCONCED, if not embattled, in a myriad of valuation issues. What is surprising is that the more we apparently learn about them and how to deal with them, the further we get from any consensus on method or application.

The courts to date generally have limited themselves to valuation issues that focus on setting monetary values on traditional assets such as businesses, pensions, licenses, and degrees. Included in this array have been both tangible and intangible assets, such as the value of "goodwill" and the enhancement of earnings from advanced education and training. In this latter area, the courts have had to be more tolerant of financial theories that rely on heroic assumptions and statistical probabilities to prove value (or loss). But if current economic thinking on the subject of what has value finds its way into matrimonial matters, we are going to have to prepare cases based on entirely new and admittedly novel areas of appraisal theory.

The U.S. Court of Appeals for the 7th Circuit affirmed a decision in *Sherrod v. Berry*, 629 F. Supp. 159, Illinois, to allow testimony on the theory that life (in general) has a measurable monetary value greater than that derived from traditional valuation measures of financial damages. The court upheld an award to the deceased's estate for the loss of life and pleasure of living, the "hedonic" component of the monetary value of life and an award for lost earnings as well. (*See ABA Journal*, September, 1988.) When making such a decision, the court supported the notion that life is worth more than merely what one can "earn" in the marketplace. More important from an appraisal standpoint, the distinction now has been clearly made between the value of life in terms of its financial or monetary attributes (measured routinely by valuators as "lost earnings and benefits") and the separate and additional value of the quality and pleasure of life.

Measuring this incremental component of value is difficult but not impossible. Economists are quick to point out that society already values the hedonic attributes of life on a regular basis. For example, workers are paid premium wages for high-risk work; the government insists that monies be spent over and above the cost of construction to ensure that automobiles, airplanes, and buildings are safe. We often assign "value" to a job in a convenient location or a home in the pristine suburbs and pay more for items of health and personal safety such as vitamins, smoke and burglar alarms, and protective clothing. Thus, we can be guided in measuring the hedonic attributes of life such as "convenience," "safety," "health," "happiness," "comfort," and even "pleasure" by looking at the value society puts on their counterparts in everyday activities. The same rationale might be applied to those elusive but very real aspects of divorce that had not heretofore been customarily valued.

What are the hedonic attributes of divorce? Is there a value to these, and should this value be factored into the monetary awards in matrimonial litigation? Among those areas where hedonic value measures might apply are as follows:

- Companionship: loss of companionship or custody of a child
- Consortium: loss of relationship with a partner
- Paternity: loss of relationship with a father
- Maternity: loss of relationship with a mother
- Parenting: loss of the pleasure of raising a child on a daily basis
- Consultancy: loss of assistance in budgeting, financial decision making, and investment planning
- Privity: loss of sharing in total resources necessitated by the maintenance of two separate households

The economist's or valuator's task would be to find the surrogate, if not the direct, measure of worth, to adequately assess the value of any or all of these areas in a particular case. The judge or jury's job would be to integrate this knowledge with the other financial data in the case and arrive at net settlement or distributive shares of the marital estate.

Hedonic value assessment is an appealing concept, but caution needs to be exercised in its application. First, the very real problem of selecting the proper measure of hedonic value must be met head-on. Second, hedonic value is spouse-neutral; that is, it is independent of plaintiff–defendant issues and is equally applicable to either side. As with many decisions related to the divorcing couple and equitable distribution, the length of the marriage, the number and age of any children, career and social alternatives available to both parties after divorce, and even separate property may well influence the extent to which hedonic values will enter the court's final assessment.

In the final analysis, we will undoubtedly have to learn to deal with hedonic values, as we have had to deal with the equally troublesome concepts of goodwill, merger, and enhanced earning capacity in the context of the value of marital assets. What remains is the challenge of selecting proper measurement techniques and the economic logic to support them. Only then will the courts have the proper data to make difficult, albeit necessary, decisions on the total value of all the assets in the marital estate.

97

Using Rules of Thumb in Valuation

Harriet N. Cohen

A POTENTIAL CLIENT is in your office sitting before you. You have come highly recommended. You want to look good. You are eliciting the material issues in the case (the numbers) and taking copious notes. In about an hour, you will want to give a "blueprint"—your best initial analysis of what you think the case is worth to them and you. If you are like me, you will be charging for that meeting at your consultation rate, and you will want to give that client his or her money's worth. And maybe more. But to do that, you will need to be able to fill in that big blank at that first meeting—your best estimate of the worth of the source of the family's support—the professional practice, the celebrity status, the business, the license, the store, the agency, so you can say what you think the payor will pay or the payee will get at the end of the day.

Rules of thumb help you to fill in that blank for that meeting and even later. How do you do rules of thumb? A good expert on board is nice. You also can educate yourself and work from recognized precedents and authorities. Get the *Handbook of Small Business Valuation Formulas and Rules of Thumb,* Third Edition, by Glenn Desmond, Valuation Press, 1993, P.O. Box 1227, Camden, ME 04943. Ronald L. Brown's *Valuing Professional Practices and Licenses: A Guide for the Matrimonial Practitioner,* Prentice Hall & Business, 1987, is indispensable. Study "The Problem with Rules of Thumb in the Valuation of Closely-Held Entities" by Jay E. Fishman, in *Fairshare,* Vol. 4, No. 112, p. 13 (December, 1984), Law & Business, Inc. Read "Rules of Thumb: Some Positive Observations" by Maxwell J. Taub, AM, CBA, *Business Valuation Review.* Look over the books and articles in the bibliographies. Prepare your own rules of thumb from the cases in your own courts. Prepare an outline for yourself and your clients. Keep the cases and the citations handy as well as a list of the recent values of law practices, of medical practices, of teaching licenses, and of various businesses.

Learn the questions to ask the client at that first meeting. How long has the dentist been at that location with that telephone number? (I have heard that people make dentist appointments more frequently when they have the telephone number memorized, and that is worth money.) Is there a partnership agreement in that law practice that says how much the partner gets on retirement, on voluntary or involuntary withdrawal? Do you know how much the new partner paid and owes to buy into the accounting practice? How long does the business lease have to run? Are the terms favorable?

Rules of thumb have been called "a sanity check" on valuation. Experts will be asked whether they have considered the rules of thumb and the industry standards, and if not, why not? On the other hand, too much reliance on rules of thumb is foolish. But for you at that first meeting with your potential client, you had better be able to add, subtract, and divide quickly and decisively enough to impress that client with your astute perceptions and recommendations. And you cannot finish the arithmetic example without that one major component—the value of the source of the earning power—the business, the practice, the celebrity status.

I use rules of thumb a second time (after landing the client who leaves our first meeting with a more concrete understanding replacing the unsettling sense of vagueness) in my negotiations and court conferences. In appropriate cases, when the other side says, "We'll need an appraiser," I may say, "Let's use one times annual receipts, and give each party half. That will save our clients the time and money for an appraiser, and the rule of thumb for this practice is pretty reliable." Depending on the ballpark and the total dollars involved, that approach may be economical from every point of view.

The author acknowledges her own "sanity check" on this article by submitting it to Henry Guberman, CPA, Lazar Levine & Co., New York City. A potpourri of rules of thumb follows.

Rules of Thumb for Valuation

OCCUPATION	RULES OF THUMB
Accounting Firms	Net assets plus 75 to 150 percent of annual gross revenues.
Auto Repair Shops	33 percent of annual gross revenues.
Beauty Shops	16 to 40 percent plus net assets.
Cafes and Diners	45 percent of annual gross sales; add inventory.
Celebrity Goodwill	One quarter of a year's earnings, or average annual net earnings over three to five years minus the annual salary of an average employed person in the same field.
Dental Practices	Net assets plus 30 to 40 percent of annual gross revenues.
Drug stores	25 to 40 percent of annual gross revenue plus net assets.
Dry Cleaners	66 to 100 percent plus net assets.
Fast Food Franchises	Net assets plus 25 to 58 percent of annual gross revenues.
Grocery Stores	11 percent of annual gross sales.
Insurance Agencies	6 to 10 percent of net commissions plus book of business, lease, and intangibles.
Medical Practices (Small Family Practice)	20 to 40 percent of annual fee revenue.
Optometric Practices	Net assets plus 25 to 58 percent of annual gross revenues.
Restaurants	40 to 50 percent of annual gross sales plus inventory.
Retail Businesses	25 to 50 percent of annual gross sales plus inventory.
Travel Agencies	35 percent of annual gross sales plus fixtures and equipment.

98

Stock Options: Be Aware/Beware

Donald C. Schiller

STOCK OPTIONS ARE A GROWING TOOL being used by companies as a source of executive and employee compensation. Effectively they give the employee a chance to profit in the growth of a company's value in addition to earning a salary. At the time of dissolution, stock options may be one of the more substantial assets a couple have in their marriage. Dealing with stock options can be very complex, in part because each company may make its own terms concerning the awarding and exercise of options and the development of the law relating to options in a marital dissolution at its early stages. The subject of stock options is well covered in articles and treatises and it is not the purpose of this "hot tip" to define or explain them. This tip is intended to raise your consciousness to a few practical issues that are too often overlooked.

I. WATCH FOR RELOAD PROVISIONS IN STOCK OPTIONS.

Some companies use reload stock option grants. Typically the "reload" means that if the employee in exercising a current stock option pays for the price of the option using the company's own stock instead of cash, the employee will automatically be given new options for future exercise. Since stock options are generally not assignable, most settlements provide for the employee to provide the non-employee divorced spouse with a division of the proceeds of the exercise of stock options on an "if, as, and when" basis. The employee spouse could, on exercising the options that were divided by the divorce judgment, use corporate stock, pay for the exercise, and without disclosing it retain for himself all of the reloaded options that are actually an outgrowth of the divided marital options.

II. STOCK OPTIONS LOST WHEN EMPLOYEE/SPOUSE LEAVES THE COMPANY.

Assume that the employee/husband has an option grant to purchase 1,000 shares of ABC Corporation. According to the grant the husband must remain employed for three more years before the options are exercisable.

The husband and wife are to equally divide the options upon dissolution. At the time of dissolution the husband has to remain employed for two more years before his options are exercisable. One year after the divorce the husband leaves ABC Corporation and goes to work at XYZ Company. The ABC Corporation options become worthless. Unless the Marital Settlement Agreement provides for more, the spouse gets nothing, but the former employee is likely to have received something of value that caused him/her to leave ABC Corporation to join XYZ Company. The former husband, therefore, did receive something of value for losing the ABC Corporation options, but the former wife did not. Marital Settlement Agreements should be drafted to prevent this type of unfair result.

III. NOT ALL TIME RULE FORMULAS ARE THE SAME.

How does one characterize stock acquired from an employee stock option granted to the employee *before* the marriage but that required continued service after the marriage before becoming exercisable? How does one characterize stock options that are granted during the marriage that require the employee's continued service after the dissolution before they become exercisable? Frequently, to resolve these issues attorneys employ a time rule formula that determines a portion of the stock or options as marital and the remaining portion as non-marital. It is important for the attorney to not just use the same time rule formula used or cited in a prior case as the basis for making allocations of marital and non-marital portions in all cases. There are different time rule formulas courts have employed that may achieve very different results. Attached is a sampling of time rule formulas.

SAMPLES OF *TIME RULE FORMULAS*

1. In measuring unvested options that were granted during marriage but *solely to encourage future employment efforts,* the following formula is frequently cited (*Garcia, supra,* citing *In re Marriage of Harrison,* 179 Cal.App. 3d 1216, 225 Cal. Rptr. 234, and *In re Marriage of Nelson,* 177 C.A.3d 150 (1986):

$$\text{Marital share} = \frac{\text{Number of months from date of grant until (dissolution) separation}}{\text{Number of months from date of grant until vesting}}$$

2. In measuring when unvested options are in consideration of *work performed* and like a salary bonus (*In re Marriage of Hug,* 201 Cal. Reptr. 681, 685) formula:

$$\text{Marital share} = \frac{\text{Number of months of employment during marriage prior to separation (divorce)}}{\text{Number of months husband employed until options vest}}$$

3. The *Supreme Court of Nebraska* in *Davidson v. Davidson*, 254 Neb. 656, 578 N.W.2d 848 (Neb. S.Ct. 1998) (a marital property state) reviewed a number of different formulas:

   (a) Regarding *grants during marriage* vesting after dissolution where for *future services:*

$$\text{Marital portion} = \frac{\text{Number of months from date of } \textit{grant} \text{ until } \textit{dissolution}}{\text{Number of months from date of } \textit{grant} \text{ until option vests (similar to \#1 above)}}$$

   (b) Regarding grant *before marriage* vesting during marriage or grant during marriage, including pre-marriage services:

$$\text{Marital portion} = \frac{\text{Number of months from date of marriage to grant}}{\text{Number of months from date of employment to grant}}$$

   (c) Regarding *grant before marriage* vesting during marriage where grant was to encourage *future efforts:*

$$\text{Marital portion} = \frac{\text{Number of months from marriage to vesting}}{\text{Number of months from grant to vesting}}$$

   (d) Regarding grant for *past service* where the employee has had *previous option grants:*

$$\text{Marital portion} = \frac{\text{Number of months since last grant (while married on marriage date if later) until date of current grant}}{\text{Number of months from last grant until date of current grant}}$$

397

XI

Settlement

IS THERE A MORE BEAUTIFUL WORD in the legal language than "settlement"? I think not. There is a saying in divorce law that a bad settlement beats a good trial. Whether that is true or not, it cannot be denied that a *good* settlement beats a good trial.

Settling family law cases is a unique art form. We start with incredibly angry clients. The issues frequently are mushy and the money to pay for investigating them is minimal. Furthermore, many a divorce lawyer has been accused of recommending a settlement that the client later regretted. It is no wonder that many divorce lawyers have gray hair, if they have hair at all.

The experts have plentiful advice on settlement—both on how to settle and what to watch out for in recommending a settlement.

99 Most divorce settlements contain what is called boilerplate language. How much thought do you give to what is in that boiler? **Bev Groner** presents some thoughts on the purpose of these standard clauses and suggests some useful language.

100 Ever handle a divorce with a Jewish couple? Were you aware that the provisions for a Jewish divorce, known as a "Get," may be invaluable in the civil divorce settlement? **Max Goodman** explains why.

101 When you're inserting those boilerplate clauses, **Bev Groner** warns to be careful of the one containing releases. You may be doing more than you really intend.

102 Having trouble settling a case because the other side is overaggressive? **Sam Groner** discusses countermeasures to employ against the overaggressive opponent.

103 There is a magic-of-the-moment concept to divorce settlement, but often that moment occurs at an inconvenient time—such as on the courthouse steps. **Elaine Rudnick-Sheps** has been there and reveals how to prepare for last-minute settlement and still be a hero to your client.

104 Monday-morning quarterbacking occurs in more than just the National Football League—you can drive yourself nuts worrying about the "what ifs . . ." that you might have forgotten in settlement. **Bev Groner** has thought of a few that you might want to insert into an agreement *before* Monday morning.

105 Prenuptial agreements, once rare, are now relatively common. With the prevalence of cohabitants increasing dramatically, it is safe to assume that cohabitation agreements will also become common. While there are similarities between these two types of agreements, **Sondra Harris** points out the differences, which any lawyer practicing in this area needs to know.

106 A lawyer of my acquaintance handles simultaneous divorce and bankruptcies, calling his services a "happiness package." Many times, however, the bankruptcy comes after the divorce and is not welcomed. **Bruce Steinfeld's** hot tip suggests ways to "bankruptcy-proof" a divorce agreement.

107 More and more family law cases are being settled through mediation. As **Carlton Stansbury** points out, preparation for mediation is every bit as essential as preparation for a contested trial. In his hot tip, Carlton provides a "punchlist" of topics to be discussed with the client and the procedures to be followed when the case goes to mediation.

99

Special Clauses for Marital Settlement Agreements

Beverly Anne Groner

EVERYTHING INCLUDED in your marital settlement agreement should be there for a purpose. Nothing should be there by rote, and it is constructive to occasionally review and update your general format to reflect changes in the law, new trends, and judicial interpretations.

Here are some thoughts that you may find useful:

SEVERABILITY CLAUSES

This clause often is included simply because no one has truly thought about it. If you analyze the consequence of including a severability clause you will readily see that no one knows where the ax may fall. It often is unlikely that you can ascertain in advance whether your client would be benefited or disadvantaged by the inclusion of such a clause. The severability clause was originally a creature of statute draftsmanship and somehow found its way into contracts. There may be specific contractual situations in which it is useful, but in my opinion these situations are few and far between and, worse yet, unpredictable in their consequences. If counsel on the other side seems determined to include the severability clause, I sometimes insist on an interdependence clause. The net result of that usually is that both clauses are omitted from the agreement and it is left to the operation of law, applied to the facts of the specific case, as to the legal consequence.

JOINT WORK PRODUCT

There still exists a general rule, the rule of *contra proferentem*, that a contractual clause is stringently construed against the person who drafted it. For this reason, it is appropriate to consider inclusion of "joint work-product" phraseology in a marital settlement agreement. Such a provision should state that the agreement is the joint work product of counsel for both parties and shall not be construed more stringently against one party on the ground that his or her lawyer drafted or participated in the drafting.

NO LEGAL ADVICE TO OTHER PARTY

Consider including a statement in your legal representation clause that neither party has received legal advice from counsel for the other side. At first glance this may seem unnecessary, but, in fact, during the pendency of the case there often is some exchange between both lawyers and both clients, such as in a four-way meeting, in a deposition, or even at a court recess. It could occur that one party could later "remember" that the lawyer on the other side expressed certain opinions that were really directed toward that party and that proved to be detrimental to that party. It is certainly reasonable to suggest that no one with much good sense would rely on advice given by counsel for the other side; notwithstanding the presence or absence of good sense, however, people sometimes do take seriously what is said by the other lawyer. Or they may merely later say they did.

CATASTROPHE CLAUSE

When your client is a professional person or someone who relies on his or her own efforts, as well as those of employees, to create the substantial income and assets that are being divided by the marital property settlement, it is important to recognize that life brings many changes, not all of them welcome, and that the person who is responsible for making the payments may suffer a decline in health or other catastrophe that makes it impossible either permanently or temporarily for that person to maintain the level of payments set forth in the agreement. In this eventuality you and your client both would be thankful if you have provided in the agreement that in the event of such detriment to your client, he or she may ask a court to determine whether the otherwise unmodifiable payments set forth in the agreement should be diminished and if so for how long. Most spouses are unwilling to agree to an automatic diminution; however, many agree to simply leaving the door to the courtroom open in the event it appears to be needed. Also be aware that when the inclusion of a catastrophe clause is requested, it is not unusual for the other side also to request inclusion of a catastrophe clause that could provide that on a serious decline in the health of the spouse whose alimony is otherwise unmodifiably limited or terminated, that person may request reconsideration of possible entitlement to ongoing or increased alimony. Sometimes, when this reciprocity is requested, counsel will decide to recommend forgoing the protection rather than exposing the client to the additional potential liability.

UNDISCLOSED ASSETS

Consider this clause for inclusion in your marital settlement agreement:

> Each party recognizes, and it is his or her intention, that the other is relying on the representations contained in their respective Financial Statements in entering into this Agreement. Further, this Agreement is made upon the assurance that each party has made a full, complete, and total disclosure to the other of his or her income and the nature, extent, and value of all of the

spouses' respective assets and obligations, for the purpose of inducing the other party to enter into this Agreement, and therefore, to the extent that a party has failed to make such full and complete disclosure, then the releases and waivers contained in this Agreement shall be null and void as to any income, property, or asset of the other which he or she has not disclosed; and any such property is unaffected by this Marital Settlement Agreement. In the event that by reason of such nondisclosure by one party, the other party incurs additional counsel fees or incurs or expends suit money or costs in order to protect or assert his or her rights or claims, the nondisclosing party shall be obligated to and shall forthwith pay to the other party all such reasonable attorney's fees, court costs, and suit money, and further, that party shall hold harmless and indemnify the other from all financial detriment thereby incurred by that party.

100

Anticipating the Need for a Get

Max A. Goodman

UNDER THE JEWISH RELIGION, a divorce—Hebrew word: *Get*—can be obtained only by the husband. Even if the husband has mistreated the wife, he is obligated under Mosaic law to secure the Get. Should the errant husband fail to apply for a Get, the wife is hapless and helpless. She remains, under the Jewish religion, a married woman, even though a secular divorce is granted by a state court.

When representing a spouse or intended spouse—especially a female—who is Jewish, the lawyer should be sensitive to this area of Jewish law. The lawyer should be dissuaded from discussing the matter even though the client says she is not that observant a Jew as to care about a Get. She should be advised to consider the possibility that she may in the future become engaged to an observant Jew who will refuse to marry her unless she has received a Get from her first husband.

So, tip number one: When preparing a prenuptial agreement for a client of the Jewish faith, discuss the advisability of inserting a clause to the effect that the parties will cooperate in obtaining a Get if the contemplated marriage is dissolved.

Tip number two: When preparing a marital settlement agreement, inquire of your client whether he or she wants the Get cooperation clause, and if so, at whose expense. Without prior agreement, can a court order the parties to cooperate in obtaining a Get? Although Ohio has said no, holding that such an order would violate the separation of church and state provision of the constitution, other states have said yes. Jurisdiction is based on the Ketubba, which is the marriage contract that is signed by the parties prior to every marriage ceremony performed by a rabbi. The Ketubba contains a provision to the effect that the parties agree to be bound by the laws of Moses and Israel. One of those laws is that marital disputes will be referred to a Beth Din, the Jewish Ecclesiastical Court, which has the power to grant Gets. This provision, say the cases, can be specifically enforced. An *American Law Reports* annotation on this subject is found in 29 *ALR* 4th 747.

101

Releases—Think before You Leap!

Beverly Anne Groner

RELEASES IN MARITAL SETTLEMENT AGREEMENTS are, of course, an important part of consideration that is bargained for. However, careful thought must be given to both sides of the release question. It can be a double-edged sword. For many years it was routine that both spouses would be expected to waive all rights other than those explicitly set forth in the agreement. Nevertheless, there may be some rights that you do not wish your client to waive. One example is infliction of emotional distress, a frequent concomitant of most divorce actions. However, *intentional* infliction implies excessive and purposefully destructive behavior designed to "break down" the other spouse. This may, in certain circumstances, be actionable. On balance, some lawyers believe that this cause of action is within the ambit of what is routinely released within the general release clauses. Nevertheless, there may be cases in which it should not be. An example would be the wrongful withholding of a child from the parent to whom custody has been awarded by a court. In some states, this also is recognized as a separate tort, and in some states it is considered a felony.

Bearing in mind that one's client should not be waiving future rights, it could be argued that when there is a general release, it includes an exoneration from such wrongful behavior as one of the considerations flowing between the contracting spouses.

Another right that arguably can be construed as being waived by a general release clause could be rights, flowing from Social Security benefits, that may accrue to a spouse without any detriment to the other spouse. Because those benefits in many cases can be obtained and enjoyed by one spouse without incurring any financial detriment, perhaps, on reflection, counsel might decide to reserve that right to preserve future benefits for the client. The current state of the law on eligibility for these benefits could be reviewed in this context from time to time. Few entitlement statutes are written in stone.

Consider the effect on assets of "general" release clauses. Do you really want a client to waive any entitlement to assets that were unknown and unrevealed at the time of settlement? If not, then saving language should be considered to the effect that assets not revealed are not affected by the waivers and release clauses of the marital settlement agreement.

The foregoing are among those releases that first come to mind. This is not to suggest that these rights should not be waived, but simply that counsel should reconsider waivers and releases by implication because of inclusion within the boilerplate language. "Waiving all rights except as may be explicitly set forth herein" might simply be too broad.

Attentiveness to detail is requisite to express exactly what one means and to neither broaden nor diminish the scope of what is intended.

Consider also a provision for a remedy, if those payments so diligently sought and provided for are not forthcoming for whatever reason. Why not state that the waivers are conditional on the spouse receiving the benefits set forth in the agreement? Even the most partisan advocate on the other side should be able to appreciate the necessity for reserving some remedial rights. For example, a waiver could be structured to become effective only on receipt of a certain consideration. If the consideration is not received, the spouse may have a right to enforce these remedial rights. These protections require careful structuring. These provisions are, of course, likely to be affected by incorporation into the divorce decree.

102

Countermeasures versus an Overaggressive Opponent

Sam Groner

TWO CATEGORIES OF OVERAGGRESSIVE BEHAVIOR

A. Not Clearly Unethical
 1. Excessive use of what would otherwise be legitimate and appropriate tools;
    a. Discovery modalities: depositions, requests for the production of documents, refusal to allow deposition or to produce documents;
    b. Motion practice: frivolous motions, excessive formality;
    c. Refusal to stipulate;
    d. Abuse of powers of subpoena; or
    e. Harassment of surveillance.
 2. Obstructive pretrial tactics generally;
    a. Overuse of court process and procedure;
       (1) Motions practice: frivolous motions, excessive formality, emergency hearings on short notice and at inconvenient times.
    b. Applying pressure by financial measures;
       (1) Refusing to pay voluntarily;
       (2) Recalcitrantly complying with court orders, not complying until just within hours of the availability of sanctions;
       (3) Defying the court order altogether, refusing to comply at all.
B. Clearly Unethical or Illegal
 1. Communicating *ex parte;*
    a. With the court; or
    b. With your client.

Such communications are sometimes executed in very subtle ways in an effort to avoid detection and ensuing reproach.

2. Deliberate misstatements of fact by counsel or false attribution of statements to your client;
3. Wiretapping; or
4. Subornation of perjury.

OBJECTIVE OF OVERAGGRESSIVE BEHAVIOR

A. Psychological Warfare
   1. To inspire you and your client with fear and awe;
   2. To gain and keep the initiative in setting the tempo and establishing the decisive issues in the case; or
   3. To impress the aggressor's own client.
B. Delay
   1. To exert pressure;
   2. For aggressor's own convenience; or
   3. To convey impression of control of the case by aggressor.
C. Economic Pressure

WHAT YOU CAN DO: AMELIORATIVE OR CURATIVE MEASURES

A. First, Check Your Perception
   1. Review in your own mind whether or not your adversary's conduct really *is* excessive. Mere aggressive representation is, after all, not improper, and may even be the most appropriate course of action in a given case.
   2. But if you conclude that your sibling-at-the-bar's aggressiveness is excessive, or even merely that it needs countering, there are some measures you can take.
B. General or Overall Responses
   1. Take the high road, if possible, without incurring detriment to your client, so that the judge can contrast your professionalism with the overaggressiveness of your opponent.
   2. Become more aggressive yourself. Outaggress your opponent; often, that quiets him or her down.
   3. Seek sanctions, in proper cases;
      a. Under State Rules such as Rule 11 of the Federal Rules of Civil Procedure, which authorizes the court to assess a fine and costs to be paid to the aggrieved party by either the lawyer personally or by his or her client (or by both) for filing frivolous suits or motions;
      b. More serious disciplinary sanctions, where warranted, against the lawyer; or
      c. Even criminal sanctions, for such offenses as perjury or wiretapping.
C. Responses in Specific Situations
   1. Abuse of discovery modalities;
      a. The ordinary remedies;
         (1) Object, and instruct your client not to respond;

      (2) Seek protective order from the court; or

      (3) In the case of refusals to make discovery, first move to compel, and then for sanctions in the form of limiting the other side's proof, deeming certain facts established, or even dismissal of the action.

  b. Less ordinary remedies;

      (1) Comply excessively; load your adversary up *ad nauseam* with documents; or

      (2) Make a motion *in limine,* foreclosing the other side with respect to certain issues.

2. Motioning you to death;

  a. Again, the Federal Rules of Civil Procedure 11 sanctions remedy, where the situation is clear.

  b. Make a record, in your responses, of the lack of necessity for the court appearance or other formality, or the refusal to stipulate regarding acknowledgedly undisputed or minor matters, to build a case for sanctions, or at least for some remark or recognition of your adversary's conduct by the judge either on or if not then off the record.

3. Refusal to stipulate;

  Do not overlook the availability of the demand for admissions! But you must be careful to draft the proposed admissions carefully, for the other party might validly deny the whole statement, if not every detail in it is true.

4. Abuse of subpoena power;

  It is difficult to deal with this tactic, unless the abuse is clear. But, if it is, it may be useful to move for a limitation, supporting the motion possibly by (a) an offer to stipulate or (b) accepting a proffer of what the witnesses would say if they were to testify.

5. Harassment by surveillance;

  a. If you have the client for it, it sometimes helps to lead the detective on a merry chase.

  b. If not, you need to document your case, particularly with instances where the surveillance is interfering with your client's freedom of action or causing him or her disadvantage in reputation or business, and seek an injunction with perhaps a suggestion of damages or disciplinary professional action against the detective.

6. Overuse of court process and procedures;

  a. Excessive motions practice. See paragraph 2.

  b. Unwarranted emergency hearings.

    It is always awkward to be in the position of denying anyone his or her day in court. Where the other side abuses this tactic, it is well to (a) explain the absence of any emergency, on the record and (b) keep a record that supports your contention and documents your opponent's abuse of this right.

A more delicate tactic, but one that sometimes is effective if it is available, is to respond in kind, with your request for emergency relief sought at inconvenient times and on short notice.

7. Financial pressure;

Where the other side actually defies and disobeys a court order, you have the usual means that the law affords to enforce your award. Where he or she stays just this side of violation, however, it is as difficult in a litigation situation to overcome financial pressure imposed by someone having superior resources as it is in life generally. As always, an additional source of funds offers the best recourse. Parents, paramours, IRAs each may be able to provide funds. Alternatively, it may be necessary to tighten one's belt and to grin and bear it to avoid yielding to the pressure for a long-term and possibly impractical loss.

It is sometimes possible, although experience teaches that it rarely is the actual event, to go before a judge, explain the situation, and obtain relief, in the form of a double-size first month's payment, an increase in the amount of award, or at least to have the judge remember the evil conduct when it is time to hand down a final decision.

8. Unethical or illegal conduct.

If your adversary goes this far, it is likely that it is not the first time that he or she has done so. You owe it, not only to your client but to the Bar and the public generally, to take some action about the offense in enforcement of your rights. Complaining on the record about *ex parte* communications may seem a bit awkward to the judge who has accepted them without reprimand, but a complaint is more likely to prevent other such communications in the future than remaining silent is.

Misstatements of fact by counsel, or persistent misattribution of statements, should be corrected vigorously and on the spot. In relation to this matter, as in others, your ability to call attention to specific other instances, from an accurate and detailed record you have kept, assists greatly in augmenting the persuasiveness of your accusation. Actually, illegal actions, such as wiretapping and the subornation of perjury, should be announced promptly, objected to, and made the subject of disciplinary or actual criminal procedure.

A FINAL WORD

You do not have to yield to overaggressive behavior by other lawyers. You may have to put up with it, but you can and should fight it, to win. Above all, do not be overawed by blowhard or bullying tactics. There are actions you can take, and you should take them. You will be helping to improve the professionalism of the Bar, improve your own chances in the proceeding at hand, and enhance the respect of your client and the reputation that you enjoy and that entitles you to be treated fairly and with civility.

103

The Fable of the Courthouse Steps

Elaine Rudnick-Sheps

IN MANHATTAN, the Supreme Court of the State of New York is a very imposing structure. The facade of the courthouse resembles that of a Greek temple. There are no less than forty huge stone steps, each more than thirty inches in depth, encompassing the entire width of the structure that occupies an entire city block, culminating in a portico of more than six magnificent Doric columns leading to an impressive rotunda.

In all my years of practice, however, I never observed a court reporter on the steps of the courthouse nor have I witnessed parties to an action executing a stipulation in the presence of a notary on the courthouse steps.

The massive courthouse steps become just another impediment to overcome to reach the courtroom. As we know, when a lawyer says that the case will "settle on the courthouse steps," what is implied is that the matter will settle immediately before trial. The actual settlement, by custom, does not take place on the steps of the courthouse but is dictated on the record by counsel for one of the parties in the presence of the litigants and the court.

Unless the lawyers are prepared to move swiftly, however, the "golden moment" of settlement can be lost forever.

Because it requires as much skill to settle a contested matter as it does to litigate the issues, it is surprising, when the golden moment does occur, that neither lawyer except for brief notes from various meetings is prepared to place a stipulation on the record that embodies not only all of the terms agreed on but all of the safeguards and waivers necessary to protect the client.

How many times have we been part of a scenario in which the court will request the lawyers to return the next day with a fully drafted stipulation only to have the terms collapse, sometimes irrevocably. The magic moment is like a bird in the hand. Grab it when you see it. To allow time to elapse, even overnight, could be fatal. The prudent lawyer will have with him or her a fully drafted stipulation of settlement as part of a trial notebook with alternate clauses in disputed areas such as custody, visitation, property distribution, and support, so that substitution can be quickly made if a dispute arises regarding language.

Furthermore, with the advent of the notebook-size computer, a fully drafted stipulation can be brought to court on a floppy disk and changes swiftly made and printed in a matter of minutes.

If the lawyer is not technically oriented, alternate drafts for each article can be brought to court and easily added to the record.

Essential to the process of swift resolution when the magic moment occurs is that there is no delay in placing the stipulation on the record. Even an overnight hiatus can pierce the resolve of the best-intentioned settlement. The client always will think of one more thing and the magic moment disappears.

So that the client does not feel pressured into a settlement, the prudent lawyer will spend time with the client prior to trial discussing settlement alternatives and provide the client with a full copy of a proposed settlement so that the client is familiar with the language and the terminology utilized.

Also, by handing the client a copy of the proposed stipulation, a trap is avoided in which the client can complain that he or she did not comprehend the full impact of what was placed on the record or was so swept up in the excitement of the moment that the actual settlement terms were not understood.

There is an exquisite timing to courtroom settlement that can make the lawyer "hero of the day." A few extra hours of preparation will lift the lawyer aloft, not only in the client's eyes, but also in the court's.

While settlement actually may not take place on the steps of the courthouse, it is the courthouse steps that lead the well-prepared lawyer and his or her client to resolve the matter on the record to the ultimate satisfaction of all concerned.

104

What Ifs

Beverly Anne Groner

THIS IS THE ERA of "what if" in the matrimonial practice. The law moves fast, and many apparently anomalous judicial opinions must be dealt with. Counsel and client must share an awareness that certain usually unexpected results are not impossible. The suggestions presented in this chapter address some of those possibilities. For example, what if the obligor of a large lump-sum payment goes through bankruptcy and your client has waived his or her right to claim other benefits in exchange for that promise to pay? It might be possible to work it out, and yet the preferable way to deal with this would be for the agreement (merged into a decree in most jurisdictions) to have provided for such a contingency. There are no panaceas, but these tips may result in added protection for your client and her or his lawyer.

PROTECT YOUR CLIENT AGAINST BANKRUPTCY OF A FORMER SPOUSE

When structuring lump-sum payments in satisfaction of property rights in connection with a marital dissolution, bear in mind that lump-sum payments are sometimes deemed extinguishable by an intervening bankruptcy. Many times they have been elected in lieu of alimony payments but without incurring tax to the recipient. Unless there is language to protect the continued longevity and viability of the payment, however, it may be a case of the two-edged sword. Thought should be given to a provision that provides for the survival of the lump-sum obligation even through a bankruptcy or, if that proves not to be possible, for other benefits to be substituted. The payee could retain reservation of the right to seek other judicial relief until certain promised benefits are received.

ALIMONY WAIVER TO BE CONDITIONAL ON PROMISED BENEFITS BEING RECEIVED

In many cases a spousal waiver of alimony rights is obtained in exchange for the promise of other benefits. These could include the family home or other valuable property, pension rights, a lump-sum payment, or transfer of valuable personalty. Sometimes these promises are not fulfilled for one reason or another. One school of thought propounds that the provisions of the contract may be considered interdependent, in which case the disappointed client might be eligible for exoneration from the obligations or waivers he or she undertook in the contract in reliance on that now broken promise. However, it seems preferable to provide in the contract itself that the waiver of alimony rights depends on the spouse's actual receipt of the other promised benefits and furthermore that the disappointed spouse would have a right to seek alimony payments in the absence of receiving the promised benefits. This rationale also could apply to the receipt of other promises of benefits in exchange for which waivers were made. A lump-sum payment is one such example. In this situation it would be well to have had the marital settlement agreement incorporated without merger into the divorce decree with, of course, all due consideration for the legal significance of that incorporation in the total legal and fact situation presented by that case.

DISABILITY INSURANCE FOR THE BENEFIT OF A DEPENDENT SPOUSE

Disability insurance to cover the obligated spouse increases the security of the recipient when it is specifically required by the agreement.

DETERMINATION AS TO WAIVER OF TORT CLAIMS

Do you wish to recommend waiver and release of claims sounding in tort? This may depend on whether your client is the victim or the perpetrator. In any event, the matter should be discussed with your client in sufficient detail to enable him or her to make a knowledgeable decision. This consideration has become more vital now because of the availability and proliferation of interspousal tort claims. Actions in tort are relatively new between spouses. Authority often can be located on both sides of many of these questions. However, the issue is not whether your client should bring such a suit but whether the availability should be retained or, if your client is likely to be the defendant in such a suit, whether you can obtain such a release.

BECOME FAMILIAR WITH DECISIONS OF YOUR LOCAL COURT AND WITH UNREPORTED APPELLATE DECISIONS

Most matrimonial lawyers focus their primary attention on the reported appellate cases emanating from their state courts and, of course, on those few Supreme Court cases that have bearing on this area of expertise. However, an analytical approach will result in recognition that among the data most useful to a matrimonial practitioner is the knowledge of how the individual state court judges are handling cases. In Montgomery County, Maryland, for a period of several years the circuit court cases were printed by a commercial professional publisher who enjoyed a good subscription market for these decisions. Prior to that time, the CLE Institute collected the cases and made them available to practitioners primarily in lecture format.

On reflection, the reason this information is so valuable is very clear. Percentagewise, relatively few matrimonial cases are appealed, and those that are appealed more often than not are affirmed. Therefore, you must make your case in the original presentation. Because courts dealing with family law matters inevitably have more than one judge, it becomes very useful to know the individual propensities and preferences of the judges to whom your case may be assigned.

Although justice is supposed to be applied blindly, it very often is applied predictably. Accordingly, to the extent you can do so, it is beneficial to be aware of what individual judges are doing within a specific factual framework. It is quite a compelling argument to be able to point out to a judge that he or she recently made a holding under similar facts that could reasonably be applied to your then current case as well. It is nearly an irresistible argument.

Attention to theretofore unpublished appellate cases is a useful adjunct to other professional material that should be beneficially studied by lawyers in the field. In most situations the unreported cases cannot be cited as precedent. However, the precedental value is only one aspect. It is a fact of legal life that unreported cases often constitute as much as 80 percent of the appellate docket of a given court. When you consider the hazard of being oblivious to what is happening in 80 percent of the cases in your area of law, it becomes a formidable thought.

Maryland recently has begun to publish the unreported cases in book form in the belief that the body of information provided by the unreported cases is vastly beneficial to counsel.

105

Secrets of Cohabitation Agreements

Sondra I. Harris

WHEN WRITING A COHABITATION AGREEMENT, most lawyers look to a prenuptial agreement as a model, since, even today, prenuptial agreements are far more common than cohabitation agreements. While it is true that there are many similarities between the two, it is also true that there are differences that could be fatal to the unwary practitioner.

For example, an area almost considered boilerplate, or a "no-brainer," is the consideration clause of the agreement. In a prenuptial agreement, the consideration is the marriage itself, as is usually stated in the introductory paragraphs of the agreement. In a cohabitation agreement, however, there is no marriage. Indeed, the parties state that this is not be construed as an agreement to marry. Thus, other consideration must be listed and the lawyer must be careful to include consideration that is legal in his or her jurisdiction. Thus, consortium, love, or affection is probably not sufficient consideration in any jurisdiction, and specific consideration should be listed.

Another example of where cohabitation agreements differ from prenuptial agreements is when considering children. There is, in every state, a presumption of legitimacy of children born in a marriage. The same is not true in cohabitation relationships. Thus, it is possible that after living together for many years, a cohabiting couple might have a child who is not the child of one of the partners, giving the biological parent the right to take that child away forever. One way to avoid this is to have the parties agree to have genetic testing at the time of the birth of the child. If they agree to that (usually with a joke or a nervous laugh), they cannot then refuse at a later date when the question is far more important. If the child is not the child of the partner, the relationship may break up, or the partner might then choose to adopt the child, thus solving problems in the future.

More important, perhaps, is the issue of children with same-sex couples. If the parties are planning to have children either through artificial insemination or through adoption (adoption by same-sex couples is permitted in every state but Florida), it is important to spell that out in the agreement and make sure that both parties have equal rights to custody and support of the child through adoption. (It is interesting to note that recently in New Jersey, the court has held that the psychological parents of the child have visitation and custody rights similar to that of a biological parent.)

A final example of the difference between prenuptial agreements and cohabitation agreements is what happens upon the illness of a party. While all persons, married or not, should have living wills and health care proxies, it is critical that these be done for cohabitants. While a spouse is considered to have the right to make health care decisions for another spouse, a cohabitant will be consulted only if there is no other relative available. Indeed, it is not unknown for cohabitants to be excluded from a partner's hospital room by the patient's family and for that family to make decisions that are different from what the person truly wanted. Health care proxies give a partner the right not only to make "do not resuscitate" orders but also to make decisions about extraordinary measures, such as the withholding of nutrition and hydration. It is also possible to allow a partner to make a decision as to donating organs if the worst happens, and a partner passes away.

Thus, it is clear that when drafting a prenuptial agreement, an attorney must be careful to take into consideration the special needs of unmarried partners, and not to treat these agreements as simply modifications of prenuptial agreements.

HEALTH CARE PROXY

1. DESIGNATION OF HEALTH CARE AGENT.

I,Z_____, hereby appoint
     (principal)

_____
(Attorney-in-fact's name)

_____
(Address)

Home:_____   Work:_____

as my attorney-in-fact (or "Agent") to make health and personal care decisions for me as authorized in this document.

2. EFFECTIVE DATE AND DURABILITY.

By this document I intend to create a durable power of attorney, also known as a health care proxy, effective upon, and only during, any period of incapacity in which, in the opinion of my agent and attending physician, I am unable to make or communicate a choice regarding a particular health care decision.

3. AGENT'S POWERS.

I grant to my Agent full authority to make decisions for me regarding my health care. In exercising this authority, my Agent shall follow my desires as stated in this document or otherwise known to my Agent. In making my decision, my Agent shall attempt to discuss the proposed decision with me to determine my desires if I am able to communicate in any way. If my Agent cannot determine the choice I would want made , then my Agent shall make a choice for me based upon what my Agent believes to be in my best interests. My Agent's authority to interpret my desires is intended to be as broad as possible, except for any limitations I may state below. Accordingly, unless specifically limited by Section 4, below, my Agent is authorized as follows:

A. To consent, refuse, or withdraw consent to any and all types of medical care, treatment, surgical procedures, diagnostic procedures, medication, and the use of mechanical or other procedures that affect any bodily function, (including but not limited to) artificial respiration, nutritional support and hydration, and cardiopulmonary resuscitation;

B. To have access to medical records and information to the same extent that I am entitled to, including the right to disclose the contents to others;

C. To authorize my admission to or discharge (even against medical advice) from any hospital, nursing home, residential care, assisted living or similar facility or service.

D. To contract on my behalf for any health care related service or facility on my behalf, without my Agent incurring personal financial liability for such contracts;

E. To hire and fire medical, social service, and other support personnel responsible for my care;

F. To authorize, or refuse to authorize, any medication or procedure intended to relieve pain, even though such use may lead to physical damage, addiction, or hasten the moment of (but not intentionally cause) My death;

G. To make anatomical gifts of part or all of my body for medical purposes, authorize an autopsy, and direct the disposition of my remains, to the extent permitted by law;

H. To take any other action necessary to do what I authorize here, including (but not limited to) granting any waiver or release from liability required by any hospital, physician, or other health care provider; signing any documents relating to refusals of treatment or the leaving of a facility against medical advice, and pursuing any legal action in my name, and at the expense of my estate to force compliance with my wishes as determined by my Agent, or to seek actual or punitive damages for the failure to comply.

4. **STATEMENT OF DESIRES, SPECIAL PROVISIONS, AND LIMITATIONS.**

I specifically direct my Agent to follow any health care declaration or "living will" executed by me.

422

5. SUCCESSORS.

If any Agent named by me shall die, become legally disabled, resign, refuse to act, be unavailable, I name the following as successor to my Agent:

A. First Alternate Agent _____Address: _____

_____Telephone Number: _____

B. Second Alternate Agent _____Address: _____

_____Telephone Number: _____

6. PROTECTION OF THIRD PARTIES WHO RELY ON MY AGENT.

No person who relies in good faith upon any representations by my Agent or Successor Agent shall be liable to me, my estate, my heirs or assigns, for recognizing the Agent's authority.

7. NOMINATION OR GUARDIAN

If a guardian of my person should for any reason be appointed, I nominate my Agent (or his or her successor), named above.

8. ADMINISTRATIVE PROVISIONS.

A. I revoke any prior power of attorney (health care proxy) for health care.

B. This power of attorney (health care proxy) is intended to be valid in any jurisdiction in which it is presented.

C. My Agent shall not be entitled to compensation for services performed under this power of attorney (health care proxy), but he or she shall be entitled to reimbursement for all reasonable expenses incurred as a result of carrying out any provision of this power of attorney (health care proxy).　　　　D. The powers delegated under this power of attorney (health care proxy) are separable, so that the invalidity of one or more powers shall not affect any others.

E. If my health care provider refuses to honor my Agent's decisions, my Agent is empowered to direct the health care provider responsible for my care to transfer my care to another health care provider who will comply; if this authority is thwarted, undermined or not honored to its fullest extent, I further instruct and empower my Agent to initiate action for battery against such providers.

BY SIGNING HERE I INDICATE THAT I UNDERSTAND THE CONTENTS OF THIS DOCUMENT AND THE EFFECT OF THIS GRANT OF POWERS TO MY AGENT.

IN WITNESS WHEREOF, I have set my hand and seal to this Health Care Proxy this   day of   ,   .

My current home address is: __

Signature:_____

Name: _____

_____

_____

WITNESSES

WITNESS STATEMENT

I declare that the person who signed or acknowledged this document is personally known to me, that he/she signed or acknowledged this durable power of attorney (health care proxy) in my presence, and that he/she appears to be of sound mind and under no duress, fraud, or undue influence. I am not the person appointed as agent by this document, nor am I the patient's health care provider. I further declare that I am not related to the principal by blood, marriage, or adoption, and, to the best of my knowledge, I am not a creditor of the principal nor entitled to any part of his/her estate under a Will now existing or by operation of law.

Witness #1:

Signature:_____ Date:_____ , _____ Print name: _____ Telephone:

_____Residence Address: _____

_____ Witness #2:

Signature_____ Date:_____ , _____ Print Name: _____ Telephone:

_____Residence Address: _____

_____

NOTARIZATION

STATE OF NEW YORK)
              ss.:
COUNTY OF NASSAU)

    On this   day of   ,   , the said

known to me (or satisfactorily proven) to be the person in the foregoing instrument, personally appeared before me, a Notary Public, within and for the State and County aforesaid, and acknowledged that he or she freely and voluntarily executed the same for the purposes stated therein.

_____
Notary Public

<u>**MY LIVING WILL**</u>
<u>**TO MY FAMILY, MY PHYSICIAN, MY LAWYER,**</u>
<u>**AND ALL OTHERS WHOM IT MAY CONCERN**</u>

Death is as much a reality as birth, growth, maturity, and old age—

it is the one certainty of life. If the time comes when I can no

longer take part in decisions for my own future, let this statement
stand as an expression of my wishes and directions, while I am

still of sound mind:

FIRST: If at such time the situation should arise in which there is no reasonable

expectation of my recovery from extreme physical or mental disability, I direct that I be

allowed to die and not kept alive by medications, artificial means, or "heroic measures."

I do, however, ask that medication be mercifully administered to me to alleviate suffering

even though this may shorten my remaining life.

SECOND: Measures of artificial life support in the face of impending death that

I specifically refuse are:

(a) Electrical or mechanical resuscitation of my heart when it has stopped beating.

(b) Nasogastric tube feeding when I am paralyzed or unable to take nourishment

by mouth.

(c) Mechanical respiration when I am no longer able to sustain my own breathing.

THIRD: I would like to live out my last days at home rather than in a hospital if it

does not jeopardize the chance of my recovery to a meaningful and sentient life or does

not impose an undue burden on my family.

FOURTH: If any of my tissues are sound and would be of value as transplants to

other people, I freely give my permission for such donation.

FIFTH: This statement is made after careful consideration and is in accordance

with my strong convictions and beliefs. I want the wishes and directions here expressed

carried out to the extent permitted by law. Insofar as they may not be legally enforceable,

I hope that those to whom this Will regard themselves as morally bound by these provisions.

BY SIGNING HERE I INDICATE THAT I UNDERSTAND THE CONTENTS OF THIS DOCUMENT AND THE EFFECT THEREOF.

IN WITNESS WHEREOF, I have set my hand and seal to this Living Will this

day of   ,   .

My current home address is: _____   Signature:_____

_____   Name:_____

WITNESSES

WITNESS STATEMENT

I declare that the person who signed or acknowledged this document is personally known to me, that he/she signed or acknowledged this living will in my presence, and that he/she appears to be of sound mind and under no duress, fraud, or undue influence. I am not the patient's health care provider, or an employee of the patient's health care provider. I further declare that I am not related to the principal by blood, marriage, or adoption, and, to the best of my knowledge, I am not a creditor of the principal nor entitled to any part of his/her estate under a Will now existing or by operation of law.

Witness #1:

Signature:_____Date:_____Print Name:_____Telephone:_

_____Residence Address: _____

Witness #2:

Signature:_____Date:_____Print Name:_____Date:____

_____Residence Address: _____

_____

NOTARIZATION

STATE OF NEW YORK   )

SS.:

COUNTY OF NASSAU

On this   day of   ,   , the said
known to me (or satisfactorily proven) to be the person named in the foregoing instrument, personally appeared before me, a Notary Public, within and for the State and County aforesaid, and acknowledged that he or she freely and voluntarily executed the same for the purposes stated therein.

_____
Notary Public

106

Pre-Bankruptcy Planning for the Divorce Practitioner

Bruce R. Steinfeld

It is important to clearly distinguish alimony/support payments from division of property payments in the divorce proceeding, order, or agreement, in order to avoid complications in a later bankruptcy case. Some tips for distinguishing property from support and for seeking to otherwise "bankruptcy-proof" the agreement follow. No assurances are made that these tips will work, only that they may assist your clients in the event a bankruptcy case is filed.

1. In order to clearly delineate alimony/support payments as such, prepare a detailed record of the facts and circumstances leading to such an award. Explicitly recite any intention to create a support obligation. Specific facts making an award of support appropriate should appear in any written agreement or court order creating a support obligation (e.g., the length of the marriage, the relative earning powers of the parties, their age, health, and work skills).

2. Provide for alimony/support payments to cease upon the death or remarriage of the recipient spouse in order to maintain a "support" argument and for an even stronger case, have the payor treat the payments as alimony for tax purposes.

3. Courts will consider labels given to an obligation as support or property settlement even though such labels are not necessarily determinative. Support obligations should not be labeled as property settlements in written agreements or court orders and should be set forth in the written document in a separate section from property settlement debts and should be clearly labeled.

4. Protect the creditor-spouse by creating a lien or other security to ensure the repayment of the support or property debt. Try to place the lien on jointly owned property rather than property held in the name of the grantor-spouse only. The 1994 Bankruptcy Reform Act

prohibits the avoidance of a lien placed for support payments. Seek to avoid extending credit from one spouse to the other. Seek to obtain a deed to secure debt or mortgage deed and properly record it, to secure such payments and lien.

5. Obtain a Qualified Domestic Relations Order (QDRO) whenever possible to secure divisions of retirement or pension funds. This protection may be taken into consideration when negotiating a settlement agreement: take the retirement funds via QDRO rather than payments over time to protect against discharge. Try to include the following language in the provision: "the wife's share of the retirement funds shall be paid directly to wife" (or husband, as the case may be) so that there is little doubt that the decree intends to transfer debtor's interest in the funds to the spouse and does not create a "debt" that may be subject to discharge.

6. Parties may also consider including a provision in a settlement agreement that the "parties mutually covenant, represent, warrant, and agree that it is their mutual intent and bargain, which goes to the very essence of this entire agreement, that the monetary payments, obligations, and liabilities assumed and set forth herein for the benefit of the parties, shall be considered, for the purposes of federal bankruptcy law, exempt from discharge and nondischargeable in bankruptcy."

You can also try to include a bankruptcy indemnification provision such as: "The parties acknowledge that husband's payment of marital debts provided for in Paragraph _____ of this agreement, as part of an equitable division of marital property, shall not be deductible to husband for income tax purposes nor taxable to wife. The parties also acknowledge that, but for said payments, Wife would not be financially independent and would depend upon husband for support on a regular basis in order to provide herself with necessaries and meet her monthly expenses. Therefore, it is the parties' intention that if husband ever seeks bankruptcy protection, the amounts payable under this agreement shall not be dischargeable in bankruptcy under 11 U.S.C. § 523(a)(5), as the payments are in the nature of alimony, support, and maintenance. Alternatively, said payments shall be nondischargeable in bankruptcy pursuant to 11 U.S.C. § 523(a)(15)."

These provisions are not binding on the bankruptcy court but can only help an argument that the obligations should remain due and owing.

7. Prior to concluding the divorce, it is a good idea to have the husband and wife execute joint letters to all credit card companies closing all accounts in which the spouse who is paying the obligation is not the sole party on the account in order to preclude the other spouse (who during the marriage was a party to the debt) from running up the balance (this is true for accounts that have a $0 balance

but have not been closed in writing). Once the run-up occurs, the credit card company will look to both parties (particularly the one with the greater assets) to recover the debt. Also have anyone who believes that their names have appeared on credit card accounts through the other party's fraud (forgery) contact the credit card company's fraud division and file an appropriate complaint. The party should avoid "ratifying" the action by making payments. It is a good idea, also, to obtain copies of all credit card applications to see who is liable for the debt and to verify signatures. It is imperative that a paper trail is retained regarding the actions taken to close the account.

107

"Prepare, Prepare, Prepare" Is Not Just for Trials

Carlton D. Stansbury

WHEN A CASE IS HEADED FOR LITIGATION, we say "prepare, prepare, prepare." Thorough preparation is key to a successful trial. We march into court knowing our facts, knowing the law, and maybe even scripting out an opening statement or closing argument as eloquent as ones we hear on television. Unfortunately, many lawyers do not treat mediation with the same level of preparedness. Just as in trials, preparation is key to a successful mediation.

Mediation is a cooperative process involving the parties (and maybe lawyers) and the mediator that is intended to help the parties resolve their own disagreements. The mediator is a neutral third person equipped with communication and dispute resolution skills who helps the parties reach an agreement by focusing on the key issues in the case, exchanging information between the parties, and exploring options for settlement. A mediator is not a decision maker.

In some states, at least one mediation session is required in a custody dispute. The exception to this mediation requirement is if mediation would cause undue hardship or would endanger the health or safety of one of the parties. Such a situation could exist in a case where a party has engaged in child abuse, interspousal battery, or domestic abuse or where either party has a significant problem with alcohol or drug abuse.

With the exception of the mandatory mediation session in a custody dispute, mediation is a voluntary process available to all parties. Mediation may cover both custody and financial issues. If financial issues such as property division, maintenance, and/or child support are to be considered in the mediation process, the parties must agree in writing. This is usually covered in the mediator's agreement to mediate. Because the mediation process is voluntary, either of the parties or the mediator can terminate the process at any time. Sometimes specific disputes such as the division of household furnishings are referred to mediation.

The first session with the mediator is a screening and evaluative session to determine whether mediation is appropriate and whether both parties wish to continue in mediation. If mediation is pursued, future mediation sessions will be scheduled by the mediator. The lawyers and guardian ad litem, if one has been appointed, can be present at the sessions if the mediator and parties agree. Although mediators can interview a child, even if a party is not present, it is rarely done and should not occur without the agreement of the guardian ad litem, both parties, and their lawyers.

The mediator may require the parties to provide written disclosure of facts relating to the custody or financial issues. This is usually done in conjunction with disclosure and data exchanged between the parties' lawyers. For the mediation sessions to be productive, it is important that the parties have the necessary financial information available at the mediation session.

In many states, oral or written communications made or presented in the mediation process either by the mediators or the parties are not admissible in evidence. A mediator cannot be subpoenaed to court or compelled to disclose oral or written communications made during the mediation or to render an opinion about the parties. There are limited exceptions to this rule. The purpose of this rule is to encourage the cooperation and candor of the parties and to encourage parties to explore facilitated settlement of their disputes without fear that their claims or defenses will be compromised if the mediation fails.

A mediator may suspend the mediation process to enable a party to obtain an appropriate court order or to obtain therapy. An example of this would be a situation where one of the parties does not want the divorce and counseling would assist that party in adjusting to the divorce.

The mediator may choose to meet separately with each party. Such a meeting is referred to as a caucus. An understanding should be made in advance of a caucus as to whether any information disclosed in a caucus is to be shared with both parties.

It is important for the mediating parties to seek advice from their lawyers on legal issues that arise during the mediation sessions prior to reaching an agreement. Usually the mediator will anticipate which legal issues will be relevant at the next mediation session and will request that the parties discuss the legal issues with their lawyers prior to the mediation.

At the conclusion of the mediation, if an agreement is reached, the mediator will prepare a mediation agreement that will be signed by the parties and the guardian ad litem if one is appointed. If the mediation involves custody, the mediator will certify that based on the information provided to the mediator, the custody agreement is in the best interest of the child or children.

The mediation agreement will be reviewed by each party's lawyer. The mediation agreement may need to be supplemented after review by the lawyers. Supplemental issues can be either referred back to mediation or resolved by the parties' lawyers.

If the parties are willing, cooperative, and flexible, the mediation process will likely be satisfactory and successful in bringing the parties to agreement.

MEDIATION PUNCHLIST

- Discuss the mediation process with the client

- Emphasis the fact that a mediator is not a decision maker and carefully chose the style of the mediator and the qualifications of the mediator (accountant, psychologist, attorney) that fits with the facts and personalities of the case.

- Discuss the benefits of mediation and explain why the client is being referred to mediation

- Review the agreement to mediate with the client

- Discuss the pros and cons of caucuses with client

- Determine whether the client would benefit from your attendance at the mediation session

- Clarify the issues in dispute with your client and make certain that the mediator is aware of the disputed issues

- Instruct the client to keep you informed of the mediation process

- Encourage the client to be flexible and explore the ranges of options with the client

- If placement is an issue, make certain the client has a placement plan to present in mediation

- Consider alternative placement plans prior to the mediation

- Get copies of all documents or work papers which client provides to the mediator

- Advise your client on the law in advance of the mediation session

- Make certain that the mediator is aware of stipulated facts

- Review the mediated agreement with client

- Be clear as to the issues to be submitted to mediation

- Prior to a mediation session on financial issues, prepare a financial disclosure to be submitted at the mediation and run through tax calculations with the client

XII

Torts

A GROWING FAMILY LAW FIELD is that of marital torts. In the divorce action, we can divide the property and make arrangements for custody and support. Yet, some of the relationships between the parties may give rise to other legal remedies, and the divorce lawyer must be aware of them and be prepared to deal with them.

108 Domestic torts is a relatively new field and theories on its use still are developing. **Leonard Karp** provides an overview of various theories on causes of action.

109 The reverse side (isn't there always one?) is that the lawyer for the potential tort feasor should close the door after the divorce so that the former spouse does not sue for the other half later. **Jim Friedman** explains how to protect the client against such a possibility.

108

Domestic Torts—An Ace in the Hole

Leonard Karp

MATRIMONIAL LAWYERS frequently represent clients whose spouses have violated court orders—domestic violence protective orders, support and maintenance orders, preliminary restraining orders, custody and visitation orders, maintenance of insurance orders, or a myriad of other orders.

In addition to the traditional remedies of contempt, arrearage judgments, incarceration, fines, or other sanctions, the lawyer for the aggrieved spouse, under the right set of circumstances, ought to consider filing a domestic tort action.

For many years, courts and legislatures throughout the country attempted to preserve domestic harmony by refusing to allow an injured family member to bring a cause of action against other family members. The doctrines of interspousal, parent/child, and intrafamilial immunity have until recently precluded pursuing domestic tort actions in most jurisdictions. In the past twenty years, however, these immunities have been eroded or abrogated in the majority of states.

The weakening of family immunities has been accompanied by increasing numbers of marital dissolutions and a realization that existing legal remedies for certain types of marital misconduct are inadequate. Together, these phenomena have combined to produce an explosion of new domestic tort actions.

The most likely cause of action arising out of conduct that violates a court order is the intentional infliction of emotional distress. To maintain such an action, a plaintiff must prove the following: (1) extreme and outrageous conduct, (2) engaged in intentionally or recklessly, (3) causing emotional distress, and (4) which is severe. Approximately three-fourths of our jurisdictions have recognized this tort.

When the marriage turns sour, spouses often engage in obnoxious or offensive behavior and outrageous conduct toward each other or the children. In addition to the traditional claims of assault and battery, tort actions for invasion of privacy, illegal wiretapping, parental kidnapping, child snatching, as well as intentional infliction of emotional distress, are potential remedies for the willful violation of an existing court order.

Evidence of physical and emotional abuse or sexual exploitation of the children often comes to light when the marriage deteriorates. Hundreds of thousands or even millions of cases of emotional abuse, sexual molestation, and physical mistreatment of children are reported annually, although the real incidence is probably much higher. Cases range from malicious beatings to cruel and humiliating punishment for misbehavior to incestuous relationships.

Violence, abuse, and disease within the family thus are serving as the bases for an emerging body of tort law, the exact parameters of which have yet to be determined.

Damages can be collected from the separate property or marital property distributed to the offending spouse in the divorce case. When the spouse who has violated the court order does not have sufficient assets to satisfy a judgment for damages, the lawyer should examine the facts to see if there are other sources of recovery. Insurance coverage may be available for the damage done by tortious conduct. Third parties with "deep pockets" who wrongfully damage, or assist in damaging, the aggrieved spouse, parent, or child are target defendants in a domestic torts case. Substantial verdicts are being reported throughout the country on a regular basis. New or expanding tort theories or claims such as federal § 1983 civil rights actions, infliction of emotional distress without physical injury, custodial interference, and wiretapping under the Omnibus Crime Control and Safe Streets Act of 1968 are successfully breaking ground to provide a means of compensation for aggrieved spouses and their children. Most states have taken the fault out of divorce proceedings and provide for an equal division of marital property regardless of culpability. As a result, there is a growing emergence of courts recognizing tort claims for behavior that exceeds reasonable bounds of marital or parental conduct during or after coverture.

The 1980s have brought enormous changes to the family law and personal injury litigator. Recent developments and current trends probably will lead to a proliferation of tort claims arising out of divorce cases and family disputes. Only the lawyer who is prepared to meet the challenge of this new wave of domestic tort actions arising out of a matrimonial litigation will be able to effectively represent the ever-changing needs of his or her clients in a rapidly evolving society.

109

Covering Your Backside against Interspousal Tort Claims

James T. Friedman

PUBLICITY GIVEN THE RECENT DECISION in the case of *Patty Sue Childs v. Jerry E. Childs* spotlights the potential for substantial money damages arising from interspousal physical or emotional tort claims. In *Childs,* after a short marriage, a Texas jury awarded the wife $900,000 for her property division and $500,000 for the husband's intentional infliction of emotional distress.

While the unavailability of alimony in states like Texas tends to encourage alternative causes of action, the fact remains that all but twelve states allow spouses to sue each other for tortious injuries. (The antitortious twelve are Delaware, Florida, Georgia, Hawaii, Kansas, Mississippi, Missouri, Montana, Ohio, Oregon, Tennessee, and Wyoming. Illinois repealed its immunity statute in 1988 and Mississippi abrogated its immunity doctrine by Supreme Court decision.) Some states limit these awards to physical damages; others require that the injury be intentional.

The problem that is of particular concern arises when the suit for tortious injury is brought *after* a dissolution judgment, to the surprise of the alleged tort feasor and the chagrin of the lawyer. One would think that the standard clauses contained in most dissolution judgments waiving claims "arising out of the marital relationship or otherwise" would be adequate to bar such suits. A developing body of case law has held to the contrary.

In the case of *Stuart v. Stuart,* 410 N.W.2d 632 (Wisconsin Appellate, 1987), the wife sued for assault, battery, and intentional infliction of mental distress arising from incidents occurring during the marriage. The husband claimed *res judicata,* waiver, and equitable estoppel based on the language of the parties' dissolution judgment. The appellate court disagreed.

In *Aubert v. Aubert,* 529 A.2d 909 (New Hampshire, 1987), a prior divorce decree was held not to bar a subsequent civil action in tort that the court held to be fundamentally different from a divorce proceeding.

Delaware has retained the doctrine of interspousal immunity in tort claims, but in the recent case of *Hudson v. Hudson,* 532 A.2d 620 (Delaware Sup., 1987), the appellate court held that immunity did not apply where the personal injury suit was heard after the dissolution decree. In all of these cases, the courts noted that fault and punitive damages are not to be considered in the award of property or support under divorce law. The injury suits were found to be necessary to provide the constitutionally mandated judicial remedy for every wrong.

TIP

The lawyer who drafts or approves judgments and agreements with standard waiver language is in jeopardy of potential malpractice claims for failing to add protective language. Therefore, add the clause "including claims arising from tortious conduct between the parties" to your waiver clauses. That simple addition should not cause a great deal of controversy (nobody reads boilerplate) and could save a great deal of client shock after the divorce. If, on the other hand, a party does intend to sandbag your client with some post-dissolution litigation, this clause will smoke them out. Better you should know now before you give away half the farm than later when they take the other half.

XIII

Trial Tactics

Most family law cases reach settlement—most, but not all. Those that reach trial tend to be complicated and to present very difficult issues.

Family law trials usually lack the excitement of, say, the O. J. Simpson trial. Many are technical and complex. They can entail reams of written documentation. This, of course, does not make them any less important to the client. It does, however, make it more of a challenge to keep the court interested.

Besides keeping the court interested, we must impress our clients with our litigation ability. Clients are used to the fast-moving trials they see on shows like *L.A. Law.* Yet few of our trials end neatly right before a commercial break. In fact, many are like the continuing episodes—you're not sure whether they're ever going to end.

Conducting an effective trial requires, like many other things in life, a great deal of practice. Because the vast majority of family law cases are settled out of court, our trial skills tend to atrophy. Thus, trial tips are especially helpful—they remind us of things we once knew and they educate us about new technology that can help make the trial both interesting and effective.

110 Preparing a budget for a client's trial has caused more than one family lawyer to go gray. Do you present what the client spent during the marriage or during the divorce? Or do you present what the client wants to be able to spend? **Ed Snyder** suggests that lawyers may want to present more than one budget at trial to reflect different considerations.

111   If a divorcing party has an incentive to undervalue assets in a divorce, the reverse is true when preparing a financial statement for a bank. The party usually has an incentive to *overstate* values to qualify for a loan. **Marshall Auerbach** discusses how to use such financial statements at trial.

112   No builder would start construction without blueprints. **Sandra Morgan Little** shows how to present the court with your blueprint in the form of requested rulings to give the judge a guide to the relief you are requesting.

113   Another form of request for relief is presented by **Arnie Rutkin**. As like Sandra Morgan Little, Arnie provides a sample request that can be adapted easily.

114   "Counsel, call your first witness," says the judge. The reply: "Your Honor, I call—the other side!" **Harvey Golden** discusses the tactical advantage that can be gained by calling the opposing spouse adversely as your first witness.

115   It was stated earlier, in pointing out the value of video evidence at trial, that we live in a visual society. By the same token, witnesses can be prepared for trial better by being shown, rather than by being told, how to be a good witness. **Donn Fullenweider** explains how to obtain videotapes to show to potential witnesses, and how to prepare your own tapes to fit your style as a litigator.

116   The audience at a family law trial is, of course, the judge. Therefore, the best advice on trial strategy comes from a judge who has been there. **Judge David Main** tells which strategies have impressed him and, just as important, which have not.

117   The first family law trial I ever witnessed nearly kept me from entering the field. I greatly admired the judge for remaining awake through mounds of boring numbers and statistics. Fortunately, with modern computer graphics, **Ken Raggio** can bring these numbers to life in a fashion that is not only entertaining but speaks volumes with only pictures.

118   For years, I prosecuted criminal trials, giving many closing arguments. I realized that the best closing arguments were not the ones I gave in front of the jury with the pressure of time and place. Rather, my most brilliant presentations were the ones I "gave" walking back to my car *after* the trial. Fortunately, divorce cases are tried to the court, and most courts think about the testimony before reaching a decision. **Herndon Inge** describes how to use the posttrial brief to present the arguments you thought of while walking to your car and wish you had presented to the court.

119 To project confidence, it is necessary to be organized. While many experts suggest using a trial notebook, **Howard Lipsey** believes that, in some complicated cases, individual files are a better way to stay on top of witnesses and exhibits.

120 Few things are more boring than listening to transcripts being read into evidence. How do you keep the court awake then, if all you have is a transcript? **Monroe Inker** suggests using a summary of the deposition, and he provides the legal authority for it.

121 Everyone loves a story. One way to keep the judge awake is to present the case as if it is a story. **Bill DaSilva** describes how to construct a theme of the case and shows how to use it throughout the trial.

122 **Willard DaSilva** notes that the core of a client's case lies in the credibility of the client. As the court's first impression usually comes during direct examination, it is critical to prepare the client appropriately. **Willard's** hot tip is an outline of issues to be discussed and advice on how to prepare a client to overcome the trepidation of their day in court.

123 The evidence is in, and it is now time to convince the judge of the righteousness of the client's cause. In her hot tip, **Kimberly Quach** gives five easy steps to draft a persuasive closing argument.

124 In real estate, the three most important factors are "location, location, location." In trial practice, the three most important factors are "preparation, preparation, preparation." For an effective lawyer, part of the preparation is building an organized trial notebook. **Mark Sullivan** describes how to prepare and use a trial notebook.

125 Communications experts tell us that an audience is most likely to remember facts that they both see and hear. In a divorce trial, the audience is the judge, and the same rule applies. **Ken Raggio** discusses how to combine sight and sound in your opening statement to maximize the judge's retention of your case.

126 Cross-examining a mental health expert is fraught with difficulties. Many are truly professional witnesses in that they have had a great deal of experience on the witness stand. Their testimony is frequently given great weight by the court. **Monroe Inker** provides some suggestions for cross-examining these critical expert witnesses.

127 While we try cases to win, where there is a winner, there is a loser—and it may be you! Under such circumstances, your client may want to appeal. As pointed out by **Andrew Berman**, you can significantly improve the odds of prevailing on appeal by how you conduct the trial.

110

How to Effectively Present Your Client's Budget at Trial

Edward S. Snyder

ANY JUDGE SITTING in family court can tell you that most of the budgets submitted on behalf of litigants can be included in a listing of the best fiction of the year. Therefore, the lawyer who submits a realistic budget on behalf of the client—one that is not an exercise in creative writing—will take a significant step toward achieving the client's goal. The focus of this tip is on the budget form and suggests that, where appropriate, litigants may use more than one budget at trial.

How often do our clients tell us that they do not live as they lived before the separation? Similarly, when preparing the budget, how frequently do clients ask either of the following questions: "Should I fill out the budget to reflect what I now spend based on the money presently available to me, or based on the way we [as a family] lived before the separation?" Or "Should the budget reflect what it will cost me to live with the children or without them?"

The simple answer is that there is no reason not to include more than one budget. The only caveat is that each separate budget that is included should be clearly labeled to reflect its contents. For example, a budget intended to reflect how the parties lived before separation should be labeled as such; and a budget to reflect how a support recipient is living now, based on limited resources, should be labeled accordingly.

The advantages of including more than one budget are easily understood. Contrasting an "as is" budget with an "as was" budget will very graphically illustrate why a significant award should be entered. For example, if a wife and three children were living on $7,500 per month before separation, but now are receiving only $4,000 per month, by preparing two budgets counsel is able to highlight the specific expenditures to which the family became accustomed and that no longer are possible given present finances. The differences between the two budgets should be further highlighted.

With all of this in mind, attention must be paid to assuring that whatever budgets are prepared are realistic. The client must be advised to avoid the temptation of inflating the budget. A simple way of ensuring that the figures are realistic is to "prove" the budget by checking the expenditures against the family's annual income. Quite clearly, something is wrong if the budget significantly exceeds the income after taxes. The reverse also is true. If the budget submitted by your client is significantly lower than annual income, you should investigate the family's savings habits. Have monies been saved? If so, where are the savings?

If counsel can present a picture of realism within the realm of the family's history of expenditures, multiple budgets provide the client with an opportunity to prove his or her case with more clarity.

111

Use of a Party's Admission in a Financial Statement

Marshall J. Auerbach

THE THOROUGH MATRIMONIAL LAWYER may want to consider discovery of financial statements submitted to lending institutions by the opposing party. These frequently reveal the identity of assets that otherwise may not have been disclosed, but they also may contain representations of value and income that are higher than those being asserted in the matrimonial litigation.

Your potential use of the admissions contained in these financial statements submitted to lenders can be devastating to your opponent. If the opponent admits that these representations were accurate, you have struck gold. On the other hand, if the opponent denies the truthfulness of those financial representations made to the lender and asserts that the figures were "hyped" or "puffed" for credit purposes, you have a powerful impeachment tool.

It is a federal crime if the opponent knowingly makes any false statement or report or willfully overvalues any land, property, or security for the purpose of influencing a lender, the deposits of which are insured by the Federal Deposit Insurance Corporation, the Federal Home Loan Bank System, the Resolution Trust Corporation, or the National Credit Union Administration Board. The opponent would be subject to a fine of not more than $1,000,000 or imprisonment for not more than twenty years, or both. 18 U.S.C. § 1014 (1989).

So strict is the application of this federal statutory provision that even false statements in a loan application regarding an applicant's Social Security number and date of birth qualify as material statements, and thus properly form a basis for a conviction under this section. *United States v. Phillips,* 606 F.2d 884 (9th Cir. 1979). The essence of the offense does not depend on the accomplishment of influencing the lender, but rather the crime is one of subjective intent requiring neither reliance of the bank officer or an actual defrauding. *Id.* at 886. The offense is committed even though the loan already had been made and the false statement could not be said to have influenced the action of the bank. *United States v. Kennedy,* 564 F.2d 1329 (9th Cir. 1978).

The use of this harmful financial admission is not to fuel a criminal prosecution but rather to bind the opponent to the higher value contained in the financial statement. Everyone is presumed to know the law, and your opponent would certainly not have risked a federal criminal prosecution by misrepresenting the value to a federally insured lender. Therefore, the opponent must be misrepresenting the value in the dissolution of marriage proceedings to obtain a better result.

It has been regularly determined that a husband who asserts a lower value for assets in a dissolution of marriage proceeding than that which he represents in a personal financial statement will be bound by the representation in the financial statement. *In re Marriage of Block*, 441 N.E.2d 1283 (Ill. App. 1982) (husband's representations of $35,000 in financial statements for value of "Weldon Square Apartments" venture was binding though he testified it had no value); *Selchert v. Selchert*, 280 N.W.2d 293 (Wis. App. 1979) (husband bound by his statement in financial declaration regarding value of lot in Florida and court rejected his testimony to lower amount); *Johnson v. Johnson*, 277 N.W.2d 208 (Minn. 1979) (husband's testimony that property was worthless because of recent developments in the area was rejected where husband represented in a signed financial statement to a fair market value of $25,000, and value of $24,000 was placed on the property by the court); *Esposito v. Esposito*, 385 A.2d 1266 (N.J. Sup. Ct. App. Div. 1978) (court adopted husband's net worth figure in his financial statement submitted to General Motors before trial). There is an obvious benefit to a party to minimize the value and existence of assets and income in dissolution of marriage proceedings that ordinarily does not exist in the case of earlier financial statements prepared and filed for business purposes.

112

Requested Rulings— Give the Judge a Guide to Your Case

Sandra Morgan Little

REQUESTED RULINGS are a shorthand method to give the court a preview of your case. A judge cannot know what your case is about or where your evidence and testimony are headed without a guide. Tell the judge in the opening statement what you want him or her to find on particular issues and what result you ultimately want. Because most judges cannot remember from your opening statement all the evidence you will present, your purpose for presenting it, and its relevance, give it to the court in writing. If your state follows the federal rules of evidence, you can give the court requested rulings as a trial aid at the end of your opening statement. The court will be delighted to have it and will use it throughout the hearing or trial to make notes. What could be better than to have the judge using your numbers, theories of the case, and division of property? You can use it for a hearing with one or two simple issues or for a complicated trial. It is simple and useful and I try not to go to court without it.

SECOND JUDICIAL DISTRICT COURT

COUNTY OF BERNALILLO

STATE OF NEW MEXICO

No. DR 96-00009

MARY SMITH,

       Petitioner,

  vs.

JOHN SMITH,

       Respondent.

REQUESTED RULINGS

Mary Smith, by Little & Gilman, P.A. (Sandra Morgan Little), for her Requested Rulings states:

1.   <u>CUSTODY</u>:

    a)   Joint custody of:

       KEVIN CHRISTOPHER, age 12, born May 10, ____
       KATHERINE ANN, age 9, born November 5, ____

       with primary residence with Mary Smith;

    b)   Decision making as set out on Schedule A;

    c)   Time-sharing as set out on Schedule A.

2.   <u>CHILD SUPPORT</u>: John Smith has annual gross income of Eighty Thousand Dollars ($80,000) and annual imputed income of Twenty-five Thousand Dollars ($25,000). Child support should be as set out on Schedule B.

3.   <u>ALIMONY</u>: John Smith should pay Mary Smith Three Thousand Dollars ($3,000) per month for thirty-six (36) months.

APPENDIX - 1

4. PROPERTY:

    a)   Characterization: The Indian Springs residence is the separate property of Mary Smith and the community has a lien of Thirty-four Thousand Six Hundred Dollars ($34,600) on it as is shown by Schedule C;

    b)   Valuation & Division: The community property should be divided as set out on Schedule E.

5. ATTORNEY FEES: John Smith should pay Mary Smith attorney fees of Twenty-five Thousand Dollars ($25,000).

LITTLE & GILMAN, P.A.

By _____
SANDRA MORGAN LITTLE
Attorneys for Petitioner
P.O. Box 26717
Albuquerque, NM 87125
505/246-0500

We certify we have hand-delivered a copy of the foregoing to opposing counsel of record this _____ day of _____, ____.

LITTLE & GILMAN, P.A.

By _____

APPENDIX - 2

SCHEDULE A - <u>CUSTODY</u>

A. <u>Decision Making</u>: Mary Smith shall have the sole
responsibility in the decisions pertaining to the children's
religion. The parties shall consult with each other on major
decisions involving residence, education, child care, recreational activities and medical and dental care. Neither party shall
make a decision or take an action which results in a major change
in the children's lives until the matter is discussed and the
parties agree. If the parties cannot agree they shall submit the
dispute to mediation with Dr. Polly Annah. If the parties cannot
agree with mediation, Dr. Polly Annah shall make the decision.

B. <u>Periods of Responsibility</u>: John Smith shall have the
following periods of responsibility:

    1)   <u>Weekdays</u>: Each Wednesday from 5:00 p.m. until
        8:30 am.Thursday;

    2)   <u>Weekends</u>: First and third weekends from 5:00 p.m.
        on Friday until 6:00 p.m. on Sunday;

    3)   <u>Summer</u>: Six weeks each summer;

    4)   <u>Holidays</u>:

        a)   One-half the school Christmas vacation,
            including Christmas Eve and Day in odd-
            numbered years;

        b)   Father's Day each year;

        c)   Each child's birthday in even-numbered years;

        d)   School spring break each even-numbered year.

APPENDIX - 3

SMITH v. SMITH   DR 96-00009
Bernalillo County, New Mexico

IMPUTED INCOME

1. John F. Smith, M.D.

Reported Annual Income	$ 80,000
Deferred Annual Excess Pension Contribution	25,000
	$105,000

BASIC VISITATION MONTHLY CHILD SUPPORT OBLIGATION

		Custodial Parent	Other Parent	Combined
1.	Gross Monthly Income	$2,500	$8,750	$11,250
2.	Percentage of Combined Income	22%	78%	100%
3.	Number of Children			3
4.	Basic Support from Table A			$1,744
5.	Health/Dental Insurance	$ -0-	$ -0-	$ -0-
6.	Work-related Child Care	800	-0-	800
6B.	Private School	-0-	450	450
6C.	Music Lessons	40	-0-	40
7.	Total Support			$3,034
8.	Each Parent's Total Obligation	$ 667	$2,367	
9.	Subtract Direct Payments	840	450	
10.	Each Parent's Net Obligation	($ 173)	$1,917	
	Father Pays Mother			$1,917

455

SMITH v. SMITH   DR 96-00009
Bernalillo County, New Mexico

MARY SMITH'S ESTIMATED APPORTIONMENT OF INDIAN SPRINGS

			COMBINED	COMMUNITY	SEPARATE
1.	Apportionment:				
	Indian Springs Acquisition (Purchased Prior to Marriage)				
	a)	Down payment	$ 57,200	$ 57,200		$ 57,200
	b)	Family Loans:				
		(1) Prin Pd Prior Marr 4,800	4,800		4,800
		(2) Prin Pd During Marr 27,400	27,400	$ 27,400	
		(3) Prin Unpaid 4,600	4,600		4,600
	c)	Total Purchase Price $ 94,000			
	d)	Landscaping:			
		(1) Prior Marriage	5,000		5,000
		(2) During Marriage	none		
	e)	Total Apportionment Value	$ 99,000	$ 27,400	$ 71,600
	f)	Share	100%	28%	72%
2.	Apportionment:				
	Indian Springs Value				
	a)	Appraisal	$123,650	$ 34,620	$ 89,030
	b)	Share	100%	28%	72%

456

SMITH v. SMITH   DR 96-00009
Bernalillo County, New Mexico

JOHN SMITH & MARY SMITH'S ESTIMATED COMMUNITY PROPERTY

ASSETS:	VALUE	JOHN SMITH	MARY SMITH
1. Checking & Savings Accounts:			
a) 1st. Security Ck. #1234	$ 15,000	$ 15,000	
b) 1st. Security Sav. #4500	20,000		$ 20,000
c) Dean Witter Invest. Acct. #8911	150,000	100,000	50,000
2. Bonds/Stocks:			
a) 450 Sh. PNM ($13.25/Sh.)	6,000		6,000
b) 500 Sh. AT&T ($52/Sh.)	26,000		26,000
3. Insurance: [Face Amt]			
a) NYLIC #20478 [$500,000]	7,500	7,500	
b) Mass Mut. #50078 [$350,000]	3,800		3,800
4. Personal Effects	25,000	10,000	15,000
5. Household Goods	60,000	20,000	40,000
6. Real Estate:			
a) 6510 Rio Granada $295,000			
Mtg. ($1,800/mo) (150,000)			
Cost of Sale (10%) (29,500)	115,500		115,500
b) 1210 Indian Springs $123,600			
Separate Interest (89,000)	34,600		34,600
c) Colorado Condo	120,000		120,000
7. Vehicles:			
a) 1994 Suburban	21,000	21,000	
b) 1993 BMW	25,000		25,000
8. John F. Smith, M.D., P.A.	320,000	320,000	
9. John F. Smith, M.D., Pension Plan	780,000	390,000	390,000
Total Assets	$1,729,400	$ 883,500	$ 845,900

LIABILITIES:			
a. Credit Cards	$ 25,000	$ 20,000	$ 5,000
b. 1st Security Credit Line	55,000	55,000	
c. 1993 Tax Liability	40,000	40,000	
Total Liabilities	$ 120,000	$ 115,000	$ 5,000

ESTIMATED NET ASSETS	$1,609,400	$ 768,500	$ 840,900
Equalization of Assets		$ 36,200	($ 36,200)
EQUAL ASSETS		$ 804,700	$ 804,700

457

113

Trial Techniques—Requests for Relief

Arnold H. Rutkin

WHILE THERE IS NO RULE OF PRACTICE or statute in Connecticut calling for a request for relief in dissolution cases, nevertheless there has arisen a common practice to file such a document in dissolution cases in most of the judicial districts in Connecticut. I believe that this practice arose in Fairfield County, and now judges require the filing of a request for relief at the beginning of the case or in some circumstances will permit it to be filed at the conclusion of the case.

It is an extremely effective tool. It can be used both as an offensive weapon and as a defensive weapon. For example, in a case where the other side is being completely unreasonable in its negotiations, that will show up in its request for relief because its unreasonableness will be immediately obvious to the court.

In one case, the other side made no offer and, in fact, asked my client to pay counsel fees. It showed the judge right at the beginning that this was a case that was being tried because one side was making no offer, and the judge then looked at the rest of the case about why that fact would or would not be justifiable.

The request for relief in all cases should be extremely short, usually two or three pages. It should be nothing more than a road map for the judge to follow regarding what you believe to be fair in this case. You want to put in each and every item you are requesting, including alimony, child support, visitation, personal property, life insurance, medical insurance, indemnification requests for debts, etc.

Many judges in Connecticut read these requests at the beginning of the case and then review them at the end of the case; and, in fact, when writing their memorandum of decision, they frequently pull out language from these requests for relief. A lawyer who fails to file a request for relief at the beginning of the case runs the risk of having the other lawyer's request for relief shape the judge's ideas about the case. If you are a lawyer who regularly appears before that judge and you indicate to the judge that in this particular case you feel you cannot file the request for relief for whatever reason, however, that failure to file a request for relief can be just as significant.

An example of a simple request for relief follows this chapter. In that particular case, the judge's memorandum of decision was virtually verbatim to the requests that I made. The other side failed to file a timely request for relief, although it did file a request for relief at the end of the case, and the other side's request for relief showed why the case was being tried.

I highly recommend to those of you who do not use such a tool to introduce it into your practice, for it will become an extremely valuable tool for you and your client.

Incidentally, you always should prepare and review this request for relief and include your client's input. It will make life much easier for your client when he or she is on the witness stand and the other lawyer attempts to ask questions regarding the client's claims in the case or if the judge happens to ask a few questions regarding the same subject. Having helped you to prepare this request for relief, the client will be very clear regarding what he or she wants from the court.

NO.   : SUPERIOR COURT

                             : JUDICIAL DISTRICT OF FAIRFIELD

VS.   : AT BRIDGEPORT

                             :

DEFENDANT'S CLAIMS FOR RELIEF

The Defendant in the above-captioned matter hereby requests that the following orders enter regarding the respective rights and liabilities of the parties:

1. That the Husband during his lifetime pay to the Wife, until her death or remarriage, the sum of Three Thousand Five Hundred Dollars ($3,500.00) per month in alimony. Notwithstanding the foregoing, the amount of the alimony should not be terminated by reason of the Wife's remarriage, for at least a period of ten (10) years. Said payments shall be taxable as alimony to the Wife and deductible to the Husband. (See Net Disposable Income Analysis—Exhibit A Attached.)

2. Said alimony payments are based upon the aggregate of the Husband's 2003 gross base salary plus bonus. If the aggregate of the Husband's gross base salary and/or gross bonus increases in future years, the Husband shall pay to the Wife as additional alimony twenty-five percent (25%) of any such increase.

3. The marital home shall be immediately sold. The sale proceeds which remain after satisfaction of the existing first mortgage, payment of the home equity line of credit, brokerage commission, usual and necessary closing costs, shall be divided two-thirds (2/3) to the Wife and one third (1/3) to the Husband. The Husband shall pay the fix-up costs necessary to sell the marital home as reflected in Exhibit B.

4. Until such time as the marital home is sold, the Husband shall pay the mortgage, equity credit line, taxes, insurance, lawn service and utilities (except telephone) associated with the marital home. Said Payments are neither deductible from income to the Husband nor includible as income to the Wife for tax purposes.

5. For all future years, on or before April 15th of each year, the Husband shall provide to the Wife on an annual basis documentation of his income, including copies of his federal and state tax returns, W-2 forms, and 1099 forms.

6. The Husband's pension through PepsiCo International shall be divided by assignment pursuant to a Qualified Domestic Relations Order one-third (1/3) to the Wife and two-thirds (2/3) to the Husband to be drafted by the Plaintiff. The Court shall retain jurisdiction to supervise and enforce the payment of retirement benefits in accordance with the above, including the filing of a Qualified Domestic Relations Order.

7. The parties shall each be responsible for federal land state capital gains tax resulting from the sale of the marital home, on an equal basis. Each shall indemnify and hold the other harmless from any liability arising by reason of any deficiency assessment in connection with his/her share of federal and state capital gains taxes.

8. The Husband shall pay to the Wife the sum of Ten Thousand Dollars ($10,000.00) for attorney's fees.

9. The parties shall share equally the individual retirement accounts (IRAs) in their names jointly and in the Husband's name solely.

10. The parties shall share equally in any savings accounts.

11. The Husband shall pay to the Wife the sum of Five Thousand Dollars ($5,000.00) toward a down payment for a new automobile. The Husband shall retain the 1996 Hyundai, valued by him to have an equity of One Thousand Seven Hundred Dollars ($1,700.00). The Wife shall retain the 1994 Chevrolet, which has a value which does not exceed its equity.

12. The Wife shall retain the Refund in the amount of $1,099.00 from the parties' joint 2002 New York State tax return.

13. The parties shall file a joint tax return for 2003, and shall share in any tax refund or tax in proportion to their income.

14. The Husband agrees to indemnify and hold the Wife harmless with respect to any and all future claims or demands and suits with respect to foreign, federal, state or municipal income taxes for any year in which the parties filed a joint income tax return, except that the Husband shall not be responsible for any omissions or mistakes in the reporting of the Wife's income. If either party receives notice of an audit or tax proceeding involving any such joint tax return, each shall immediately notify the other or his or her representatives of such proceeding and the parties shall have the right to defend said return. In the event the Wife is obligated to pay any amount assessed as a deficiency, interest, penalty or otherwise with respect to a federal or state income tax return (except with respect to her income) she shall, upon demand, be reimbursed in full by the Husband unless such charge resulted from an omission or mistake in the reporting of the Wife's income, in which case she shall be solely responsible.

15. The Husband shall be responsible for the following liabilities: auto loan, $2,500.00; visa $1,213.00; loans on life insurance policies; $4,400.00 (Phoenix Mutual), $1,781.00 (Metropolitan Life).

16. The Husband shall retain his interest in the employee stock option plan with PepsiCo International.

17. The Husband shall maintain the Wife as beneficiary of a life insurance policy on his life in the amount of $250,000.00, which amount shall be paid in a lump sum upon the death of the Husband. The Husband shall at least on an annual basis provide to the Wife satisfactory evidence demonstrating his compliance with the above. Said policy shall remain even if the Wife remarries and the death benefit shall be modifiable if the Husband's employment provides less.

18. The Husband shall cooperate with the Wife in obtaining any documents or information necessary for continuation of her medical insurance coverage through his employer. The cost of said continuation shall be solely the expense of the Wife.

19. The Husband shall retain the interest in the cash values of the Metropolitan Life insurance policy and the Phoenix Mutual life insurance policy.

20. The Husband shall transfer to the Wife fifty percent (50%) of all "Frequent Flyer" certificates owned by him or due and owing to him as of this date. In addition, for a period of five (5) years after the date of the decree of dissolution of mar-

riage, the Husband shall transfer to the Wife, on an annual basis, fifty percent (50%) of all "Frequent Flyer" certificates which he accumulates in any given year. The transfer shall be made on or before December 31st of every year.

THE DEFENDANT
BY_____
ARNOLD H. RUTKIN
RUTKIN & EFFRON, P.C.
315 Post Road West, P.O. Box 295
Westport, CT 06881
227-7301 Juris No. 101515

This is to certify that a true copy of the foregoing was delivered this date to all counsel of record.

_____
ARNOLD H. RUTKIN
Commissioner of the Superior Court

EXHIBIT A
NET DISPOSABLE INCOME ANALYSIS

	HUSBAND	WIFE
1. Gross Income (Employment)*	$116,050.00	$18,720.00
2. Other Income (Interest, Dividends)		
3. Alimony (Unallocated Alimony & Support)	(42,000.00)	(42,000.00)
4. TOTAL ADJUSTED GROSS INCOME	74,050.00	60,720.00
Less:		
5. Exemptions @ $2,000.00	2,000.00	2,000.00
6. Deductions: (a) Standard	3,100.00	3,100.00
(b) Itemized		
7. TAXABLE INCOME	68,950.00	55,620.00
8. Tax—Federal (Tax Bracket)	18,065.00	13,627.00
9. Tax—State 4%	4,642.00	
10. FICA	3,600.00	1,406.00
11. TOTAL TAXES (8, 9 & 10)	26,307.00	15,033.00
12. Child Support		
13. NET DISPOSABLE INCOME (HUSBAND)		
(4–11–12)	47,743.00	
14. NET DISPOSABLE INCOME (WIFE)		
(4–11+12)		45,687.00
15. Percentage of Total Net Disposable Income	51%	49%

*Husband: Based upon 2003 salary of $94,200.00 plus $21,850 bonus

Wife: Based upon current salary

EXHIBIT B
PROJECTED REPAIR COSTS FOR SALE OF MARITAL HOME

1.	Handyman (est)	$ 500.00
2.	Septic (new leach fields)	Undetermined
3.	Pipe for storm drain	3,500.00
4.	Roof (est)	5,000.00
5.	Painting - Living Room	1,400.00
	- Hallway	
6.	Replace Window (est)	125.00
	TOTAL	$10,525.00(+)

114

Calling Defendant as Plaintiff's First Witness

Harvey L. Golden

MANY STATES, either through adoption of Federal Rule of Civil Procedure 43(b)(2) or as part of their case law, allow a family court litigant to call an adverse party as a witness and cross-examine or at least interrogate by leading questions without the need for proving surprise or hostility. By calling the enemy spouse as your first witness, when the judge's attention is fresh and the opposing party and counsel least expect it, you can obtain a significant advantage that may carry you through the entire trial.

This technique allows you to "bookend" your case with the most important testimony: your enemy's admissions at the beginning and your client's testimony at the very end, after he or she has heard all of the previous testimony and can wrap up the loose ends. Your client is the one witness who cannot be sequestered from the proceedings and thus may be present in court throughout the trial and may "go to school" on everything that has transpired before having to testify. Most important, using this tactic, the judge has heard the other party's admissions as part of his or her first impression of the case. And, *if the discovery deposition has been performed, correctly,* it can create a strong tactical advantage at the earliest stage of trial, because I believe a pound of the other party's admissions is worth a ton of your testimony.

115

Using Video for Trial Preparation

Donn C. Fullenweider

INTRODUCTION

A. Technical advances make this a worthwhile, inexpensive tool;
B. Kinds of equipment and cost; and
C. Professional photographers.

USING VIDEOTAPE TO PREPARE WITNESSES FOR TRIAL

A. Preprepared tapes:
State Bar of Wisconsin Tapes
Law Office Videotape Series
P.O. Box 7158
Madison, WI 53707-7158
(608) 257-3838

1. *About Your Divorce*
This tape should be seen by the client either before or after the initial consultation. It provides basic information about major issues relating to divorce, including:
Psychological aspects of divorce;
Need for counseling;
Working with your lawyer;
Property division;
Maintenance;
Child custody;
Visitation;
Child support;
Emotional effect on children; and
Lawyer fees.

2. *Preparing for Your Deposition*
This videotape should be viewed by every client prior to having his or her deposition taken. It demonstrates the dos and don'ts of being deposed and helps alleviate some of the stress and anxiety the client experiences. These topics are covered:
What is a deposition;

What a deposition looks like;
Importance of telling the truth;
Listening carefully to every question;
Understanding the questions;
Volunteering too much information;
Guessing at answers;
Paying attention to objections;
Avoiding absolute words such as "never" and "always";
Personal appearance and demeanor; and
Opposing lawyers' personality and tactics.

3. *Going to Court: Part I—What to Expect*
4. *Going to Court: Part II—What's Expected of You*

PREPARING YOUR OWN TAPES

A. Testifying for a deposition;
B. Testifying in court;
C. How a divorce works;
D. Consider the tapes you can make, such as:
   1. *How We Will Handle Your Case;*
   2. *Meeting Our Staff;*
   3. *The Members of Our Firm;*
   4. *How to Avoid Visitation Problems;*
   5. *What to Expect for Child Support or Alimony; and*
   6. *How Child Support Guidelines Work.*

PREPARING WITNESSES FOR TESTIFYING

A. Try a practice session of direct examination of your client on video-tape.
   1. Puts the witness at ease;
   2. Helps build self-confidence;
   3. Improves the client's ability to answer properly; and
   4. Acquaints the witness with the question-and-answer format.
B. Preparing for cross-examination:
   1. Use associates or other lawyers to ask questions;
   2. Repeat questions regarding sensitive areas for desensitization;
   3. Show body language and habits that give negative impressions;
   4. Coach voice use and projection; and
   5. Use eye contact.
C. Will help you improve your skills as an examiner.

VIDEO AS A TRAINING TOOL

A. Cross-examination of a client by associates;
   1. The tape can be used to critique your association on examination technique style, following the trial advocacy institute format of learning by doing, but with an actual factual situation.
     a. May give you some new ideas.

       b. You might not want to cross-examine your own client. A client may become angry or embarrassed because of the examination. This avoids undermining the client's confidence in the lawyer to whom the client is looking to try to settle his or her case.

B. Cross-examination by paralegal;

    1. Paralegals enjoy the chance to be a lawyer;

    2. Gives the client some training;

    3. Even when the questions are inarticulate or argumentative, which younger lawyers or paralegals tend to be, it can give you an example of how the client will hold up under confusing examination; and

    4. Later you can refine the questions to a skill level that the client can expect in trial.

VIDEO FOR SEEING DISTANT LOCATION

A. This is an opportunity to see the home and the life of the client for yourself or for use in court;

B. This also is an opportunity to see the property or the area in which the property is located;

C. Consider video depositions to show lifestyle or property values; and

D. Day-in-the-life custody tapes.

TYPE OF FORMAT

A. Solo—you appear in your own office, following a standard script;

B. Have others in your office follow the same script for use with the client;

C. A group of lawyers can share the cost by having a professional photographer and studio; and

D. Consider a group of lawyers in a talk-show format to discuss why someone was a good or bad witness, or how to be a good witness.

116

Trial Strategies

Hon. David R. Main

CROSS-EXAMINATION

A multitude of texts and articles have been written about the art of cross-examination. In most cases, the typical witness in a family law matter requires a special approach to take into account the emotional issues involved and the often voluminous content that may result from the testimony if the witness is allowed too free a rein. A particularly useful approach I have observed involves what I would characterize as a soft, yet extremely leading and pointed, style that is aimed specifically at the weaknesses in the evidence in chief and that is formulated to gently, yet firmly, confine the answers to the questions within a narrow range. The key lies in keeping the witness absolutely focused and carefully leading him or her step by step to the desired answer or position.

CROSS-EXAMINATION OF THE CHILD WITNESS

During the course of my articles leading up to the call to the bar, I recall my principal apprehensively preparing for the cross-examination of an adolescent witness in a hotly contested custody dispute. When I questioned the concern this exercise seemed to be engendering, I received the following advice: "Question: How do you cross-examine a child? Answer: Don't!" By and large, most children, particularly those of tender years, are unreliable from the point of view of responding to questions as one would expect. Too soft an approach may result in a disarming response guaranteed to devastate the examiner. Too hostile an approach may result in tears and an admonition from the bench. Personally, I do everything within the bounds of fairness and the law to avoid requiring children to give evidence. There are, of course, instances in which such evidence must be taken, and in these cases, it would seem advisable to exercise great caution and, as much as possible, to prepare yourself in advance in regard to the child's life experience, emotional status, intelligence, propensity to tell the truth, etc.

CHALLENGING THE EXPERT WITNESS

I continue to be amazed at the number of lawyers who seem to be incapable of breaking down or at least weakening the evidence of a well-prepared expert witness. Simply being legally trained and displaying an icy stare is unlikely to do the trick. I know for a fact that many experts dread the prospect of cross-examination in a courtroom, and it seems to me that the difference must lie in the state of preparation between the witness and the examiner. The answer is obvious. Cross-examination of such an expert means having a firm grip on the fundamentals within the area of expertise of the witness, defining in advance from the witness's reports the flaws in the analysis, and learning, wherever possible, the human bias, if any, that may be exhibited by the witness.

KNOW THE CHARACTERISTICS OF YOUR JUDGES

One of the ingredients of a successful law practice, especially in the area of family law, is a firm and up-to-date knowledge of the views, likes, and dislikes of those who would judge your cases. This information will affect both your preparation and your presentation. The scope of the exercise of judicial discretion probably is nowhere wider than in the area of family law. It follows that a clear definition of the profile of the judicial officer exercising that discretion is absolutely critical.

MEDIATION AND SETTLEMENT AT TRIAL

Relative to where it began, the complexion of a case often alters dramatically as the evidence unfolds. At a particularly auspicious point in a trial, a judge often will seize on the moment to suggest some form of settlement, hopefully in a way that will not disqualify him or her. Some lawyers often utilize the same tactic to continue negotiations toward resolution. There is a third alternative that may be used in multijudge courts, and that is to seek, where appropriate, the intervention of another judge to explore the possibility of settlement based on the evidence led before the trial judge. We have used this technique from time to time in the court in which I sit, often at the request of the lawyers, and with considerable success, particularly in child protection matters.

HOW TO UPSET A JUDGE

Several ways to upset a judge include the following:

A. Be late;
B. Be unprepared;
C. Be unjustifiably and unreasonably argumentative;
D. Be overly verbose; or
E. Be ungracious in defeat.

HOW TO IMPRESS A JUDGE (AS EXPRESSED BY ANOTHER CANADIAN JUDICIAL OFFICER)

To impress a judge:

A. Be on time;
B. Be prepared;
C. Be brief; and
D. Be gone.

117

If a Picture Is Worth a Thousand Words, How Many Is a Chart Worth?

or

How Even a Lawyer Can Make Presentation Graphics for Court

Kenneth G. Raggio

INTRODUCTION

All of us are aware of the axiom that "A picture is worth a thousand words." Some judges would call us "wordy" in our court presentations. Many courts have intervened, requiring that parties present financial/budget information on standardized forms; some states (such as California) require many other financial disclosures to be made on a standardized form.

Two ways of focusing the court's attention and interest on particular facets of your case are by using graphs and summaries. With graphs and charts you have the ability to move the judge's focus from "writing down the information" to "looking at" a graphic depiction of testimony. It generally is conceded that a well-constructed graph containing salient information makes a great impact on the court.

SUMMARIES

Summaries are useful for detailing particular information from a great deal of source documentation:

A. Showing long-term patterns: expenditures by months (or years) to show needed level of support for necessaries;

B. Emphasizing certain "abusive" or extraordinary expenditures (restaurant visits, cash ticket withdrawals, etc.) over a period of time; or

C. Tracking bank account activity over a period of time.

SUMMARIES INTO GRAPHS AND CHARTS

Admissibility generally is governed by Federal Rule of Evidence 1006 as follows:

RULE 1006. Summaries

The contents of voluminous writings, recordings, or photographs, otherwise admissible, which cannot conveniently be examined in court may be presented in the form of a chart, summary, or calculation. The originals, or duplicates, shall be made available for examination or copying, or both, by other parties at reasonable time and place. The Court may order that they be produced in court.

Charts and graphs are efficient conveyors of data. Good uses include showing:

A. Trends;

B. Aberration from trends;

C. Precipitous reduction in income contemporaneous with divorce filing; or

D. Disparity of earnings between spouses.

GRAPH-IN-THE-BOX

Graph-in-the-Box (Version 2.0): A "Lawyer-Proof" Product (Retail $140; street $80):

A. Extreme ease of use: "Paint a box over the numbers on the screen and a graph pops up."

B. Minimal keystroking. The program captures the figures from a word-processing or other document on-screen, and places the information into a chart or graph. (Ask your secretary to explain "block" and "move" to you if you are lost.)

C. Options: Fifteen colors; eleven different graph types; small, medical, and large charts; ten different fill patterns and line types; on-monitor slide shows.

D. Limitations: hard to modify the canned formats; may have to unload another memory program to run it; cannot do 3-D charts; only one font.

DEMONSTRATION

The columns of figures in the following charts will be captured to build a graph.

NOTE: The speed of building the graph on-screen is a function of the computer and disk. Your desktop PC will be faster.

A. The "Jaw" Chart

Comparative Income, Husband v. Wife

	Wife	Husband
1982	$ 0	$ 25,000
1983	5,700	60,000
1984	14,000	75,000
1985	15,000	83,000
1986	16,500	125,000
1987	16,000	175,000
1988	18,000	210,000

COMPARATIVE INCOME, HUSBAND V. WIFE

COMPARATIVE INCOME, HUSBAND V. WIFE

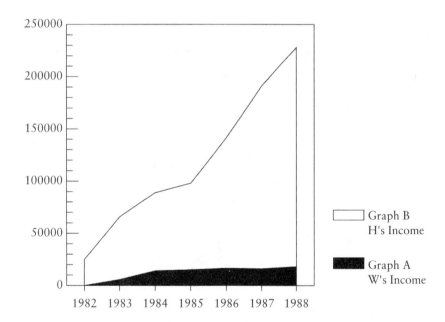

B. Husband v. Wife, 1988 Deposits & Withdrawals

1988	Deposit	Bank Account W/D
Jan	$4,010	$2,270
Feb	4,120	2,120
Mar	3,755	1,850
Apr	4,305	2,310
May	4,700	2,080
Jun	3,210	3,550
Jul	2,102	3,810
Aug	1,721	3,420
Sep	1,595	3,985
Oct	1,380	3,880
Nov	1,750	3,225
Dec	1,660	3,660

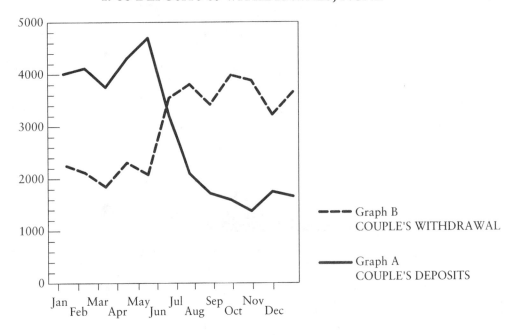

HUSBAND V. WIFE
1988 DEPOSITS & WITHDRAWALS, NCNB

Graph B
COUPLE'S WITHDRAWAL

Graph A
COUPLE'S DEPOSITS

GUESS WHEN THE DIVORCE WAS FILED?

C. Dr. Jones Billings, Receipts, and Receivables

Month	Fee	Payments	Adjustment	EOM A/R
Jan	$21,335	$ 6,524	$ 280	$ 54,689
Feb	34,765	16,952	129	72,372
Mar	33,360	8,581	625	96,524
Apr	28,024	31,601	137	92,810
May	32,154	21,665	3,739	99,559
Jun	29,100	23,263	3,056	102,339
Jul	24,530	21,319	1,267	104,282
Aug	43,392	24,002	13,110	110,562
Sep	38,200	14,640	14	134,107
Oct	21,880	14,079	4,912	136,996
Nov	23,010	45,115	−414	115,305
Dec	32,665	16,773	10,395	120,801

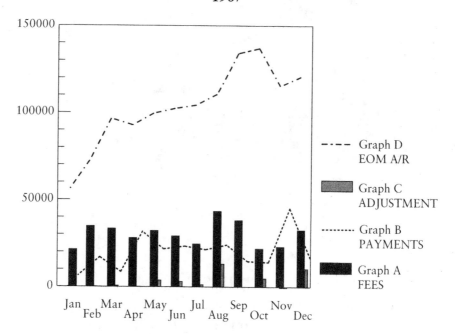

DR. JONES BILLINGS, PAYMENTS,
ADJUSTMENTS, AND RECEIVABLES
1987

481

D. Proof of Effective Services

Mr. Leah's Claimed Separate Property

	M/L	DEBENTURE	REALTY	OTHER
Inventory	$400,000	$500,000	$300,000	$100,000
Interrogs	320,000	500,000	200,000	100,000
Deposition	300,000	300,000	200,000	100,000
Amended Inv.	200,000	200,000	100,000	100,000

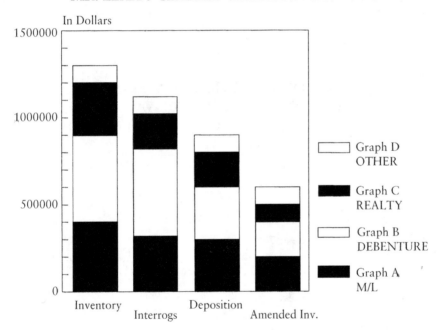

MR. LEAH'S CLAIMED SEPARATE PROPERTY

CONCLUSION

A graph is not mandated for every presentation; however, a few minutes viewing reams of data in graphic form can only aid the lawyer in making a more concise, clearer, and more effective court presentation.

118

Posttrial Brief

Herndon Inge III

YOUR EXPERT'S TESTIMONY was not so persuasive as you expected. The judge had twenty motions set for hearing that day and was not so patient as your case required. You got the necessary documents into evidence, but the opposing counsel objected to your questioning the witnesses or isolating the information found in the documents. The trial judge did not allow oral argument after the evidence was closed. The trial judge would not allow you to explain the fine distinction between conflicting legal authorities. Nevertheless, your case is over, or is it?

Domestic relations cases are especially fertile territory for posttrial briefs because the decision is made by the judge alone. The judge always has exercised his or her discretion to allow evidence to be submitted after the day of the hearing, allow the introduction of additional legal authorities, and even allow argument of the case after the day of the hearing. We are all familiar with these uses of a posttrial brief. There may be other uses, however.

In any domestic relations hearing or trial with complicated figures, documents, or unfamiliar medical conditions, an expert witness may be needed, e.g., accountant, physician, or social worker. Your client already has identified and the judge has admitted into evidence the underlying facts, figures, or documents and you had planned to present an expert witness to explain, summarize, and compare the significance of these facts or figures that already are in evidence. What if the opposing lawyer is successful in proving that your expert is not qualified in this particular area, the judge is impatient and does not want expert testimony that may prolong the hearing, or the only expert available is unaccustomed to vigorous cross-examination? A posttrial brief may be your only remedy. The post-hearing brief can include charts, graphs, comparisons, and distinctions merely arguing facts already admitted into evidence. Reasonable inferences may be drawn from these facts and figures and argued effectively in the brief.

If you see that your motion is one of twenty set on the docket that day and you see the judge is impatient, then you may need to present the underlying facts, introduce the necessary documents in bulk, and present an expedited hearing and ask the judge to delay ruling until you have submitted a posthearing brief. As long as the underlying facts and figures are admitted into evidence, you can take the necessary time and space to make such arguments, comparisons, and distinctions by posthearing brief.

Often prior years' income tax returns, financial statements, corporate records, or even medical records are introduced at the trial or hearing but the judge rules that he or she will take the documents under submission and review them after the hearing. He or she often does not have the time to extensively and meticulously review the documents and to make the comparisons and distinctions to recognize the relationships that you believe are necessary to your client's position. These relationships can be isolated, explained, and argued in a posthearing brief.

Trial lawyers are used to arguing their client's position, identifying inconsistencies of the other party's evidence, contrasting the opponent's present testimony with prior testimony, and even commenting on the nonverbal communications of the opposing party or his or her witnesses during the trial. This also can be covered in a posthearing brief, drafted in the peace of the trial counsel's office, considering the trial in retrospect, now that all of the evidence is in. A posttrial brief may make that extra difference.

Occasionally, all trial lawyers are surprised at trial when their opponent presents an unexpected legal theory or authority and further legal research is required to defend this new issue. Now that you have heard your opponent's full explanation of the importance of his or her legal authorities, a posthearing brief will allow you the opportunity to judge the application of your opponent's authorities, present opposing legal authorities, or at least argue that your opponent's legal authorities can be distinguished.

Not every hearing and trial requires a posthearing brief. It is only suggested that the posthearing brief be filed away in your toolbox to be used when appropriate.

119

The Individual Trial Files

Howard I. Lipsey

I HAVE ATTENDED MANY of these tips seminars with respect to how to properly prepare your papers for trial. The most popular vehicle seems to be the trial notebook. As a matter of fact, in one recent seminar, the entire topic was the trial notebook.

From the inception of my law practice, I have tried different vehicles or methods to make life easier at trial. At the outset I used some form of trial notebook, then discarded it. I then went into the big file, which became cumbersome and difficult to sort out at the time of trial. After going to some of the more recent seminars, I then started to use the trial notebook referred to as, and manufactured by, Euro Files. I found that the notebook itself was excellent and the mechanism of getting to and from the documents was excellent as well. The problem I found in using it at actual trials was that I was constantly constantly thumbing through the trial notebook, even though I had an index and tabs, and finding that one trial notebook was not sufficient and that I constantly had to use additional trial notebooks. Furthermore, when it came to putting into evidence certain documents, taking them from the trial notebook usually left a void unless I had a separate trial notebook just for evidence and copies of evidence that I was going to introduce.

At the risk of being a heretic—to the trial notebook brigade—I am going to suggest that you throw away your trial notebook and try an approach that many of us have always used, sometimes used, or, in fact, never used, and that is the individual file folder.

Let me suggest a scenario: You have a fairly large domestic relations trial; you are going to have several witnesses and you know that there are going to be several witnesses for your opponent; you have certain important pleadings; you have documents that must be introduced into evidence somewhere along the line; furthermore, you have information such as medical texts, economic texts, accounting texts, business valuation texts, or child custody texts that you will utilize to cross-examine the other expert or even, depending on your rules of evidence, to put in the documents as substantive exhibits.

There are various portions of a trial. For example, in the preliminary stage you may have certain motions. You can have a motion and your answer or your motion and the other side's answer in an individual file; any particular law or notes with respect to that motion can be in that particular file, so when you do, in fact, go to court, you will not have to drag every bit of your voluminous files, but only the particular motions and areas of concern that are in the individual file.

Whatever the categories are that you wish to individualize is up to you. Examples are as follows:

1. Investigation
2. Settlement
3. Costs
4. Custody Issues
5. Property
6. Appraisals
7. Experts
8. Discovery
9. Direct Examination of a Witness and
10. Cross-Examination of a Witness

The point is that you can individualize each aspect. When you need a particular file, you do not have to thumb through a notebook, which could be so voluminous that the notebook itself becomes the chore.

For example, you might have a particular witness who is an expert on the valuation of a business. In that particular file would be all of the pertinent data, with a separate individual index about that expert. You might have his or her curriculum vitae, an outline of specific questions that you want to have him or her cover, certain backup information, law with respect to evidentiary issues that may arise with his or her testimony, and, not last, but certainly as part of it, research materials that you utilized with that expert. The opportunities are as broad as the nature of the case.

Another example: Have a deposition available, together with your notes and outlines of the portions of the deposition you want to zero in on as well as any other material for impeachment purposes. Thus when the witness gets on the stand, all you will have to do is take out the individual file and utilize it for your examination.

You may have a separate file for final arguments. As you go along, you may add to that file when you have a thought about something you may want to say in the final argument. You always have that particular file available and you will not have to search all over the place later on before preparing for your final argument.

Another file may have "things to do," order of trial, and law and specific issues involved. It is helpful and probably will be required, in any of the individual files, to have an individual file index that is right in the file itself.

Certainly what I am suggesting is not to reinvent the wheel or tell any of you things that you already know and may have already used. The purpose is to point out that each trial lawyer has his or her own way of handling the files. I would suggest that we rethink the use of individual files for individual topics and not become slaves to the beautiful blue, red, or green notebooks that seem to be the latest craze.

120

The Use of Deposition Summaries at Trial

Monroe L. Inker

LAWYERS OFTEN MUST RELY on vast amounts of deposition testimony in complex cases or when witnesses cannot be present at trial. The verbatim reading of these depositions is tedious, boring, and time-consuming work. To keep the attention of jurors and the judge, to help them better understand the case, and to minimize wasteful expenditures of court time, lawyers should consider using deposition summaries at trial.

Authority for the use of deposition summaries is based on the Federal Rules of Civil Procedure, the Federal Rules of Evidence, and the Manual for Complex Litigation. FED. R. CIV. P. 1 states that "[The Rules] shall be construed to secure the just, speedy and inexpensive determination of every action." FED. R. EVID. 403 says that "Although relevant, evidence may be excluded if its probative value is substantially outweighed by the danger of unfair prejudice, confusion of the issues, or misleading of the jury, or by considerations of undue delay, waste of time, or needless presentation of cumulative evidence." FED. R. EVID. 611(a) gives the court power to control the submission of evidence to "make the presentation effective for the ascertainment of truth" and to "avoid needless consumption of time." More specifically, the Manual for Complex Litigation § 22.332 explicitly advocates the use of summary depositions for both bench and jury trials when counsel can agree on a narrative synthesis.

Courts have allowed using deposition summaries under three different circumstances: as part of an agreement between the court, counsel, and a master in advance of trial; on the recommendation or insistence of the court as part of a general policy; or simply mandated by the court *sua sponte* in the course of a confusing or lengthy proceeding.

In *In re Air Crash Disaster at Stapleton International Airport*, 720 F. Supp. 1493 (D. Colo. 1989), for example, the court suggested and the lawyers agreed before the trial to summary presentation of the relevant portions of a deposition in a one- or two-page narrative, prepared by the offering lawyer.

Id. at 1503. The opposing counsel then was given the opportunity to review the summary for accuracy. *Id.* Disputes that arose during the trial over the contents of the summaries were resolved by the court in camera. *Id.* Sometimes resolutions took the form of allowing opposing counsel to supplement the summary by reading limited portions of the deposition transcript to the jury. *Id.* at 1504. Summaries in this case were used for expert witnesses unable to attend the trial and for presenting corroborative testimony to lessen the time spent on repetitive testimony. *Id.* A U.S. district court's general policy that deposition testimony be reduced to a five-page narrative summary was upheld by the Seventh Circuit in a medical malpractice case. *Oostendorp v. Khanna,* 937 F.2d 1177, 1179 (7th Cir. 1991); see also *Nigh v. Dow Chemical Co.,* 634 F. Supp. 1513, 1519 (W.D. Wis. 1986). The court affirmed the use of such summaries as a "reasonable means of implementing the mandate of Rule 611." *Oostendorp,* 937 F.2d at 1180.

Other courts that do not have a regular policy concerning deposition summaries have decided extemporaneously to order their use. For example, in *Kingsley v. Baker/Beech-Nut Corp.,* 546 F.2d 1136, 1141 (5th Cir. 1977), a case dealing with severance compensation under an employer's personnel policy, after the plaintiff's lawyer read lengthy deposition excerpts to the jury, the court ordered the lawyer *sua sponte* to reduce the testimony to summary form and read only the summary to the jury. *Id.* Despite objection by the opposing lawyer that the summary was not accurate, the decision was upheld because the court found that counsel had had ample opportunity to rebut any contested testimony. *Id.*

Courts have permitted the presentation of deposition summaries in many types of cases. Judges have allowed deposition summaries not only in the tort and labor cases cited previously but also in domestic relations, corporate, and criminal trials. In a 1977 case in which a former wife was seeking a modification of child support, the trial court made findings based in part on the defendant's summary of the deposition testimony. *Addington v. Addington,* 363 N.E. 2d 151, 153 (Ill. App. 1977).

In a case involving a corporate tender offer, a U.S. district court required the plaintiff to present oral summaries of lengthy depositions, rather than reading them verbatim to the jury. *Walerk v. Action Industries, Inc.,* 802 F.2d 703, 712 (4th Cir. 1986). The Fourth Circuit Court upheld the policy of the judge, recognizing that the practice of requiring deposition summaries was a "legitimate exercise of [the court's] inherent discretionary power to ensure the orderly and expeditious administration of the trial." *Id.*

In a recent first-degree murder, arson, and sexual battery case, the trial court insisted that a summary of a witness's deposition be presented to the jury because defense counsel was unable to get the witness to come to court. *Holton v. State of Florida,* 573 So.2d 284, 289 (Fla. 1991). Both the defense and the prosecution objected to the use of summary deposition testimony. The defendant urged the trial court to grant a continuance and the prosecution complained about its inability to cross-examine the witness. *Id.* at 289, n. 4. Yet, the Supreme Court of Florida found no error on the part of the trial court because both the defendant and the prosecution had been involved extensively in the preparation of the summary. *Id.* at 289.

Deposition summaries also may be videotaped or used along with videotaped testimony. In *ESTI Pipeline Project v. Burlington Northern, Inc.,* No. B-84-979-CA (E.D. Tex. 1987), an antitrust case involving charges of a decade-long conspiracy among six companies, lawyers took 300 depositions. C. Michael Buxton and Michael Glover, "Managing a Big Case Down to Size," 15 *Litigation* 22 (Summer 1989). Faced with a case that promised to take many months to try, an innovative federal district court judge devised many procedures to shorten the time and expense of the trial. *Id.* Among them was giving lawyers wide latitude to edit and rearrange videotaped depositions and intersperse narrated summaries with excerpts of deposition testimony. *Id.* Each party chose its own mechanics and method of video presentation. *Id.* at 23. The plaintiffs produced a videotape that included the lawyer narrating a summary along with deposition excerpts. *Id.* The defendants' lawyers read the summaries in person and interspersed them with videotaped excerpts of deposition testimony. *Id.*

Summaries in *ESTI Pipeline* were used for a variety of purposes, from providing background for the excerpts to explaining technical issues. *Id.* The only requirement was that the end product be fair and accurate. *Id.* The use of deposition summaries along with well-edited deposition excerpts kept the interest of all concerned and saved an enormous amount of time. As a result, the trial was completed within eight weeks. *Id.* at 22.

There is authority and precedent for using deposition summaries, either read in person by counsel or videotaped, in many types of trials. While some courts already have policies governing the use of deposition summaries, others may be open to the idea if counsel suggest it. Summaries can keep the interest of a jury and judge, make the trial more understandable, and conserve time and money. See Hon. Leonard S. Sand, "From the Bench: Getting Through to Jurors," 17 *Litigation* 3 (Winter, 1991).

121

Theme of the Case— A Winning Technique

Willard H. DaSilva

Whether litigated to conclusion or negotiated to a settlement, every case should have a theme, that is, a central focal point of attention consisting of the major objective of the client. It is the theme of the case that holds it together, that gives it form and direction, and that becomes the most persuasive tool in convincing an adverse party or the trier of fact of the superiority of your client's position in the case.

WHAT IS THE THEME?

Each case has one overriding issue that overshadows all others, with rare exceptions. It is that issue that should receive the prime attention of the court and of the lawyer and client in preparing the case to present to the trier of fact. The theme is the bond that holds the case together and maintains the focus of the court on the issues as you present them and want them to be considered.

Packaging is an extremely important marketing tool in the world of business and commerce. It is no less important in the handling of matrimonial cases. The packaging of the issues and evidence in a case determine the credibility of the client's position and the ease (or difficulty) of persuading the court of the justification of the position of the client on the most critical issues to be determined. A case that is prepared without a theme is a case with inadequate preparation. The presentation of the case undoubtedly will be a litany of facts and information that are disjointed and that do not come together for the support of a client's position in a convincing and persuasive manner.

Picture the creation and development of the theme of the case as similar to the construction of a house. Before the first shovel is put into the ground to dig the foundation, plans have been made. The plans essentially give a picture of the overall appearance of the house as it is to be completed, in addition to providing the working detail to accomplish the end result. One of the first considerations in building a house is: What should it look like?

Will it have the appearance that is desired? Similarly, the theme of the case is to develop an overall picture of the issues in the case so that they all may be viewed as a whole and seen as a total, composite picture.

After the foundation is dug for the house, the structure then is framed in and a roof put on. The house has begun to take form in a general way. Likewise, the opening statement of counsel will be the first opportunity to construct the foundation for the case, and as witnesses and evidence are presented, the framework is developed.

As the house construction proceeds, interior walls are installed, and all of the accoutrements, fixtures, and frills are added. So with the matrimonial case, once the overall structure of the case has been presented, details then may be provided to give the structure vitality, form, and the appearance that the lawyer wants the court to view.

Finally, the house is decorated, which puts the finishing touches on it and makes it livable. The summation and "windup" of the matrimonial case pulls together all of the issues supported by the evidence in the manner that the lawyer has developed.

Throughout the entire process of building the house and of building the case, the blueprints are followed and changed only if necessary to cover circumstances not originally contemplated. In each instance the overall form of the house and of the case is known and visible and kept in mind.

HOW IS THE THEME DEVELOPED?

Perhaps the easiest way to start to develop a theme for the case is immediately following the conclusion of the initial conference with the client. This may occur even before the lawyer is retained. By the end of that conference, the lawyer should be aware of the overall picture and the ultimate goals of the client. It is the earliest and best time to conceive of a theme for the case. If, for example, it appears that the major issue in the case will be the custody of children, that will become evident in the very first conference with the client.

The development of the theme depends on information furnished by the client, and the preparation for trial is planned with the ultimate goal in mind. If custody is to be the prime issue, unquestionably you will initially evaluate, at least on a cursory basis, the priorities of the parties with respect to their responsibilities toward the child or children. It may very well be that the priorities of one parent for self-indulgence, other activities, and outside business or social pursuits have demonstrated a history of a higher priority than attending to the needs of the child. This often is reflected by the attitude of the child, who looks to one of the parents as the primary psychological, nurturing parent. The entire custody case can be developed around the theme of the priority of the parent's responsibility and dedication to the child's welfare and the child's view of that parent as the primary psychological caretaker.

If equitable distribution of marital assets or a division of community property is an issue, there may be a question of commingling of separate property and marital (or community) property, which becomes the primary focus of the case. That, then, is the pervasive theme for the case from the opening statement to summation.

THE SUMMATION TIES THE CASE TOGETHER

An impressive speech is one where the speaker at the outset states what subjects will be covered, then discusses those subjects, and, finally, concludes by summarizing what has been said. The summation of the case is part of the wrapper, together with the opening and the intervening evidence, which ties the entire case together. The theme of the case is a picture and gives structure to the case from the outset through its development by way of evidence and, in conclusion, by way of summary.

If effectively presented, the theme will make the difference in many cases between a successful result or a disappointing failure. It makes the case vibrant and alive and keeps the trier of fact focused on the major issues throughout the entire case. Just as a house should not be built without a previously developed set of plans, no case (and certainly no trial) should be undertaken without a similar blueprint with focus on the theme—the overall picture of the end result sought to be accomplished.

122

The Client's Direct Examination— The Real Challenge

Willard H. DaSilva

EXPERIENCED LITIGATORS are of the common opinion that the most difficult, the most important, and yet the most neglected area of trial practice is the client's direct examination. Trial lawyers revel in taunting witnesses in cross-examination, in breaking down their positions, and in reinforcing the case for the client. Mental health experts are particularly vulnerable to cross-examination techniques.

The core of a client's case, however, lies in the credibility of the client. Usually, the first impression of the client by the trier of fact is the client's testimony in the presentation of his or her case. It is rare that a client has had any considerable experience in a trial courtroom. Consequently, to that person the courtroom scene is often met with trepidation, anguish, and sometimes even fear. It is, therefore, prudent to prepare the client properly for the ordeal of the trial.

ORIENTATION

The Courtroom Setting

A vital part of the preparation of a client for trial is to give the client a degree of comfort in knowing what may be expected. From a physical viewpoint, the client should become familiar with the actual setting in which the trial will take place. If it is possible to have the client visit the courthouse and, if known, even the particular courtroom that will be used, there can be a certain advance familiarity so that the client will not be in a strange and unfamiliar place. The locations of the judge, court stenographer, court clerks, security guards, the tables used by both parties, the possible presence of visitors (where courtrooms are open to the public), and other physical aspects of the courtroom should be explained in detail. Similarly, the client should be informed of the function and expected activities of each of the persons in the courtroom.

A View of the Courtroom

If there is a trial taking place in one of the courtrooms and the courtroom is open to the public, it may be helpful to escort the client into the courtroom and observe the activities of an ongoing trial. All too often clients have an impression that a trial is what is portrayed in the movies or on television, which frequently is not a particularly accurate rendition of what actually takes place. It is preferable to have the client in the actual courthouse and a courtroom located therein so that the event of the trial occurs in a place of physical familiarity.

Dress

In all cases, the client should be advised of the manner of dress that is appropriate to the case. The client should be neither under- nor overdressed. If the client is the economically disadvantaged wife who has enjoyed a luxurious style of living, she should be dressed in accordance with the style to which her husband has accustomed her. On the other hand, if the husband is suffering financial reverses, he should not come to court sporting a gold Rolex watch, diamond cuff links, and a custom-tailored suit. Neither should he come into the courtroom wearing disheveled or threadbare clothing. He should dress neatly but not luxuriously. After all, even before a word is spoken in the courtroom, the judge will form an opinion of the client by his or her appearance. That appearance should be consistent with the legal position that is to be espoused and should be supportive of the credibility of the client. There was a memorable custody case in which the mother was charged with promiscuity in front of the children of the parties. Obviously, she had not been prepared by her lawyer as to her garb. She came to court wearing a skin-tight wool dress that outlined in explicit detail every feature of her body. When the judge came on the bench, his reaction was readily noted. After the lunch break, and no doubt with the belated advice of her lawyer, the mother returned to court wearing a prim and concealing business suit. However, the damage had been done, and that initial impression no doubt counted significantly toward the loss of her case.

SUBJECT MATTER

Theme of the Case

Every case has a theme, whether it is recognized or understood by the lawyer or not. Consequently, it is critical that the lawyer develop a theme for the client's cause and explain to the client the nature of that theme. If the client understands the overall parameters of the case and the manner in which his or her testimony will help develop that theme, then a tremendous step forward will have been taken to establish the client as a good and credible witness.

Word Pictures

Frequently, a client will believe that the function of direct testimony is to "tell my story to the judge" and to ventilate feelings and emotions. To dispel that attitude, the lawyer should explain to the client that the direct testimony is similar to a simple question-and-answer game. A question is asked, and then an answer to that question is given by the client. The response gives no more and no less than the complete and direct answer to the question actually asked.

Because leading questions are extremely limited in direct testimony, a party often talks about extraneous matters, testifying about impressions and other conclusory thoughts. The client should have a full explanation that he or she is simply a fact witness, and nothing more. Being a straightforward purveyor of fact is precisely what a judge usually wants and what helps give credibility to the client. The client, therefore, should be advised that he or she is to create a specific and detailed picture by the use of words of what has taken place.

It is obvious that word pictures create credibility. The client should be rehearsed to create those word pictures and to develop a technique so that the language flows readily. One technique is to tell the client to assume that the judge or jury is blind. It is, therefore, necessary to describe in detail the exact physical setting of the place where an incident took place and then to describe in detail the activity at that location. It is though a snapshot had been taken of the scene, and the party must describe the detail of that picture to a person who cannot see it.

Sample Questions

There should be introductory questions of a leading nature so that the client can begin to feel comfortable in giving responses. "Yes" or "no" answers are easy at the beginning, with other questions following, which require short answers, such as the names and birth dates of the children of the parties. The client should have reviewed an outline of the questions with key words or key dates. In that way, a question that is not leading may be asked, but that nevertheless will be sufficiently clear to the client as to the information to be imparted to the court. Caution should be taken not to over-rehearse the client for fear of allowing the client to memorize responses. It is better that the client "get the feel" of answering questions. A rule of thumb is that a client should be prepared at least two hours for each hour of testimony.

Objections to Questions

The client should be aware that questions may be asked that the other lawyer may consider to be improper. The client should be trained in advance that when he or she hears the word "objection" from the other lawyer, the client is to become instantly silent, even in the middle of a sentence, until the judge has made a ruling. The client should be aware of the meaning of "objection sustained" and "objection overruled." It may be helpful in preparing the client to have an associate or other person play the role of the adverse lawyer and state "objection" during the rehearsal process.

In order to avoid objections, a full explanation of the word "hearsay" should be given. The client need not have a full law school explanation of the meaning of hearsay and all of its exceptions, but he or she should nevertheless be aware that hearsay is not acceptable (in most jurisdictions). The client should also be aware that it is permissible to quote the other party, even though the other party's statement to the client contains hearsay information.

Talk to the Judge (Jury)

If the client is to be convincing, it is important that he or she give testimony to the person or persons who make the determination of fact. Specifically, the client should be advised not to look at his or her lawyer or to the opposing lawyer or party but rather to the judge (or jury). It is important to assume a conversational role with the judge (or jury) and to make eye contact.

Interruptions

Advise the client that it is not improper to ask for a glass of water, if the occasion should arise. Nor is it improper to request a recess to go to a rest room. However, any such request should not be made when it would appear that the reason is simply to gain time in answering a question or series of questions.

Use of a Professional Preparer

If warranted, it may be advisable to use a professional preparer of witnesses. Usually, that person charges less than the lawyer and is often more skilled in preparing the client for trial. The use of such a person is particularly important when the client would otherwise make a poor impression as a witness, has a volatile temper, has emotional instabilities, has memory failures, or for any other number of reasons. However, the lawyer who will be conducting the direct examination of the witness should nevertheless participate at least in some degree in preparation of the client so that the client will feel comfortable in answering questions of the trial lawyer.

Credibility

The key to success in a trial is credibility. The direct testimony should start with a strong point, should acknowledge weaknesses in the case, and then end on a particularly strong point. The testimony of the client should be structured to carry out that sequence of events in most cases. The first impression and the last impression of the client on the witness stand are extremely important. Confessing weaknesses with suitable explanations (if they exist) often deflates the position of the adverse party.

Conclusion

Preparation, preparation, preparation! That is the key to success. Because of the difficulty in leading the client in direct testimony, even more care and more time are necessary so that the client will be succinct, accurate, and convincing.

The client should feel comfortable sitting on the witness stand (at least as much as possible under the circumstances) and should feel a direct relationship to the judge (or jury) in making statements. The testimony should be factual and directly to the point. All of the questions and answers should be part of the development of the central theme of the case. The trial is akin to a Broadway theatrical production. It should have a scenario and a theme which are convincing and credible. The lawyer is the director, but the client is the principal player. There is only one performance. And the critic is the judge.

123

How to Draft a Persuasive Closing Argument in Five Easy Steps

Kimberly A. Quach

A S TRIAL LAWYERS, we all dream of drafting a beautifully crafted, compelling closing argument—a solid summary of the evidence that leaves the Court breathless to draft an opinion in our favor, and our clients clamoring to pay our bills in gratitude for excellent advocacy. We have big hopes about closing when we hear bits and pieces of our client's and other witnesses' comments, the judge's rulings and thoughts, and the other lawyer's arguments. And we can practically taste how wonderful our closings will be as we view the trial during each of these stages. Oh, yes, we think, I must remember to include the judge's comment during that evidentiary ruling.

But when until we actually sit down to write this "masterpiece," we become overwhelmed by the magnitude of the task. Suddenly, incorporating all of those wonderful ideas seems an unattainable goal. We have no idea where to begin. How can we reduce the case to its substance without sacrificing the one factor that might tip the scales of justice in our client's favor? How can we change the judge's mind if she was otherwise inclined to rule in favor of the opposing position?

This Hot Tip is designed to help with the task of drafting a closing argument in five easy steps. It is hardly a panacea for good preparation, but it can help to allow the lawyer's nonjudgmental, brainstorming juices flow rather than slow the process of drafting when perfectionism looms.

THE FIVE EASY STEPS

The five easy steps to drafting a persuasive closing argument are based on the premise that closing argument is drafted, in part, while trial is going on rather than after the trial. Certainly, one cannot draft a good closing argument until the end of the case, but why not brainstorm about ideas for closing as you listen to the case? Pull out your highlighters, colleagues, as you are listening to opening statements and testimony so that you can easily refer to what you found compelling as you listen to the case. Then, when you finally have the opportunity to draft your closing argument, you can collect all of these bits and pieces and quickly incorporate them into your argument.

Lest I get ahead of myself, though, the steps in drafting your closing argument should include at least the following:

- **Listen to the Case Carefully.** Listen to the witnesses, the evidence presented, and the Court and opposing counsel with the theme of your case repeating like a well-memorized mantra. Also, look for the Big Mistake made by the opposing client.

- **Highlight Supporting Information for Future Reference.** Highlight any testimony, and comments by the Court that support your theme in the case, as well as your perception of the Big Mistake made by the opposing client.

- **Identify Two or Three Main Points in the Case.** Identify two or, at most, three main points relevant to the Court's consideration.

- **Fit the Supporting Information into Your Outline.** Take all of the highlighted information that you thought was helpful and place it into the outline that you have created.

- **Create a Catchy Introduction That Summarizes Your Assessment of the Case.** After you have created an outline, complete with supporting information, craft a pithy, catchy introduction with which to start your closing.

LISTEN TO THE CASE CAREFULLY

It is important to establish a theme to your case in your opening statement, which is beyond the scope of this Hot Tip, so I will not address how to develop that theme. Your task, as you listen to the case, is to listen for how your theme plays through the evidence. Is it being supported? Does the theme need to be modified? If so, what additional evidence should be submitted to support the modified theme? How do you plan to pitch the justification for the modified theme to the Court in closing?

It is also important to see how the opposing client's theme plays through the evidence. Has he made promises that were not kept during the case? Has he introduced testimony or evidence that contradicts his theme? A Big Mistake is the part of a case in which the opposing client submits testimony or evidence that substantially undercuts his initial assessment of the case. Listen to the case carefully to identify that Big Mistake. At some point in the middle of your closing, make sure to identify the opposing client's Big Mistake to undercut the opposing case. It is best to do so in the middle of the case so that the court does not view this technique as unnecessarily negative or overzealous.

HIGHLIGHT SUPPORTING INFORMATION FOR FUTURE REFERENCE

There is no reason to artificially compartmentalize tasks as a trial advocate. Being a good trial lawyer is a lot like flying an airplane on instruments—one has several critical functions to negotiate simultaneously, and it is perfectly fine (perhaps even expected) to multitask. So that listening to the evidence for closing argument does not become overly burdensome, I suggest you simply use one color of highlighter to identify the information you feel might be valuable for your closing. If you highlight the important tidbits, you will be more likely to stop worrying about remembering them later. (Those lawyers that are highlighter-happy might use another color for cross-examination.)

Remember that there are several sources of information for your closing. The judge may make preliminary comments on the record or in chambers that you wish to address in closing. Your client or an expert might have used a clever phrase to describe a feature of the case. In one of my recent trials, the expert said the father was "consistently inconsistent" in his positions during a custody study, a statement I found particularly helpful in my closing. And do not forget exhibits as a source of closing argument materials, which should be identified by exhibit number in your closing so the Court has a clear outline of why you are making your arguments. The judge may not prepare a ruling for several days after the trial, so specific references to exhibits and testimony will be helpful to refresh her recollection. Even more important, use of exhibit numbers and specific references to testimony will vest your argument with an air of credibility, making the Court more secure in its willingness to trust your perceptions of the case.

IDENTIFY TWO OR THREE MAIN POINTS IN THE CASE

The Court can process only so much information. After reviewing all of your highlighted information in a very summary fashion, try to think of two or three main ideas that summarize the evidence and testimony. This *should* be the hardest part of drafting your argument, so do not be hard on yourself if it takes a little time. A cohesive structure for your argument is the very foundation of what makes it compelling and easy for the Court to digest completely, with all of its nuances.

FIT THE SUPPORTING INFORMATION INTO YOUR OUTLINE

This is truly the fun part. Make a list of all of the information you highlighted, and fit it into the structure you have created. Start grouping the ideas within the structure you prepared. If the evidence is duplicative, or related, in its content, for example, use the information as a list in your closing. Consider the following:

- You can state, "All of the lay witnesses agreed that the Mother was the child's primary caretaker, including . . ." and list the witnesses' names.
- The wife's spending habits, as summarized in the year-end VISA and American Express Statements (Exhibits 31 and 32), show that she spent at least $3,000 a month after taxes.

If a witness provides a good anecdote about the evidence, place it in the outline. At this point, do not be judgmental about what you include. Just list it all.

If you are like me, the closing argument you have drafted is about an hour long. If your judge does not have this level of patience, now is the time to start cutting out detail that you feel is not essential to the argument, or to summarize the detail more briefly. Your choice about what to omit from your closing argument should be based, in part, upon how the judge responded to the evidence. If she was annoyed by one particularly uneventful turn in the evidence, it is a good bet you can safely omit that discussion from your closing. If your judge was careful not to reveal her leanings, put your best argument together. Know that you may need to adapt if the judge appears to wince at your approach during closing.

CREATE A CATCHY INTRODUCTION THAT SUMMARIZES YOUR ASSESSMENT OF THE CASE

Your argument is drafted. You breathe a sigh of relief. But now, according to communications experts, you need a catchy introduction. This introduction will grab the Court's attention and give you the momentum to deliver your closing with an appropriate level of enthusiasm. It should complement your theme. Perhaps you will quote a witness, or read from an exhibit, or provide an analogy for the way in which your client or the opposing client is approaching the case. Whatever it is, make it simple. Your goal is to have the Court repeat your introduction and theme in her ruling.

CONCLUSION

Drafting a closing argument is hardly brain surgery, but sometimes we treat it that way because we want it to be excellent. This Hot Tip hopefully provides some ways to help the lawyer quickly draft a compelling closing argument by treating it like a brainstorming exercise, rather than like Chagall's irreversible splotch of oil paint on a clean canvas. There are very few times when practicing law feels like artistry; closing argument is one of them. Be creative, and be credible by preparing for closing argument throughout the trial.

124

Using a Trial Notebook

Mark E. Sullivan

IT IS SOMETIMES AMAZING how disorganized domestic trial lawyers can be in cases which have a very important bearing on the future of the client's welfare and financial condition. The truly excellent personal injury lawyer, dealing with a case worth thousands or possibly millions of dollars, would never think of preparing for trial and appearing in court with a set of manila folders and a handful of notes to be strewn over the counsel table. It is a fact, unfortunately, that domestic relations lawyers all too often fall into this practice.

Can you imagine the subtle impressions on the trial judge created by the lawyer whose counsel table is covered by a mass of papers, notes, orders, and motions? Even more important, consider the impact of a disorganized lawyer upon the jury in those domestic cases where they sit as finders of fact. Juries often pick up hidden messages from such things as the appearance and demeanor of witnesses, the body language of the lawyer, the way a client dresses and, of course, the relative organization of counsel for either side in one of these important areas of family law. As elsewhere, having the edge on organization may make a difference in the trial of the case, and this advantage cannot be overlooked by the competent lawyer.

An additional advantage that comes from organization is *peace of mind*. A well-organized lawyer who has prepared properly for the case and has his or her notes, questions, motions, psychological evaluations, expert evaluation reports, and other documents organized in an efficient manner will be more likely to get a good night's sleep before the trial than an lawyer who is not so well organized. If the organization is clear and the preparation has been done, the case will virtually try itself, with minimum intervention by (and few surprises for) the trial lawyer.

The best method of organization of substantial cases, such as custody, property division, alimony, and paternity, is through the use of a trial notebook. An excellent source of information on trial notebooks is found in James W. McElhaney's outstanding primer on trial advocacy, *Trial Notebook,* published by the American Bar Association's Section of Litigation. A copy of this fine treatment of how to prepare a trial notebook is available at a reasonable cost from the American Bar Association, 750 North Lake Shore Drive, Chicago, Illinois 60611.

HOW TO PREPARE A TRIAL NOTEBOOK

The way to prepare a trial notebook in a custody case, for example, is to first concentrate on the topics to be contained in the notebook and to obtain tabs from a stationery supply store for listing the documents contained in each area. Sample tabs would obviously be needed for the following items:

Initial Pleadings	Lay Witnesses for Client
Motions	Documentary Exhibits for Client
Orders	Notes on Cross-Exam of Opposing Party
Financial Affidavits of the Parties	Notes on Cross-Exam of Their Witnesses
Interrogatories, Answers	Psychological Evaluation of Children
Document Requests, Responses	Pretrial Order
Deposition Transcripts	Briefs on Issues of Law
Outline of Client's Testimony	Summation
Expert Witnesses for Client	Proposed Findings of Fact for Judge

In any alimony case, on the other hand, some of the above would be deleted and additional tabs would be prepared for such items as jury selection and proposed instructions for the jury. In a paternity case, tabs would be prepared for results of red-cell and HLA tests and stipulations as to laboratory tests and the chain of custody.

TESTIMONY TABS

The next question involves what goes into the testimony tabs. At this point, it is best to sit down with your client and explain the nature and purposes of a trial notebook. In this way, you can form a "partnership" with your client that will allow the client to do the majority of the work in preparing the custody trial notebook. Some lawyers, in fact, will not agree to undertake the trial of a custody, alimony, or paternity case unless the client agrees to prepare the entire trial notebook, except such items as pleadings, orders, and discovery matters. Thus your client, Mr. Green, will not be asking you, "Ms. Jones, what are you going to ask me on the witness stand?" Instead, he will say: "Ms. Jones, here is *what I want you to ask me*!"

The client should ordinarily be responsible for preparing entire sections of the trial notebook regarding testimony of the witnesses, except for matters involving laying the foundation for the testimony, introducing documentary evidence, inquiring into the expertise of the witness, and so on. Outside this obvious exception, however, a client will almost always have more information as to his own testimony and the testimony of friends, neighbors, and other witnesses than will the trial lawyer. Since these matters are intimately within the knowledge and memory of the client, it is best to have the client prepare the questions and answers for each witness.

It is important that the client prepare *answers* as well as *questions,* since this will directly involve the client in the process of interviewing prospective witnesses. After the answers are prepared and the lawyer has reviewed the proposed testimony of each favorable witness, all that is necessary is a brief follow-up interview or telephone conversation with the witness to ascertain the nature of the testimony, ask for additional insights into the case, and inform the witness of the next hearing date in the matter. As stated before, once this is done by the organized trial lawyer, the case will *virtually try itself.*

WHAT TO ASK

A client will often ask the lawyer, "What should I put down for questions?" The answer to this question will vary according to the nature of the case. In an alimony case, for example, you would instruct Mr. Green, your client, that there are certain areas that should always be included in the client's testimony or that of the witnesses. Examples of such areas include the following:

a. The wage-earner roles of the parties (as applicable);
b. The homemaker roles of the parties (as applicable);
c. The income (as applicable) of the husband and wife;
d. The monthly expenses of your client, Mr. Green;
e. The lifestyle and living standard of the parties;
f. The working hours of the parties (as applicable);
g. Fault issues;
h. Attorney's fees incurred by Mr. Green;
i. Tax issues according to the CPA for Mr. Green.

The use of an outline to assist the client in deciding on specific areas of inquiry will be of great assistance in helping the client in the preparation and trial of the case, making him a better witness in the process and a more satisfied client, regardless of the outcome.

125

The Assisted Opening Statement

Kenneth G. Raggio

WHO IS YOUR AUDIENCE?

The judge[1] has been hearing "the same old story" for a long time, for a lot of weeks and months, in a lot of hearings in cases, and a lot of trials. While the judge will do her best to put the pieces together as the trial unfolds, the best time to put your case forward is in an effective, well-planned opening statement. Show the judge why your case is worth listening to and why your position is meritorious.

An effective opening statement will combine sight and sound to break up the monotony that is the judge's curse of "lawyers talking." Showing the judge what is going on from your perspective as the case stars can often help determine the outcome of the proceedings in a favorable manner.

WHAT?

The "assisted" opening statement entails using technology to assist you in your presentation. A simple form is merely a typewritten listing of the high points of the case, of the witnesses, expected testimony, legal disagreements, and perhaps even a suggested division shared with the judge and opposing counsel. This is a fairly mundane, yet potentially effective, presentation. Using prints of slides or overheads is a variation on the same theme.

However, computer tools have become more powerful and easier to use to where even sophisticated technology is now not only "lawyer proof" but is "lawyer friendly." The name brand of a computer or a software package or camera doesn't really matter; they are all variations on the same theme of creating a "multimedia presentation" package. The components of a multimedia package include:

---

1. Only Texas and Georgia allow juries in Family Law cases; an opening statement to a jury should give them a "front row seat" preview. Remember a jury has seen "Law & Order," etc., and has unreasonably high expectations of a lawyer in a trial. Don't let them down in the opening statement. Having said that, jury trials are rare.

1) Notebook computer with DVD/CD burner, video and digital inputs/ outputs;
2) Presentation software such as PowerPoint or Presentation;
3) Digital still camera;
4) Mini-DV camcorder;
5) Speciality timeline/charting software;
6) Scanner;
7) Fast internet access.

Not all tools will be used in all cases; so when planning your assisted opening statement, go through the analysis that you would make with any opening statement:

- What do I want the judge to know about my case?
- What is unique about my case?
- What egregious facts/positions can I have on the opposing party?
- How can I combine sight and sound to demonstrate this?
- How can I make my presentation bulletproof?
- Can I get my entire presentation completed within the Court's allocated time limits?
- Does the Court have equipment on site that I can plug into?[2]

HOW?

Our friends in the P.I. practice have pioneered the use of tools for us; many P.I. lawyers have even formed their own A.V./litigation support firms to specially produce major presentations.[3] If your budget and/or fear factor support it, get professional help. Otherwise, combining some or all of the following elements can make a compelling presentation:

- A video clip with a damning statement ("her job in those early years was primarily to screw me")
- Images of documents with key phrases blown up and highlighted
- Timeline of events
- Factors indicating why the Court should rule your way on particular issues including attorney's fees

CAVEATS

- Be accurate in your depiction.
- Be sure your key assertions will be covered by competent, admissible evidence.
- Don't oversell.
- Have your script prepared to read, and handouts of your images and slides for backup if your high-tech show crashes for any reason.

---

2. It is rare that a Court won't have some AV equipment available. Check it out. Make sure your computer will display on the Court's equipment.

3. Besides, it's an expense in a contingent fee practice and therefore can be recovered in addition to attorney's fees.

126

Some Suggestions for Cross-Examining Mental Health Experts

Monroe L. Inker

I. Research
   A. Research all technical aspects of witness's testimony.
   B. Research witness's background.
      1. Everything she has published
      2. Transcripts of prior trials
      3. Professional affiliations
      4. Past clients
      5. Government positions
      6. Certain theoretical "positions" she holds
      7. Observe her testify at another trial.
   C. Get reports of treatment if available and not privileged.
   D. Speak to other psychological experts in the vicinity.
   E. Know the different psychological orientations, i.e., behavioral, psychoanalytic, and the major research in each field on children and divorce.

   *Remember that psychologists like to write about things. Look for inconsistencies.

II. Challenge Witness's Credentials
   A. To exclude expert's testimony, challenge the legal sufficiency of the testimony.
   B. Attack the weight the testimony should be given.
   C. Attack the remoteness of her credentials.
   D. Point out the inapplicability of her credentials.
   E. Point out the lack of general acceptance of her area of expertise.
   F. Point out the unreliability of the data.
   G. Never stipulate to an expert.

H. 3 basic techniques to discredit witness's expertise:
 1. Limit the scope of the witness's expertise.
 2. Stress missing credentials.
 3. Contrast your expert's credentials.
I. Question whether witness has any special education in the unique aspects of the case such as alcoholism, homosexuality, over-parenting, etc.
J. If testifying witnesses is treating psychologist, challenge her with American Psychological Association (APA) Guideline that states treating psychologist should not be evaluator.

III. Obtain Favorable Information
 A. Always do this at the beginning of the witness's testimony.
 B. Affirm your own expert.
 C. Elicit areas of agreement.
 D. Get expert to criticize opposing party's conduct or make adverse comments about the other side.
 E. Ask questions to which the expert may give a positive or reasonable answer.
 F. Get expert to reveal admissions made by opposing party to expert, if disclosure is not privileged.

IV. Use Learned Treatises
 A. Confront witness with published treatises, periodicals, pamphlets so long as they have been established as reliable.
  1. Use the DSM-IV, American Psychological Association positions, etc.

V. Challenge Witness's Impartiality
 A. Confront her with fees she is receiving in connection with the case.
  1. Generally this is productive only when the fee is extraordinarily large.
  2. Contingent fees are unethical.
  3. Find out if she is receiving government reimbursement for supervised visitation or to render a report against one party or another.
 B. Challenge witness's status of always testifying for the same law firm.
 C. Challenge why expert is wedded to a certain professional or scientific position.
 D. Confront her with bias.
  1. Is she receiving a bonus at the end of the case?
  2. Does she socialize with the lawyer or make professional presentations together?
  3. Does she make a habit of always testifying and never treating patients?

VI. Point Out Omissions
 A. Point out failure to conduct essential tests or procedures or neglect to consider all significant factors (use discovery to find this out).
 B. Point out failure of the witness to have actually done a test or procedure herself, but is negatively commenting on it.

C. Point out that the witness spent insufficient time on an evaluation or failed to obtain enough background information.

D. Ask if favorable characteristics of your client were part of the history available to the examiner/expert or negative characteristics of the other party were available.

VII. Substitute Information

A. Ask the expert to alter an assumption for one you believe to be more in keeping with evidence in the case.

B. Vary facts the expert relied on or suggest additional facts.

VIII. Challenge Degree of Certainty

A. Suggest alternative scenarios or explanations.

B. Challenge whether the conclusion expert arrived at is sensible.

C. Point out if expert didn't evaluate other parent, she can't make the comparison between parents legitimately.

IX. Dependence on Other Testimony

A. Challenge an expert's testimony by challenging its factual underpinnings during cross-examination of the fact witness upon whose testimony the expert based her conclusions.

X. Challenge Technique or Theory

A. Challenge witness's method, theory, or logic. But it is unlikely she will admit to any deficiency. It is better to use your own expert to point out these weaknesses.

B. Know the important psychological tests like Rorschach or MMPI and what certain results tend to indicate.

C. Challenge use of Rorschach or MMPI data for divorce cases because APA Guidelines state clinical data should not be overinterpreted or inappropriately interpreted. Neither test is designed for use in divorce, therefore use of them in divorce cases is overinterpretation.

XI. Attack Clinical Judgment

A. Use the DSM-IV, ask what symptoms of disorder are, how they were assessed, and why competing diagnoses were ruled out.

XII. Attack the Field of Psychiatry

A. Point out lack of reliability.

B. Point out disagreement debates within the scientific community regarding the field of psychiatry or psychology.

C. Challenge the scientific status of the field.

D. Challenge classification systems employed.

E. Attack unreliable nature of judgments of psychiatrists and other mental health professionals. (Much has been written on this—see book "Challenging Psychologists and Psychologists as Witnesses.")

F. Point out that psychologists have tendency to disregard scientific evidence in favor of theories that have not been proven or validated.

G. Point out that psychologists have overexposure to maladjusted individuals, resulting in "exaggerated sensitivity to psychopathology" or "predisposition to find disorders and abnormality where none exist."

H. Note that expectations of psychologists can lead them to believe symptoms consistent with their diagnostic impressions were exhibited when they were not.

I. Note that research indicates that psychologists typically reach their diagnostic conclusions early on in interview and as a result rely on minimal data in making conclusions and disregard evidence that contradicts initial impressions.

J. Note that psychologists use spontaneous questions rather than comprehensive checklists, which can bias data.

K. Point out problems with diagnosis because psychologist may rely on patient information and may mislead the examiner, especially if involved in litigation, and that psychologists often have no means of verifying patient information.

127

Establishing the Foundation for Successful Appeals during Trial

Andrew S. Berman

"AN APPEAL, HINNISSEY, is where ye ask wan coort to show its contempt f'r another court." Finley Peter Dunne, *Mr. Dooley Says: The Big Fine* (1906). While this notion might be a tad cynical, statistics in Florida reveal that less than one in five appeals results in a partial or complete reversal. Lawyers seeking appellate relief should assume that an appellate court must be left with no choice but to reverse. Achieving this level of certainty is a daunting task. The process begins, and the groundwork is laid, at trial.

I.   Appeals have always been an uphill battle.
    A. Decisions of trial judges arrive on appeal clothed with a presumption of correctness. It is the burden of the appellant to show reversible error.
    B. Appeals are generally not successful if judgments are supported by substantial competent evidence or do not constitute abuses of discretion.
    C. The real test is whether, but for the error complained about, a different result would have been reached.
II. As far as the appellate court is concerned, if something is not in the record, it did not happen.
    A. Apart from fundamental errors of law, appellants should never bring new issues to the appellate court that were not before the trial court. Nothing will draw the court's ire more or lower one's chances of success quicker than raising such matters on appeal.
    B. Remember, it is the duty of the trial lawyers to properly establish the record and preserve error. Appellate courts commonly affirm judgments because of inadequate records or error not preserved. On the flip side, retrials have been ordered due to the loss of trial records or transcripts through no fault of the appellant.

C. Under certain circumstances it is possible to reconstruct a record or supplement it to provide missing material, but this is subject to strict standards and limitations.

III. The importance of framing issues for appeal during and after the trial

A. Since litigants cannot ordinarily raise issues for the first time on appeal, it is critical for attorneys to raise objections to perceived errors on the record as they occur *and secure rulings on those objections.* This reflects a practical necessity and the basic fairness of the judicial system; objections place trial judges on notice that a perceived error has been committed and provides them with the opportunity to correct them at a time when it is most efficient to do so.

B. It is the responsibility of trial lawyers to obtain rulings on their objections from the trial court. Making a motion or objection is not enough. *Without a ruling on the motion or objection, you have nothing to appeal.*

C. Only matters involving pure errors of law or fundamental errors going to the foundation of the case or the merits of the cause of action can be raised at any time, even for the first time on appeal. And they are rare. If you must rely on the concept of fundamental error, you are in trouble.

D. Posttrial motions present ideal opportunities for trial lawyers to frame issues for appeal. These motions also give the trial judge a final opportunity to correct errors. However, lawyers should use posttrial motions only if they feel that there is a good probability of success before their particular trial judge or if it is required in order to make the record (viz., motions for new trial or judgment as a matter of law).

IV. Conclusion: By paying attention to detail in trial, lawyers can significantly increase their likelihood of success on appeal.

XIV

Evidence

A FAMILY COURT JUDGE I know tells a story of a divorce trial in which one of the lawyers objected to a question, citing the code of evidence. When the judge asked the opposing lawyer for a response to the objection, the answer she received was: "But, Your Honor, this is a divorce trial!" The objection was sustained. The point of the story is twofold: First, many lawyers pretend that the rule of evidence does not apply to family law cases. Second, unless we have a better understanding of the laws of evidence than the lawyer quoted previously, we run the risk of not getting important parts of our case into evidence.

Following are some tips from the experts on divorce evidence:

128   Few evidentiary rules are applied as incorrectly as the Best Evidence Rule. Yet, it may be a major weapon in the arsenal of a family law trial lawyer. **Monroe Inker** describes the Best Evidence Rule and its application to different circumstances, including modern technology.

129   For the divorce trial with reams of financial documents, proving authenticity of each one can serve as a cure for insomnia. **J. Lindsey Short** suggests means of establishing authenticity of each document at a deposition to clear the way for admissibility at trial.

130   What do you do when an evidentiary ruling goes against you? If you may want to appeal, you need to know how to make an offer of proof. **Monroe Inker** explains how to make an offer of proof and provides the legal basis.

128

The Best Evidence Rule

Monroe L. Inker

Litigators frequently misapply the Best Evidence Rule, codified in the Federal Rules of Evidence at Rules 1001–08, by demanding the production of tangible evidence to bolster oral testimony introduced to prove a matter. *See McCormick on Evidence* § 230 (3d ed. 1984). Parties are not required to use all available evidence. For example, the 10th Circuit held that a prosecutor need not produce whiskey bottles to prove that the revenue stamps were missing in violation of a criminal statute. *Chandler v. United States*, 318 F.2d 356 (10th Cir. 1963). In a trial charging a defendant with possession and manufacture with intent to sell adulterated bologna, the court held that the Best Evidence Rule did not require that the prosecutor produce and introduce a piece of bologna. *See Meyer v. State*, 218 Ark. 440, 236 S.W.2d 996, 998, 1000 (1951). As these examples demonstrate, the rule applies to documentary, rather than to tangible, evidence. *See id.; see also* Advisory Committee's Notes to Fed. R. Evid. 1002 (if party could prove an event through nondocumentary evidence, rule would not apply even if parties executed a written document). The rule applies only to writings, recordings, or photographs that relate to contested or material issues in the case. *See* Advisory Committee's Notes to Fed. R. Evid. 1002.

Lawyers further complicate the rule by demanding an original communication any time a party seeks to introduce *any* writing, photograph, or recording. McCormick, however, described the rule by stating: "[I]n proving the terms of the writing, where the terms are material, the original writing must be produced unless it is shown to be unavailable for some reason other than the serious fault of the proponent." McCormick, *supra* at § 230. The rule, therefore, applies not to *all* writings but only to writings, photographs, or recordings introduced to prove the contents of the communication. *See* Advisory Committee's Notes to Fed. R. Evid. 1002; *see, e.g., People v. Doggett*, 83 Cal. App. 2d 405, 188 P.2d 792 (1948) (court required original photograph of bank robber); *Daniels v. Iowa City*, 191 Iowa 811, 183 N.E. 415 (1921) (original x-ray required). Courts then must consider first whether the communication offered is material and whether it is offered for its independent probative value.

Even finding materiality, however, does not necessitate production of an original document, photograph, or recording, unless the opposing party questions the authenticity of the original. Because the rule treats duplicates, produced with the methods discussed in Rule 1001(4), as originals, the rule amounts to a rule of preference rather than to a mandate. *See* Fed. R. Evid. 1003; *see also United States v. Balzano*, 687 F.2d 6, 7–8 (1st Cir. 1981) (court permitted government to play a copy of a tape containing a statement made by defendant to undercover agent). Rule 1001(4) identifies a duplicate as a "counterpart produced by the same impression as the original, or from the same matrix, or by means of photography, including enlargements and miniatures, or by mechanical or electronic rerecording, or by chemical reproduction, or by other equivalent technique which *accurately* reproduces the original." Fed. R. Evid. 1001(4) (emphasis added). The advisory committee believed that these duplicates would provide accurate copies that removed the possibility of error. *See id.* The definition includes carbon copies of documents, but whether photocopies or Xerox copies constitute duplicates remains unsettled law.

If the purpose of the original preference rule is to secure the most reliable documentary evidence when a party contests its terms, then all modern-day forms of copying should fall within the 1001(4) and 1003 definitions of duplicates. The state of authority suggests that photocopies, unless kept in the regular course of business or as public record, however, are inadmissible unless the court accepts the reason for the original's nonproduction. *See* McCormick *supra* at § 236. It would appear that the fear of fraud provides a second, ancillary justification for compelling an original document when its terms are in dispute. *See id.* at §§ 231, 236.

Many courts have focused on accuracy as the key determination to whether a particular duplicate should or should not be admitted. *See United States v. Cortellesso*, 663 F.2d 361 (1st Cir. 1981); *Amoco Production Co. v. United States*, 619 F.2d 1383 (10th Cir. 1980). The courts have held that once the government proves the accuracy of a copied tape recording, the susceptibility to tampering should not override the value of a copy unless the opponent could bolster allegations of tampering. *See United States v. Cortellesso*, 663 F.2d 361 (1st Cir. 1981). The 3rd Circuit upheld the tapes' admission and held that if the defendant suspected tampering, he could have engaged an expert to examine the tapes. *United States v. Cortellesso*, 663 F.2d 361 (1st Cir. 1981). Furthermore, the courts could use their discretion and demand an original over a photocopy if the court viewed the admission of the photocopy as unfair. *See Amoco Production Co. v. United States*, 619 F.2d 1838, 1391 n.8 (10th Cir. 1980) (court had discretion to exclude copies if admission would be unfair). Where the offered document does not provide a clear and exact duplication of the writing, photograph, or recording, courts have excluded the duplicate's admission. *See id.* at 1391.

Modern technology raises more questions regarding the admission of new forms of communications. As computers gain popularity, more information will be stored in computers' diskettes and hard drives. Yet, computers create problems because of the ease with which documents can be altered. Furthermore, any newly printed document could be proffered as the original. The 4th Circuit, however, has held that a computer printout, which provided base data from which the government codified a chart of houses sold by the defendants, qualified as a duplicate. *United States v. Foley*, 598 F.2d 1323 (4th Cir. 1979). The court authorized the computer printout's admission. *See id.*

Whatever new forms of communications arise in the future, parties arguing for the admission of a duplicate should focus on the copy as an accurate representation of the original piece. Lawyers should avoid unnecessary use of the rule and remember that it applies only to documentary evidence. Finally, lawyers should impose the rules only when the contents of the documentary evidence raise important and material issues for the court or jury to decide.

129

Authenticity and Admissibility

J. Lindsey Short Jr.

A DEPOSITION IN A PROPERTY CASE is a good place to deal with arriving at a stipulation regarding the authenticity, as well as the admissibility, of documents for consideration by the court at the time of trial. This concept is particularly useful when a number of different people have control of some of the documents that will be necessary, but not all of them.

When there are a large total number of exhibits in a divorce proceeding that generally relate to characterization and/or valuation of the assets or of a particular asset, as you are deposing the people who are knowledgeable about all or part of a company or business enterprise, you should present to the witness as well as to counsel for the opposing party a carefully copied and organized number of documents that would be necessary for proof, generally by both sides, of character, value, or whatever other area might be at issue.

Once the witness has identified the document, the deposing lawyer then may ask for a stipulation from opposing counsel regarding the authenticity (if it is a copy) and admissibility of the document into evidence. By this method, the lawyers should be able to present to the trial judge, at the time of trial, a stack of documents for which there is no dispute of their appropriate consideration by the court.

A great deal of time will be saved. Preparation for actual trial will be easier and less costly and time-consuming, for only certain documents will be needed for briefing or argument regarding their role, if any, in the case.

130

Offer of Proof

Monroe L. Inker

WHEN A JUDGE SUSTAINS an objection to a question on direct (cross-examination will be addressed later) and excludes evidence, the proponent should consider making an offer of proof. The primary purpose of the offer of proof is to inform the trial and appellate courts of the substance of the excluded evidence. An offer of proof enables the judge to reconsider his or her ruling and receive the evidence. The secondary purpose is to preserve the record for appeal. 19 Hughes Mass. Prac. § 214; *see U.S. v. Rayco, Inc.,* 616 F.2d 462, 464 (10th Cir. 1980) (court will not consider evidentiary objections where no offer of proof made part of record); *U.S. v. Cook,* 608 F.2d 1175, 1186 (1979) (proponent must make the record through offer of proof, or point of appeal will be abandoned).

A party may waive the right to claim error on appeal by not presenting an offer of proof at trial, unless the substance of the evidence is apparent from the context of the question. *See Palmer v. Palmer,* 27 Mass. App. Ct. 141, 149 n. 9 (1989) (issue waived on appeal where trial judge invited counsel to make offer of proof and counsel declined); *Virta v. Mackey,* 343 Mass. 286, 292 (1961); *Richmond v. Warren Institution for Savings,* 307 Mass. 483 (1941). The judge has discretion to delay the offer of proof until the close of the party's evidence, but commits error by completely denying counsel the opportunity to make an offer of proof. *In re Marriage of Strauss,* 539 N.E.2d 808, 811 (Ill. App. 1989).

Offers of proof must be "reasonably specific," *U.S. v. Winkle,* 587 F.2d 705 (5th Cir. 1979), and must state the purpose of the proof unless the purpose is apparent. *Davey Bros., Inc. v. Stop & Shop,* 351 Mass. 59 (1966); *see* Federal Rules of Evidence, Rule 103(a)(2) (setting forth procedure for making offers of proof). The proponent should limit the substance of the offer of proof to information sought from the question. When making an offer of proof, however, counsel should state all grounds for admissibility, for, on appeal, counsel may not state new grounds for admission of evidence not previously presented at trial. *See U.S. v. Grapp,* 653 F.2d 189 (5th Cir. 1981); *Huff v. White Motor Corp.,* 609 F.2d 286 (7th Cir. 1979). Counsel can prevent this problem by including all possible grounds for admissibility in the offer of proof.

The trial judge has broad discretion regarding whether the offer of proof will be in narrative or question-and-answer form. *Fidelity Savings & Loan v. Aetna Life & Casualty Co.*, 647 F.2d 933, 937 (9th Cir. 1981) (Federal Rule of Evidence 103(b) provides that form of offers is left to discretion of trial court). The narrative form allows the proponent to advise the court of the substance of the witness's proposed testimony. The lawyer must state factually how he or she expects the witness to testify, and may not provide conclusions or any summary unless the question calls for one. *See Gildwani v. Wasserman*, 373 Mass. 162, 168 (1977) (offer of proof must contain information showing witness's ability to present admissible evidence). Counsel objecting to a question on direct examination may prefer that the proponent use the narrative form outside the witness's hearing to prevent the proponent from refreshing the witness's memory through the offer of proof. The question-and-answer form, however, is the most reliable and accurate method of making the offer of proof because there is no speculation involved. *Lane's Goldstein Trial Technique* § 13.30 (3d ed.). The proponent will address questions to the witness as though the testimony was being received into evidence.

Historically, requirements for an offer of proof are relaxed on cross-examination, for the cross-examiner does not know how the witness will respond. Some jurisdictions, however, require an offer of proof even during cross-examination. The Federal Rules of Evidence make no distinction between the exclusion of evidence on direct and cross-examination. *See Saltzman v. Fullerton Metals Co.*, 661 F.2d 647, 653 n. 8 (7th Cir. 1981) ("Federal Rules of Evidence do not differentiate between the exclusion of evidence on direct and cross-examination and have not been applied to create such a distinction"); *U.S. v. Vitale*, 596 F.2d 688, 689 (5th Cir. 1979) (failure of lawyer to make offer of proof during cross-examination waived issue on appeal). Other jurisdictions, such as Massachusetts, still apply a relaxed standard for offers of proof on cross-examination. Although an offer of proof normally is not required, a rare group of cases exists where "if the purpose of significance of the question is obscure and the prejudice to the cross-examiner is not clear, . . . the record must disclose the cross-examiner's reason for seeking an answer to an excluded question." *Breault v. Ford Motor Co.*, 364 Mass. 352, 357–58 (1973); *see also Commonwealth v. Barnett*, 371 Mass. 87, 95 (1976) (offer of proof ordinarily not required, but cross-examiner should be allowed to make an offer if he wishes). A Massachusetts appellate court, however, held that where a trial judge invited counsel to make an offer of proof during cross-examination and counsel declined, counsel waived his right to appeal. *Palmer v. Palmer*, 27 Mass App. Ct. 141, 149 (1989); *cf. Saltzman v. Fullerton Metals Co.*, 661 F.2d 647 (7th Cir. 1982) (conclusory offer of proof failed to disclose need for cross-examination). On cross-examination, counsel generally can do no more than make a hypothesized general offer because he or she cannot know how the witness would respond. *See Palmer*, at 149 n. 9 (1989); *Barnett*, at 95 (1976).

XV

After the Divorce

THERE IS A SAYING that it is possible to win the war, but lose the peace. I do not think I understood that saying until I started doing post-judgment divorce work. No matter how good the divorce judgment, unless it is completed properly, the case is not over.

Ever feel like you are the divorce lawyer for life? Closing the file can take longer than the divorce itself. Yet, this is critically important work. Here are a couple of tips on how to do it well.

131   Do you routinely ask clients what type of business documents they signed before the divorce started? I did not until I read **Sandra Morgan Little**'s tip on revocation of continuing guarantees.

132   Your client's property division settlement or support payment is secured by life insurance. Can your client rest easy? He or she can if the insurance company is solvent. **Bob Moriarty** tells how to ensure that there will be insurance.

133   **Jonathan Levine's** hot tip is a checklist of steps that need to be taken to close a file. The checklist can easily be adapted into a closing letter to the client, which will be appreciated by the client and will serve as written proof that the client was informed of what needs to be done to wrap matters up.

134   So now the case is over. The client goes on with his or her life and we go on to our next case. **Mark Chinn** posits that this is the perfect time to conduct an exit interview with the client. Mark includes a "checklist" form, which includes warnings to the client of pitfalls that might lie ahead.

131

Revocation of Continuing Guarantees

Sandra Morgan Little

MANY CLIENTS HAVE SIGNED continuing guarantees to banks or other financial institutions because of convenience or because the institution requires it. Unless the client is sophisticated in dealing with financial institutions, he or she may not know what was signed or what the implications can be. Your client may have guaranteed:

1. Debts of a spouse;
2. Debts of a business; or
3. Debts of an investment partnership.

Your client's spouse may have guaranteed:

1. Debts of a partner;
2. Debts of a business; or
3. Debts of an investment partnership.

It is wise to question your client regarding all banking relationships whether personal, business, or investment-related. Send revocations to each institution. Even if the loan to which the guarantee applied has been paid, under the terms of particular guarantees, the guarantor can be liable for future debt incurred. A revocation can terminate the guarantee to future borrowings but cannot alter responsibilities for debts already incurred. If additional borrowing takes place by the spouse and the borrowing spouse later has financial difficulties, your client may be required to pay the debt. It is safer to send letters to all financial institutions involved even if a guarantee has not been signed rather than be sorry.

Following is a sample Revocation of Continuing Guarantee and Future Indebtedness form.

_____(Date)_____

<u>HAND-DELIVERED</u>

OR

<u>CERTIFIED MAIL</u>

_____(1)_____
_____
_____

          Re: Revocation of Continuing Guarantee
               and Future Indebtedness
               _____(2)_____

Dear _____(3)_____:

I revoke any continuing guarantees I have made to your institution, including the instrument dated __(4)__, a copy of which is attached. Notice is given pursuant to __(5)__ of the attached instrument. The guarantee is revoked effective __(6)__.

I will not be liable for any other indebtedness incurred by __(7)__ after __(8)__.

                   _____
                   (9)

__. <u>CONTINUING GUARANTEES</u>:   The parties have [been extended credit and have] executed continuing guarantees:

    a.   Continuing guarantees and the amounts of the related debts are listed on Schedule A;

    b.   Husband/Wife shall cooperate with husband/ wife and shall do all acts necessary to obtain a release of any continuing guarantee from husband/wife to any creditor by husband/ wife;

    c.   Husband/Wife warrants that he/she shall not incur any debt in addition to those listed on Schedule A at any institution holding a continuing guarantee from husband/wife;

    d.   Husband/Wife warrants he/she shall provide wife/husband with timely notice of any claim made under any continuing guarantee;

    e.   Husband/Wife warrants there are no undisclosed debts being secured by a continuing guarantee of husband/wife;

    f.   Husband/Wife indemnifies wife/husband for any claim made by any creditor holding wife's/ husband's continuing guarantee for any loan made to husband/wife by that creditor. This indemnification includes repayment of all amounts by husband/wife pursuant to such claim and all costs incurred by husband/wife pursuant to such claim, including reasonable attorneys fees.

_____ v. _____ DR _____
_____ County, New Mexico

_____ & _____ 'S CONTINUING GUARANTEES

Date of
Guarantee   Creditor   Names of
                                                                   Guarantors

132

How to Know When the Life Insurance Policy Securing Your Client's Property Settlement Agreement Will Do the Job

Robert B. Moriarty

OK, SO YOU HAVE DONE A GREAT JOB for your client, wife of the president, and sole stockholder of the XYZ Widget Company. You have maximized your leverage in this thirty-year marriage, using it and your client's age and lack of employment history to obtain long-term maintenance and a substantial distributive award. And best of all, it is secured by life insurance, so if Mr. Jones leaves this good earth before his time (which from your client's point of view means before she does), an insurance policy kicks in to protect the award you have worked hard to obtain.

Or does it? In 1991 two industry giants, Executive Life and First Capital Life, failed, and a third, Mutual Benefit Life, also collapsed. If you had tried to determine the viability of these companies, chances are you would have consulted A.M. Best, Standard & Poor's, Moody's, and/or Duff & Phelps, the four best rating agencies. Chances are also their ratings would not have helped you.

In June 1990, Standard & Poor's and Duff & Phelps rated Executive Life "BBB" and "BBB−," respectively, meaning good. A.M. Best, the oldest and biggest of the agencies, issued an "A" rating, meaning excellent, although it said the company could be downgraded.

Moody's was more on top of the situation, although it equivocated by issuing a "Ba2" rating, meaning questionable. But would you have understood what a "Ba2" rating meant? Again, chances are you would not have.

TIP

If you want a quick, understandable rating on an insurance policy, consult Weiss Research, Inc., 2200 North Florida Mango Road, West Palm Beach, Florida 33409, (407) 684-8100. It also has a toll-free number, 1-800-289-9222.

Weiss rates in an easily understandable manner—A+ through F—and will give you a quick rating over the telephone for $15. It is something of a pariah in the insurance industry because its views are bearish, and Weiss has been accused of encouraging consumers to worry for its own financial gain.

But from the point of view of a matrimonial lawyer who wants to be sure the life insurance policy used to secure a client's property settlement is a good one, Weiss's conservatism is just the ticket. Lending credence to its ratings is the fact that the biggest companies in the insurance industry pay big sums of money to Standard & Poor's Corporation, Moody's, A.M. Best, and Duff & Phelps to rate their companies, and therefore certainly cannot be considered neutral or independent in the services they render. Weiss receives no income from insurance companies.

133

How to Properly Close a File

Jonathan R. Levine

AFTER MEETING A NEW CLIENT and receiving the retainer, perhaps the divorce lawyer's favorite task is returning from the courthouse with the Final Judgment and Decree and shipping the file to storage. Unfortunately, obtaining the Final Judgment and Decree is only the beginning of the end. Simply mailing the client the Final Judgment and sending the file to storage is one of the biggest malpractice traps in family law today. It is of the utmost importance that you send your client a closing of the file letter that begins the closing process.

Below is a list of issues and items to consider in a closing of the file letter to your client.

1. **Thank your client for choosing you to represent them.** Let the client know it was an honor and a pleasure.
2. **Have your client procure a current Last Will and Testament.** Generally speaking, a will is automatically revoked upon divorce, unless it was specifically made in contemplation of that divorce. Therefore, your client will need to procure a new Last Will and Testament. You should refer them to three estate planners to help them with the process (and then call all three to inform them of the referral).
3. **Refer your client to a certified public accountant** to assist them in future tax issues as well as with the tax implications of the settlement agreement. Again, give them three recommendations.
4. **Advise your client of the possible need to file IRS form 8822.** It notifies the IRS of where to send correspondence or notices to the client.
5. **Advise your client to notify all insurance companies,** including, but not limited to, health, life, disability, automobile, property, and homeowners and notify them of the divorce. It is possible that an insurance company could consider the divorce a change in condition sufficient to deny your client coverage. If appropriate, recommend three insurance agents, because many times the current agent is a friend of the former spouse and your client may not want to deal with that agent.

6. **Notify your client to change the beneficiary of certain assets** such as an IRA, retirement accounts, and life insurance policies, as a divorce does not automatically do so.

7. **If your client is the recipient of certain funds** from their spouse's retirement account and a QDRO is required, it is imperative that you follow up on preparing the QDRO, having it submitted to the judge for signature and, finally, having it approved by the plan administrator. It is also important to confirm that the funds have actually been transferred.

8. **Tell your client to diary the critical dates** in the agreement such as when they will be receiving child support, alimony, and/or lump sum payments.

9. **Confirm with your client that you have no original documents belonging to the client.**

10. **Inform your client of all issues relating to medical insurance** and COBRA and the need to act within thirty days to ensure they are properly and adequately covered.

11. **Discuss the transfer of both real and personal property** and whether a quit claim deed or title transfer form must be signed, and who will bear the responsibility to prepare that form.

12. **Inform your client to close and/or cancel all credit cards,** and to notify the financial institutions of the divorce and your clients non-responsibility for any future issues.

13. **Tell your client to provide the settlement agreement to their children's school,** so that the school is adequately informed of custody issues as well as their duty or responsibility to provide school records to your client.

14. **Inform your client of remedies for nonpayment** of child support, alimony, and property division payments.

15. **Tell your client to keep accurate records** of all payments made and/or received.

16. **If any fees are owing,** first inform your client that you will not provide them with a copy of the Final Judgment and Decree until you are paid in full. While more of a psychological factor than anything else, most clients want that piece of paper granting the divorce, as it helps them with the closure issue. If that tactic fails, inform your client that if you are not paid within thirty days from the Final Judgment, you will place an attorney's lien on their property to ensure payment.

17. **Inform your client of issues relating to Social Security** benefits and their automatic entitlement if they were married for more than ten years.

18. **Tell your client *specifically* the actions that your firm will be taking** to assist them in closing the file.

19. **Tell your client that he or she must do the following things themselves** and then specifically list each task your client must do.

20. **Enclose a questionnaire.** Now is the perfect time to do a short questionnaire, having your client evaluate your firm and the services provided.
21. **Make your client sign a copy of the letter and return it to your office** acknowledging that they have read and understand all instructions.
22. **Thank your client again.**

By failing to properly close the file you could easily undo much of what you obtained for your client. It is also a great marketing tool, in that it allows you to make referrals to tax specialists, estate planners, insurance agents, and others, as well as getting feedback from your client in the form of the questionnaire.

Finally, and most important, you and your client now know what must be done, and by whom, to properly conclude your representation of the client.

134

The Exit Interview

Mark A. Chinn

MANY LAWYERS PERFORM wonderful work and then fail to conclude their work properly. The exit interview is a wonderful technique to make sure that you have "tied a ribbon around your product package."

The exit interview should be scheduled when all activity in the file has been completed. It should be scheduled for approximately fifteen (15) minutes, and you have the option of whether or not you want to charge for it.

Begin the exit interview by congratulating the client on a successful legal product. Then go back through your file from the very beginning and tell the client when you opened the file and what problems the client faced. Let the client know the actions that you took at the outset to help them. Walk the client through the trials and tribulations and successes and decisions that you both went through during the process of the case. Let the client know where you helped them. Legal business is a specialized and sophisticated art, and clients oftentimes do not know or appreciate what you have done for them. In the exit interview, you should **tell them.** This will give them an appreciation for what you did for them and what they have received as a result of retaining you. After you have walked them through the process of the case, go through the end product with them. In most cases, this is a judgment of divorce with an award, or an agreement. Walk through each paragraph of the agreement, explaining how each paragraph was arrived at and what it means. Ask the client if they have any questions about any of the provisions. Point out any potential problems for the future. Also point out any successes you might have had in getting a particular provision in the agreement.

Educate the client about the future. Explain some of the pitfalls of the post-divorce process. Let the client know what might happen in the future. Explain legal doctrines such as "Modification" and "Contempt Actions." Give the client pointers on how to protect herself or himself. Let the client know that when there are problems, they should contact you immediately. Also, let the client know that they should probably touch base with you once a year to do an audit of their circumstances.

After you have walked the client through the process of the case and educated the client about the future, celebrate the moment and the conclusion of the struggle. Give the client a gift that will help them to enjoy the end of a long struggle. In our firm, we present the client with a wine cooler and a bottle of champagne. Clients are almost always tickled to death to receive this gift. They are unprepared for this and have not thought before that they might celebrate the conclusion of this long battle.

If you use the exit interview, you will find that you generally end with clients who have a lot more appreciation for the work you have done. You will also find there is a clear ending to your work in each case, and both you and the client will know that your work is over and that you have done a job well.

POST-DIVORCE EXIT INTERVIEW AND WARNINGS

DATE: _____
ATTORNEY: _____

❏ MODIFICATION

Pertains to all but a lump sum. It can be obtained where there has been a substantial change in circumstances, such as the following:
- increase or decrease in either party's earnings or wealth
- increase in either party's expenses
- increase or decrease in needs of children

Warnings:
1. Do not act contrary to the decree without consulting Chinn & Associates
2. Do not wait if there is a change in circumstances. Contact Chinn & Associates *immediately*.
3. Check with Chinn & Associates at least once a year to make sure you are not entitled to a modification.

❏ CONTEMPT

Failure to comply with the decree is punishable by confinement in jail. Failure to pay child support or alimony or to perform other obligations can result in contempt and possible confinement.

Warnings:
1. If you owe child support and cannot pay, contact Chinn & Associates *immediately*.
2. If you are owed support, wait about ten (10) days and consult with Chinn & Associates about a course of action.
3. Do not retaliate against the other party for their contempt (e.g., withholding visitation to non-supporting father). Your own failure to comply with the decree may prevent you from seeking to enforce it.

❏ ALIMONY

Alimony is terminable upon remarriage or death, or on other circumstances stated.

Warnings:

1. Consult with Chinn & Associates if an event terminating alimony has occurred or is about to occur.
2. Alimony may be terminable if the receiver engages in "immoral conduct." Consult with Chinn & Associates before beginning any "serious" relationship.
3. Monthly alimony is "deductible" to the payer and "includable" in the receiver's income. Consult your accountant.

❏ CHILD SUPPORT

Child support lasts until each child reaches majority, which is twenty-one (21) or becomes emancipated (married or self-supporting) or otherwise self-supporting. Support can be modified by either party for a substantial change in circumstances.

Warnings:

1. If you can't pay it, contact Chinn & Associates *immediately.*
2. If you are not receiving it, wait about ten (10) days and consult with Chinn & Associates.
3. If there is any change in circumstances, consult with Chinn & Associates.
4. If either party wishes to do something different from the decree, *do not do it* without consulting Chinn & Associates.
5. Consult with Chinn & Associates once each year.

❏ MEDICAL BILLS

The best way to handle payment of medical bills is for the person obtaining the service to send the bill to the other person with an enclosure letter, keeping a copy. The courts will view thirty days as a reasonable time to reimburse. Extraordinary, non-emergency expenses should not be incurred without prior notification to the other parent. Orthodontic expenses should *never* be reimbursed or incurred without *prior* consultation with Chinn & Associates. Documentation of medical expenses is essential to obtaining reimbursement. In court, the person seeking reimbursement will have to *prove* they submitted the bill to the other party before the court will hold them accountable for failure to reimburse.

❏ CUSTODY

Can be modified if there is a substantial change in circumstances. Although many factors are important, the key inquiry is what is best for the children. The law is that a child who reaches the age of twelve (12) has a say in custody but the overall best interest of the child is still the key inquiry.

Warnings:

1. Consult with Chinn & Associates as any child reaches the age of twelve (12).
2. Consult with Chinn & Associates if your spouse moves.
3. Consult with Chinn & Associates once a year.

❏ VISITATION

This is an area that causes trouble. Adhere to the letter and "spirit" of the Decree. Try to cooperate. The courts expect healthy cooperative visitations.

Warnings:

1. When you have a question, consult the Decree and try to do right.
2. Consult Chinn & Associates if problems arise.
3. Do not withhold visitation in retaliation.
4. Consult with Chinn & Associates if you think visitation may constitute a danger to the children.

❏ MOVING

The Court requires each party to advise the other of changes of address or phone number. Moving by either party may constitute a change in circumstance.

Warnings:

1. Advise Chinn & Associates immediately if either party plans to move.

❏ CREDIT CARDS AND OTHER DEBTS

❏ AUTO TITLES

❏ BANK ACCOUNTS

Do any need to be closed or name changed?

❏ INSURANCE POLICIES, ETC.

Beneficiaries should be changed on insurance policies and pension funds, etc.

❏ HEALTH INSURANCE

1. Claim Forms
2. Card
3. Pre-certification
4. COBRA—Warn about deadlines for election

❏ WILL

❏ BOOKS ABOUT DIVORCE (See attached lists)

❏ TAX RETURNS

CHINN & ASSOCIATES DOES NOT FURNISH TAX ADVICE. YOU ARE DIRECTED AND ADVISED TO OBTAIN INDEPENDENT TAX ADVICE FROM A QUALIFIED TAX ACCOUNTANT OR TAX COUNSEL AS TO YOUR PROCEEDINGS, AGREEMENTS AND ANY OTHER DOCUMENTS.

1. Child support is *not* includable nor taxable.
2. Monthly alimony is includable and taxable.
3. Lump Sum distributions are not includable or taxable.
4. Dependent tax exemptions. Custodial parent gets the exemption unless waived or otherwise specified in the return.
5. Part or all of Attorney fees may be deductible.
6. Send the IRS a change of address form 8822, attached.

Warnings:

1. Check with an accountant now and obtain advice now about tax issues.

❏ **RETURN OF CLIENT DOCUMENTS**
LIST ALL DOCUMENTS RETURNED TO CLIENT

_____

_____

_____

_____

❏ **FILE DESTRUCTION**

Part or the entire file may be destroyed at any time for storage purposes.

❏ **THANK WITNESSES AND OTHER SUPPORTERS**

❏ **DOCUMENTATION**

Try to document what you and your former spouse do. Keep a diary or log of things. Confirm arrangements in writing and keep a copy. If you are making payments, get documentation. Use a check or get a receipt.

❏ **OTHER PROBLEMS**

Chinn and Associates handle a wide variety of problems and cases. If any legal question arises, such as an auto accident, on the job injury, contract issue, business formation, loan closing, or any other problem, call Chinn and Associates for assistance or proper referral.

❏ **DIVORCE GROUP**

Below are some books for men, women, and children who are going through the divorce process:

Crazy Time, Surviving Divorce by Abigail Trafford
Coping: A Survival Manual for Women Alone by Martha Yates
Women in Transition by Carolyn Kott Washburne
Part-Time Father by Edith Atkin and Estelle Ruben
The Boys' and Girls' Book about Divorce by Richard A. Gardner, M.D.
The American Way of Divorce: Prescription for Change by Sheila Kessler, Ph.D.
The Courage to Divorce by Susan Gettlemen and Janet Markowitz
Creative Divorce by Mel Krantzler
Dear Dad by Lee Shapiro, J.D.
101 Ways to Be a Long-Distance Super-Dad by George Newman

About the Editor

Gregg Herman is a shareholder with the law firm of Loeb & Herman, S.C., which practices exclusively family law, concentrating in cases with significant assets or income. He is a 1974 graduate of the University of Wisconsin and 1977 graduate of the University of Wisconsin law school.

From 1977–1984, Mr. Herman was an assistant district attorney for Milwaukee County, prosecuting nearly 100 jury trials ranging from white-collar crime to first degree murder. He joined Leonard Loeb in the practice of family law in October 1984.

Gregg Herman is the founder of the Collaborative Family Law Council of Wisconsin, Inc., and was its first state-wide chair. He is currently a member of the Board of Governors of the State Bar of Wisconsin (1999–2003) and a member of council of the ABA Family Law Section (1996–2003).

Mr. Herman is a former president of the Milwaukee Bar Association (1998–99), the Wisconsin Chapter of the American Academy of Matrimonial Lawyers (1999), and is a past chair of the State Bar of Wisconsin Family Law Section (1996–97).

Gregg Herman is editor-in-chief of the *Wisconsin Journal of Family Law* and co-author of *The System Book for Family Law* published by the State Bar of Wisconsin.

In his personal life, Gregg's passions are his family (including three children), the Wisconsin Badgers, and his yellow Labrador Retriever, not necessarily in that order!

About the Authors

Michael J. Albano graduated from the University of Missouri at Kansas City in 1965 and received his J.D. from the University of Missouri at Kansas City School of Law in 1968. Currently a shareholder and officer in the law firm of Welch, Martin, & Albano, LLC, in Independence, Missouri, he is a past chairperson of the American Bar Association Section of Family Law and a past president of the American Academy of Matrimonial Lawyers.

Marshall J. Auerbach, who heads a law firm bearing his name, concentrates his practice in matrimonial litigation. He is the principal draftsman of the 1977 Illinois Marriage and Dissolution of Marriage Act. After graduating from the University of Illinois, he received his J.D. from the John Marshall Law School in Chicago in 1955.

Robert J. Barnard Jr. currently limits his private practice to domestic relations and matrimonial law in Kalamazoo, Michigan. He received his B.S.M.E. from Purdue University, his J.D. from Northwestern University Law School, and his M.P.L. from John Marshall Law School. He is a fellow of the American Academy of Matrimonial Lawyers, a diplomate of the American College of Family Trial Lawyers, a council member of the Family Law Section Council of the State Bar of Michigan, and a member of the Family Law Section of the Illinois State Bar Association.

Lewis Becker is a professor of law at Villanova University School of Law. He has authored many book chapters and law review articles pertaining to Family Law. He is an at-large member of the Family Law Section's Council and has served as chair or co-chair of the Section's Custody and Ethics Committees.

Andrew Berman graduated from Brandeis University in 1980 and from the University of Miami School of Law, with honors, in 1983. He is a member of the Association of Professional Responsibility Lawyers (director 1998–2000) and is a Founders Circle member of the American Bar Association Center for Professional Responsibility. He is also president of the Spellman/Hoeveler American Inns of Court. Mr. Berman specializes in appellate practice and concentrates in the areas of complex commercial litigation (including business torts, unfair competition, and contract disputes), healthcare–related litigation and the representation of lawyers and other professionals in professional disciplinary and malpractice matters.

Phyllis Bossin practices law in Cincinnati with the firm of Phyllis G. Bossin Co., L.P.A., concentrating her practice in the field of family law. She is a Certified Family Law Specialist in Ohio, a fellow of the American Academy of Matrimonial Lawyers and the International Academy of Matrimonial Lawyers, and a diplomate of the American College of Family Trial Lawyers. She is an Adjunct Professor at the University of Houston Law School and a member of the faculty of the Trial Advocacy Institute sponsored by the Family Law Section of the American Bar Association. She was recently elected to the position of chair-elect of the Family Law Section.

Mark Chinn received his undergraduate degree from Iowa State University in 1975 and his law degree from the University of Mississippi in 1978. He is admitted to practice in all courts in Mississippi, the Fifth and Seventh Circuits, and the United States Supreme Court. He is listed in *The Best Lawyers in America* and Martindale-Hubbell's *Bar Register of Preeminent Lawyers* in the field of Family Law. He is vice chair of the Supreme Court's Gender Fairness Task Force and was appointed by the governor to the Children's Justice Task Force.

Harriet N. Cohen is a founding partner of the matrimonial and family law firm of Cohen Hennessey & Bienstock P.C. in New York City. She is a graduate of Barnard College where she received her B.A., Bryn Mawr College where she received her M.A., and Brooklyn Law School where she received her J.D. cum laude.

Sharon L. Corbitt is a shareholder in the law firm of Sneed Lang, P.C. in Tulsa, Oklahoma. Ms. Corbitt is a fellow in the American Academy of Matrimonial Lawyers and is also past chair of the American Bar Association Family Law Section and serves on the American Bar Association Commission on Domestic Violence. She currently serves on the Board of Domestic Violence Intervention Services of Tulsa and on the Board of the Parent Child Center of Tulsa.

William C. Darrah is the immediate past chair of the Family Law Section of the Hawaii State Bar Association and is the editor of the *Hawaii Journal of Family Law*. He is a 1970 graduate of the University of North Carolina and a 1975 graduate of the New York University School of Law. He founded the Family Law Mediation Center of Hawaii.

Willard H. DaSilva, a member of DaSilva, Hilowitz & McEvily LLP, is a veteran matrimonial law practitioner with offices in Garden City and in New City, New York. He is a past president of the American Academy of Matrimonial Lawyers, New York Chapter, and is currently editor-in-chief of the ABA's *Family Advocate* magazine and a council member of the American Bar Association Section of Family Law. He is a magna cum laude graduate of New York University, member of Phi Beta Kappa, and received his law degree at Columbia University Law School.

Ellen J. Effron is a custody expert practicing law in Morristown, New Jersey. She is a candidate for vice chair of the Section of Family Law and has been a committee chair or officer in the section for the past twelve years. She has been section liaison to the American Psychiatric Association since 1990.

Linda Elrod is a professor at Washburn University School of Law, where she has been teaching since 1974. The editor of the *Family Law Quarterly* for the ABA's Section of Family Law, she is a former chair of the Kansas Bar Association's Family Law Section and has been vice chair of the Kansan Advisory Committee on Child Support since 1984.

Joy M. Feinberg has practiced law for over 25 years, concentrating her practice in family law. Ms. Feinberg is a past president of the American Academy of Matrimonial Lawyers Foundation; past president of the Illinois Chapter of the AAML; past co-chair of the ABA Family Law subcommittees on Custody, Continuing Legal Education and Domestic Violence; past chair of the Illinois State Bar Association Family Law Section and Continuing Legal Education Section. She has written extensively on custody and psychological testing issues; divorce-related pension issues (and has testified as an expert witness to juries on such matters); and tax and business valuation issues in divorce cases.

James H. Feldman, a partner in Jenner & Block's Chicago office and chair of the firm's family law practice, is a certified fellow of the American Academy of Matrimonial Lawyers and has chaired committees in the Family Law Section of the American Bar Association on legal ethics and federal legislation affecting family law. Mr. Feldman is also a member of the Illinois State Bar Association's Family Law Section and the California State Bar Association's Family Law Section. He received a B.A. from Tufts University in 1965, obtained his J.D. in 1968 from the University of Illinois College of Law, and received an L.L.M. from New York University School of Law in 1970.

Harold G. Field is a sole practitioner in Wheaton, Illinois, who graduated from Arizona State University with distinction and received his J.D. from the Illinois Institute of Technology in Chicago, Illinois. He has served on the Board of Governors of the Illinois State Bar Association, the Illinois State Bar Family Law Council, as well as the ABA's Section of Family Law. He is Counsel for the International Academy of Matrimonial Lawyers.

John E. Finnerty, founder of and a partner in Finnerty & Sherwood, P.C., is the former chairman of the New Jersey State Bar Association's Family Law

Section. He is a 1972 graduate of the Rutgers School of Law in Newark. Awarded the Saul Tischler Award for his lifetime contribution to advancement of family law in New Jersey, he has written for the ABA's *Family Advocate* and other publications.

James T. Friedman is a partner in the firm of Davis, Friedman, Zavett, Kane & MacRae, a Chicago-based firm specializing in the practice of family law. Having received his undergraduate and law degrees from the University of Michigan, Friedman is a fellow and former counsel, treasurer, governor, vice president, and president of the AAML.

Melvyn B. Frumkes has offices in Miami-Dade County and Palm Beach County, Florida. He is a graduate of the University of Florida, College of Law. He is on the faculty of the National Judicial College in Reno, Nevada, a fellow of the AAML and the International Academy of Matrimonial Lawyers, and a diplomate of the American College of Family Trial Attorneys. He is the author of *Frumkes on Divorce Taxation,* Third Edition.

Donn C. Fullenweider has had a private practice in Houston for thirty-six years. He received his J.D. from the University of Houston in 1958. A past president of the AAML, Fullenweider planned and chaired the first ABA Section of Family Law Advanced Trial Advocacy Institute at the University of Denver College of Law in June of 1987 and served as its course director for four years.

Sharon Stern Gerstman is a matrimonial referee and confidential law clerk in the New York Supreme Court in Erie and Niagara Counties and an adjunct professor at the State University of New York at Buffalo Law School. A graduate of the Yale Law School with an L.L.M., the University of Pittsburgh Law School with a J.D., and Brown University with an A.B., she has a private practice and full-time legal scholarship on several faculties.

Gunnar J. Gitlin's family law firm, the Gitlin Law Firm in Woodstock, Illinois, exclusively handles family law cases. Mr. Gitlin received his B.A. from Kenyon College and his J.D. from Loyola University of Chicago. Mr. Gitlin is the coeditor of the American Bar Association's Family Fax News Update Service. He has lectured to various organizations including the American Bar Association, Family Law Section, the American Academy of Matrimonial Lawyers, and Law Education Institute.

H. Joseph Gitlin's matrimonial law firm, Gitlin & Gitlin in Woodstock, Illinois, is concentrated in the field of family law. He has held leadership positions in the Illinois State Bar Association's Family Law Section Council and the ABA's Section of Family Law. An author and lecturer, Gitlin was named one of the nation's top forty-three divorce lawyers by the *National Law Journal.*

Lynne Z. Gold-Bikin is managing partner of the Family Law Department of Wolf, Block, Schorr and Sois-Cohen LLP. She is a delegate from the Family Law Section to the House of Delegates of the American Bar Association. She is on the board of governors of the AAML and on the editorial board of the American Law Institute's *Practical Lawyer*. She has recently been named one of Pennsylvania's Best 50 Women in Business and one of the ten top lawyers in the country by *Worth Magazine*. She is a graduate of Albright College and received her J.D. from Villanova University Law School in 1976.

Harvey L. Golden has been a trial attorney in South Carolina for 48 continuous years with primary statewide practice in family law. Recipient in August 2001 of the American Bar Association's Lifetime Achievement Award, he has served the ABA as a member of the House of Delegates (1990–2000) and as national chairman of the Family Law Section (1987–1988).

Max A. Goodman received his J.D. from Loyola of Los Angeles in 1948 and is on the faculty at Southwestern University School of Law. He teaches community property, family law, and an advanced family law seminar.

Samuel J. Goodman is a shareholder and founder of the firm of Goodman, Ball & Van Bokkelen in Indiana. A graduate of Purdue University and the University of Michigan Law School, Goodman has served on the ABA Section of Family Law's Continuing Legal Education Committee and has chaired the Family Law Practice Committee. Goodman is the past chairman of the Family and Juvenile Law Section of the State of Indiana Bar Association.

Beverly Anne Groner is a past chairman of the Section of Family Law of the ABA and a graduate of Washington College of Law. Selected to teach at Harvard University Law School as a family law expert-in-residence, Groner is president of Montgomery-Prince George's Continuing Legal Education Institute, Inc. She is the chairman of the Maryland Governor's Commission on Domestic Relations Law.

Judge Samuel B. Groner is a graduate of Cornell University and the Cornell Law School in Ithaca, New York. He received his master of arts in economics from the American University in Washington, D.C.

Hanley M. Gurwin received his undergraduate and law degrees from the University of Michigan. He is currently practicing matrimonial law with Clark Hill P.L.C. in Birmingham, Michigan. He is a fellow of the AAML and a diplomate of the American College of Family Trial Lawyers.

Geoffrey Hamilton is both a past chair and the chair-elect of the Section of Family Law. A graduate of the Duke University School of Law in 1968, he cofounded Char, Hamilton, Campbell & Thom in 1980. Together with Thomas Merrill, he has presented papers on various aspects of the psycho-dynamics of divorce to two ABA annual meetings. He was appointed special master by the family court of the First Circuit Court in 1988.

Ann M. Haralambie is a practicing attorney in Tucson, Arizona, concentrating on custody and child abuse cases. She is a certified domestic relations specialist, past president of the National Association of Counsel for Children, and life charter member of the American Professional Society on the Abuse of Children.

Stephen J. Harhai established his Denver law practice in 1976, then began a ten-year effort to redraft statutes relating to divorce, child support, and custody while serving as chair of the Legislative Committee of the Family Law Section of the Colorado Bar Association. He was appointed by Governor Romer to chair the Colorado Child Support Commission from 1990 to 1995. Harhai received his B.A. and J.D. from the University of Pennsylvania.

Sondra I. Harris is senior partner in Sondra I. Harris and Associates in Woodmere, NY. She is a member of the ABA Family Law Section council and chair of the Alternative Family Committee. She writes and lectures extensively on family law.

David H. Hopkins of Schiller, DuCanto & Fleck in Chicago, Illinois, received his A.B. from Duke University in 1966 and his J.D. from Columbia University in 1969. He is currently the chairman of the ABA's Section of Family Law Taxation Committee, and he is a member of the Illinois Family Violence Coordinating Council.

Susan A. Hurst received her B.A. in psychology from Bowling Green State University and her J.D. from the University of Toledo College of Law. She is a family law sole practitioner in Smyrna, Georgia, and a certified mediator and guardian ad litem.

Herndon Inge III holds an A.B. degree in English from the University of the South, Sewanee, Tennessee, and a J.D. degree from Cumberland School of Law. He is an experienced lecturer who has taught family law as well as other law courses at Spring Hill College and has been a frequent speaker for CLE programs on family law for the Family Law Sections of the Alabama State Bar as well as the American Bar Association. He is a member of the Family Law Sections of the Alabama State Bar and is a Fellow of the American Academy of Matrimonial Lawyers.

Monroe L. Inker is a principal in the law firm of White, Inker, Aronson, P.C., in Boston, as well as an adjunct professor of law at Boston College Law School. He received his B.A. from Brooklyn College and his LL.B. and

L.L.M. from Harvard Law School. He is a member of the editorial board of the *Massachusetts Family Law Journal* and the ABA's *Family Law Quarterly.*

Mitchell A. Jacobs is a certified family law specialist and a principal of the law office of Mitchell Jacobs in Los Angeles, California. His firm specializes in representing high-net worth individuals in dissolution of marriage and child custody cases.

Daniel J. Jaffe is a senior partner in the law firm of Jaffe and Clemens, Beverly Hills, California, a law firm that limits its practice to high asset, complex dissolution matters. He received his Bachelor of Business Administration degree in 1959 at the University of Michigan, and his Juris Doctor degree from UCLA School of Law in 1962. He is a certified specialist in family law, a former chair of the Los Angeles County and Beverly Hills Bar Family Law Sections, a fellow of the American Academy of Matrimonial Lawyers, and a diplomate of the American College of Family Trial Lawyers. Mr. Jaffe writes and lectures extensively on divorce taxation, division of employee benefits, deferred compensation, and related family law topics.

Lewis Kapner is a senior partner for Lewis Kapner, P.A., a West Palm Beach, Florida, law firm concentrating in marital law. He is a former chief judge of Palm Beach County. A graduate of the University of Florida and Stetson University Law School, he is certified by the Florida Bar Board in marital law. He is a fellow of the American Academy of Matrimonial Lawyers and the International Academy of Matrimonial Lawyers and a member of the American Law Institute.

C. Terrence Kapp received his B.A. from Colgate University, his M.A. from Holy Apostles Seminary & College summa cum laude, and his J.D. from Cleveland State University. A practicing lawyer for over twenty-four years, Kapp is active in the ABA's Section of Family Law and lectures nationally on family law issues.

Cheryl L. Karp, Ph.D., is the clinical director of the Trauma Program at Desert Hills Center for Youth and Families, a youth psychiatric hospital and residential treatment center in Tucson, Arizona. She obtained her Ph.D. from the University of Arizona in 1978 and has been a licensed psychologist in private practice since 1980, specializing in child abuse trauma and forensic psychology.

Leonard Karp is a member of the American Academy of Matrimonial Lawyers and the American College of Family Trial Lawyers. He is a frequent lecturer on domestic relations and domestic torts and the author of numerous professional articles.

Twila B. Larkin is a founding partner of Walther & Larkin, LLP, a firm specializing in complex divorce and family law in Albuquerque and Santa Fe, New Mexico. A former chair of the New Mexico State Bar's Family Law Section, she is currently serving her second term as the Region V Representative to the Council of the ABA Section of Family Law. She is a frequent speaker on family law issues.

Jonathan R. Levine is a member of the law firm of Levine & Smith, LLC, where he practices in the areas of domestic relations and family law. Mr. Levine received his B.B.A. degree from the University of Texas, his J.D. degree from the University of Georgia and his L.L.M. degree in taxation from Emory University. He is an instructor for the Emory University Trial Techniques program and a past instructor in family law at the National Center for Paralegal Training. Mr. Levine is a frequent lecturer on family law issues. He is the chair of the Atlanta Bar Association, Family Law Section Board of Directors. Mr. Levine is a barrister of the Georgia Family Law American Inn of Court and a fellow in the American Academy of Matrimonial Lawyers.

David H. Levy is a trial lawyer with twenty-six years of experience handling complex financial and custody cases. He is the managing partner of the law firm of Kalcheim, Schatz & Berger, with offices in Cook and Lake County, Illinois. Mr. Levy is a fellow of the American Academy of Matrimonial Lawyers. He was chairman of the Illinois State Bar Association Family Law Section Council in 1995–96. He has lectured extensively throughout the United States, including presentations to the American Bar Association and the American Academy of Matrimonial Lawyers.

The Honorable Howard I. Lipsey has been an associate justice in the Rhode Island Family Court since August 1993. He received his B.A. from Providence College. In 1960, he received his J.D. from the Georgetown University Law School. He has served as chair of the Family Courts Committee and as council member of the Family Law Section of the American Bar Association and is a fellow of both the American College of Trial Lawyers and the American Academy of Matrimonial Lawyers. In 1999 he received an adjunct faculty teaching award from the Roger Williams University School of Law.

Sandra Morgan Little is a board-certified family law specialist practicing in the Albuquerque, New Mexico, firm of Little & Gilman-Tepper, P.A. She is a past chair of the ABA Section of Family Law, is listed in *The Best Lawyers in America,* and is a frequent author and lecturer.

David M. Luboff is a graduate of the UCLA School of Law. He is associated with the firm of Jaffe and Clemens in Beverly Hills, California, and is certified by the California Board of Legal Specialization as a specialist in family law.

Ira Lurvey is a former chair of the ABA Family Law Section. He previously chaired family law sections of the California State Bar, the Los Angeles County Bar, and the Beverly Hills, California, Bar; is former president of the Southern California Chapter of the American Academy of Matrimonial Lawyers and former member of its national Board of Governors; and lectures frequently on family law litigation and mediation.

The Honorable David R. Main earned both his B.S. in pharmacy and his J.D. from the University of Toronto, Faculty of Pharmacy, in 1964 and that university's law school in 1968, respectively. Prior to being appointed to the Ontario Court's Provincial Division in 1975, Main's practice was restricted to family law.

C. Ian McLachlan, a graduate of Georgetown University and Fordham University School of Law, practiced family law in Connecticut for more than twenty-five years prior to his appointment as Connecticut Superior Court judge in March of 1996. He has served as chairman of the Section of Family Law's Divorce Taxation Committee.

Thomas S. Merrill is a clinical and forensic psychologist whose practice focuses on the area of divorce and the children of divorce. Active in the development of the Kids First and Custody Guardian Ad Litem programs, and through his mediation and therapy practice, he continues to participate in those areas designed to mitigate the harmful effects of divorce on both children and their parents. Board-certified in Clinical Psychology by the American Board of Professional Psychology, Dr. Merrill is the past president of the Hawaii Psychological Association, founder and past president of the Hawaii Mental Health Center, and recipient of the Hawaii State Bar Association's Golden Gavel Award and the Family Law Section of the Hawaii State Bar's Distinguished Service Award.

Laura Morgan is an appellate family law attorney in Charlottesville, Virginia, and the owner of Family Law Consulting, a firm providing research and writing services to family law attorneys nationwide. She is the author of *Child Support Guidelines: Interpretation and Application,* and has acted as a special adviser to a dozen state child support guideline commissions.

Robert B. Moriarty of Moriarty & Dee in Buffalo, New York, has been a family law practitioner for over thirty-four years. He is a past chair of the ABA Continuing Legal Education Committee and Publications Development Board and a coauthor of two books dealing with domestic relations.

Sandra Joan Morris received her B.A. with honors from the University of Arizona in 1965 and her J.D. from California Western School of Law in 1969. She has been specializing in family law since 1970 and is a fellow of the International Academies of Matrimonial Law and a diplomate of the

American College of Family Trial Lawyers. Her practice is located in San Diego, California.

William P. Mulloy Sr. is a senior partner in the law firm of Mulloy, Walz, Wetterer, Fore & Schwartz in Louisville, Kentucky. He received his A.B. in 1949 and his J.D. summa cum laude from the University of Louisville. He is a teacher of numerous seminars annually including those for the American Law Institute and the Louisville and Kentucky Bar Associations.

Michael T. Murphy is a certified specialist in family law in Las Cruces, New Mexico. He is a fellow of both the American Academy of Matrimonial Lawyers and the American College of Trust and Estate Counsel. He is listed in *The Best Lawyers in America.*

Marjorie A. O'Connell is the founder of the Washington, D.C., law firm of O'Connell and Associates, which recently celebrated its 25th anniversary. A member of the American Bar Association House of Delegates, she has been an officer of the ABA Tax Section and served on its governing Council. She has served as chair of the ABA Tax Section's Domestic Relations Tax Problems Committee and vice-chair of the ABA General Practice Section Tax Committee, chair of the ABA Family Law Section Tax Committee, and chair of the American Academy of Matrimonial Lawyers Divorce Taxation Committee. She is chair of the International Bar Association Family Law Committee and president of the National Foundation for Women's Bar Associations. She holds a Bachelor of Arts degree, magna cum laude, from The Catholic University of America, and is a member of Phi Beta Kappa.

Theodore P. Orenstein is a principal in the firm of Rosenberg, Freedman & Goldstein in Newton, Massachusetts. He has been handling domestic relations matters in eastern Massachusetts since 1970. A graduate of the University of Texas School of Law, he has served on the Council of the Family Law Section of the Massachusetts Bar Association.

Catherine Holland Petersen is president of Petersen Associates, Inc., a Norman, Oklahoma, law firm concentrating in family law. She is a member of the Section of Family Law of the American and Oklahoma Bar Associations. She has served on the faculty of the Trial Advocacy Institute since 1995 and was named Outstanding Family Law Attorney in Oklahoma in 1988.

Peggy L. Podell, a partner in the Milwaukee firm of Podell & Podell, is the chair-elect of the State Bar of Wisconsin Family Law Section. She is a financial officer of the ABA's Section of Family Law. A member of the editorial board of the *Family Advocate,* she serves as the tax column editor for that publication.

Richard J. Podell of the law firm of Richard J. Podell and Associates was chair of the ABA's Section of Family Law in 1988–89 and a member of the

Family Law Council from 1970 to 1988. He was one of the section's delegates to the ABA House of Delegates from 1996 to 2000. Since 2000 he has been a member of the ABA Board of Governors.

James B. Preston, a graduate of the University of California and the Hastings College of the Law, was a member of the Thursten Honor Society. A certified family law specialist, he is a former financial officer and current council member of the ABA Section of Family Law and the State of California Board of Legal Specialization.

Roseanna L. Purzycki is a tax partner at Gursey, Schneider & Co., LLP. Previously, she taught accounting and taxation courses at the University of Michigan Graduate School of Business and the University of Southern California School of Accounting. She holds a master's in business taxation from USC and a master's in accounting from Eastern Michigan University.

Kimberly A. Quach is a senior associate at the Washington County office of Gevurtz, Menashe, Larson & Howe, P.C., a 25-attorney firm specializing in the practice of family law. She graduated in 1987 from Carroll College of Montana (summa cum laude) and in 1990 from the University of Washington School of Law. She divides her practice between Oregon and Washington, and is considered one of the firm's primary litigation resources. Ms. Quach is a member of this Section's Council, and co-chair of the Publications Development Board. She is a former co-vice chair of this Section's Trial Techniques Committee.

Grier H. Raggio Jr. graduated from Harvard College and Boston College Law School and now practices family law in Dallas, Texas, with the family firm Raggio & Raggio. He is a fellow of the American Academy of Matrimonial Lawyers and of the American Bar Foundation. He has published numerous articles and two books on family law.

Kenneth G. Raggio, a past chair of the Section of Family Law of the ABA, practices family law and conducts mediations with Raggio & Raggio. He is a fellow of the Texas Bar and American Bar Foundations. As the long-time author of the "Tools of the Trade" *Family Advocate* column, Raggio is regarded as an important "technological" influence in the Section.

Louise B. Raggio received her B.A. from the University of Texas and her J.D. and Honorary Doctorate of Laws from Southern Methodist University. A past chair of the Section of Family Law of the ABA and the State Bar of Texas, Raggio has earned numerous awards, including the ABA's Margaret Brent Award in 1995 and the State Bar of Texas's highest awards for family law reform.

Charles H. Robertson was admitted to the Texas Bar in 1969 after obtaining both his B.A. and his J.D. degrees from Southern Methodist University. He is a former chair of the Family Law Section of the Dallas Bar Association.

557

Kathleen Robertson, a partner in the AV-rated law firm of Norris & Robertson, LLP, located near Silicon Valley in the San Francisco Bay area, concentrates her practice in the legal and practical issues involved in complex family law matters. Ms. Robertson has extensive trial experience and litigation skills, as well as training in mediation, negotiation, and collaborative law. She is active in the local and state bar associations in addition to the Family Law Section of the American Bar Association.

Jennifer J. Rose is a sole practitioner in Shenandoah, Iowa, whose practice is limited to family law. She is a former chair of the Iowa State Family & Juvenile Law Section, a member of the ABA General Practice Section Council, and the editor-in-chief of *The Compleat Lawyer.* She serves on the ABA Standing Committee on Continuing Education of the Bar.

Lee S. Rosen is a certified family law specialist practicing in Raleigh, North Carolina. An advisor to the National Council of Juvenile and Family Court Judges, he serves on the editorial board of the *Family Advocate.* A graduate of Wake Forest University Law School and the University of North Carolina-Asheville, Rosen serves as committee chairperson of the ABA's Section of Family Law.

Elaine Rudnick-Sheps has wide experience as a lecturer at seminars on matrimonial practice and procedure sponsored by groups including the American Academy of Matrimonial Lawyers, the New York State Trial Lawyers Association, and the Law Education Institute. She is a member of the American Bar Association Family Law Section, and was chair of the Matrimonial and Family Law Committee of the ABA Litigation Section.

Arnold H. Rutkin of Rutkin & Oldham, LLC, is the former editor-in-chief of the *Family Advocate.* He is the author of *Valuation and Distribution of Marital Property,* Matthew Bender Publishing Company, 1984; and coauthor of *Family Law and Practice* (3 vols.), West Publishing Co., 2000–2001.

M. Dee Samuels of the firm of Samuels & Shawn in San Francisco, California, has specialized in family law for twenty years. She graduated from Whittier College and the University of San Francisco Law School. She is certified by the State Bar of California Board of Legal Specialization as a family law specialist.

Donald C. Schiller, a partner in Schiller, DuCanto and Fleck, has served as president of the Illinois State Bar Association and chairman of its Family Law Section. Mr. Schiller was a member of the Board of Governors of the American Bar Association in 1994–97 and chair of the Circuit Court of Cook County's Domestic Relations Management Advisory Committee from 1993 to 2000. In 1994 he became a diplomate of the American College of Family Trial Lawyers.

Samuel V. Schoonmaker III graduated magna cum laude and Phi Beta Kappa from Yale College in 1958 and from the Yale Law School in 1961. After joining Cummings & Lockwood's Stamford Office in 1961 as an associate attorney, he became a partner in 1970 and a managing partner in 1987. He founded Schoonmaker & George, P.C., in April of 1996.

Philip Schwartz practices law in Washington, D.C., and Virginia, as well as internationally, specializing in the international aspects of family law. He is the incoming president of the International Academy of Matrimonial Lawyers. With an L.L.M. in taxation, he serves on the United States Secretary of State's Advisory Committee on Private International Law.

J. Lindsey Short Jr. is currently president of the National American Academy of Matrimonial Lawyers. He is a past member of the board of directors of the State Bar of Texas, a past chairman of the Family Law Section of the State Bar of Texas, and past chairman of the Family Law Advisory Commission for the Texas Board of Legal Specialization. Mr. Short has taught semester-long courses at the University of Houston Law School, Washington and Lee University Law School, and the University of Texas Law School, all dealing with advanced family law. He was a founding fellow of the International Academy of Matrimonial Lawyers and a founding diplomate of the American College of Family Trial Lawyers. During his 35 years as a lawyer, Mr. Short has lectured on over 100 occasions and written and published over 80 articles.

Gary Neil Skoloff is a partner in the law firm of Skoloff & Wolfe in New Jersey. He earned his B.A. from Rutgers University in 1955 and his LL.B. from the Rutgers University School of Law in 1958. His practice of law is limited solely to matrimonial matters.

Patricia Garity Smits, the senior attorney at Smits & Solotoff LLC in Morristown, New Jersey, served for two terms as a council member of the ABA Section of Family Law. She is vice-chair of the New Jersey Supreme Court Family Practice Committee, a senior editor of the *New Jersey Lawyer* Editorial Board, and a master in the New Jersey Family Inn of Court.

Edward S. Snyder is a partner in the Roseland, New Jersey, law firm of Weinstein Snyder Lindeman, P.C. He is a former vice president of the American Academy of Matrimonial Lawyers and a former council member of the ABA's Section of Family Law.

Robert G. Spector is the Glenn R. Watson Centennial Professor of Law and legal director of the Interdisciplinary Graduate Training Program in the Prevention of Child Abuse and Neglect at the University of Oklahoma Law Center. He serves as the reporter for the Uniform Child Custody Jurisdiction and Enforcement Act and the Family Law Joint Editorial Board for the National Conference of Uniform State Laws, and serves as the associate editor of *Family Law Quarterly.*

Carlton D. Stansbury is a shareholder in the firm Burbach & Stansbury S.C. in Milwaukee, Wisconsin. He concentrates his practice in family law and paternity, including litigation, mediation, arbitration, and collaborative law. He is the author of the *Family Law Practitioner's Guide to Social Security* (ABA Section of Family Law 1995) and has written for other publications, such as the *Family Advocate* and the *Wisconsin Journal of Family Law*.

Barbara Kahn Stark practices family law in New Haven and Westport, Connecticut. She chairs the ABA Section of Family Law's Publications Development Board. She lectures and writes frequently in this field and is an adjunct professor at Quinnipiac College School of Law and the University of Houston School of Law Trial Advocacy Institute.

Bruce R. Steinfeld is a shareholder in the Atlanta, Georgia, firm of Steinfeld & Steinfeld, P.C., specializing in family law. He is a fellow of the American Academy of Matrimonial Lawyers, a barrister in the Charles Longstreet Weltner Family Law Inn of Court, secretary of the Family Law Section of the Atlanta Bar Association, and former editor of its newsletter, *The Family Lawyer*. He received his B.A. and M.A. degrees from Binghamton University and his J.D. degree from Emory University School of Law. He and his wife, Shayna, are coauthors of *The Family Lawyer's Guide to Bankruptcy*, published by the ABA's Family Law Section.

George S. Stern is a senior partner in the Atlanta, Georgia, firm of Stern & Edlin, P.C., specializing in family law. He is a former president of the American Academy of Matrimonial Lawyers. He is also the treasurer of the International Academy of Matrimonial Lawyers, a member of its board of governors, and a founder of its U.S.A. Chapter. Stern received his B.A. in 1959 and his J.D. in 1961 from Vanderbilt University.

Lowell H. Sucherman is certified by the California Board of Legal Specialization. He is a graduate of the University of Michigan, the University of Michigan Law School, and Brooklyn Law School. He was admitted to practice in California and New Mexico and is currently practicing in San Francisco as senior partner of Sucherman & Collins.

Mark E. Sullivan is a principal of Sullivan & Grace, P.A., in Raleigh, North Carolina. He has limited his trial practice to family law since 1981, and he has been certified by the North Carolina State Bar as a specialist in family law since 1989. He is a member of the American Academy of Matrimonial Lawyers and the Family Law Sections of the North Carolina Bar Association and the American Bar Association. He is co-chair of the Military Committee, ABA Family Law Section. He is the editor of *Family Law Practice and Procedure Manual* (N.C. Academy of Trial Lawyers, 1989, with 2000 Supplement), and he has written numerous articles on trial advocacy and the practice of family law. In September 2000, he was certified by the American Academy of Matrimonial Lawyers as an arbitrator.

Deborah Miller Tate is a past president of the Rhode Island Bar Association, concentrating her practice in family law with the firm of McIntyre, Tate, Lynch & Holt in Providence, Rhode Island. She received her L.L.M. in Taxation from Boston University and her J.D. from the New England School of Law. She is licensed to practice in Rhode Island, Massachusetts, and Florida, is a fellow of the American Academy of Matrimonial Lawyers, and is a master in the Gallogly Family Law Inn of Court.

David L. Walther practices family law in Santa Fe, New Mexico. He is a New Mexico Board–recognized family law specialist, a diplomate of the American College of Family Trial Lawyers, and a fellow of the American Academy of Matrimonial Lawyers. He is a graduate of the Marquette University Law School in Milwaukee, Wisconsin.

Jan L. Warner received his A.B. and J.D. degrees from the University of South Carolina and earned an L.L.M. in taxation from the Emory University School of Law in Atlanta, Georgia. He produced a series of audiotapes, videotapes, and print materials concerning divorce, separation, and issues affecting the elderly. He coauthors a weekly column about divorce and other transitions.

Richard A. Warshak earned his B.S. from Cornell University and his Ph.D. from the University of Texas Health Science Center in 1978. He is a clinical and research psychologist and a clinical professor of psychology at the University of Texas Southwestern Medical Center at Dallas. He has published extensively on divorce and custody.

The Honorable Francis T. Wasielewski graduated from Marquette University with a B.S. in mathematics in 1964 and from the University of Wisconsin Law School in 1968. He has been a circuit court judge in Milwaukee County since 1983.

Joanne Ross Wilder, a principal in the matrimonial law firm of Wilder & Mahood in Pittsburgh, Pennsylvania, is the author of *Pennsylvania Family Law Practice and Procedure,* now in its fifth edition, and is a frequent lecturer at continuing legal education programs. She is editor-in-chief of the *Journal of the American Academy of Matrimonial Lawyers,* a past president of the Pennsylvania Chapter of the Academy, and a diplomate of the American College of Family Trial Lawyers.

Marshal S. Willick is the principal of a firm in Las Vegas and practices exclusively in the field of family law. In addition to a full-time practice, he writes and lectures extensively on domestic relations and legal technology issues. Mr. Willick is an elected fellow of both the American Academy of Matrimonial Lawyers and the International Academy of Matrimonial Lawyers. He has chaired several committees of the American Bar Association Family Law Section, is a member of that ABA Section's Legislative Lobbying Task Force, and has repeatedly represented the entire ABA in congressional hearings on military pension matters. Mr. Willick received his B.A. from the University of Nevada at Las Vegas in 1979, with honors, and his J.D. from Georgetown University Law Center in Washington, D.C., in 1982.

Marshall J. Wolf is president of the Cleveland, Ohio, domestic relations law firm of Wolf and Akers and past chair of the ABA Family Law Section. He received his B.A. from Miami University (Ohio) in 1964 and his J.D. from Case Western Reserve University in 1967. In 1993, he served as the keynote speaker and chief United States delegate to the First World Congress on Family Law and Rights of Children in Sydney, Australia.

Susan W. Wolfson is a partner at Susman, Duffy & Segaloff, P.C., in New Haven, Connecticut, where her practice concentration is family law. She serves as co-chair of the Alimony and Spousal Support Committee of the Family Law Section of the American Bar Association. A frequent speaker on family law, professionalism, and gender bias issues, she was a member of the American Bar Association Standing Committee on Professionalism, and serves as liaison between that committee and the Family Law Section. She is a fellow of both the American and Connecticut Bar Foundations. Ms. Wolfson received a B.A. in Economics from Barnard College and a J.D. with Honors from the University of Connecticut School of Law.

David J. Zaumeyer, national director of litigation services for BDO Siedman, LLP, has served as an expert witness, court-appointed appraiser and valuation expert, economist, accountant, and independent consultant. His business valuation and forensic experience encompass many types of civil and tort litigation. He is also a senior member of the accounting faculty at Rutgers University.